ATHENAE EPHESUS

ANTIOCHIA

IA

ALEXANDRIA

CHARAX

THEBAE

BERENICE

THE REACH OF ROME

Also by Alberto Angela

A DAY IN THE LIFE OF ANCIENT ROME

THE
REACH
OF
ROME

A Journey Through
the Lands of
the Ancient Empire,
Following a Coin

ALBERTO ANGELA

Translated from the Italian by Gregory Conti

Rizzoli
ex libris

First published in the United States of America in 2013 by Rizzoli Ex Libris
An imprint of Rizzoli International Publications, Inc.
300 Park Avenue South, New York, NY 10010
www.rizzoliusa.com
© 2013 Alberto Angela
Translation © 2013 Gregory Conti

First published in Italy as *Impero: Viaggio Nell'Impero di Roma Seguendo Una Moneta*
© 2010 by Alberto Angela
© 2010 Rai Radiotelevisione Italiana, Roma
© Arnoldo Mondadori Editore S.p.A., Milano

2013 2014 2015 2016 / 10 9 8 7 6 5 4 3 2 1
Distributed in the U.S. trade by Random House, New York
Printed in the United States of America
ISBN-13: 978-0-8478-4128-8
Library of Congress Catalog Control Number: 2013934991

To Monica, Riccardo, Edoardo, and Alessandro

Because my most beautiful journey is the one
I make each day in your eyes

Contents

Preface

Take a look at a map of the Roman Empire at the height of its territorial expansion. What strikes you most is how vast it is. It stretches from Scotland to Kuwait, from Portugal to Armenia.

What was is like to live in this world? What kind of people would we have met in its cities? How were the Romans able to create such a great empire, uniting peoples and places that were so diverse? The aim of this book is to take you on a journey through the Roman lands to find the answers to these questions.

Perhaps you are reading this after having read my previous book on Rome, *A Day in the Life of Ancient Rome*: an hour-by-hour exploration of daily life in the capital city. I had imagined that typical day as being a Tuesday during the reign of the emperor Trajan.

Now imagine that you are waking up the following day, a Wednesday, and that you are about to leave on a journey that will take you through the entire empire. A journey where you will breathe the atmosphere of exotic places, the smells in the alleyways of Alexandria, Egypt, the fragrances used by the noblewomen strolling on the streets of Milan; where you will hear the sound of hammers and chisels at work in a stonecutter's shop in Athens; and where you will see the painted shields of legionnaires on the march in Germany and the painted bodies of the barbarians on the empire's northern border in Scotland.

When I was preparing to write this book, I wondered what kind of story line I could use to guide us on a journey like this through the Roman Empire.

I thought of a coin. A *sestertius* (or sesterce), to be exact. In fact, by following the peregrinations of a coin as it continually changes hands, it is possible, in theory, to reach any point in the empire within the span of a few years (even as few as three). And, even more important, by following the people who take turns possessing the coin, we can discover their faces, their experiences, the world around them, their homes, their ways of life, their customs and habits.

So we will pass from the hands of a legionnaire into those of a member of the landed nobility; from the hands of a slave to the hands of a surgeon trying, by way of a most delicate operation, to save the life of a baby boy; from a wealthy trader in *garum* (the famous sauce so loved by the ancient Romans) to a prostitute; from a singer, at risk of dying in a shipwreck in the Mediterranean, to a sailor, all the way up to the emperor. And lots of others.

Obviously, our journey will be imaginary, but nevertheless it is totally plausible. The people you will meet are, with few exceptions, people who actually lived in that same period and almost always in the same places. Their names, occupations, and personal details are real, the fruit of a long labor of research using tombstones, inscriptions, and ancient texts. We even know what many of our characters looked like, thanks to the so-called Fayum portraits, an extraordinary collection of paintings found in Egypt by archaeologists and dating back to the first centuries after Christ, to the very same period in which our journey takes place. They are portraits of ordinary people that would be hung on the walls in the subjects' homes and then applied, after their deaths, to their mummies. Several of the characters in this book are directly inspired by them.

And so, almost by magic, on the streets of a city, in the back alleys of a port, on the deck of a ship, we will come upon their ancient, but no less familiar, faces. And the spark shining in their eyes will illuminate our view of a little piece of the culture and daily life of their era.

In the same way, the dialogue that you'll hear pronounced by some of our ancient Romans is almost always "original," taken from famous works written by Latin writers such as Martial, Juvenal, or Ovid.

My intention has been to provide as realistic an idea as possible of the era, its people, and its places. If, for example, during Trajan's reign the North African city of Leptis Magna still didn't have the great baths built just a few years later by Hadrian, then you won't see them as you follow the sestertius on your tour of the city.

At times, the writing style will be very much like fiction, but every place, every climate, every monument, every landscape that you'll discover during your reading has been carefully documented in ancient sources and archaeological studies so as to be described in the book as it was seen and experienced by the ancient Romans. If there are any errors in this regard, I ask my readers to accept my apologies.

What I hope to do in these pages, in fact, is to help readers immerse themselves in the reality of daily life in the ancient world. And I want to present lovers of history and archaeology with the tidbits and sensations that are not usually described in books, like the smell of the crowd gathered to watch the chariot races in the Circus Maximus or the arabesques of light projected by the latticework of the windows.

Given that we cannot know everything exactly as it happened during the few years of our journey (which concludes in 117 CE), it has been necessary in some very rare cases to make adjustments. At times, an incident may have actually happened in an era slightly earlier or later than the moment in which I've placed it, but even in those cases it is completely plausible that the incident could have happened during our journey.

I have drawn on a variety of sources. First among them are the ancient authors. Then come the archaeologists, who in many cases have recounted their discoveries to me personally. Then, the scholars whose studies and research have provided us with extremely rich descriptions and interpretations of life at the time. It is not possible to list them all here but I will cite one of them as a representative of them all: Professor Lionel Casson, a great student of journeys.

In this behind-the-scenes view of the Roman Empire, you will see that the world of the ancient Romans, at its core, was quite similar to our own. They were the ones who brought about the first instance of globalization in human history: throughout the empire, payments were made in a single currency; there was one official language (Latin, joined by Greek in the eastern empire); nearly everyone knew how to read, write, and do arithmetic; there was a single, universally recognized body of laws; and goods circulated freely throughout the empire. You could sit in a tavern in Alexandria or London or Rome and order a glass of the wine that was being sipped in Gaul or dress your salad with olive oil that came from Spain. At the clothing store across the street you could buy a tunic made from linen grown in Egypt and weaved in Rome (a bit like what happens with T-shirts today). On the road, you might come across motels and fast-food service areas like the ones we have, and rent a vehicle to travel from one city to another. In essence, traveling through the Roman Empire might feel like a fairly familiar experience.

There were problems like ours back then too: a rising divorce rate and a falling birth rate; a slow-moving legal system congested by an overload of litigation; scandals caused by contractors who pilfered the public treasury by charging enormous amounts for public works they never built; intense deforestation to satisfy the demand for timber; the "cementification" of certain coastal areas with the construction of gigantic seaside villas. Plus there were wars in places like Iraq. Trajan's invasion of Mesopotamia—the same geographical area where the "coalition of the willing" intervened some two thousand years later—allows us to examine military and geo-political issues, which, at times, are surprisingly similar to our own.

If we think about all the centuries that separate us from the Romans, what stands out is this incredible modernity of an ancient society. As we will see, the secret to the empire's success was not only its military might but also its dominance in engineering (aqueducts, baths, roads, cities endowed with every conceivable public service), which enabled it to conquer the world of the time.

The journey in this book reflects a "magic moment" of history: for the first time, the whole of the Mediterranean and Europe were united. No other culture or civilization, up to and including the modern era, has been able to do the same. And this unity lasted throughout the first four centuries of the Christian era. It was possible to travel without borders (and without pirates or enemies) from one end to the other. Shortly thereafter, this extraordinary era came to a close, never to reopen again.

Finally, this book features a historical figure without whom our journey would not have been the same: Trajan. The history books don't pay much attention to this emperor. In Italy today nobody names their own son after Trajan (Traiano)—something that happens quite frequently, on the other hand, with a lot of greats from the past: Julius Caesar, Augustus, Constantine, Alexander, and even Hadrian, Trajan's successor. Yet Trajan is the emperor who led the Roman Empire to its greatest expansion, giving it a level of prosperity, wealth, social welfare, and a "moment of grace" never equaled in Roman history. The maps that you see in books showing the empire at the height of its expansion depict the empire during Trajan's reign.

This book hopes to reawaken our interest in this grand historical figure, this *optimus princeps,* as he was called, and above all in the extraordinary epoch that he was able to forge.

Pleasant journey. *Vale.*
Alberto Angela
Rome, November 9, 2010

THE REACH OF ROME

ROME

~ *Where It All Begins* ~

The Underworld of the Eternal City

She moves swiftly down the unpaved narrow streets, wending her way through the crowd. Her face is covered with a veil so she won't be recognized. She's elegant and refined, a woman of gracious ways. Her hands have long, tapered fingers with shiny, manicured nails. Hands that have never worked. So she is truly out of place here in the Suburra, the lowlife neighborhood of Rome, where there is no silk or marble, only hunger and poverty.

Agile as a cat, she tries to avoid contact with people but it's not easy. She passes by toothless butchers with ox quarters slung over their shoulders, little matrons, fat and fussy, talking in loud voices, slaves with their heads shaved, emaciated men with the fetid smell typical of poor personal hygiene, scurrying children. She even has to be careful about where she puts her feet. Rivulets of raw sewage form puddles in the alleyway where clouds of flies come to drink, the naked feet of the passersby futilely trying to shoo them away.

Off to her right she hears a female voice, shrill and agitated: there's a screaming match going on behind that door. She doesn't have time to look inside because the flapping wings of a chicken cause her to turn her head in the opposite direction, where she spies a shop with a pile of wooden cages full of hens emitting the unmistakable stench of a chicken coop.

The woman rushes ahead quickly, as though she wants to be in that alley as short a time as possible, and she walks by an old man sitting on a chair, who raises his head, sensing, more than the caress of her tunic as it touches his knee, the fresh smell of her wake as she passes by. The man's eyes, one of which is white, search futilely for that "fairy." His healthy eye barely glimpses the edge of a veil, fluttering in the air as it vanishes around the corner.

Here we are: this is the place. "After turning the corner, keep going down the hill, but before you get to the bottom you'll come to a sacred shrine: it's a miniature temple attached to the wall. Opposite it you'll see a small entrance with some stairs going down; you'll find her there," her old midwife had told her.

The young woman hesitates. The entrance is very small and dark. The stairs descend into the darkness. She looks around: all she can see are the high walls of tall, rundown buildings built to house the poor. The plaster is chipped and flaking, pockmarked with the signs of dampness and stained with dirt and filth; the wooden shutters on the windows are splintered and warped; the balconies look like they're about to cave in—there are ropes hanging down from them. "But how can people live like this?" she asks herself. And then, "What am I doing here?" The answer is right in front of her: in that pitch-black entryway. Her eyes meet those of an old woman, her tunic worn and wrinkled, looking out through a window with a maternal smile. The old woman gestures with her head for her to come in, as though she understands why our young woman has come here and wants to reassure her. Who knows how many she has seen arrive at her door.

The woman takes a deep breath and goes in. Almost immediately she's overwhelmed by the acrid smell of something cooking or burning, but she can't identify what. All she's able to perceive is a hell-like atmosphere that confirms that this is indeed the place she was looking for. Her heart is beating so hard she can almost hear it in the silence of the semidarkness. She takes another few steps in. A woman's face appears suddenly in the darkness. She's so scared she jumps.

It's the conjure woman.

She looks like a woman of the people, fat, corpulent, streaks of gray and white running through her unkempt hair. Penetrating black eyes, and above all, a gaze that is determined and secure. "Have you got everything?" The young woman hands her a rolled-up bundle of cloth. She reaches out as though to take it and then grabs her hands, pulling them to herself. "You want him dead?" Her eyes are devouring those of the young woman, who responds with a fearful nod.

The conjure woman already knows that she's supposed to cast a spell so that the man who is now married to the young woman, on the decision of her parents, will vanish from her life. He is a violent type who beats her regularly. For some time now, she has found comfort in the company of another man. A passionate love has blossomed between them. Now she has decided to turn to magic for a solution. . . .

The conjure woman unfolds the cloth bundle, which holds hairs from the man's scalp and fingernail clippings that the woman has managed to procure in their house. She starts preparing the ritual: she'll have to make a statuette from clay mixed with these "portions" of the man who is to be struck.

Naturally, she wants to be paid in advance. The young woman pulls out a small leather purse and hands it over to the hag. She opens it and shakes out its contents. The old woman smiles; it really is a lot of money. She turns her back and hides the money in a small crib hanging from some ribbons tied to hooks in the ceiling. Inside there's a baby girl, sleeping. The conjure woman sends the crib gently swaying. She's probably thirty-five or forty, but her flabby body and shabby appearance make her seem much older.

The place where she lives is dark and dank. What light there is comes mostly from a lit fireplace. Hanging inside it from a hook is a pot holding a strange bubbling brew, filling the air with the acrid odor that the young woman had smelled as she was entering. It must be one of the philters or potions that the hag is preparing for one of her clients.

This kind of stewpot, called a *caccabus*, is a typical instrument used by those women—witches, if you will—who cook up herbal cures or, as necessary, hexes and jinxes as described by Virgil, among others.

Throughout the passing years, the *caccabus* will continue to be part of the image of the witch. The image is a composite of all of these elements: the stereotypical witch is an old or aging woman who has lost her youthful charm (or better, who is downright ugly), is not rich, wears humble clothing, lives in a hovel rather than a palace, and makes poisons. Here's where it all begins: with certain women from the popular classes who in all eras and epochs (not only in ancient Rome) have devoted themselves to witchcraft and curses, exploiting the credulity of the common people, their weaknesses, and above all, their suffering.

That's why the bags of sesterces, drachmas, florins, shillings, or euros that have fallen into their hands over the centuries and millennia constitute one of the most wicked and least punished forms of thievery. Even in Trajan's Rome.

The statue is ready. It has all the features of a man, even the genitals. The old woman etches his body—the not-yet-hardened clay—with magic formulas that probably only she is able to decipher. Then, after a series of chants and incantations invoking the evil spirits, the statue is placed head down (a symbolic position) inside a lead cylinder, which in turn, is inserted into two larger cylinders, creating a "matryoshka doll" of malediction that is sealed with wax. The conjure woman uses a knife to engrave the outside with the sacred figures and evil formulas. Then, her face dripping with sweat, she raises the container on high, clawing it with her pointed fingernails. She chants some more spells and finally offers it to the young woman. "Go," she says. "You know where to put it." The young woman takes the container; it's about the size of a large jelly jar but a lot heavier because of the lead. She wraps it in a cloth that she holds to her side and leaves without looking at the sorceress. Out on the street the light is different from when she arrived. Even though on Rome's narrow alleyways the sunlight never reaches the ground, the young woman realizes that the sun has now dropped down behind the rooftops. Who knows how long she was inside with the conjure woman.

Now she's got to hurry on her way.

The Fountain of Anna Perenna

The next day the woman, using the excuse of going to visit a relative, leaves the city in the company of her elderly midwife. They set out on the Via Flaminia. Almost immediately, on the right side of the road, they come to two large mounds of yellow sand, completely covered with woods. These hills will survive into the modern era and eventually become the Parioli neighborhood of present-day Rome. Today it is a densely developed urban area, but a piece of that forest still exists. It can still be seen, intact, in the city center—one of the many islands of green in the Eternal City. The trees, which today's drivers and pedestrians barely notice, are actually the direct descendants of the trees that, in Roman times, were part of a sacred wood.

The two women turn down a well-beaten dirt road that veers off from the Flaminia and runs into an internal valley of these hills. The sacred wood is all around them. A place of great beauty, whose peaceful silence is interrupted only by birdsong. Quite a difference from the noisy chaos of Rome. Along the sloping sides of the narrow valley, up among the trees, there are grottos dedicated to the nymphs. These groves of trees are like temples for the Romans. Cutting down trees or gathering firewood is forbidden in these woods. And even in unprotected areas, cutting down trees is frowned upon. The Romans believe that the bark of oak trees, for example, is home to nymphs and hamadryads, who are closely connected to the life of the planet. Before a tree is cut down a priest is called in to conduct a ritual that will drive them away.

In the middle of the valley, where it widens out into a clearing, is a natural spring. A large brick structure has been built around it, with a central tub and lateral branches where the faithful fill their pails with the holy water.

This sacred spring is dedicated to a divinity with a special and potentially misleading name: Anna Perenna. Not a person (as the name "Anna" might lead one to believe), Anna Perenna is the divinity who oversees the cycle of the year and its continual renewal. Not coincidentally, one of the phrases most frequently used by Roman well-wishers is *Annarè perennereque commode,* which translates roughly as "Have a good year from top to bottom," a wish especially popular on New Year's Day.

And when was New Year's Day for the Romans? In the imperial age it was the first of January, while in the Republican era it was on the (famous) ides of March, that is, March 15. Thousands of people come to celebrate it here around the sacred fountain of Anna Perenna. And, as described by the ancients, the scene was really impressive.

Roman New Year: An Ancient Woodstock

Try to imagine it: a long column of men and women streaming out of the city of Rome and coming out here to feast, sing, and enjoy themselves. The banquet tables are set up along the Via Flaminia, but almost everyone is lying or sitting on the grass as if at a colossal picnic. They sing, they dance, and they get drunk (some of the toasts, or drinking games, are impossible: a cup of wine for every year that you still want to live). All very much like one of our New Year's Eve parties. If anything, it's even more raucous: a kind of ancient Oktoberfest.

Actually, it's even more than that. As Ovid tells it, the feast is very playful and clearly erotic. People drink and have sex. Ovid recounts that the women, having let their hair down, sing songs with explicit sexual allusions. In effect, the feast has all the features of an initiation rite and a lot of the women use the occasion to lose their virginity. In a sort of Woodstock atmosphere, couples lie together on the grass or take shelter under improvised tents made of tree branches, bamboo, and togas. Some fragments of wood, rediscovered by archaeologists inside the main basin of the fountain, are thought to be surviving parts of these improvised love tents.

The fountain was rediscovered during the construction of an underground parking garage, and the archaeological dig conducted by Professor Marina Piranomonte of the Archaeological Superintendency of Rome uncovered a lot of objects that had been thrown into the water as offerings. Numerous eggs, for example (symbols of fecundity and fertility), and pinecones (symbols of fertility but also of chastity). The archaeologists' curiosity was especially piqued by a series of objects that have no connection at all to the Anna Perenna cult but are related to magic rituals and hexes.

Magic Objects

The digs uncovered a splendid *caccabus*, and at least five hundred coins, which the Romans were as fond of throwing into important or sacred places as they are today. And as is the case in modern times, the coins are seldom of big denominations: most of them are asses, the equivalent of a quarter of a sestertius (about fifty of today's euro cents).

Some seventy oil lamps were uncovered and, oddly enough, almost all of them were new. Why, in markedly different eras, did people carry all the way out here, beyond the city walls, so many new oil lamps—just to throw them into the fountain? According to both Ovid and Apuleius, the rites of the ancient conjure women were almost always nocturnal, so the oil lamps were an essential element for both the women and their customers. And they had to be new. So it is very likely that the ones that have been rediscovered were connected to some magic rites or incantations rather than to the cult of Anna Perenna. The hexes still conserved on the lead linings of six of the lamps provide further evidence that this is the case.

The question of the hexes (*defixiones*) is interesting because about twenty of them have been discovered in the fountain's main basin. They are in the form of little "pages" of laminated lead. Lead is malleable and rustproof, which is why it was preferred over other materials. Once it's beaten into a thin sheet, it can be engraved with magic curses against some person; then it is folded up and stuck inside a tomb, a well, a stream, or a fountain (like the one dedicated to Anna Perenna). Such places are believed to be in direct contact with the river of the afterlife or with the divinities of the netherworld, who will then put the curse into effect. It is both strange and even slightly exhilarating that amid the hexes and magic letters (*characteres*), written especially to heighten the effect, the name of the target is repeated over and over; or the person is described in precise detail (he lives here, works in this or that occupation, etc.). And all this so that the evil spirits wouldn't go after the wrong person and hurt an innocent victim. Pretty much like the instructions given to a hit man.

But who were the targets of these curses? In one of the rediscovered *defixiones,* for example, there is an etching of a human figure and then his name, Sura, and his occupation, a referee or perhaps a judge. The gods of the netherworld are implored to tear out his eyes, first the right one and then the left, because, as the inscription says, he was born of a cursed womb (*Qui natus est da vulva maledicta*).

Roman Voodoo Statues

But the most extraordinary aspect of the discovery of the Anna Perenna fountain was the emergence of seven small intact human figures used for magic rituals, similar to the famous hexes; the equivalent of voodoo dolls. Exactly the kind of ritual we saw the conjure woman performing.

Laboratory studies have suggested that these statuettes were made from flour and milk. One of them was made from wax. It is still possible to make out the eyes, the mouth, the breasts or the penis, depending on the gender. In at least one case, the feet were broken off intentionally. These extremely delicate statues have survived because, after being thrown into the fountain, they settled onto the bottom of the basin, where they gradually sank into a layer of clay that was entirely devoid of oxygen, preventing bacteria from acting on them and causing their decay over the centuries.

All of their containers are made of lead and there are always three of them, one inside the other: the repetition of the number 3 certainly had magical significance. The spinal column of the statuettes is formed by a bone, embossed with Latin letters in at least one case. And this corresponds to what was recommended in the famous Greek magic scrolls where these rituals are described.

But by examining these statuettes we can discover traces of other rituals as well. One in particular has some magic letters engraved all over its body and a deep hole in its head: it's not hard to imagine the effect it was intended to provoke in the victim.

The most surprising statuette is the one of a person wrapped in the coils of a giant crested snake that is biting him in the face. Assisting the "grip" of the snake is a thin sheet of metal that embraces the victim. As though that weren't enough, another sheet of metal with curses inscribed on it is nailed on top of the statue; one of the nails pierces its belly button and the other its feet. They probably have some symbolic meaning attached to them.

There must have been untold numbers of Romans who engaged in these practices. That much is suggested by the fact that the containers were manufactured serially. So interested parties bought them separately and took them to the conjure women. In other words, there was a flourishing market in these objects and lots of money was spent on them.

On examining the closure of one of these containers, sealed with a resin around its cork, researchers found fingerprints. The object was taken to the technicians of the police forensics team, and it was discovered that the hand that closed the lid was small, so it must have been the hand of a very young person or of a woman—a sort of confirmation of what the ancients have told us about the practices of their conjure women.

The young woman and the old midwife approach the fountain. They take a look around; there's nobody there. Her hands moving swiftly and deftly, the midwife unrolls a cloth bundle, grabs the cylindrical container, and hurls it into the air, high above the fountain. The cylinder vanishes from sight and an instant later comes the sound of its plunge into the water. The two women turn to each other and smile.

The fountain of Anna Perenna will continue to be the focal point of the cult of fertility, a source of good omens, and the setting for New Year's celebrations for a long time to come, at least until the third century CE. Then this religious tradition will gradually wither away until the fourth or fifth century, when the cult will be more and more "contaminated" by obscure rituals with containers and curses rooted in superstition. This decline in the tradition was accelerated by the closing of the fountain (as part of the prohibition of pagan cults ordered by the Emperor Theodosius in 391), but it is also a reflection of the widespread degeneration of the values of Roman society, by now on the verge of collapse. Less than a hundred years later, in fact, the empire would cease to exist.

This doesn't mean that the launch of the lead cylinder with its little statue inside would not have been possible during the era when New Year's celebrations were held here. It is all still quite possible and plausible. Our story has merely advanced the calendar a little.

Now the two women take their leave of the fountain. Their mission is accomplished. On the bottom of the fountain's main basin, surrounded by eggs and pinecones, there is now a dark capsule containing a request for someone's death. The man to be struck down is now peacefully riding his horse, on a business trip, completely unaware of the danger.

But for the two women it's only a question of time. They are sure of it. And tonight, taking advantage of her husband's absence, she will go again to meet her lover.

The Colors of the Night

Rays of moonlight shine through the latticework of the window, projecting onto the floor its elegant arabesque decorations. The designs are like dark vines of ivy moving through the house, climbing onto the bed, elongating themselves on the pillows, and wrapping around the bodies of the woman and her lover.

After a long, tender embrace, the man gets up and walks across the small room. The moonlight seems to be playing with his muscles, darting across his shoulders and buttocks, sculpting them in light with his every step. When he reaches the other side of the room, he steps out onto a large terrace and leans with both of his hands on the wooden railing. His chest heaves like a bellows. On this hot summer night there doesn't seem to be enough air even to breathe.

A few seconds later, he senses the light step of the woman and the touch of her body. Luckily, this terrace, attached to a palace at the top of the Quirinal hill, is always cooled by a light breeze. They stay like that, silently embracing, admiring the grandeur of the spectacle that stretches out before them. The couple, in fact, is gazing out on one of the most beautiful views in the history of civilization: the city of Rome at the height of its beauty and power.

Tonight, with a full moon shining, the Eternal City seems to have no limits. Its buildings stretch into the distance as far as the eye can see, then vanish in the darkness. The nearest buildings are in full view. They are some of the city's gigantic *insulae*, similar to our condominiums, their walls covered with white plaster and their roofs with clay tiles. We can get a good view of their windows, the shutters open wide because of the heat, but also the outline of their balconies, many of them decorated with flowerpots as is often done in our modern cities. We can also see some balconies enclosed by latticework similar to those seen today in India. They look almost like armoires hanging from the walls of the buildings.

On the inside, behind the windows, all we can see is darkness where people are asleep. But here and there the light of an oil lamp reveals some scenes of everyday life that continue well into the night. These points of light emanating from oil lamps and torches throughout the city transform it into a veritable galaxy of life hovering in the night sky.

The silence is striking. By day, this city of more than a million inhabitants is enveloped by all sorts of noise; at night it's very different. In certain alleyways and small piazzas the silence is well-nigh absolute, broken only by the thin stream of water flowing in a public fountain, a dog barking in the distance, or the blustering exchanges of drunken brawlers carousing through the neighborhood.

To be sure, the night is also the time when goods are delivered to stores, shops, and public baths, and the sound of wagons, the outbursts of profanity uttered by their drivers, by those who are denied the right of way at intersections, or by those whose goods haven't been delivered on time, flash through the streets and neighborhoods like lightning. But compared to the daytime, Rome by night recovers all of its charm—it's the same charm that one can feel today on a nighttime stroll along the city streets.

From up here on the Quirinal hill (so named for a temple dedicated to Quirinus, a pre-Roman deity), we can make out in the milky glow of the moonlight the dark masses of some of the seven hills upon which Rome was built, but also the familiar silhouette of the Colosseum.

The couple whispers words of love, leaning their heads against one another. Their gaze is fixed on the gigantic amphitheater that stands out against the brightening dawn. The white mass of its marble, with its torches and lamps hanging from the vaults of its arches, is like a magnet for their eyes as they remain absorbed in their sweet dalliance. What they don't know is that just beyond it, where their eyes are following some lights on the horizon, something is happening that will allow us to undertake an extraordinary journey, reaching the most faraway corners of the Roman Empire and its most glorious parts as well. It is taking shape in a frightening place, a real inferno located in the vicinity of the Colosseum: the Roman mint.

The Sestertius Is Born

The heat is oppressive. Outside it's tough to breathe, but in here it feels like we've entered a furnace. The colors of the place only add to the sensation. The light from the oil lamps seems to envelope everything, tingeing the rooms with an orange-yellow hue. Our attention is drawn to a long wall on the other side of a heavy studded door. There are a lot of spots where the plaster has fallen off and dark shadows flitter over the mottled surface of the wall, appearing and disappearing, as if engaged in a frenetic dance. They are the luminous echo of something that is happening in this great space.

We go through the door. The sound of heavy blows pummels the air and penetrates deep into our ears. Mighty blows, with metallic reverberations. We turn around and before our eyes a scene out of Dante's *Inferno* opens up: half-naked, sweat-soaked men are gathered together in small groups. Above their heads we can see heavy sledgehammers rising up, only to plummet down with a mighty clang. This is the birthplace of the sesterces that circulate throughout the empire. And that's not all. At certain times of the year silver coins (denarii), gold coins (aurei), and then all of the minor coins in bronze (dupondii) and copper (asses and semisses) are also made here.

In accordance with a rigid monetary system established by Augustus, which laid the foundation for commerce in the Roman Empire, one aureus (gold coin) equals:

25 denarii (silver coin)
100 sesterces (bronze coin)
200 dupondii (bronze coin)
400 asses (copper coin)
800 semisses (copper coin)

We approach one of the groups of men. These are the workers in the mint and something about them strikes us: they are slaves. They belong to a so-called *familia monetalis*. They are under constant surveillance. Depending on the time of year, they handle silver and even gold. It is an operation that requires enormous attention on the part of the guards. At the end of their shift they are subjected to a painstaking search, one by one, in order to prevent theft. Their sandals are brushed, their hair and mouths are examined, and so forth. Even the floor is made out of grates to collect any fragments that might have fallen.

Today they are coining sesterces, and we can see how they are made. The first step is to make bronze bars. In a nearby room, there are some small foundries where the metals are melted down in an unimaginable heat. Using two pairs of long pincers, the smith takes the crucible from the oven and empties it into a fireclay mold. The bronze is now a dense searing-hot liquid that disappears into the mold. A cloud of smoke billows out of the entrance hole, and the smith squints, his eyes inflamed by this ceaseless labor. His face is red, maybe even redder than his hair. He'll have to wait until the bronze cools down. In the meantime another slave opens some other blocks of already cooled clay and extracts the raw bars of bronze.

These will then be chiseled into slices, just like slicing salami. Each slice will become a sestertius. Naturally, it will have to be shaped to make it perfectly round (which is why in slang it's called a *tondello* or a "round"). Practically speaking, it is now a raw coin, still without any images or inscriptions.

It will be weighed carefully. This is a fundamental detail because a coin's value is not based on what it represents but on how much it weighs (this might be obvious for gold but the same is true for the bronze sestertius, the silver denarius, and so on).

Finally, it will be heated and taken to the men who imprint it with the face of the emperor on one side and all the inscriptions and figures on the other (heads and tails, in other words).

And now we are standing right next to these men. They are all irritable and worn out from the exhausting shifts and the abuse of the guards, who behave like real tyrants every time someone makes a mistake.

One of the slaves comes over to us, using a pair of tongs to hold the hot round, which he lays down on a small round anvil. Not just anywhere but right in the center, where the die is; the sculpted figure of the emperor. When the die is struck with the hammer, it will impress the face on one side of the future coin. And on the other side? Simple, the same technique. While the slave holds the future coin in the center of the anvil, a second slave places a metal cylinder on top of it with another die, the one for the "back side," as they say. At this point everything is ready for the hammer blow. A third slave raises a massive sledgehammer.

The three men look each other in the eye for a fraction of a second. The slave with the hammer, a huge red-haired Celt, rips the air with a tremendous blow. The other two close their eyes. The Syrian, especially, grimaces so intensely that his black eyes drown amid the wrinkles on his face. The African's face, meanwhile, is creased by a line of gritted white teeth.

The hammer blow is so powerful that the grated floor trembles. For a second, everyone turns to look, even the guard watching over the next group. Such a strong blow is not common. The Syrian's ears are ringing and his hands are tingling. But he thanks the gods that the giant did not miss his target; otherwise his hands would have been crushed. The African doesn't say a word. The red-haired Celt has a satisfied look on his face. Suddenly, an act that is so routine in this environment has become the center of attention. Everyone is staring at the coin. It's the die master who comes over to pick it up with his tongs. He's a heavyset man with a snarly beard. He examines it. The hammer blow was perfect. The face of the emperor is well positioned in the center of the coin. The inscriptions are legible. There's just one defect: the coin has a crack along one side. It's nobody's fault. The die is "tired," as they say. It has stamped too many sesterces, and maybe it's broken. The man takes a last look at the coin and throws it into the strongbox of newly minted sesterces. Then he yells at the three slaves to get back to work immediately. They instinctively take a last glance at the coin as it lands on the pile of its look-alikes and start hammering again. This time the blows are not so powerful.

Freshly cast bronze is the color of gold. And the coin with the crack in it shines as though it were alive. On its surface are reflected, as in an old mirror, the figures of the slaves as they go on hammering out new coins.

This is the sestertius that is going to take us on our voyage through the Roman Empire. Nobody here at the mint can imagine it, but it's going to be an incredible journey.

LONDON

~ *Roman Inventions* ~

The Dawn of a Long Journey

The soldier gives a whistle. Husky white horses begin pulling on thick ropes tied to the big twin rings of a double wooden door. The hinges, inactive for too long, first start creaking, then emit little explosions of dust, and finally give way with a long metallic groan.

The two sides of the double door open slowly, like the arms of a still-sleeping giant. With the help of the dawning sunlight, they project ample black shadows on the lichen-encrusted walls of the fort. The sinister sounds of the creaking hinges are echoed by the barking sound of military orders, spoken in Latin with a strong Germanic accent. Indeed, the little fort is occupied by a detachment of auxiliaries from Tungria, who come from the lands to the north of the Ardennes plateau, a tribe of Gauls who have been "Romanized" now for generations.

The heavy double door is still not completely open when a *turma*, that is, a squadron of thirty horsemen, comes riding out at a gallop. They are military couriers. They're all carrying large saddle bags, draped over the flanks of their horses, containing newly minted coins. They are transporting them to the northernmost parts of the empire: forts, provincial capitals, governors' seats, the empire's key economic centers, strategic military outposts.

This is routine practice: every time a new coin is minted, it must be shipped immediately to the four corners of the empire. In an age in which television, radio, and the telephone do not exist, the coin is not only an economic instrument; it is also an instrument of propaganda and information. Even more than that, the coin amounts to a sort of public address by the emperor, complete with its own publicity poster and policy achievement.

One side of the coin, in fact, bears his profile. Emperor Trajan is serious, his head crowned by a laurel wreath, always facing right, as tradition warrants. The subliminal message to his subjects is reassuring: the most powerful man in the empire (the only one with a lifetime appointment) believes in the classic values; he is a soldier, a "son" of the Senate, chosen by the emperor Nero, a champion of tradition and continuity.

The other side of the coin shows an accomplished objective. Sometimes it's a monument, which he has built for the Roman people (the Circus Maximus or the new port at Ostia, a colossal bridge across the Danube, a great aqueduct for Rome, the forum in the heart of the city, etc.). Sometimes it's a military victory and pictures a nation, such as Dacia (the future Romania), represented by a defeated foot soldier.

Other times, instead, there is a deity with a very specific symbolic meaning (Abundance, Providence, Harmony, etc.), so as to underline that the gods are favorably disposed to this leader.

Every conquest, every new monument, appointment, or acclamation must reach the ears of all the subjects of the empire: the task performed by radio broadcasts in early-twentieth-century regimes. Coins performed this same exact function: through them, the most powerful man in the empire spoke to his subjects.

You can imagine how important this all is when a new emperor comes to power. In the span of a few hours, new coins stamped with his portrait are already being serially produced, in order to be sent throughout the empire. Sometimes they are made by way of a simple alteration of the portrait of the previous emperor, deceased just a few hours before, making changes directly on his die (a sort of Photoshop for classical antiquity). Usually, however, the job was entrusted to true geniuses of the art of engraving, who rushed to chisel out a new die with the profile of the new sovereign so that everyone could get to know his face, thus making his rise to power official.

The importance of image for political leaders is not a modern invention. The Romans were among the first to understand the effectiveness of good images and used them on a large scale. They made the best possible use of the media that were available to them: from coins to statues, from inscriptions on plaques and buildings to bas-relief sculptures on monuments, and so on.

In normal situations, like the one we find ourselves in now, the sestertius was designed and made with great care, and there is a lot of satisfaction in the mint. Now, this little masterpiece, duplicated in the hundreds of thousands, is ready to be put in circulation throughout the empire.

The coins we are now following are a small example of coins being used for propaganda, as we have already described. The thousands of other look-alike coins will follow a much more orthodox distribution channel. From the mint they will be delivered to the treasury, and from there they will begin to circulate, mostly in Rome, passing from hand to hand in the markets, in the shops, in the taverns. Then they will arrive almost everywhere, following the streams of commerce, land journeys, sea voyages, and so on. Their capillary circulation will also be made possible by figures such as the *argentarius*, or money changer, antiquity's living version of our banks.

Naturally, not all of the coins will travel about in the same way. The silver coins will be the fastest; having a greater value and being smaller in size, they are ideal for travel. A few of them are enough to add up to a good amount of money, taking up less space and weighing less (a little like today's fifty- and hundred-euro bills).

Gold coins, on the other hand, will travel even farther because gold is sought after and accepted as tender everywhere on the planet. It's amazing to think that archaeologists have come across Roman gold coins as far away as the Mekong Delta in Vietnam and on the northern tundra of Afghanistan. The Romans themselves will not get that far, but their coins will, transported by local merchants.

The career of our sesterce will be altogether different. Given their lower value, sesterces tend to be used mostly in and around their place of origin. But many will travel far, like the one that we are following now.

The cavalry squadron has been on the road now for several days. These couriers passed through the Alps, went through Gaul, and crossed the English Channel on boats. Then they landed at Dubris (Dover), in Britain and spent the night in this small fort in the hinterland, unaccustomed to visits of this kind (the noise made by the great double door is evidence that it isn't opened very often). Along the way, each time they arrived in an important city or fortress, they delivered, in accordance with their orders, small quantities of coins to the commanders or functionaries in charge. And then they were on their way.

Now the squadron of horsemen, with their flowing red capes, is galloping away again, heading north, with their final destination the northern boundary of the empire, what today we call Hadrian's Wall. Later on, the boundary will be moved even farther north, with a second wall, the Antonine Wall, named for Antoninus Pius. But before they reach the border they have to make an important stop: London.

The auxiliary on watch in the fort they've just left squints to follow them as they ride off into the distance; the cavalry squadron has become a small colored cloud floating away on the long gravel-topped road.

When they disappear beyond the horizon, the soldier looks up to scrutinize the clouds in the sky. They're running low, almost as though they were chasing after the couriers. They are heavy with rain and don't promise anything good for the near future. He pulls his helmet down tighter on his head and grimaces. In Britain the weather never changes; winter or summer it's always rainy.

London: A Roman Invention

The cavalry rode along for hours, passing by small wagons driven by merchants and groups of people on foot. The soldiers figured they had to be nearing the city because the traffic on the road was gradually getting thicker. Then the first wooden houses appeared, essentially log cabins, scattered here and there along the side of the road. Minute by minute, these houses became increasingly more numerous, until they finally formed a continuous wall on both sides of the road. Proceeding along this urban corridor, the horsemen expected to end up in the heart of the city, perhaps in the forum. But they were in for a surprise. Now they all come to a halt and are looking around in amazement. The road has come to an end and in front of them is an enormous river. It's the Thames. Beyond it, on the opposite bank, lies London.

Now, at the beginning of the second century after Christ, London is truly unrecognizable. It's the size of a small town. None of the horsemen can even imagine the metropolis that will rise up here in two thousand years.

There is already something, however, that makes it resemble modern London: a long bridge across the Thames, with the center span that opens to let ships pass through. It is a true ancestor of London Bridge, and the surprising thing is that it was built in almost the same place, as some English archaeologists discovered just a few years ago. Unlike modern bridges, it's made of wood, not iron. And now, thirty horsemen are riding across it.

The clopping hooves of an entire cavalry squadron make the bridge resound like a gigantic tom-tom, attracting the attention of the fishermen on the banks and the sailors on the boats tied up at the docks. Everyone stops what they're doing to stare at the red capes of the soldiers crossing the bridge. But the horsemen are surprised too: none of them have ever been here before and their eyes are fixed on the approaching city.

We are about to come ashore on the side of the river that will be the future home of London's financial district, the City, but it really seems as though we're on a different continent. There are no large buildings at all, just low-level houses made of wood. The skyline of the modern era is still far off into the future. And that's not all. The sites of all the city's future landmarks, like Buckingham Palace, the Palace of Westminster, and Big Ben, even Number 10 Downing Street, the residence of the British prime minister, are still part of the open countryside, crisscrossed by little streams and rivulets. The same goes for the other modern tourist attractions like Trafalgar Square, Piccadilly Circus, and Regent Street.

London, or Londinium, as it is called, is truly a Roman invention. Before the legions arrived here there was nothing but countryside, with little islands of sand sticking out of the Thames.

We can't exclude the possibility that there were some small hamlets of log cabins like the ones that tend to rise up, from time to time, on the banks of large rivers. But one thing is certain: it was the Romans who founded the city of London.

From here, halfway across the bridge, you can understand why they chose this spot. At this point the Thames narrows (facilitating the building of a bridge), but it is still deep enough to allow cargo ships to dock along the shore. The city has a very long dock area where dozens of cargo boats, big and small, many of them sailboats, are tied up.

The constant operations being carried out along the docks make the area a beehive of activity. One ship is unloading amphoras of wine from Italy, another, just arrived from Gaul, delicate "sealed" pottery, the color of red wine, with reliefs of figures and decorations, to be used at important banquets. And we get a glimpse of lots of other products, like fabrics and linen tunics from Egypt, fine blown-glass pitchers from Germany, amphorettes of *garum* from southern Spain.

Oddly enough, there aren't any large warehouses (archaeologists will find only two of them along the entire waterfront). This means that the goods were not stored here but were shipped out again right away. The long loading areas of London, in other words, were more like an airport than a river port, with goods in perennial movement toward the hinterland.

All of these things are evidence of a city in the midst of rapid development, in accordance with the typical Roman model and in contrast to Celtic cities. But they also tell us something else: London was built up from nothing, not for military reasons, but essentially for commerce. Archaeologists have not found any evidence of a military camp that could have served as a base for the birth of the city, as was often the case in other places.

It was money, or more precisely the sestertius, that brought about the foundation of London. Indeed, the city is located in just the right place to bring in goods by sea from points all over the empire, and to send them from here by land to places throughout Britannia.

In exchange, Britain supplies the empire with a host of products: slaves, hunting dogs, minerals.

It is curious to think that London was born for mercantile reasons and that its nucleus rose up in exactly the same place occupied today by the City, the financial heart of London and all of Great Britain. Its economic spirit seems to have been a part of it from the very beginning.

The "Prefabricated" Houses of London

We've arrived on the other side of the bridge and, together with the horsemen, we're making our way into the city. The most striking thing is that London looks like any other little country town, very anonymous. The houses are all made of wood and very low, two stories at most. The streets are muddy in winter and dusty in summer. The traffic is composed of horses, pedestrians, wagons, and carts. We're a long way from the marble and brick cities of the Mediterranean world. In these parts, in fact, masonry buildings are few and far between.

The horsemen pass by a house under construction and are curious to see that it is in large part "prefabricated." Londinium has been built with a really modern construction technique. Almost every house has a framework of oak beams that fit together perfectly. The beams are made elsewhere and transported here, and all the workmen have to do is assemble them on site.

The system is simple. Have you ever seen the way a wooden ladder is made, the ones from the old days that had rungs rather than steps? There are two long pieces of lumber with a series of holes where the rungs are inserted; all the parts fit together without nails or screws.

The walls of the houses in Londinium have a very similar structure. The workmen lay a predrilled beam on the ground, insert the smaller crosspieces into the holes, and then close the whole thing off at the top with another predrilled beam.

Each wall, in other words, is reminiscent of a huge ladder sitting sideways on the ground. By joining together a number of these wooden frames, the skeleton of the house is put in place. At this point the walls have to be filled in with bricks made from mud or horizontal wood strips (the end result looks something like a trellis) that are thatched with reeds or straw. Care is taken to leave openings here and there for doors and windows. A smear of plaster covers everything and gives it a uniform surface. An ingenious system of joints to hold the beams together, some of them laid diagonally, inside the thickness of the wall, makes the structure of the house quite resistant and stable. Finally, this jigsaw puzzle of Legos is topped with a wide roof supported by a rigid framework of trusses. Most of the neighborhoods of Roman London were built with this Ikea-style assembly system.

But it's not only the buildings of London that impress the horsemen from Rome. It's also their inhabitants. The people come rushing outside to see these soldiers in their red capes. Their facial features are those of a Celtic population: fair skin and freckles, blond or copper red hair. Very seldom, on the other hand, do they see someone with a dark complexion and curly hair: essentially only slaves, merchants, or soldiers. Just the opposite of what you see in the Mediterranean cities of the empire.

An Eighty-Year-Old Youth with a Tragic Past

By Roman standards, London is a very young city, less than eighty years old. It's astonishing how late it was that Britain became part of the empire. To put it in perspective, when Jesus was crucified, Britain was still only a large island, beyond the boundaries of the empire. Another ten years went by before Claudius, in 43 CE, decided to invade it, a sort of D-day in reverse. After that the Roman legions and merchants spread out slowly over the island.

London was born shortly thereafter (the remains of a wooden drainage ditch, on the sides of a Roman road, indicate that it was founded in 47 CE). But it took a lot of courage to live in the city in those days. It was a frontier town, surrounded by very hostile populations. In fact, a little more than ten years after its founding, London was totally razed to the ground by a woman, Boudicca, at the head of a tribal army that rebelled against the Romans.

It was the year 60 CE, and as Tacitus recounts in Book XIV of *The Annals*, the rebels had already destroyed Camulodunum (present-day Colchester), defeated a legion, and were marching on London. The legionnaires sent to defend the city were too few to fight off the massive forces of the enemy, so they decided to sacrifice the city to save the rest of the province. They opted for a strategic retreat. "Steadfast in the face of the supplications and protests, [the Roman general Suetonius Paulinus] gave the order to leave. The inhabitants were authorized to follow him. Those who remained, because they were women, old men or too attached to the place, were massacred by the enemy."

The Roman reaction was not long in coming. In a big battle, the legions of Suetonius overwhelmed the rebel tribe, and Boudicca, it seems, killed herself by poison. Tacitus reports that seventy thousand rebels were killed, a veritable slaughter.

So the London that we are visiting accompanied by the cavalry, though still quite young, has already gone through a reconstruction.

A Meeting with the Governor

The *turma*, now on the other side of the city, has reached the palace of the governor, the Pretorium, overlooking the Thames. With their customary precision, the soldiers on horseback have lined up in typical muster formation: three rows of ten, with their respective commanders, the decurions, on the ends.

In accordance with classic Roman military rationality, the first decurion to be selected commands the other two. And indeed it is he, together with his deputy commander, a giant blond Batavian (that is, a Dutchman), who heads toward the entrance to the palace where two guards are standing at attention.

After exhibiting his credentials, he hands over to the chief guard a sealed scroll to be delivered to the governor. While he waits to be received by a member of his staff, he observes the palace, totally out of line with the simplicity of the rest of the city.

The building sits high over the banks of the Thames in a spectacular setting, developing internally on several levels, with long colonnades, indentations, reflecting pools and terraces. From where he is standing, the decurion is able to see one wing of the palace, but there must be another one, symmetrical to it, on the opposite side. The eye of the decurion studies the capitals, columns, and statues of white marble, brought here from the most famous quarries of the Mediterranean. Imagine the cost of building such a beautiful palace in such a faraway place.

The only place he's seen something like this is in Cologne, when he was stationed in Germany. That was the governor's palace too and it overlooked the Rhine, in a very similar setting. "Is it the same architect or the same intent to inspire awe?" he asks himself.

He breaks into a smile, interrupted, however, by a man at his back, who salutes him, stamping the floor with his foot. The noise from the metal studs on the bottom of his sandals betrays his military identity. As the decurion turns around, his blue eyes transfix the soldier. He's one of the governor's bodyguards. He asks the decurion to follow him.

Passing through a heavy oak door, the two cross through an elegant series of rooms and small courtyards. Their footsteps resound through empty spaces, occupied only by imperial statuary and small fountains. In other rooms, offices, they pass by members of the administrative staff with scrolls under their arms.

The decurion walks shoulder to shoulder with the governor's bodyguard. He can't stand walking behind him, not least because of the dreadful smell of perfume he leaves in his wake. If a soldier uses perfume it can only mean he's going soft on the life of the palace. The days of Boudicca are long gone! By now London is a pretty cushy assignment.

The two men climb a wide staircase, at the top of which two guards snap to attention. Beyond them a large garden opens up, surrounded by a lovely colonnade. By the decurion's eyeball estimate, it's about forty yards long and twenty yards wide. The center is dominated by a huge tub with rounded edges. The decurion notices some water-spurting statues, bushes, carefully clipped small hedges, and large grottos housing water lilies. A real paradise compared to what he has seen riding through the city.

The bodyguard signals him to stop. In front of them is a man standing with his back to them. He's looking out at the Thames, his hands resting on the balcony ledge. His gaze is fixed on a sailing ship coming into port with all its sails unfurled. He lets out a sigh and turns around, exclaiming, "What's the word in Rome?"

He's a handsome man, tan, with salt-and-pepper hair kept unusually long given the responsibilities of his office. His wide-set eyes are deep blue. But what strikes you is his smile, open, sincere, with lines on the sides of his mouth and gleaming white teeth. He is Marcus Appius Bradua, appointed to this post only recently. The decurion is surprised and also a little intimidated by the openness of a governor that he's seeing for the first time. He knows only too well that these people can be deceitful and ruthless. But this time he feels an immediate sympathy for the man.

Governor Appius Bradua has been in London for a very short time. His tan is left over from years past and another post on the shores of the Mediterranean. And his nostalgia for those warmer climes is all in his admiring gaze at the tall ship coming into port. He stares at the decurion and then raises his hand: his fingers are holding a shiny coin. It's our sestertius that the *turma* has brought all this way.

On a marble table, under a colonnade, the decurion spies one of the open sacks filled with more coins. The governor has beat him to the punch, having his coins delivered to him directly, without waiting for the bureaucratic protocol. That's one of his powers.

The decurion is surprised and a little annoyed; he realizes that it is thanks to this capacity to surprise and anticipate the moves of his adversaries that Marcus Appius has risen so fast in the hierarchy.

The governor senses the decurion's discomfort and immediately snaps his fingers, ordering two cups of wine to be brought in. This is not according to protocol. During this unusual and rather informal meeting, the governor plays host to the decurion, asking him for news about Rome, about the halls of power, about some of the people who count, but also about the atmosphere in the city's back alleys, in the Circus Maximus and along the roads that have brought him here. As they are chatting, he turns the sestertius in his fingers and holds it up to his face, tapping his lips with it instinctively.

When their chat is over he looks the decurion in the eye, tells him to open his hand, lays the sestertius on his palm and closes his fingers around it, crowning it all with a big Mediterranean smile, showing all his pearly white teeth, "in memory of our meeting." Then he turns around and goes back to watching the ship in the harbor. Now its sails have been lowered and it has begun to unload its cargo.

The decurion takes his leave, accompanied by the same perfumed bodyguard. Before leaving the garden he glances distractedly at the sestertius in the palm of his hand. It seems a little heavy for a bronze coin; and actually he notices that it's not alone. The governor has also given him a silver medal, with the symbol of victory on it. Yet another magic trick from this man who never fails to surprise. He smiles and heads down the stairs.

When the City Was Just a Frontier Town

The thirty horsemen have found lodging in the fortress of Londinium on the north end of the city, where its mission in this period of peace is not so much defending the territory as providing housing for the troops. And now they can all enjoy a well-deserved visit to the baths. It is one of the city's few large building complexes, and it's located right along the Thames, below the Pretorium, where the meeting with the governor took place.

The best time to go is during the lunch hour, when the water, in everyone's opinion, is warmest. After sharing some laughs in the water and the ritual massage, many of the soldiers head out to the city's bordellos in search of pleasure. The chief decurion, on the other hand, together with his deputies, goes for a walk around the future city.

After the luxury of the Pretorium and the perfect hydraulic technology of the baths, the city looks to the three of them like a very simple place, akin to a frontier town in the Wild West. And the analogy is not at all far-fetched: like the European pioneers who settled the American continent by moving farther and farther west, the Romans carried out their own brand of westward expansion on the continent of Europe. And Britain is indeed one of the destinations of Europe's "far west."

So, just as the pioneers introduced into the lands of the native Americans technologies, cities, and ways of life typical of seventeenth- and eighteenth-century western civilization, the Romans introduced their own civilization into the lands of the Gauls, Britons, and Germans. With problems and solutions, all things considered, often quite similar.

In a lot of ways, in fact, the Londinium of the age of Trajan resembles those small frontier towns of the old West: in addition to the mainly wooden houses, the products of very simple construction techniques, in this land where it was difficult to procure everyday tools and instruments there are stores that sell all sorts of things, exactly like the general stores in the pioneer villages. There are also saloon-like taverns and inns, where the girls who wait on tables may also bed the customers. Not unlike Dodge City, Kansas, or Tombstone, Arizona, there were also stables and blacksmiths, barbers ready to pull a tooth when the occasion arises, and even some native Celts crossing the street decked out in the typical symbols of their culture: tattoos and ornamental jewelry, and instead of a tunic, an overshirt and striped or checkered plaid pants.

Walking Around the City:
The World's Oldest Washing Machine?

One of the three decurions has stopped to buy a splendid torque, the horseshoe-shaped collar worn by Celtic warriors, that a street vendor has been showing him, along with other bronze and iron ornaments, including a lovely misshapen dagger. These are all objects commonly found in, and evidently stolen from, the tomb of a Celtic male; the swords and daggers of the deceased were bent so they couldn't be used anymore.

In the meantime, the other two decurions have gone to look into a doorway where they've heard the strange sound of water, clanking iron, and creaking wood. The whole place is enveloped in darkness; the only thing they can discern is that it's a large space. Their eyes adjust quickly to the dark and they begin to make out, on one side, a whole lot of little tubs, and on the other, men who seem to be walking in slow motion, under the feeble light of oil lamps. They are slaves and they're walking at a slow pace inside two large wooden wheels, a lot like the ones you might find inside a hamster cage, except these have a diameter of ten feet!

As they turn, these wheels set in motion other wheels that wind up long chains with buckets full of water. This system makes it possible to draw water continuously from wells that are fifteen feet deep. It's a movement that never stops because the chains, like the ones used on bicycles, form a ring that keeps on turning incessantly. But to what end? The decurions, standing in the doorway of this strange place, are asking themselves that same question.

Then an obsequious little slave boy asks them to let him by. He's carrying a small mountain of clothes to be washed. He empties his load into a tub. At this point the decurions realize that what they are looking at is an enormous laundry. None of them has ever seen anything like it. And even in modern times this place piques our curiosity.

In September 2001, when some English archaeologists announced their surprising discovery of this site, a lot of observers immediately dubbed the structure the "oldest washing machine in history." It was a little cumbersome, certainly, but capable of satisfying the needs of thousands of Roman-era Londoners.

Not everyone agreed that this is what it was, however. When you think about it, what sense did it make to invent a washing machine in an era when there were thousands of slaves ready to do the same job? Moreover, even today, even though there is electricity available almost everywhere in the world, you can still see hundreds of laundrywomen at work along the river banks of India and Pakistan, wringing out clothes all day under the hot sun. I was once told that if you ask one of these women what they think of the washing machine, they answer, shrugging their shoulders, that they are an invention without a future.

It can't be ruled out, therefore, that this strange site with all those tubs is actually a place for tanning leather, like the ones that can be seen in modern-day Marrakech. We reserve judgment, in part because according to a recent hypothesis the water wheel might have had a different purpose: to supply the city with water. From where we are we can't figure it out. It's too dark and we're too far away. All we know is that it's a surprising technological structure.

But the washing machine hypothesis is intriguing. How many of the inventions or habits that we think of as modern were actually thought up by the Romans? Lots of them, from the characters that we use in our computers to many of the laws that contain the principles of our jurisprudence; it would be impossible to describe them all.

Here are a few, however, that may surprise you: the bikini, stockings, cured ham or prosciutto, ball bearings, candles, the pulley, glass marbles, baloney and grilled sausage, scissors, room heating (the baths), election campaign posters, the screw press, fritters (*frictiliae*, a popular sweet on Shrove Tuesday or Mardi Gras), concrete, sewers, curling irons, the magnifying glass.

Even the names of the week, which come from the names of the planets, already known in antiquity, are products of the Roman system: *Luna* (Moon) for *lunedì* (Monday), *Marte* (Mars or Tiw) for *martedì* (Tuesday), *Mercurio* (Mercury or Woden) for *mercoledì* (Wednesday), *Giove* (Jove or Jupiter or Thor) for *giovedì* (Thursday), *Venere* (Venus or Frigg) for *venerdì* (Friday). In modern Rome, Saturday and Sunday have been Christianized into *sabato* for the Sabbath and *domenica* for the day of *dominum* or the Lord's Day, while in English their names still derive from Saturn and, of course, the Sun.

It must be said, however, that some of these inventions are not properly Roman. Actually, they had already been sketched out in even more ancient times, but the Romans acquired them, modified them, and made them more efficient.

One example is the lens used for eyeglasses. The lens was already known to the ancient Greeks, but it was used primarily for lighting a fire by concentrating the rays of the sun. The Romans were the first to use lenses to see better. Pliny the Elder, in fact, claimed that Nero used to look through the concave section of a precious stone (perhaps an emerald) to get a better view of the gladiators in the arena. Many thought that this was his way of correcting for myopia. While the benefits of lenses were already known to the ancient Romans, the first eyeglasses would not come onto the scene for over a thousand years. They will make their appearance at the end of the 1200s, at the height of the Middle Ages, and they are an Italian invention.

The Romans' inventions include more than machines and tools that we still use today. There are even some very widespread superstitions, like, for example, not spilling salt at the dinner table (or olive oil, they would have added). Actually the reason behind it was quite practical: in Roman times salt was very costly.

The Slave Who Bought Himself a Personal Slave

What's the population of Londinium? It's difficult to make an estimate. It has been calculated, however, that in 60 CE it was between five thousand and ten thousand. Now, under Trajan, it should be closer to twenty thousand. But it's a third-world–style population, with lots of young people and very few seniors.

In Roman-era London, as in many other cities of the empire, as many as half of all newborn children died before making it to adulthood, and only a quarter of the population made it to old age. And don't think in terms of today's life expectancy; for the Romans anything beyond age forty qualified as "old age."

The three decurions have gone back to their walk and are promptly bumped into by a laughing couple. She looks almost like a little girl. They are really an unusual couple. During the collision a waxed tablet falls on the ground. One of the decurions picks it up and opens it. He shows it to his two comrades-in-arms and reads the names on it out loud: Vegetus and Fortunata. The couple turns around, surprised to hear their names and, alarmed, come back to the three soldiers.

What fell to the ground is a contract for the purchase of the girl! She is a slave and the man who is holding her by the hand has just bought her.

This tablet will be discovered by archaeologists (who will date it to between 80 and 120 CE, hence, in our same period) and it will constitute a big surprise for scholars. The contract reads, in fact, that Vegetus, the man who is holding her by the hand, bought Fortunata for 600 denarii (€4,800 in today's money, or about $6,000).

But there is also another curious contract clause: Vegetus is in turn the "assistant" slave of a certain Montanus, who is also a slave of the august emperor (that is, he works in some public service, in the public administration, or as a manual laborer, etc.). The surprising thing about this document, therefore, is that it demonstrates the existence of three different levels of slavery, making plain just how complicated and stratified this world was.

As we will discover during our journey through the empire, there are many categories of slaves: from the most downtrodden and mistreated, who work in the fields, to those who are treated very well because they are cultivated and educated, who perform very delicate functions in the heart of the public administration or in the most powerful families. Evidently, the latter (such as Montanus) can decide they need to have assistants (such as Vegetus), who in turn manage to save up a little nest egg to buy a slave girl (such as Fortunata).

We don't know what use Vegetus will make of this slave girl, but we like to imagine, given how much he paid for her, that the purchase is the happy ending to a tormented love story in which a slave has finally been able to embrace the woman he loves, ransoming her from her owner. The Roman era had plenty of stories like that. . . .

"Flip Him the Bird, Sextillus!"

The decurions give the tablet back to the couple and turn off the main street down a little alleyway. The smell of fresh-baked bread draws them like an invisible magnet. After opening a door made of three vertical pieces of wood held together by two slabs of oak nailed crossways, the decurions are presented with a scene quite common in all Roman cities: the back room of a bakery. Some slaves are standing over a table, turning small grindstones by hand to make flour. Others are kneading dough into thick round loaves of bread with deep grooves radiating from the center (the precut "slices" of the future).

Over in a corner, two slaves are using sieves to separate out the impurities from the flour, creating a beautiful effect: the light pouring down into the room from some small windows up above hits the flour suspended in the air, forming bands of light that cut all the way across the room, akin to what one used to see in movie theaters when smoking was still permitted. All the slaves are covered with this thin layer of white flour. But they are also very sweaty, because along one side of the room two ovens are engaged nonstop in baking loaves of bread; some very shaky shelves nearby hold piles of freshly baked loaves.

The bread is sold at the other end of the house. The decurions have opened up the back door, the one that leads out to the alley. Our visit will lead us through the entire house: in some neighborhoods of London, many houses are arranged adjacent to one another, with the front opening onto one street and the back onto another. The decurions buy some loaves and walk off, savoring the taste of the bread fresh out of the oven. As they leave they close the door to the back room again.

One minor but interesting thing that has almost certainly escaped your notice, because it is so familiar to us, is that Roman doors always open toward the inside of the house, never toward the outside, onto the street. The reason for this is simple: otherwise they would use a portion of public property for private purposes. In effect, the area in front of the entrance to the house is used for the movement of the door, "robbing" it from the public. Only a rich or powerful Roman can afford to do that. No one else. This rule has been handed down through the centuries. The same thing happens with the street doors of our houses, from the doors to single apartments to the main doors of apartment buildings. Check it out: go see how the door to your house works.

Among the many Roman legacies that we have conserved there is another, rather vulgar one, which may surprise you. The three decurions are now standing in front of the London amphitheater. It is one of the city's prized possessions. After a morning of fights between wild animals and after the lunchtime executions, it's probably time for the gladiators to fight. And in fact the decurions can hear cheers and chiding coming from the spectators in the grandstands. But the noise of the crowd is nowhere near as loud as what the three men are used to hearing in Rome. The Colosseum holds between fifty thousand and seventy thousand spectators, but here a capacity crowd is only six thousand, one-tenth the size. Furthermore, the London amphitheater is still made of wood. The fans will have to wait until Hadrian's reign before it will be rebuilt in brick and marble.

Turning a corner, the three decurions happen onto an argument. A man is pulling his friend away from a dispute with another man who keeps insulting him. And he says to his friend: "Look, Sextillus, just laugh in the face of anyone who insults you, and flip him the bird." His friend follows his advice: turning toward his adversary, he spits at him and shows him his middle finger. The argument then turns into a brawl, one of the many that can be seen every day on the backstreets of London. The decurions walk away. They don't want to be involved.

But this scene has been very interesting for us. We've discovered that one of the most offensive gestures of our own time, the raised middle finger, is not the product of our own vulgarity, but comes down to us from antiquity; it was already used by the ancient Romans. Confirmation of this comes from the Roman poet Martial, in his epigrams.

We rejoin the three decurions. They have just turned a corner onto the decumanus, one of the main streets of the future city of London. We lose ourselves together with them in the crowd of "Londoners."

An Ancient Feast of Purification

The cavalry squadron has gotten back on the road toward the northern boundary of the empire. This means several more days of riding. Their destination is Vindolanda (present-day Chesterholm), one of the farthest-flung forts in the Roman system of defense, the stronghold of what will become Hadrian's Wall. They will be entering what is still a hot zone of the frontier, where frequent skirmishes and battles break out with tribes who inhabit all of Caledonia (present-day Scotland) beyond the boundaries of the empire.

The soldiers on horseback are excited by this prospect and they're on alert. But there is still no need; although the cities, the villas of the wealthy, and the hovels of the poor are steadily thinning out, Rome is still in complete control of this part of Britain.

With the passing days the weather has gotten cooler, and by now it's fairly cold at night. Even the lowest hilltops are covered with snow. The sky is constantly overcast with thick layers of gray clouds, almost like a winter fur coat. The horsemen are hit by rain every day, and the cold wind transforms the raindrops into freezing needles that sting their hands and faces.

The *turma* has passed through the city of Lindum (now Lincoln) and then Eboracum (York), where an entire legion is based, the Legio VI *Victrix* (Sixth *Victorious* Legion). At every stop they deliver the new sesterces, and the next morning they climb back into the saddle and get on the road again.

Now they will spend their last night in a town before reaching their destination. They'll be staying in the small city of Cataractonium (now Catterick, in North Yorkshire), which is located next to a military fort.

While the soldiers have been scattering about town in alleyways, taverns, and bordellos, the three decurions have been accompanied by a colleague to participate in a feast of the local tribe to celebrate the advent of summer. We are now about midway between the spring equinox and the summer solstice, sometime around May 1.

The sun has gone down and the small group of soldiers are walking single file in the still snow-covered countryside. Summer arrives late at these latitudes. The trees in the forest still seem to be wrapped in in their winter torpor. They stop at the top of a hill where a lot of people from nearby villages are starting to gather with their farm animals. Many of them are shirtless, despite the cold. The decurions remain aloof from the crowd, but they observe the scene with curiosity.

There is a big pile of firewood and tree branches in the middle of the hill where the arriving crowd converges, as though attracted by it. Oil lamps and torches combine to form a myriad of lights that seem to be hovering in the darkness like fireflies. The same thing is happening on hilltops all around in a mesmerizing scene. In the crystalline cool night air the hills are topped with crowns of shimmering light that rival the stars in the sky.

Suddenly the crowd falls silent. One man speaks. He is the druid. In the semidarkness of the night all faces are turned toward this aged man, who intersperses his words and phrases with many pauses.

The Romans don't understand a word, but they can sense perfectly the solemnity of the moment. Their guide explains that they are looking at a feast of purification in honor of the sweet season that is approaching. The druid will light a big bonfire and the farm animals will walk by it to be purified by its smoke. Then it will be the people's turn.

The druid surveys the surrounding hills; on one of them you can see a torch swaying back and forth rhythmically. It's a signal. He points his bony index finger at the stack of firewood and pronounces some sacred words. Some bare-chested young men carrying torches go over to the pile and set it on fire. In the torchlight the Romans can make out the elegant tattoos wrapped all around their torsos like vines of ivy.

This is it; the fire rises up, envelops the pile of wood, and becomes a cathedral of flame. The decurions observe the crowd, whose faces are gradually illuminated in the rising glow of the fire; they all have such intense looks in their eyes.

The animals are pushed and prodded to get them to file past the bonfire. It's not easy because they are understandably frightened. As they pass by, torches are waived over their backs in symbolic purification.

The chief decurion looks out at the other hilltops. They are lit up like volcanoes and the snow reflects the flashes from the bonfires, projecting them out into the darkness. It looks like the world is on fire. From all those hills comes the sound of savage yelling and screaming. It is a true feast that now, once it has moved beyond the sacred and solemn phase, explodes in a great collective euphoria. Winter is behind us; now comes the growing season.

"It's a ritual to summon the fertility of life," one of the decurions thinks to himself. He still hasn't completed his thought when a swarm of torches carried by naked young men springs up from the base of the hill. Their muscles seem to seethe under their skin. And they are shouting. With them are a lot of young girls, also without clothes but with glimpses of ritual body painting. Their only clothing is leather stockings with laces. They run about shaking their torches; their shining bodies look like living flames defying the cold and the snow.

At the top of the hill, they push people in the crowd to make them jump, one by one, over little fires lighted in the snow. It's part of the ritual: you have to jump the fire to purify yourself. Old people and children are spared the jump in favor of a symbolic wave of the torch over their heads.

A small group of young people breaks away and run toward the Romans. Leading them is a girl with hair down to her shoulders. Behind her is another, with big hips, a bit less agile. Their breasts bounce with each step. Their torches light up their bodies, with a reddish orange light that softens their shape. When she gets within a few feet, the girl shouts something at the Romans, throwing open her jaws as though she wanted to bite them. She stares at them for a second, hints at a smile, and then "unsheathes" her torch and waves it at them before turning to vanish back into the darkness.

The flames from the torch pass in front of the Romans' eyes like a banner of fire. By the time they've gotten used to the darkness again, the group of girls and boys has gone back to their people, pushing, shoving, and laughing at those who hesitate to jump the fires.

To the chief decurion the girl's "bite" contained the roar of the tribal culture subjugated by the Romans. The empire has won the conflict of arms, certainly, but the tribal traditions are still strong. How far away Rome seems in these parts of the empire.

The tradition of lighting bonfires on hilltops and mountains has been conserved in modern times. There are still traces of this ancient tradition in many small-town feasts and festivals. It is difficult, however, to establish how much they are descended directly from ancient purification rituals and how much they are derived from more recent influences and propitiatory feasts to welcome the new season (by burning what is old or, symbolically, "burning" the harsh weather of winter), not least because many of these celebrations are held in the summer time.

Time to Say Farewell

With the coming of dawn the sky has gradually grown lighter, but the thick cover of gray clouds keeps everything colorless, wrapped in a cold metallic tint, including a little log cabin, with moss-covered walls.

Then, suddenly, the first rays of sunlight burst onto the horizon. It's like a breach in a wall; the bright beams of sunlight cut through the cold air, fend off the gelid wind, and come to rest on the roof of the cabin, like tired birds. Then, slowly, they slide down to the door, caressing it, almost wanting to knock. It's incredible how the sunlight makes the door change color. It's as though it has come back to life. From black it turns lighter and lighter, until it takes on the color of wood. Now the sun is a bright shiny ball, sitting on the horizon. Soon it will disappear, devoured by the thick gray clouds that seem to be eternally present in these climes.

Just then the door bursts open. The chief decurion comes out, his hand resting on the hilt of his sword, ready to use. He looks around, then relaxes, turning his face to the sun and nearly closing his eyes, savoring this magic moment that will soon be gone.

He's not alone. A woman comes out the door, wrapped in a warm blanket of brightly colored plaid. On her pale white legs she walks over to the decurion. The man turns and puts his arm tenderly around her, pulling her to him. She looks at him smiling, her face leaning against his chest. It's the girl from last night; the one who almost bit the Romans. Evidently, the decurion had tarried a while on the hilltop, and the two of them had taken advantage of the confusion of the feast. . . .

But now he has to be ready before his cavalry squadron is given the order to muster outside the fort in Cataractonium. The two of them wrap themselves in a passionate embrace before saying farewell. Both of them know that it is highly unlikely that they'll see each other again. After a last, long look from the girl, the decurion heads off toward the place where the unit is to assemble. Then he stops, turns back toward the girl, and launches a last, intense look, with a smile that lights up his face. The girl's cheeks are lined with tears and she pulls the blanket tighter around her.

What the two of them don't know is that part of the decurion will be staying here. In nine months the girl will have a baby, who over time will display one of his father's characteristic features: two mischievous lines on the sides of his mouth, the same ones that are now framing his smile. The decurion closes his eyes and goes off again to join his unit.

As he is walking he feels something inside the little purse on his belt that keeps knocking against his hip. He thought the purse was empty. He sticks his hand in it and finds the sestertius that the governor had given him. He looks at it, smiles, and gives it a squeeze before starting to walk again.

When he gets to the parade ground, his gigantic blond attendant has already saddled his horse and is waiting at attention, confirming for him that the other two decurions have already picked up the last load of sesterces to be delivered, which they had deposited in the fort for safekeeping.

It takes just a few minutes for the squadron to assemble, all present, outside the fort. Some of the soldiers cough. One blows his nose with his fingers. The rain and cold of the last few days have taken their toll. And it's not just the weather: One of the soldiers has a swollen face from a fight. Another, looking glum, is still hung over from an epic night of drinking. Most of them are going to remember this layover in Cataractonium for a long time.

The decurion smiles, knowing, however, that now he's going to have to be on alert for the threat of possible attacks. He looks at his men, then puffs up his chest and shouts the order to march. The squadron moves slowly down the main street, its insignias and *vexilla* in plain sight, attracting glances and curiosity.

Then, in just a few minutes the squadron exits the city and follows the road to the top of a rise. A gaze follows the squadron until the last purple cape vanishes beyond the hilltop. It is veiled in tears. It's the gaze of the girl.

Vindolanda

It has been a march where even the slightest sound was reason for alarm, especially when they were moving through wooded areas, but now the final destination of their long journey is near. The fort appears on the horizon, a long line of towers and rooftops looming under a blanket of enormous gray and white clouds. All around it the woods have been cut; all that's left are acres of intensely green grass. Snow is still hunkered down in the shady patches of the landscape, not willing to accept the fact that the season for nasty weather is over.

Next to the fort, on one side, a small village extends outward, home to the soldiers' families, a few craftsmen, and so on. Officially, the soldiers are not allowed to marry before the end of their period of service (which lasts twenty-five years), but inevitably bonds of affection are created, especially in faraway posts like this, where soldiers can be holed up for years. Children are born, giving rise to "spontaneous" families, which the army administration agrees not to notice.

The squadron presents itself at the entrance to the fort, and the chief decurion provides his credentials to the commander of the guard. Procedures have to be followed; the column is waiting for permission to enter. The chief decurion takes the opportunity to have a look at this frontier outpost. The walls are made of wood and they are not all that high (about twenty feet), but in case of attack it's difficult to get over them because the fort is surrounded by a deep moat, which makes the walls much higher. The walls are also topped by a layer of earth and grass to protect against attacks by fire. It's interesting to note that as far back as the Roman era there were already battlements with alternating merlons and crenels, like we associate with medieval castles.

Overlooking the walls are some wooden towers with naked structures. They look like trellises supporting a sort of square terrace, where the soldiers stand guard. They are placed at regular intervals, and the distance between them is not left to chance. Each terrace is within the firing range of a Roman war machine so that, in case of attack, one tower can protect the next.

The fort has a square floor plan with a fairly big surface area, about the size of four football fields. From where the chief decurion is now, you can see the roofs of the barracks, the stables, and all the buildings that make up this large frontier garrison.

One final curiosity: the camp has four entrances, one on each side, and it's easy to see where they are, even from far away, because there are always two paired towers keeping guard over each entrance. This is something that can still be seen today in many cities with a Roman design, including Rome itself. The main gates to the city, located along the defensive perimeter walls, can always be recognized from the two rounded towers that watch over them like sentinels. This is the case at the beginning of the famous Via Veneto, near the Pincian Gate in Rome. Two cylindrical towers indicate that this was the starting point of the ancient Via Salaria, which then flows into and follows the Salaria Nova.

The chief decurion is given permission to enter with his squadron. He dismounts and orders his men to go to the lodgings that have been reserved for them. He and the other two officers have to report to the commander and deliver the sesterces. The three of them make their way down the main street of the fort, together with the Batavian giant, who is carrying the last bag of sesterces with such ease it looks like a sackful of dry leaves.

The fort looks like a little city of soldiers, full of life. A stable boy passes by leading a horse. The sound of laughter can be heard coming from the open doors of the barracks. Some soldiers, their backs leaning against the wood columns of a shelter, are listening to some other soldiers explaining with gestures the maneuvers of a recent battle they fought in. After so many days in armor, the decurion finally meets up with some groups of soldiers in regular uniforms: no more chain mail and helmets; just a tunic and a belt from which are hanging, naturally, a short sword (*gladius*) and a dagger, ready for use (we're still in an operations zone).

As he passes he hears some unusual names. Names that are surprising to us too because they're foreign, certainly not Latin. Some of them are of German derivation: Butimas (the first part of the name means "booty"), Vatto, Chnisso, Chrauttius, Gambax (from the ancient Germanic *gambar*, "vigorous") and then Hvepnus, Hvete. Other names are typically Celtic: Troucisso, Catussa, Caledus, Uxperus, Acranius, Cessaucius, Varcenus, Viriocius. (Archaeologists have actually found all these names in the Vindolanda fort.)

After a long period of operation by Batavian soldiers, the fort is now occupied by the first cohort of Tungrians (from the northern part of the Ardennes plateau, in what is now France, Belgium, and Luxembourg). This is an important detail, for these soldiers are not legionnaires but soldiers recruited from peoples conquered by the Romans generations ago. These peoples, now faithful to the empire, are asked to provide soldiers who will serve alongside Roman legionnaires. They are usually under the command not of a Roman but of a member of the nobility of their nation. So they are units that are very unified from a cultural and linguistic point of view, but who fight and sacrifice themselves for the cause of Rome. Indeed, the forts manned by legionnaires are located well behind the front lines. So it is actually these "colonial" troops who suffer the first impact of an enemy attack, whether in battlefield formations (they are always in the front line) or in frontier forts. The legendary legionnaires are always ready to intervene, but only after the initial engagement. That's how the Roman army is organized.

As soon as they finish their military service, the prize for these auxiliary soldiers (so-called, to distinguish them from the legionnaires) is a piece of land, permission to legalize their marriage (and their offspring), and above all Roman citizenship, the most desired compensation. From then on they will no longer be Romanized ex-barbarians but fully legitimate citizens of Rome and the empire, as will their children. It's a sort of golden parachute that pushes these soldiers to grit their teeth and fight to the end. If indeed they make it to the end: on the front line, as we have seen, death is a daily occurrence.

The fort has a number of quarters, low buildings covered in white plaster with a long dark green stripe running all around the base. These are the barracks of the soldiers, their centurions, and their officers. But they are also used by the horses of a detachment of soldiers from the first cohort of Varduli, from northeastern Spain. As we can see, the frontier forts are the homes of the true "foreign legions" of Rome.

Sandals and Socks from Almost Two Thousand Years Ago

The meeting with the commander of the fort was intense and cordial. He spoke to the chief decurion in his typical Batavian accent—Nordic with a bit of a drawl. And he couldn't help but shake his head when he saw the sack of sesterces sitting on the table. He's a practical man and considers it a true waste of military energy to use an entire squadron to transport a simple supply of coins all this way. But he smiled when he saw the emperor's new conquest represented on the back of the coins. Another victory for Rome. As a good soldier, he views Trajan as one of his peers, that is, a man who has earned his stripes in the army. And he and all the other soldiers feel the utmost respect for him.

Some days ago, news reached the fort that a small group of Caledonians, a band of commandos, had infiltrated the Roman lines. The tracks of their wagon had been found in the snow, but then they disappeared near a river. "They are demons that come from the cold," he said. "They move with surprising skill through the most impervious terrain, and then they attack our positions behind the lines, with sneak attacks." The only way to stop them would be to build a wall from one coast to the other, with forts at regular intervals. "It's the only way; everybody who's been stationed here is convinced of it. That way we could put a stop to the infiltrations and get better control over trafficking in goods."

His view of the problem was adopted just a few years later, with the next emperor, Hadrian, who built a single wall, 20 feet high, 7 to 10 feet thick, and 108 miles long, across the entire width of northern Britain, from the Irish Sea to the North Sea. A true European "great wall," with guard towers every 1,500 feet and small forts placed at every mile to guard little passageways through the wall: a real "filter" for the passage of goods and people. In front of the wall, on the side facing the barbarians, there was a parallel ditch, 10 feet deep, to impede enemy attacks. Behind the wall, on the Roman side, there was a road connecting the forts and, curiously, another defensive ditch, reinforced by an embankment, showing that attacks were also feared from inside "friendly" territory. Numerous other large forts (like the one in Vindolanda) served as strongholds along Hadrian's Wall, like guard dogs ready to spring. The work was so well executed that a large part of this long stone snake is still visible today.

Exiting the commandant's room, which looks out onto the main courtyard of the general quarters, the decurion happens upon a scene that is in breach of protocol. A little boy with long blond hair and big bright eyes runs toward the commandant, shouting, "Papa, Papa."

A servant woman tries futilely to stop him, but the little boy is too fast for her. Nimble and quick, he runs up the three stairs to the wooden portico where the two men are standing and jumps into the arms of his father, who gives him a hug and picks him up. "Here's my little Achilles. Ready to do battle."

The decurion notices that the little boy's shoes have cleats on the soles, exactly like those of the legionnaires. He also notices the boy's heavy and colorful socks. Here almost all the soldiers wear heavy socks under their sandals (*caligae*).

Even though today a similar combination (which some designer fashion houses like Burberry, Givenchy, and Dior have recently brought back) might make people turn up their noses, a cold day like this one is enough to make you immediately opt for the "socks and sandals" style (*udones et caligae*, as the Romans would have said).

The commandant's wife also makes an appearance. She's an elegant woman with delicate features, almost certainly the daughter of an aristocratic family. She hands over a few of her letters to one of the commandant's secretaries, who nods and will see to their being sent. Writing and receiving letters from here might seem like a routine activity but for archaeologists it has turned out to be a true gift for the information that it has allowed them to discover, as we will see shortly.

The decurion bids farewell to the commandant. The difference in rank between the two is nearly unfathomable, similar to the gap between a corporal and a general. Yet the farewell, despite its martial nature, is quite cordial.

Heading toward the lodging he shares with the other two decurions, he quickens his step, having felt in his bones the cold and the humidity that has penetrated the fort. The climate here may be the true enemy of the Roman soldiers; it attacks them every day. And not only that, it attacks their buildings too.

As we have already noted, the fort is made of wood; not until a few years from now will it be replaced by a smaller one made of stone. And these buildings don't hold up very long in the humid air and damp terrain—less than ten years. Each time a building is torn down or part of the fort is restored, everything is covered, ruins and detritus, with a layer of impermeable clay, and the new structure is built on top of it. But this layer of clay has suffocated the terrain. Without oxygen, bacteria have not been able to act on and decompose objects underground, where they have thus been perfectly conserved by the high humidity of the layers of soil (which, in certain points, is almost muddy). As a result, over the last forty years the archaeologists and volunteers of Vindolanda, led by the tireless Robin Birley, have dug up thousands of intact objects, after a big sleep of almost two thousand years.

Many of these finds are on exhibit today in the museum on the site, and their uniqueness has made Vindolanda one of the most interesting areas of the Roman world. All kinds of artifacts have been found: from gold coins with the portrait of Trajan to precious rings with engraved seals, but also rings that are quite simple and emotionally moving, one of which, small and made of bronze, bears the inscription MATRI PATRI ("To Mom and Dad").

It's not possible to describe all of the finds: they range from a comb in its flat leather case (identical to the ones a lot of men carry in their pockets today) to dishes sent from France and never used because they were damaged en route, from fragments of wine amphoras to a glass cup with fighting gladiators etched on the sides, from a medallion with a Roman couple kissing (exactly like you might see on the cover of a gossip magazine) to sacrificial altars.

In addition, the archaeologists discovered more than two thousand sandals and shoes of all shapes and sizes. They are incredibly well preserved; you can even see the latching mechanisms and decorations. It has thus been ascertained that during their military service soldiers often wore midcalf boots, just as ours do today. A lot of them had metal cleats on the soles to keep them from wearing out and to ensure better traction. The clay-protected terrain has even yielded up socks used by soldiers to keep their feet warm. But the most striking finds are a baby's shoe (it too has cleats) and a little wooden gladius. They were found in the home of the commandant of the fort, Flavius Cerialis. Maybe they belonged to his son.

Another strange find is a wig made with long, dark, vegetable filaments (it may have been a woman's hairnet for use against insects, but it's not certain). It probably belonged to the commandant's wife, Sulpicia Lepidina. We know quite a bit about this couple, thanks to the archaeologists' discoveries. They lived here in the fort for ten to twelve years before the decurions' arrival, and now they are somewhere else in the empire. We know they have at least two children. The archaeologists have found buried under the house several small shoes for children ages two to ten. They couldn't have been the shoes of only one child as he grew, because the family lived in the fort for just four years, at which time the entire cohort of Batavians under the command of Cerialis was sent to Dacia to help conquer it for Trajan. (It seems that this transfer of the cohort caused numerous desertions by soldiers who didn't want to leave their "spontaneous" families behind without any means of support.) But the most complete news about this family comes from the letters that it sent and received.

"Send Me Two Pairs of Underpants": Letters from the Edge of the Empire

The Vindolanda site earned its honored place in the history of archaeology for the nearly two thousand letters and documents found there by researchers. They give a vivid description of life on the edge of the empire, supplying us with information about the Roman military organization, from logistical systems for supplying the troops to the costs of tents, wagons, and clothing. The letters even bring to light a crime, perhaps a case of corruption inside the fort, in which the guilty party was deported from the province in chains. An exemplary punishment for a very serious crime.

In the case of the commandant, the letters and various documents that he sent and received were supposed to have been destroyed. His aides lighted a fire to burn them but a providential storm extinguished the flames, permitting their conservation.

Before we look at what is written in the letters, let's examine how they were written. First of all, what did the Romans write on? On wooden tablets with raised borders around a layer of wax where the text was written, or scratched, with a long metallic pen. Or else on thin wood strips about six-hundredths of an inch thick, made from trunks of alder and birch trees. These strips, about seven inches long and four inches wide, were written on with ink. The pens were cigarette-size wooden cylinders with a metal ring on the tip that stuck out like a filed fingernail. It was a very effective system. Modern experiments have demonstrated that one dip of the pen in ink was enough to write three or four words. Even more impressive is the fact that the little wooden cylinders are often hollow, which raises the possibility that they could be used much like our fountain pens, with a small supply of ink on the inside (but as of now this is only a hypothesis). In all, more than two hundred pens have been rediscovered.

The Romans had an interesting system for "folding" their letters. Envelopes did not exist. The wooden strips were put in a row, like dominoes, and tied together with a little cord through holes. Most of the time there were two of them and they closed like a restaurant menu. But sometimes there were more than two, and in such cases they were folded in on one another much the way we do with road maps (or did, before the arrival of digital navigators). On the first "page" they wrote the name of the recipient, just as we do today on the front of the envelope.

These delicate letters have been miraculously preserved for centuries, thanks to the humid terrain that was free of bacteria and—at the time they were discovered—some twenty to twenty-five feet underground. At first, the archaeologists didn't understand what they were. In some cases the writing was faded. Using infrared light they managed to read the texts in their entirety.

Here is an extract from a letter sent by Solemnis, a solider at the edge of the empire, to a fellow soldier named Paris.

Report of 15 April on the IX cohort of Batavians: all the men are present and their equipment is in order!

I'm sending you a few pairs of socks, two pairs of sandals, and two pairs of underpants.

The Britons don't have armor; they have a good cavalry that doesn't use the spear, however. These poor little "Britoninnies" don't even know how to launch a javelin on horseback.

The men are out of beer. I ask you to order someone to go get some more.

Thanks for giving me such a splendid vacation.

I inform you that I am in excellent health, and I hope the same is true for you, lazybones; you haven't sent me even one letter!

But the most touching letter, perhaps, is the birthday party invitation from Sulpicia Severa, the wife of the commandant of another fort, to Lepidina, the wife of Cerialis. It's the most ancient letter we have from one woman to another.

Sepulcia Severa to her Lepidina, greetings! The third day before the ides of September [September 11], sister, for the day of my birthday celebration, I'm sending you my heartfelt invitation to see to it that you can come be with us, so that by your presence you can make my day even happier, if you come (?).

My best to your Ceriale. My Elio and our son send their regards to him. I await you, dear sister! Be well, sister, my dearest soul, just as I hope to be well too, and farewell.

To Sulpicia Lepidina [wife] of Ceriale, from Severa.

What's more, the back of one letter has a dictation exercise written by the son of Commandant Cerialis! There is a line from Virgil's *Aeneid* (IX, 473) that his tutor, the "erudite" house slave (perhaps named Primigenius) had dictated to him. And there are some mistakes made by his student. It is easy to imagine the voice of the slave, enunciating slowly: *Interea pavidan volitans pennata per urbem nuntia Fama ruit matrisque adlabitur auris Euryali.* ("Meanwhile, winged Rumor, flying through the frightened city, reaches the ears of his mother Euryalus.")

Today, from a distance of nearly two thousand years, we can discover what the student wrote: *Interea pavidam volitans pinnata p'ubem.* We can't help but sympathize with this lad who had to study the *Aeneid* in such a godforsaken place. But we can also appreciate the effort his father made to give him a good education, even while living on the edge of the known world of the time.

All this is beneath the floor of the Pretorium, the house of the commandant, which our decurion has just left. Now, chilled to the bone, he may go for a dip in the hot water of the baths, which are located right outside the fort. He deserves a little relaxation after all these days on the road. Plus, don't forget, these are the northernmost baths in the entire empire—something to tell his friends about when he gets back to Rome.

To see how far it is to the bath complex, the chief decurion climbs to the top of the fort's defensive walls, but when he gets to the top of the stairs a glacial wind hits him right in the face, forcing him to take cover behind a merlon. Two young soldiers on guard duty, numb, observe him, their eyes tearing up from the cold.

The chief decurion takes a quick glance outside. Just forty or fifty feet from the walls of the fort a group of soldiers are practicing with a *scorpio*, a sort of enormous dart launcher mounted on a tripod. Their target is the head of a cow that's standing about seventy-five yards away.

The dart takes off, whistles through the air, and strikes the cow square in the head, which is already full of holes from previous launches. The precision of these weapons is astounding, as we will discover in subsequent chapters. As the crew reloads, executing the orders barked by a centurion, the decurion notices something lying in a ditch off in the distance. It's a man's body, mutilated, and he realizes that it must be one of the Caledonians involved in the attack on the *mansio*. He had heard that the soldiers had captured a warrior who had managed to escape from the scene of the assault. They interrogated him, tortured him, and killed him. Now his body is lying in that far-off ditch.

The chief decurion doesn't know it, but many centuries from now, during an archaeological dig, two skulls will be found: one of a cow riddled by projectile blows and, in another location, one of a young man between twenty and thirty years old with evident signs of other kinds of blows.

The chief decurion casts a glance northward, into the territory of the Caledonians. The low-lying hills are lined up from here to the horizon, covered with patches of snow and woodlands. Out there it's no longer the empire. The known world ends here. He is truly on the edge.

From the world of the barbarians a sudden gust of ice-cold wind rises up, hitting him like a slap in the face. The chief decurion instinctively takes a step backward. Then he narrows his eyes and launches a grimace of defiance toward the horizon.

This place is really damned by the gods, he thinks to himself. Far away from the warmth of Rome and the Mediterranean, far away from the cities, from the inhabitants of the empire who don't even know that these forts and these men are here. It's a world inhabited only by the hatred of the populations beyond the frontier and the harshness of the climate.

He turns around and quickly descends the stairs to go to the baths: the last sign of Roman civilization in these parts; beyond them only nothingness.

PARIS

~ *When It Was Smaller than Pompeii* ~

Our coin is back on its journey through the Roman Empire, having changed hands by sheer accident. In the baths of Vindolanda, as the decurion undressed and hurriedly rolled his clothes into a bundle, his mind occupied by his desire for a nice bath, the purse hanging from his belt turned upside down and the sestertius fell out, dropping to the floor of the little niche that served as a locker in the dressing room.

Nobody noticed it for several days, until another customer of the baths, passing by with an oil lamp, noticed a little twinkle of light, reached out his hand, and grabbed it.

Now it's in the purse of a wine merchant who has just delivered some amphoras of wine to the edge of the empire and is on his way back home. Britain is behind him, and the coin has returned to the continent and is traveling along a big road in the province of Lugdunensis, in the heart of what today is known as France. The merchant is on horseback together with his trusty slave. They've been riding along at a slow pace for hours, under the pouring rain.

How do the Romans protect themselves from the rain? If you think that umbrellas are a modern invention, you're mistaken. They existed even before the time of the Romans. Archaeologists have discovered several of them in Etruscan tombs. They were a little different from ours, lacking thin metal spokes or springs. They were very similar, however, to Chinese umbrellas, with thick, rigid wooden staves. But the use they made of them was quite different. The Etruscan umbrella preserved in the Villa Giulia museum in Rome, for example, is made of ivory, which means it was used by wealthy people, a true status symbol of the aristocracy. And it was used for protection not from the rain but from the sun. To keep their skin from becoming tan, noblewomen carried umbrellas, or parasols, exactly as women did in Europe in the eighteenth, nineteenth, and early twentieth centuries, and as women still do today in the Far East. In fact, the Latin name was *umbrella*, from *umbra*, meaning "shade," the same name that is used today in English and Italian (*ombrello*).

So how *did* they fend off the rain? With an invention we wouldn't necessarily associate with the Romans: the poncho! The two men on horseback, and some of their fellow travelers on foot, are wearing leather ponchos (*paenula*), made waterproof by a coating of grease. Others, like the legionnaires, use ponchos made of boiled or felted wool, soaked in olive oil to keep water out.

The poncho always includes a hood, which is often pointed. From far away, therefore, a group of Romans in the rain looks like little walking pyramids, with their faces peeking out through a round opening.

The Skeleton of Roman Globalization

Neither of the two men on horseback realizes it, but the gravel-covered road they have been traveling on for hours will go down in history as one of humanity's greatest masterworks. It is part of the incredible network of roads that radiate throughout the empire.

To be sure, when we ask ourselves what is the greatest monument built by the ancient Romans, we instinctively think of the Colosseum, the Circus Maximus, or the baths of Caracalla. But actually it's the roads. They are without a doubt the most enduring monument left to us, constituting a network measuring over eighty thousand kilometers, or forty-eight thousand miles. In other words, with the roads they built, the Romans could have ringed the earth twice—an extraordinary accomplishment in any age. Why did the Romans build such an extensive network of ground transportation and communication? Initially, their purpose was military:

the roads enabled the legions to deploy rapidly anywhere in the empire in order to deal with possible threats. In this sense we can think of the Roman roads as the aircraft carriers of antiquity.

They served this purpose for centuries. But almost immediately they came to be used for other purposes as well, especially economic ones, with the circulation of merchants, merchandise, and sesterces. And for cultural purposes too, because they permitted the circulation throughout three continents of people and ideas, artistic styles and fashions, information and knowledge, laws and religions.

The roads, along with maritime routes, allowed Roman civilization to expand and put down its roots everywhere, and also to acquire ideas, ways of living, and products from other cultures, creating a society that was diverse, multiethnic, and dynamic, as we are only now beginning to do again. In this sense, the roads were initially the muscles of the Roman civilization; then they became its circulatory system, and finally its nervous system.

Without the roads and maritime skills, history's first globalization, the one brought about by the Romans, would never have happened. Roman culture could still have spread in a limited way along the seacoast, as the Phoenician, Aegean, and Greek cultures did, but it would not have united millions of people with the same language, the same body of laws, the same way of dressing, eating, and living. And our world would look very different today.

The Highways of Antiquity

What was so special about the Roman roads?

Firstly, the Roman concept of the road is incredibly similar to our own. The proof of this is right before our eyes every day. We in Italy don't notice it, but in our cities we continue to use Roman roads to go to work, go into town, take our children to school, go shopping, and leave the city for an outing in the countryside. In many cases, modern asphalt has simply covered over the ancient roadbed designed and built by Roman engineers; or else it runs parallel to it. This is the case for the famous consular roads, such as the Flaminia, the Cassia, the Appia, the Salaria, and the Aurelia.

Then there is also a whole network of lesser roads in rural areas, which are still unchanged, demonstrating the validity of Roman transportation planning and design. Their needs were very similar to ours because their world was very similar to ours.

If you take a close look at a consular road like the Appia Antica, which runs straight for miles, you realize that the Roman engineers had already come up with the modern concept of the highway: a road that cuts through the territory in a straight line, bypassing smaller towns and settlements, and not succumbing to obstacles such as mountains, valleys, or cliffs, but overcoming them in spectacular fashion (whereas before, roads adapted to the terrain, going around hills or valleys, winding up and down mountainsides, etc.).

Indeed, when the Romans had to build a road that was important for the legions and for the economy, they didn't adapt to nature but rather, in many cases, they adapted nature to their needs: they pulled down entire coastal cliffsides (like the *tagliata*, or cut, near Terracina, a mighty cliffside that was cut away by picks on orders from Trajan to let the Appia continue on its way); built tunnels (like the Furlo tunnel on the Flaminian Way in the Marche region, authorized by Vespasian, where you can still see the marks left by Roman chisels); or carved roads or arches directly on rocky mountainsides (as can be seen at Donnas in Val d'Aosta).

The Romans had the capacity to build roads through mountain passes at altitudes over eight thousand feet (like the Great Saint Bernard Pass) that were then used by wagons and carriages for centuries until the advent of the automobile. Viaducts, arches, and bridges allowed for relatively swift passage through valleys and passes while maintaining a maximum slope of 8 to 9 percent (with rare exceptions of 10 to 12 percent).

All of this made the Roman roads (it has not been said often enough) a truly revolutionary accomplishment: for the first time Europe was united by a network of stable and sturdy roads, an achievement that has endured even in language. The Roman name for a road is *via strata*, which means "paved way"; hence the Italian *via* and *strada* but also the English *street* and the German *Strasse*.

The Secrets of Roman Roads

When we examine a Roman road in Rome or at an archaeological site, we ask ourselves how it is possible that it is still intact after almost two thousand years, when our roads, without regular and careful maintenance, deteriorate so easily into fields of potholes. The same question was asked during the Middle Ages when people continued to use Roman bridges and ways, calling them "paths of the giants" and "bridges and roads of the devil."

The secret is in their structure. They were roads that were designed to last.

The two travelers carrying our sestertius can see it with their own eyes. It has stopped raining, but the road has not turned into a quagmire and there are no puddles. The water hasn't stagnated, the internal structure of the road has allowed the water to run off and drain, just as on our highways. How did they do it?

The two travelers are now passing an area where some roadwork is in progress. The road has been opened up as for a surgical operation, and the two of them stop, curious to see its anatomy.

Generalizing and simplifying, we might say that building a road starts with digging a big ditch, from fifteen to twenty feet wide and maybe six or seven feet deep. Basically it looks like a long canal running through the countryside.

Then it's filled in with three layers of stone: on the bottom, a layer of large rounded rocks, followed by a layer of medium-sized stones, and finally the layer closest to the surface, which is a mixture of gravel and clay (which must not come from the local area; that's something the Romans are adamant about). The use of concrete, starting around the time that we're talking about, made the road sturdier.

This layering of the stones, from the largest and coarsest to the smallest and finest, is the real secret of Roman roads. Like a filter, the road carries the rainwater down off the surface, keeping it from stagnating.

And it's not over yet: the whole road surface is now covered with a last layer of large volcanic stones, arranged in a tortoiseshell pattern. When we see these stones today, they seem like thin flat slabs placed one against the other. But actually they are very thick, real blocks of stone similar to large cubes; their weight and mass are what make the road so stable. They are placed in such a way that the surface looks rounded, like a donkey's back, so that whatever rainwater hasn't drained down through the various layers will run off to the sides (exactly what happens on our streets).

This description of the structure of a Roman road refers to an ideal type. In actual fact, more often than not the engineers find themselves confronted with soils so geologically diverse that they have to make adjustments to their construction methods each time. And it is exactly this great (and complex) variety of solutions that allows us to appreciate the surprising capabilities and competence of Roman engineers.

Local conditions permitting, the roads are about thirteen feet across, wide enough to allow two wagons to pass. On the sides there are ten-foot-wide walkways for pedestrians. You can see, then, that a lot of films and paintings are mistaken when they show people walking in the middle of the road; it's much more comfortable to walk on the raised, flat sidewalk than on the convex road surface. If you were to ask a modern legionnaire (a member of those historical associations, the so-called reenactors, who perform a precious service of experimental archaeology by dressing and living as soldiers or people of antiquity) to walk on a Roman road paved with volcanic stone like the ones you see in Rome, Ostia, or Pompeii, he would find it difficult. Why? Because his military *caligae* with their metal cleats will cause him to slip and slide as though he were walking on ice.

So we must conclude that the legions, when presented with roads paved with stone slabs, preferred to walk in rank and file on the sidewalks. And that's not all. There are a lot of little details that seldom get mentioned. The border of the sidewalks is usually made of long stone beams laid end to end, like our city sidewalks. But there's a difference: at regular intervals, every few yards or so, a little stone block (*gomphus*) would appear, like a wayside post. What might this be used for? For dismounting or mounting a horse. In an age when stirrups still didn't exist, these blocks were the equivalents of a stool. And they are useful to someone who needs to get down off a wagon.

The Romans' practicality emerges from the details of their roads. Another curiosity is that in flat areas the roads tend to be raised, so that they can be recognized under the snow and protected from water. In the Veneto, for example, they are raised fifteen to twenty-two feet above ground level and built on embankments that are forty yards wide. Moreover, they tend to be built on hillsides rather than on the valley floor, to avoid flooding from overflowing rivers and to ensure a favorable position in case of enemy attack. Finally, in the mountains, the roads are often scored with concave tracks, like tiny canals, so wagon wheels won't skid or slide off the road into the valley below.

But is it really true that Roman roads never had potholes like our roads today? Actually, the quality of the roads changed depending on the location. While in Italy every road had a *curator*, a superintendent in charge of maintenance carried out by a sort of service guard (similar to a highway administration), in the provinces things were done differently. By order of the proconsul, it was the local communities that had to provide for the proper functioning and maintenance of the roads. And in many cases, since they were already oppressed by taxes, they didn't always provide adequately, or at least not quickly. So in certain parts of the empire there certainly were potholes, or their ancient equivalent, and then some—a further resemblance to the modern era.

Another myth to be dispelled is the idea that Roman roads were always covered, throughout the empire, by slabs of basalt, as was the Appia Antica. This is absolutely not the case. In reality, you only find paved road surfaces on the main streets of cities (not on side streets). Outside of urban centers the pavement continues for only a short distance and then disappears, replaced by a fine crushed stone. The reason is that it cost too much. Between one city and another, in other words, a road, even though it still has all of its deep "draining" layers of stone and rubble, no longer has its stone slab pavement and it becomes essentially *glarea strata*, as the Romans call it, that is, a road of gravel or crushed stone. A curiosity: these roads were very dusty, so much so that numerous Latin authors complained about them. In his Letters to Atticus, Cicero speaks openly of *aestuosa et pulverulenta via* ("a burning and dusty way," *Att.*V., 14, 1). These roads turned into a real nightmare when they went through tunnels, as Seneca notes, when he describes his passage through the Crypta Neapolitana, the tunnel that connects Naples to Pozzuoli (*Epist.* V., 57, 1–2).

One feature that is always present, however, and which is essential to travelers, is the milestone. These are small pillars placed, as the name suggests, "a thousand paces," or one Roman mile (4,860 feet), apart.

If you do the math, a stride of nearly five feet might seem to be rather long for the person who is walking, but "pace" is defined here as the moment that the same foot touches the ground for the second time, completing the cycle of the step. So, in reality, it is a double step (exactly like a marching platoon counting cadence).

The pillars are the travelers' odometer. Written on them are the number of miles traveled from the city of departure and sometimes other information as well, for example, how far it is to the final destination or to some important place along the road, or even the names of the magistrates who have provided for road repairs, etc.

The zero point of the empire's vast network of roads was the *miliarium aureum,* or golden milestone, a marble column clad in gilt bronze and placed by Augustus at one end of the Roman Forum, on which were engraved the distances between Rome and the most important points in the empire.

Part of this concept of the centrality of the Roman Forum to the system of consular roads still survives today. If you take the Via Cassia from the center of Rome you will read on the marble street signs that the numbering of the houses corresponds to the metric distance from the Capitol, that is, from the place that was the heart of ancient Rome, right next to the Forum.

When Paris Was Smaller than Pompeii

It's stopped raining, and the two men on horseback are making their way down a road with a long aqueduct running alongside it. Through the aqueduct's arches you can see the tombstones of a necropolis, a sign that the city is near. Cemeteries, in fact, are always just outside the city. At the end of the road the first houses come into view. Very soon the two men find themselves in the midst of a noisy crowd of people on the main street. But what city is this?

They notice a sign on the entrance to a tavern. Along with the prices there's also the name of the establishment and a figure: Lutetia's Rooster. So, we're in Lutetia Parisiorum, the future Paris!

It's unrecognizable, an anonymous town with maybe eight to ten thousand inhabitants. It's smaller than Pompeii, which has a population of twenty thousand. The area it occupies is just a little bigger than the future Latin Quarter of Paris.

It's astounding to see that the future capital of *la grandeur française* is the size of Punxsutawney, Pennsylvania, and that today Paris, Texas, has three times the population of its namesake. But that's the way it was in the Roman era.

Right now we're making our way along the *cardo maximus*, a main north-south axis that the French will call Rue Saint-Jacques, ignoring its true origins. The houses are low, at most two stories high.

It's intriguing to try to recognize in the Roman city the signs of the modern city of the future. There are plenty of surprises. First of all, the Roman city is not a capital but just one of many provincial towns. The provincial capital is Lyon (Lugdunum), which is much bigger, maybe the biggest city in Europe west of the Alps. Paris will be given its current name toward the end of the Roman era and will become a capital city in four centuries, in the year 508, under the Franks, who will give their name to the entire nation. Even though these barbarians gave rise to the first dynasty of kings, it's surprising that the French, always proud of their own Gallic origins (to the point of defining almost any Roman object found on their territory as "Gallo-Roman") have kept the name of the Franks, an invading Germanic people.

Let's continue our visit to the city. On horseback, we pass one of Lutetia's bistros, but actually it's a *popina*, a bar-tavern like the ones that can be seen anywhere in the empire. We overhear a discussion between some men standing at the counter drinking white wine from terra-cotta glasses, literally the *blanc* served today in French bars.

"Not long ago, Gellanius the auctioneer was selling a girl with a less-than-sterling reputation, one of the ones who are always sitting in the middle of the brothel. Since the bids were all very low, he tried to convince everyone that the girl was a virgin and started pulling her toward him while she waved her finger at him to say "No, no." And he kissed her one, two, three, four times. You want to know what he got for those four kisses? The guys who had been offering 600 sesterces changed their minds and lowered their bids!" A burst of laughter from his listeners.

We don't know if the speaker's tale is a true story or if he simply used a famous story from Martial's *Epigrams*, passing it off as his own.

Let's examine the other customers. Their faces are those of Celts and merchants who have come ashore from ships arriving on the Seine. Indeed, the situation here is reminiscent of London. Paris, too, was "invented" by the Romans.

This area was originally inhabited by the (possibly nomadic) tribe of the Parisii, a branch of the Senones. During the campaign for the conquest of Gaul, the legionnaires of Julius Caesar defeated the Parisii warriors in 52 BCE, and the whole basin of the future capital of France fell into Roman hands. Just a few decades later the city baptized Lutetia Parisiorum (Lutetia of the Parisii) was founded. The river made it possible to bring in goods and transport troops. And right in the middle of the Seine there were two islands that made it easier to ford the river and that must have reminded the Romans of Tiber Island in the heart of Rome.

So Paris was born, thanks to the Romans, in part on the left bank of the Seine and in part on the river's main island, the future Île de la Cité.

Now, under Trajan, though still very small, Paris has all the features of a typical Roman city. The forum of the ancient city will be the site of the big buildings on the future Rue Soufflot, and the two bath complexes of Lutetia will be either overrun by throngs of tourists who have just gotten off the Métro between Boulevard Saint-Michel and Boulevard Saint-Germain, or home to the solemn environs of the Collège de France.

What stood on the site of the cathedral of Notre-Dame? We can see it now with our own eyes. We have crossed the whole city in almost no time and have arrived on the banks of the Seine, near the location of the future Petit Pont. Anyone standing here in the modern era has the romantic view of the bridges of Paris, the *bouquinistes,* and in the background the imposing silhouette of the cathedral. And in the Roman era?

No *bouquinistes* selling old books, only merchants and slaves busy unloading goods from the ships moored at the wooden docks attached to the muddy banks of the Seine. No *bateaux mouches* overflowing with tourists, just boats loaded with casks of wine, amphoras, and even slaves captured beyond the borders of the empire to be sold here at auction.

And above all, no Notre-Dame. It won't be built for over a thousand years. In its place now is an imposing temple dedicated to Jupiter, with its columns and its gilt-bronze friezes. In many ways this island is to Paris what the Capitoline Hill is to Rome. After the Temple of Jupiter this same site will host a Christian basilica, then a Romanesque church, and finally the great cathedral. The sacred vocation of the place first selected by the Romans will be passed down over the course of the centuries, as in a relay race, until it is crowned by the marvelous architecture of Notre-Dame.

It all seems so different in the Roman era—or perhaps not. The romantic charm of Paris already exists. Two lovers, she blond and buxom, he tall and Celtic, are leaning against the parapet of the bridge that crosses the Seine, lost in a passionate kiss. It's the ancient version of the famous photograph by Robert Doisneau that is admired today in so many post-cards and posters of Paris.

We continue on our way. The two men, master and slave, must arrive at the last stop on their journey to organize another wine trade. Their destination is the area that produces one of the most renowned wines in the northern part of the empire, the area near the shores of the Moselle.

TRIER

~ *Making the Nectar of the Gods* ~

The Wine of the North

After several days' journey in the rain we arrive at Augusta Treverorum, the present-day city of Trier, now a pleasant German city near the border with Luxembourg. Still, today, anyone would find this city surprising; you just don't expect to find so many vestiges of Rome in northern Europe. The whole city is sprinkled with the remnants of baths, bridges, amphitheaters, ovals for chariot races, and an immense basilica, where the emperor Constantine once sat. And it must also have surprised those who, after days of journeying through forests, woods, and lakes, suddenly found themselves confronted with a large, wealthy, Roman city, so far north, in such a cold climate.

But there is another monument that we haven't yet encountered that will last even longer and better than the city and its buildings, coming all the way down to our own time: the vine.

The two men arrive in the late afternoon, exhausted from the journey. They leave their horses in a stable, paying for the animals' lodging with a few coins, among them our sestertius, which thus changes hands once again. We won't see the two men again; they'll be lost in the folds of daily life in the empire.

But neither will the sestertius stay long in the hands of its new owner. The next morning, a well-dressed young man enters that very stable. He had left his horse there very briefly, long enough to grab a quick bite to eat in the city. It's a gorgeous horse, powerful and fast, the equivalent of a modern-day sports car. That's why he put it in a safe and supervised "garage." When he came back he paid with a denarius and was given several sesterces, including ours, in change.

His horse, his finely crafted clothes, and his denarii indicate that the young man belongs to the upper ranks of society. In fact, he's the son of a vineyard owner and he's on his way to one of his family's farms. For us it's a nice piece of luck; there's some Moselle wine waiting for us.

In less than an hour by horseback we are in the heart of where it's produced. The road runs alongside the Moselle River, which flows majestically through the wooded hills and mountains, creating lots of loops and bends. It looks like a gigantic sleeping snake. The countryside is breathtakingly beautiful, one of those landscapes that soothes the soul, but the most impressive thing is the vast expanse of vineyards that cover the sweetly rolling slopes as far as the eye can see, right down to the river's edge.

It's like that even today. And if we are still able to savor the renowned wines from this area, we owe it to the Romans, who understood the potential of these hills, giving an incredible boost to the production of wine.

The Romans' policy on wine is really curious. For several centuries they maintained an absolute monopoly. Wine was popular, especially among the Celtic populations of the north (they had first gotten to know it thanks to the Etruscans) who entered the Roman orbit with the conquests of Julius Caesar. They liked it so much, in fact, that Roman slave traders were able to purchase men and women just by offering amphoras of wine. The barbarians themselves captured other barbarians from nearby territories to sell them to the traders. Wine, in other words, followed the legions like a faithful dog and arrived wherever new settlements were established. It was one of the fuels of daily life.

Then as now, wine was very much appreciated and the demand for the "nectar of the gods" on the part of Roman settlers and conquered peoples was pressing. You can imagine the volume of traffic in amphoras northbound from Italy on ships. On the docks of port cities amphoras were lined up in rows like soldiers, ready to be loaded on board. In fact, the most beautiful amphoras in museums today, the Dressel 1 and 2 models, with their tapered bodies and long necks, date back to this period of conquest and expansion. To see them now is like capturing a photo of that era. It can be asserted with confidence that they date back exactly to the decades immediately before the birth of Christ, that they were manufactured solely in the workshops of Campania, and that they contained wine produced in the vineyards that extended more or less from the south of Lazio to just north of Naples. Those amphoras were also used to export the famous Falernian wine, so praised by the ancients. They arrived everywhere throughout the Mediterranean, especially in the three Gauls. But not all of them reached their destinations. A large portion of the Roman shipwrecks loaded with amphoras that now lie on the bottom of the northwest Mediterranean come from this exact period of history: the colonization of the north.

It's no wonder, then, that the Roman administrators realized the potential profits that could be made in the wine business. They even prohibited grape growing in the new territories, forcing the populations to pay high prices for imported wine.

Later, with the expansion of the empire, they initiated a policy of concessions, but for a long time the only authorizations to grow wine were issued to legionnaires. Their presence on the frontiers (*limites*) led to a delocalization of wine production, not least because they were such heavy consumers of it. Wine growing was often entrusted to veterans who were given farmlands in frontier areas as rewards for their period of service. Finally, wine production was also granted to private growers, and this created huge areas of production, like the one we are exploring now.

On both sides of the river vineyards cover every possible square inch on the slopes of the hills. But how do they manage to produce wine so far north in the empire, and with what systems?

How the Romans Produce the Nectar of the Gods

The young man on horseback meets and passes a lot of four-wheeled wooden wagons pulled by oxen and loaded with baskets full of grapes. There are a lot of farms that produce wine in this area. It's harvest time, and along the rows of vines you can see columns of slaves going up and down with panniers chock-full of grapes. The glories of these vineyards will be sung a few generations from now by the poet Decimus Magnus Ausonius.

The surprising thing is that the vines are much different than ours. The shoots are not stretched out for twenty yards or more on suspended metal wires. Instead they are made up of so many little "trees" extending down the hillside from top to bottom in single file. And they have a curious shape: the shoots have been curled and bent like a wire until they form a figure eight the height of a man. It's an ingenious system: in this way a rather long piece of vine is folded up on itself to occupy a relatively small space. The grape bunches grow on both sides of this figure eight, with the interior ones splendidly framed by the double ring of which it is composed.

The vineyard owner's son arrives in front of a large wooden gate. His horse stamps its feet. The rider and his beautiful white horse, a sign of his family's ample profits, have been spotted from far away. A slave opens the gate immediately and greets him obsequiously. The young man advances without returning the greeting. He proceeds at a gallop, up a hill, to a low building where the grapes are pressed. Upon his arrival, a group of slaves in single file stop working and put their panniers on the ground, lowering their heads in deference. They are half-naked and sweaty, their skin sticky from the resins seeping out of the cut vines. He orders them gruffly not to stop and to keep on working. Then he goes into the building, rudely pushing out of his way a slave standing in the doorway. The inside is a single large room—we might compare the entire structure to an industrial shed—with a line of slaves. The slaves empty into a large tub the heavy baskets of grapes they have been bearing on their shoulders. During the harvest they will carry tons of grapes here and empty them into this tub, basket after basket without interruption.

Other slaves, the *calcatores*, completely naked and soaked with sweat, are stamping the grapes. This is an exhausting job; they have to "march" for hours and hours, crushing grapes that never seem to end, amid clouds of stinging wasps and screaming overseers. To lighten the burden they sing songs from their native lands and lean on strange walking sticks that look like crutches to keep from losing their balance.

All of this takes place under the vigilant eyes of two divinities painted on the walls and much venerated around these parts: Sucellus, of Gallic origins, the protector of Moselle wine growers, often represented with bunches of grapes, casks, and wine presses; and Bacchus, of Mediterranean origins, who is the protector of wine drinkers.

The grape juice pours out copiously from several openings in the form of a lion's mouth and flows into a smaller tub, sunk below ground. The liquid flows through some wicker baskets that function as filters, holding back the grape skins and dead wasps. The juice that passes through the baskets gradually fills up the smaller tub. At regular intervals it is then poured off into small amphoras.

In an endless assembly line, other slaves slide sticks through the handles of the amphoras and carry them out into the courtyard of the farmhouse. There, they pour the grape juice into large terra-cotta jars that stick up out of the ground. These jars, called *dolia*, are about the size of washing machines; the juice will age and ferment inside them. The *dolium* is the Roman solution for aging wine. But the Gauls have invented an alternative that is very effective: the cask.

The Romans adopted it immediately, and in a very short time they introduced it in numerous areas of the empire. The cask will continue to be used over the centuries down to our own time. Here both systems are used. Other slaves, in fact, are pouring grape juice into a line of large casks.

These farms, like all farms throughout the empire, have very modern techniques for optimizing productivity. The aim is to maximize profits by literally squeezing the source of earnings (in other words, the grape) down to the last drop. After the first pressing, done by foot, grapes can still yield a lot of juice. And the Romans know this only too well. But how to obtain the juice? By using a gigantic press, the *torculum*.

The *torculum*, which is enthroned in the center of the building, is an immense beam, forty feet long, made from the trunk of a single oak. This is how it works. The pulp and skins of the pressed grapes (that is, the dregs) are left to steep for several days. This makes them softer, watery, and easier to squeeze. Then the mixture is put into a single container, a wooden tub with a lot of openings in the bottom, and the beam is centered horizontally over the tub. The beam will act as a huge weight, crushing the pulp and skins.

At first glance the weight of this immense beam seems capable of giving a pretty good squeeze. But it's not enough. The Romans devised an ingenious method for infusing the *torculum* with a force never seen in all of antiquity. The beam is anchored to the wall on one side, while on the opposite side it has an enormous wood screw that goes all the way down to the ground where it is fixed to a massive block of stone weighing a ton. When this screw is turned, the beam descends toward the block of stone, like an enormous nutcracker, crushing the skin and pulp with extraordinary force.

When everything is ready a signal is given. Two husky slaves position themselves near the wooden levers inserted in the screw so as to form a cross and slowly begin to turn it. The whole structure emits loud creaking sounds. With each turn, the screw penetrates inside the huge beam, which steadily moves downward, transforming itself into a pitiless press that squashes the pulp and skins, squeezing them to the last drop. The wood groans noisily, and everyone present can see the liquid spill forth from the openings in the wooden tub, flowing into a collector tub. This last juice will be poured into *dolia* and into casks like the juice from the first pressing.

The owner's son looks on with satisfaction at the sweet "liquid gold" flowing steadily out of the *torculum*. He doesn't know it, but this invention, the screw press, will remain unchanged until the nineteenth century, when the screw will change from wood to iron. (Today hydraulic presses are used.)

At this point what happens to the grape juice? It will be left to ferment for ten days or so (the must will literally start to boil). Then the large semi-interred jars will be sealed with terra-cotta lids and the aging process, which will last months or years, will begin. In antiquity, in fact, "young" or new wine does not exist; wine that is aged for several years, in some cases even as many as forty years, is more prized. Naturally, this is the theory. The actual practice is established by the wine-producing companies which have to sell it as soon as possible in order to realize their profits, maybe even after only one year. In this they are assisted by the Roman system of distribution, which is slow. Between storage and transport in stages on roads and ships (which cannot sail for six months out of the year because of the terrible storms at sea), months and even years pass before the amphora is opened and the wine poured at table.

Under the press, what remains after this last squeezing is an organic mush that is not thrown out. Dried and shaped into little bricks, it will be used for lighting fires in fireplaces and kitchens. Nothing is wasted. It is an example of true recycling in antiquity.

We now leave the building of the *torculum*, known as the *torcularium*, and immerse ourselves again in the panorama of the vineyards. What varietals of grapes did the Romans grow here, along the Moselle?

Archaeologists have discovered the answer by analyzing the grape seeds unearthed during their digs: they were somewhere between wild vines and cultivated ones, select varietals that demonstrated their resistance to the climatic conditions of northern Europe. Probably their distribution path followed the Rhone, passing through the farms that had spread into the Lyon area. From there they migrated northward, eventually arriving in this area.

On the banks of the Moselle white wine is produced, but there is one curiosity: here and there we step on some cherry pits. What are they doing on farms where wine grapes are grown? This is not an accident. Archaeologists have found cherry pits here too. They are added to color the wine red. It's not considered an adulteration, just as it is not considered an adulteration to add honey to the wine so that the fermenting sugars will increase the alcohol level. As the Romans see it, this has two advantages: the wine is more pleasing because it's stronger; and it travels better and doesn't deteriorate during the long journey to distant places in the empire (the high concentration of alcohol inhibits degradation caused by microorganisms, a bit like what happens with high-alcohol-content wines, such as port).

What the Romans don't like at all, however, is the smoking of wine, as originally done in Narbonese Gaul. This is a system for making the wine age more quickly, but it leaves an unpleasant smoky aftertaste, as Martial notes. Clearly, the wines of this era are very different from ours. Very often they have the consistency of molasses. In the winter they are diluted with hot water, in the summer with ice-cold water, and spices are often added.

Furthermore, the fact that the grapes are squeezed without separating them from the grape stalks, or twigs, makes the wine rather bitter. Quite often, therefore, the wine is seasoned in big containers made of lead— or even worse, lead powder—or else little blocks of lead are added to sweeten it. (Over time, lead develops a whitish patina with a sweet taste.) Naturally, the Romans don't know about the health hazards of lead: lead poisoning, or saturnism, provokes anemia, jaundice, convulsions, cerebral edema, and finally death.

Here we have to interject a small parenthetical observation. It has often been said that the fall of the Roman Empire was caused by lead poisoning stemming from the use of lead pipes to transport drinking water in the cities. But this story is as false as it is widespread. Undoubtedly lead claimed some victims in the Roman era, just as it does today. But it was not absorbed in such massive and widely distributed doses as to weaken and annihilate an entire empire, from the ruling class, to the army, down to the level of ordinary people. Not even serious epidemics, like the terrible plagues that killed emperors like Marcus Aurelius, were capable of doing that.

Despite all these adulterations, people in the Roman Empire like their wine. And evidently they like it a lot, considering the boats filled with wine casks going up and down the Moselle right before our eyes. On the roads, too, we run into wagons piled high with casks. Wine from the Moselle region is exported throughout the empire. This area is a true El Dorado of wine that has enriched many local families.

Archaeologists working in the Moselle area have unearthed many pitchers and cups used at banquets. They are made of dark, much prized pottery, with bright decorations and eloquent inscriptions. The latter are toasts that were recited at banquets, engraved on the cups almost as though they were the fossilized voices of the invited guests. These were dedicated to the guest of honor, to a lover, to life . . . or to the host so he wouldn't water down the wine (but how can you blame him, given that the wine often had percentages of alcohol commonly found in whisky!).

One of these toasts has come down to our own time. When a German raises his glass and says "Prosit," he is actually speaking Latin. A Roman in the era we are exploring would have understood him instantly. *Prosit* means "That it should be good for you" or "To your health." That wish, that gesture, embraces an entire world.

When the Dead Speak to You: A Roman Spoon River

The young man on horseback is on his way back to Trier. As in all Roman cities, the access roads to this big urban center of the north are lined with cemeteries. A proper city of the dead greets incoming visitors: on both the left and right tombstones emerge out of the grass, along with stone sarcophagi, monuments, and mausoleums. All around us is a sea of names, and busts and statues observe us with a severe gaze. We're passing a lineup of the faithfully departed, and inevitably our gaze is directed toward the inscriptions. They are a precious font of information.

Thus we discover that the Romans don't live very long. Most of the gravestones are in memory of people that today we would consider young. There are lots of teenagers and even more children. Many are adults who died long long before their hair would have started turning gray. The statistics are cruel: in the Roman Empire men have an average life span of forty-one, women a paltry twenty-nine. The big difference in the longevity of men and women was caused by the fact that women began giving birth at a very young age, and frequently they died in child-birth or its aftermath.

It must be kept in mind that these numbers are averages. Some Romans live very long lives, but very few. These data tell us that in the Roman Empire, among the people you see on the street there are plenty of young people while seniors are rare. Exactly like the situation today in the Middle East or in third-world countries.

But there are exceptions. In a Roman cemetery for the poor, discovered in Vatican City, I happened to see an inscription in honor of a certain Abascantus, who died at the age of ninety! He lived more than twice as long as the average Roman. At the time he must have been considered a real immortal.

It's intriguing that the Romans seem to have used their tombstone inscriptions to create a dialogue between the dead and the living. While on our modern tombs the inscriptions are almost always a dedication to the deceased, with the Romans it's just the opposite: it's the deceased who do the talking.

It's the location of the cemeteries that is responsible for this desire to communicate. Contrary to today, the necropolises are not fenced off and separated from the world of the living, but are still part of it: the tombs line the sides of the city's most-traveled access roads. It's only natural, therefore, that a dialogue is created between the living and the dead. And it's not a dialogue between the deceased and their relatives but between the deceased and the people who happen by the graves.

The dead, in a certain sense, are like those genteel old people that you run into on the backstreets of the city, sitting on the stoop in front of their houses. If you pass by they will almost certainly start up a conversation.

The Romans also have another reason to "humanize" their tombs. They believe that after death the soul of the deceased wanders around the gravesite. There is no afterlife (paradise, hell, or purgatory); at most there is only the gray world of the dead (Hades) where souls, cold and pallid, wander around without memory in the semidarkness (as is written in Book VI of the *Aeneid*, which recounts the descent of Aeneas into the world of the dead). The Elysian Fields were reserved for the deserving few, heroes of grandiose deeds, who had the good fortune of being able to meet the great figures of the past.

Roman epitaphs, therefore, synthesize the personality of the deceased: sometimes they are romantic, sometimes sarcastic, sometimes endowed with a sense of humor that lasts through the centuries, making us smile even today. Here are some of the epitaphs that have been discovered by archaeologists in various places in the empire, many of which have been collected by Lidia Storoni Mazzolani in *Iscrizioni funerarie romane* (Rizzoli, 2005).

Hymn to life
> Baths, wine, and Venus ruin our bodies. But baths, wine, and Venus are what life is made of.

The tomb of a great worker
> Here lie I, Lemisus. My death was my only dispensation from work.

Anyway, there's no escape
> Hey you, walking by, come over here. Rest for a while. You shake your head; don't you want to? Yet someday, like it or not, you'll be back here.

> Here it is, your asylum. I come here against my will, nonetheless obliged.

You who are still living, take advantage of life
> Here are the bones of Prima Pompea. Fortune promises much to many but maintains its promises for no one. Live day by day, hour by hour. Because nothing is ours.

Until the age of eighteen, I lived as best I could, beloved by my father, and all my friends. Have fun, enjoy yourself, that's my advice. This place is a realm of serious rigor.

I'm out of play

I've escaped, I'm out of it. Hope, Fortune, I bid you farewell. I no longer have anything to share with you. Make a fool of someone else.

Death has its advantages

The thought of suddenly finding myself reduced to hunger doesn't frighten me, and this way I am immune to gout. Nor will it ever happen to me again to be the guarantor on an installment loan. I have the benefit of free lodging forever.

Take your leave with peace of mind

Having lived to a ripe old age, chock-full of years, I am called by the gods; children, what have you to cry about?

To die of childbirth

The cause of my death was childbirth and impious fate. But you stop crying, my beloved companion, and hold onto your love for our son. Because by now my spirit is among the stars in the sky. (Rusticeia Matrona, lived twenty-five years)

Medical malpractice two thousand years ago

Here lies Efesia, good mother, good wife. She died for a malign fever provoked by her doctors and outlived their predictions. For this crime there is only one consolation: that the death of such a sweet woman I believe happened because she was more suited to the company of the gods.

Death of a centaur

I, Florius, here I lie, boy charioteer. Too soon I wished to race, too soon I plummeted into the darkness.

Extraordinary for its sense of humor is the epitaph of an actor who had acted the part of a dying man many times. His words make him quite likable and inspire us with the curiosity (never to be satisfied) to know him:

Here is buried Leburna, a maestro of recitation, who lived a hundred years more or less. I've died so many times! But like this, never. To you up there I wish you good health.

One of the surprising things on Roman gravestones is the life span of the deceased: it is specified almost obsessively and in certain cases, in addition to the number of years, months, and days the inscription even counts the hours, almost as if to count every "drop" of lived life:

Callista lived sixteen years, three months, six hours. She was to be married on the 15th of October. She died on the 11th.

Gravestone inscriptions are full of curiosities. Some tombs added warnings to be respectful, like the one admonishing the wayfarer to refrain from taking care of his bodily needs nearby, addressing him with a very direct term: *cacator* or "shitter."

Lucius Cecilius Libertus of Caius Lucius Florus lived sixteen years and seven months. That he who shits or pisses on this tomb should suffer the rage of the gods above and below. (*Focus Magazine*)

In effect, precisely because they are usually unpeopled places and rich with monuments to hide behind, cemeteries are often used by travelers as toilets. And, it's also easy to find prostitutes here, plying their trade. The reason is simple: as is the case today, prostitution is practiced on the outskirts of the city, on roads frequented by men who travel for work. And the tombstones do offer some privacy.

Skyscrapers for the (Wealthy) Dead

These epitaphs allow us to get to know directly the people who lived in the past: ordinary people, certainly, but also and especially the most powerful families. And we can get a better idea of this as we continue on our way through the necropolis of Trier.

Here they have built some imposing tombs that stand out like skyscrapers; some of them look like square towers with pointed tops more than seventy feet high (as in the Igel cemetery). If the rich have the biggest and most beautiful houses while they're alive, the same is true after they die. It's still possible even today to admire these tombs in a very special place, the Rheinisches Landesmuseum in Trier. Many of them date back to the third century, but we can plausibly imagine that there were already similar monuments in the second century.

Sometimes they are real masterpieces, with a lot of sculpted scenes showing the deceased during their lives, involved in their daily routines. Never depicted by chance, these scenes are always status-symbol moments immortalized for the viewer.

The most surprising thing is the tendency to tell the story of how the family became rich, sometimes showing, in a rather coarse way, their piles of money. And so we can see the head of the family sitting at a table, with his clients or servants lined up and carrying sacks full of coins that they empty out onto the table. The deceased is represented carefully recording his profits in a big ledger, with the precision of an accountant.

Sometimes on the other side of the tomb the wife is represented, sitting in a wicker chair with a high back as her slaves ritually comb her hair. On other tombs we can see the scions of these families, sitting at their desks while their tutor teaches them languages and other subjects. (Rich families were all at least bilingual. They knew Latin and Greek as well as the local language.) All of these scenes are painted in bold colors—blue, red, yellow, green—and you can see every little detail.

There's no mistaking the mountain of sculpted amphoras that, quite often, are the crowning element of the funeral monument. They are piled one on top of the other in an orderly manner, like oranges at a fruit stand. That's how the deceased made his money, in the wine trade. And we also discover an extraordinary detail: the amphoras are all encased in woven straw, which covers everything except the neck and handles. This is clearly a way to avoid breakage during transport. We can't help but be reminded of our own glass wine flasks, which are protected in the same way. We may not have noticed it before, but it's possible that every time we've sat down to the dinner table, we've had right before our eyes an ancient custom that has come down to us directly from the Romans, a true archaeological fossil.

Kill Your Father?

Another tomb along the way is truly spectacular. It is in the form of a Roman boat, cutting through the water. In the front, as on a Viking ship, the head of a dragon. In the back, on the curled stern, the muzzle of a bear. The boat is propelled by a host of oarsmen and, at its center, are five enormous casks of wine. The deceased is sitting in the boat, his hand indicating the casks, as if to say "Look how much wine I've managed to sell. Imagine how rich I am." No one today would be represented like this on a tombstone, but in an era in which the only important things are money and social status, such memorials are quite normal.

And you can also imagine what is going through the head of our young man on horseback. In such a competitive society, which values only the size of one's bank account, the sons of the rich are in an uncomfortable position. As long as their fathers are alive, they are under their tutelage, under their control, and have no say whatsoever in how the family holdings are managed. Nor do they have property of their own. This is certainly normal if they are still young. But the situation is a little more delicate and embarrassing if an elderly father manages to remain alive and insists on keeping the reins of the family estate even though his children's hair is starting to turn gray.

It is not so surprising, then, that every once in a while some of these sons try to kill their fathers. Sometimes the motive is debt: killing your father, by poison or with the help of a hired killer, means finally having access to the family coffers and being able to pay one's creditors. This was the reason that Macedo, a man who lived under the emperor Vespasian, used to justify the murder of his father. The case caused an uproar and the Senate approved a law, *senatus consultum Macedonianum*, which prohibited anyone from collecting money from people who were still under paternal authority.

What was the punishment for a son who kills his father? It was particularly gruesome: the convicted patricide was tied up inside a sack with a snake, a chicken, a monkey, and a dog, all still alive. The sack was then sewn up tight and dumped in a river. This punishment was applied frequently in Rome. We have documentation of it under Constantine and under Claudius, who, according to Seneca, "sacked" more patricides during his short reign than all of his predecessors put together.

Iced Wine

The young man is now entering the city. He doesn't know it, but in the future the place where he is now will be photographed by thousands of tourists from all over the world who have come to admire the Roman ruins of Trier. It may well be the most impressive city or Roman site that one can see in all of northern Europe. This entrance gate, in particular, is a true symbol of the city. It is the Porta Nigra, or Black Gate, composed of two towers, three and four stories high respectively, adorned with innumerable archways and openings. It is an emotional experience today to pass through it while trying to imagine how many Romans did the same centuries ago. Not our young man on horseback, however: the grandiose gate will not be built for another couple of generations.

The Porta Nigra is so big and spacious that in the Middle Ages its lower section was transformed into a church, and the upper part into a monastery. When Napoleon arrived he dismantled all the religious coverings and architectural details, restoring the Porta Nigra to its original form, as we see it today. It seems strange how certain places can make multiple appearances on the stage of human history. Trier is the birthplace of Saint Ambrose, whose father was the prefect of the Pretorium. And many centuries later, not more than a hundred yards from the Porta Nigra, Karl Marx was born. His house, still visible today, is on the street that begins at the city's great gate.

Today the street is lined with stores, restaurants, and ice-cream shops. It already existed at the time of Trajan, and we are now riding down it on horseback. It seems like we're seeing the same things: shops, stores, eateries, and pubs. Some things never change.

Our young man dismounts from his horse in front of a *popina*. Having tied his horse to a post, he sits down at one of the tables arranged outside on the sidewalk and orders some wine. "And make it ice-cold," he adds.

The order slip arrives immediately inside the tavern. The girl behind the counter takes some ice out of a compartment and puts it into a bronze colander, pressing it into a ball as though it were a scoop of ice cream. Then she grabs a pitcher and pours some wine over the ice. The ice turns the color of the "nectar of the gods" and an instant later, from the holes of the colander, the chilled wine, almost frozen, comes flowing out, filling a lovely terra-cotta cup. Then she adds a little spice. The girl's movements are rapid, sure-handed, and elegant.

Put on a tray, the cup of cold wine begins its passage among the tables. Many of the customers notice this petite, dark-haired young woman, with gracious movements and elongated eyes, who passes between their tables with surprising agility. Discreetly, she approaches the young man sitting at the table who is absently staring at the comings and goings of the crowd.

He looks up to see first the cup and then the girl's eyes: they are smiling, deep, and full of life. Almost mechanically, the young man pulls out our sestertius, never taking his eyes off the girl, and puts it on her tray. It's a nice tip, his way of saying that he is struck by her beauty. She squeezes the sestertius in the palm of her hand and smiles. Their gazes have become much more intense.

Hurrying Off to the Edge of the World

At the next table, a man observes the scene out of the corner of his eye and smiles. He is tall, blond, and blue-eyed—clearly Nordic. His short beard betrays his occupation: he must be a soldier. It's hard to shave every day when you're on the march or at war. Legionnaires, therefore, and auxiliary troops as well, are spared the requirement of being clean-shaven.

Indeed, beards are not fashionable in Trajan's time. And it has been this way for generations. A Roman man is always well shaved, following the emperor's example. But things will change when the next emperor, Hadrian, wears a beard, setting a style that will last for generations to come. In the era in which we now find ourselves, a man who lets his beard grow is in mourning, or on trial (to soften the heart of the tribunal); or he is a barbarian, or else a soldier.

The young officer signals to the waitress that he would like to pay for the lunch he has just eaten. As his change he receives our sestertius. He gets up and heads toward his horse, and our sestertius is setting off once again.

The soldier is heading to the frontier of the empire along the Rhine. He is a centurion. Until a few days ago he was on leave, but he's been called up in a hurry to rejoin his century, the basic unit of a legion, composed of eighty men. He imagines that something is cooking, probably a military operation to respond to an emergency on the border.

It's curious: our coin has now gone from the northern frontier, in Scotland, to the eastern frontier, on the Rhine, which may be an area even more at risk. Beyond the big river, in fact, lies the home of the most dangerous of the barbarian peoples: the Germans.

During his journey, the centurion will come to realize more and more that the operation is an important one. On the long road that will take him to the Rhine he'll encounter some sizable units and detachments (*vexillationes*) sent by other legions or frontier forts. Some have been on the march for several days. At the head of their ranks are their emblems and banners (*vexilla*) displayed for all to see by the *signiferi*, or standard bearers, in the front line.

Thus the centurion discovers that all of the principal northern legions have sent reinforcements, like the VIII Augusta, stationed in Argentoratum (Strasbourg). Founded by Augustus, the legion has distinguished itself in many battles, first and foremost in the battle of Actium against Marc Antony and Cleopatra.

Or the I Minervia, headquartered in Bonna (Bonn), with the goddess Minerva on its emblems, the same legion that fought the Dacians just a few years ago in terrible and bloody battles during the conquest of Dacia (Romania) under Trajan's command.

They are all war-fighting professionals, trained to kill a human being in just a few seconds. Now they are marching in silence toward a new mission, with their heavy equipment and their lances held high. All you can hear is a rhythmic, metallic beat, the choral rattling of weapons and armor in cadence with their marching feet. It can be heard from very far away, as though it were a drum announcing their arrival. Some units sing military songs, to give rhythm to their steps, with the commanders themselves leading the chorus. The centurion salutes his colleagues as they pass by but he doesn't ask any questions. From the way they're marching, at a constant, sustained rhythm, it's clear to him that they have orders to arrive as fast as possible.

It is really impressive to see the speed with which these legionnaires are able to move. They are trained to cover twenty Roman miles (a little over eighteen miles) in just five hours, and they do that carrying sixty-five pounds of gear on their backs. Their training demands that they each carry their own equipment: armor, weapons, cooking implements, digging tools, even two pointed poles for building a defensive enclosure: in enemy territory, at the end of the day's march, they have to set up camp immediately.

This means digging a long trench around the perimeter, in all about two miles long, three to ten feet deep and wide (according to the degree of danger at the moment). Using the dirt they've dug up, they build an embankment on the inside of the trench in which they plant their pointed poles. Inside this defensive perimeter, they set up tents for six hundred soldiers. (These are goatskin tents; this is why Roman soldiers say they are going *sub pellibus*, under the skins.) The final shape of the camp is a quadrilateral measuring about 875 yards long on each side, with the tents lined up close together and divided into quarters, each with its own main street, headquarters, etc.

And how long does it take them to build this camp? About two hours! This is because each of the five to six thousand soldiers in a legion knows what he is supposed to do, and he does it quickly in a precise location.

It is clear, therefore, why the legions have been a victorious army for generations: in an era when the typical mobilization for war consisted of rounding up as quickly as possible the largest number of warriors available, relying only on numbers and violence (that's what most of the barbarian peoples do), the Romans have created a permanent army of professional soldiers, an army in constant training. Even in peacetime, in fact, the legionnaires do three 20-mile marches per month, carrying sixty-five pounds on their backs. And this for every one of the twenty-five years of their military service!

Naturally, there were no jogging shoes or easy trails in city parks: the soldiers march wearing their *caligae* on unpaved roads or cross-country, in the suffocating heat of summer, under the pounding autumn rain, or in the penetrating chill of winter.

Small wonder that the legions are much more mobile than any of their enemies. And as we will see, they also know how to deploy in battle and which part of the enemy's body to strike with their swords. The legions are a perfect war machine, in which discipline, speed, training, and the capacity to adapt to any situation are the keys to victory. In this respect we can't help but compare them to modern armies. In reality, they are the ancient expression of the modern mentality, in which organization, strategy, and technology are the key factors in every battle.

Becoming a legionnaire is not easy; after a rigorous initial selection process, the training is intense, a bit like the training in all the elite corps of modern armies, from the marines to the special forces. We are used to seeing films depicting new recruits being terrorized by sadistic sergeants. For the legionnaires it was worse. The centurions are even more rigid and beat the recruits (and veterans as well) with heavy sticks made from gnarled olive wood. Serious violations (like falling asleep on watch in enemy territory) are punished by being beaten to death at the hands of your comrades-in-arms.

Recruits are trained to fight using the methods of the gladiators, dealing blows to a pole stuck in the ground, in order to perfect their aim against a tall, thin target. All blows inflicted along the central line of an adversary's body, from the forehead down through the nose, throat, chest, and belly to the groin, will have grave, often lethal consequences. Initially, recruits train for long periods with heavy weapons made of wood. Even the wicker shields weigh twice as much as normal. In this way, they learn to move with strength. When they are ready to move beyond this first level (there are always superior officers sitting as judges to supervise the training), they graduate to real weapons that will seem much lighter by comparison. So the blows they strike will be murderous.

According to an eyewitness account from the Roman era, "the training sessions are like real battles without the blood and the battles are like training sessions with the blood."

BEYOND THE RHINE

~ *Battling the Barbarians* ~

A Roman "Airport"

The galloping centurion finally arrives in Mogontiacum (present-day Mainz), a large port city rising on the banks of the Rhine. In front of him are the majestically flowing waters of the river. Have you noticed anything about the cities we have seen so far? Like almost all the cities of the Roman Empire they are situated on the banks of a river or at its mouth, overlooking the sea.

While proximity to a large body of water is no longer an essential feature for a large urban center, in antiquity it was fundamental, both because fresh water is an indispensable ingredient of daily life and of all artisanal and productive activities and because a river is the ideal means of intracontinental transport.

In the ancient world, rivers are the equivalent of modern aviation routes: people and goods travel on them in greater numbers and faster than on roads, where the wagons are small and slow. Mogontiacum is a virtual airport of antiquity, the ancestor of the present-day Frankfurt Airport, as Londinium and Lutetia are to Heathrow and Charles de Gaulle. But Mogontiacum is also one of the principal military bases of the Roman Empire, a base port of the *classis Germanica*, that is, the Rhine fleet.

The Romans have two kinds of fleets, marine and fluvial, that are equally important. The military presence here is essential. The Rhine and the Danube are not only strategic for commerce; they also constitute boundaries or frontiers. Their waters, therefore, are under constant surveillance by patrols made up of fast, lightweight boats. These are the boats that our centurion is now carefully examining as he rides his horse along the banks of the city dock.

Now, for example, he is approaching a slender cargo ship called a *liburna*. It is about twenty meters long, with a low, pointed bow shaped like a clothes iron that cuts through the water; the stern is adorned with an elegant curl of painted wood thrust toward the sky.

Moving with the current, the *liburna* is making a wide turn to tie up at the dock. Its large square sail has been taken down, and it is being powered by two dozen soldiers who are rowing in perfect unison, making the boat look like a centipede skimming across the surface. Responding to a single grunted order they pull their oars, just under fifteen feet long, out of the water. It's amazing to see how easily the oars are able to slide back and forth inside the boat. Delicately maneuvered by the helmsman sitting in an open cabin at the stern, the galley slides sweetly up to the dock. Two soldiers hop off and swiftly fasten some lines around the wooden bollards. As though protesting the end of its long run on the Rhine, the ship pulls slightly sideways, letting out some long groans at it strains against its taut lines. Then it surrenders and nestles up against the dock. The soldiers get up from their places and gather up their gear, weapons, lances, and bows, ideal for hitting the enemy on the shore. They have finished their patrol on the river and now they're disembarking down a gangplank on the side of the boat.

The centurion notices the artillery piece on the ship's bow: the cannon of the age. It's a *scorpio*, a giant crossbow, with a tripod mount identical to the one we saw in Vindolanda, Scotland. Only this model is a little different. To reload, it uses a strange cranking mechanism, which sets in motion a true "bicycle chain," capable of stretching the powerful cable that fires the darts. It looks like a design by Leonardo da Vinci.

The centurion's eye examines some of the other warships at the dock. Activity in the port is at a fever pitch. The boats are being loaded with equipment, tents, food and water, and provisions of all kinds. Something really big is in the offing.

As he is thinking about all this, he spurs his horse to pick up the pace toward the city's fort where his legion, the XXII Primigenia, has its headquarters. In a few seconds he disappears among the crowd, making his way through soldiers and civilians carrying sacks and cases down to the port.

Out on the river, meanwhile, two lightweight Roman galleys go speeding by. They are identical to the Viking longboats: oars, a lot of round shields on their flanks, and a dragon's head jutting out in front of the bow. These nimble boats are the fighter planes of the age, and their assignment is to patrol the Rhine. In the glow of the sunset their brightly painted hulls leave shimmering wakes behind them. They look like comets, skimming silently across the golden surface of the river.

Behind the two galleys, beyond the opposite shore, lies the darkness for the Roman Empire, with thick forests and bellicose populations still living in the Iron Age, ready to tear an intruder to pieces if given the chance.

The Roman Empire's Clever Border Policy

What is the best way to control a border like the one on the Rhine? Obviously, the strategies differ depending on the type of terrain and the development stage of the empire. Unlike in the modern era of nation-states, a border is not a line drawn on a map demarcating this country on one side and that country on the other. Instead it is a wide swath of terrain that is patrolled by the army and marked by roads and forts.

A good way to understand how the empire's border works is to think of our own skin. The border between our bodies and the outside world, it is not a single layer of film but a series of interacting layers. The outermost layer is made up of cells that are expendable and are subjected to the initial impact of attack by our enemies (bacteria, scratches, etc.). Then there is a very thick, living layer, made up of blood vessels and lymph nodes, which carry "troops" (antibodies, white blood cells) as well as supplies (fats, sugars, oxygen, etc.) wherever they are needed. The same thing happens on the borders of the empire. This band of territory has several layers. The key element of any Roman border is always a main road along which troops and supplies can be transported; the road branches out into secondary roads, leading to forts, fortresses, and towers in a strategic fashion.

The Romans always construct the road alongside an existing physical barrier, such as a mountain range or river (in this case the Rhine). Or they build one of their own, as with Hadrian's Wall. The idea is simple. On the outer edge of the physical barrier, surrounded by enemy territory, there are advance posts, lookout towers, and small forts, occupied not by Roman troops but by allies (the so-called auxiliaries). Not being Romans, they can easily be sacrificed. They are the ones who will undergo the initial enemy attack, giving the alarm and beginning the battle.

On the inner side of the barrier, friendly territory, there are more forts, with more numerous and better organized troops. And positioned still further back are forts manned by the legions. The legionnaires are always stationed at some distance from the front line; they are never actually the first line of defense. The logic is that it's better to let the enemy first get a taste of less professional troops and then, if the situation requires, the best soldiers of Rome, the crème de la crème of the Roman army.

Obviously, this border structure is not always applicable. In the deserts of Asia and East Africa, for example, the preferred strategy is to put forts only in the oases or in the cities, that is, in places where there is water or where commerce and trade are conducted.

Besides this military border there is another one that we might call diplomatic. The borders of the Roman Empire are never really cut and dried, with the good guys on this side and the bad guys on that side. Beyond the border there are buffer states that are "clients" of Rome. Sometimes they have this role despite themselves. They are, in fact, within striking distance of the legions, so Rome is able to obtain their allegiance first and foremost with military and diplomatic pressure.

Beyond these states, there is another layer of security constituted by peoples and tribes over which Rome has some influence, less direct perhaps, but nonetheless effective. In this regard, it must be said that many times Rome has purchased alliances with external peoples and tribes with gold coins. And it has always been clever at sowing discord and envy among its allies, at times by favoring one over the others, keeping them from uniting among themselves and becoming an overwhelming force capable of invading the empire: *divide et impera*—divide and rule.

In the period of its demise, many invasions were launched when Rome was no longer able to bring to bear its force (military or diplomatic) beyond its borders.

Our coin, along with the others the centurion had in his purse, has been hidden at the base of a tree, under an arc-shaped root. The centurion doesn't want it to fall into enemy hands if he is killed or captured. All the other soldiers hide their money in the same way. It's become a superstitious habit. Now the centurion is together with his men, marching since dawn in enemy territory.

This is an important policing operation across the border. It's taken them two days to get here. The men, their gear, and their horses were ferried across the river, using every available vessel, from the lightweight galleys to the wide, capacious river barges used for this occasion as landing craft. This operation was followed by a long march through the buffer zone, all the way to the border. The spark that set off the Roman response was an attack on some lookout towers and two auxiliary advance posts carried out by a strong contingent of one of the barbarian tribes called the Chatti.

The Chatti are a proud and warlike people, who in the past few decades have launched brutal attacks against Roman outposts and devastating incursions into Roman territory. For a long time now, their tribe has been within the orbit of the empire, putting pressure on its borders. The Romans have always found it difficult to establish stable relationships with them. In this case, it's very likely that they are taking advantage of Emperor Trajan's absence from this front and his involvement in a war in far-off Mesopotamia. The Chatti are testing the Roman defenses on behalf of the rest of the barbarian peoples. The Romans need to snuff out this offensive before the idea that Rome is weak can spread to other groups.

Now an entire legion and some supporting units are on the move against the barbarians. The XXII Primigenia, dedicated to the goddess Fortuna Primigenia, was founded by Emperor Caligula, less than eighty years ago, in 39 CE. It has faced the Chatti on a number of occasions and it has always won. Indeed, it has the reputation of being a legion of stalwarts, used to fighting the empire's toughest and most determined enemies.

To be sure, there have also been years better left forgotten, for example, the fratricidal battles against other legions after the fall of Nero, in which the Primigenia frequently chose the wrong side. But it managed to regain its good standing. It was the only legion in Germany to survive the enemy attacks during the Batavian revolt in 70 CE, which speaks to the toughness of these legionnaires. Then it participated in the defeat of the usurper Lucius Antonius Saturninus in 89 CE, earning itself the gratitude of Emperor Domitian, who bestowed on the legion the title of *Pia Fidelis Domitiana,* loyal and faithful to Domitian.

Looking into the faces of these men as they are marching, what you see are confident gazes and athletic bodies, accustomed to years of living on the border, as demonstrated by the scars that so many of them bear. But above all, you can see the determination of professional warriors, anxious to finally take part in a full-scale border protection operation against their sworn enemies.

The entire Roman column has been marching for hours across a landscape that is largely flat; hills are becoming more scarce and in the distance is the edge of the thick, dark forest. According to the survivors, it was from there that the attacking hordes first appeared, and then disappeared again like eels back into their holes.

When a legion advances, it does so in a precise order. The pathbreakers are always the cavalry, which, like a swarm of bees, clears the territory ahead, eliminating the threat of ambush. Next come the auxiliary units, armed with light weapons, and then the main body of the legion, with its cohorts, its baggage trains, and its war machines. Our centurion, Titus Alfius Magnus (from Bononia, modern-day Bologna) is near the head of the legion, and he gives the cadence to his men.

All the soldiers scan the surrounding countryside, ready to spot the enemy. Every now and again, our centurion turns his head and observes the long Roman column, including the white horse of the *legatus,* the commander of the legion, a decisive and secure man whom he holds in high esteem. The centurion has a good view of the symbols of the legion: a goat and Hercules, displayed at the top of a lot of emblems and banners waving above the helmets of the legionnaires.

Most impressive is the golden eagle, the soul of the legion; it advances with the soldiers of the first cohort, at the top of a long pole. The honor of carrying it belongs to the *aquilifer,* a soldier whose helmet peeks out from the open jaws of a lion's head, its skin draped over his shoulders like a mantle. Losing that eagle in battle is the worst dishonor. Much more than a banner, it is the spirit of the legion, almost a divinity. If it is captured or destroyed, the entire legion will be disbanded. Equally important is the gold mask of the emperor, protected inside a niche on the end of a pole, symbolizing a direct connection between him and the legion.

In this sea of lances and symbols, some other strange emblems stand out. Every century has its own extra-long lances, on which are displayed a column of gold plates and a half-moon, or *lunula*. It's not very clear what they represent, perhaps the legion's past campaigns (the plates) and the seas and mountains it has crossed to fight its battles (the half-moon). But it is also true that the number of plates is never more than six, so it's likely that they have another meaning that remains unknown. At the top of the lance, depending on the legion, are gilded laurel wreaths or symbols such as an open hand raised in greeting (representing loyalty). Whoever carries these emblems (the *signifer*, or standard-bearer) is covered by the skin of a bear or a wolf, the muzzle and teeth of which adorn his helmet.

The Numbers of a Legion

While we're on the subject, let's quickly explain some military terms that most of us have heard at one time or another. Let's start from an unusual place: the barracks of a Roman fort. Each room held eight soldiers, who formed a close-knit squad or "tent group" called a *contubernium*, the basic unit of a legion. And here's how you get from those first eight men to a legion.

1 contubernium equals 8 men.
10 contuberniums form a century: 80 men.
6 centuries form a cohort: 480 men.
10 cohorts make a legion.

Simple math would therefore suggest that a cohort is 4,800 men. But not all cohorts are the same. In a legion there are:

9 regular cohorts of 6 centuries: 4,320 men
1 special cohort (first cohort) of 5 double centuries: 800 men
120 horsemen

This makes a total of 5,240 men.

The idea of the eight-man squad making up the building blocks of the legion is ingenious: even when they march, a century deploys in ten rows of eight men. And this is one of the secrets of the Roman army: living elbow to elbow for years on end makes those eight men very united in battle, contributing to the cohesion of the Roman line of attack.

The Enemy Is in Sight

Our centurion is among the first to notice the dust rising up from behind a hill. It's very far away, but gradually it rises high overhead. The enemy is marching toward the legion!

Some returning cavalry scouts report in, confirming the news. Shortly thereafter the commander of the legion breaks away from the column and goes to the top of the hill together with the soldiers of his escort and his marshals.

The view from the hill is spectacular. The Chatti are still a few miles away, but they've gathered new forces, and now there are several thousand of them. They are marching right at the legion, cocksure, like an enormous hungry shark. Let's not forget that we're in their territory, and the legionnaires are not welcome here.

All the men of the XXII Primigenia legion, the ones sent by the VIII Augusta, the ones from the I Minervia, and all the auxiliary troops have their eyes fixed on the *legatus*, sitting on his horse. He issues sharp orders with crisp gestures. Some of his officers come galloping back to the column. The order is to go over the hill and deploy on the opposite slope in front of the enemy. The battle will take place there. This is typical of Roman generals: always choose the place to do battle. And don't engage unless you have the favorable position. The slope of that hill is tactically important. It allows the Romans to occupy a dominant position and aim downward with their weapons at the oncoming foe. Besides that, the sun is behind them, so the enemy will have the sun in their eyes.

From various points in the column comes the sound of horns blowing and orders being shouted. The banners are lowered to the side, pointing toward the hill. Rapidly but in formation, thousands of soldiers set off on the march. In just a few minutes they have gone up and over the hill and start to deploy down the slope on the other side.

The wagons of the baggage train stop on top of the hill, defended by several centuries of auxiliaries and legionnaires in the VIII Augusta. They quickly start digging a deep defensive trench all around the hilltop. Equipment is precious and must be protected. Just below the top of the hill, the artillery pieces deploy in a line where they are rapidly mounted.

The artillery are the scorpions, *scorpiones,* and their larger twins, the *ballistas.* To us they look like giant crossbows on tripods. Every legion has at least sixty at its disposal: one per century. But in this case there are more, and along with them are some unusual pieces: scorpions mounted on carts pulled by two horses. These are the ancestors of the tank, and they were also used in the conquest of Dacia in 106 CE. Inside the cart are two men: one aims and shoots the darts (the "gunner"), and the other reloads the machine with a curious system of levers that pull the chord back until it's fully stretched. The iron-tipped projectiles are two feet long and extremely accurate. The men who use them can line up a target up to a hundred yards away and hit it without fail. These weapons are amazingly powerful. There is an account of a barbarian chief, a Goth, hit by one of these darts; it passed through his armor, his body, and again through the back of his armor and nailed him to a tree.

When aimed upward to obtain a parabolic trajectory, the weapon's range increases to four hundred yards or more, and it can shoot three to four rounds per minute. Obviously, at that distance it is less accurate, but a battery of sixty scorpions can shower the enemy with 240 projectiles a minute, capable of piercing helmets, armor, skulls, and rib cages.

Below the line of artillery the legionnaires, including our centurion, are deployed in numerous lines well down the slope. His men are the row of legionnaires just behind the front line, which is formed as always by various kinds of auxiliaries.

The one in front of Titus Alfius Magnus's century are Raeti, the inhabitants of present-day Bavaria and other Alpine regions of central Europe. Their banners say they are the II cohort, so they are from the fort in Saalburg, a day's march from where we are now. Their symbol is a bear in the act of giving a paw slap, and he is pictured together with a red half- moon on their big yellow oval shields.

Our centurion examines them. They appear very different from his legionnaires. A legionnaire typically wears body armor that covers his shoulders and chest with overlapping strips, a tunic that covers his thighs like a skirt, and a rectangular shield. And above all, he is a citizen of Rome. Not so for the Raeti, who are dressed in armor made of chain mail, short pants, and oval shields. And above all, they are former barbarians, a subjugated people, very useful if, as in this case, they are powerfully built, hefty Germans.

So now it's clear: there's about to be a battle between barbarians and ex-barbarians: the Chatti against the Bavarian auxiliaries—a fratricidal conflict. The Romans are extremely pragmatic. They exploit the fighting capacity of their former enemies by putting them on the front line. To be sure, their final reward, as we have had occasion to mention, is the acquisition of Roman citizenship—if they live that long, a real issue given their continual deployment on the front line. The real slap in the face is their salary: they risk a lot more than their legionnaire colleagues, but they get paid three times less—and forty times less than the Roman centurions who command them.

Magnus sees the enemy approaching. They must be two or three times more numerous than the Romans. They're still a ways off, but he tightens his helmet straps and swivels his head to make sure the helmet is stable. The straps are so tight they leave marks on his neck.

His movements attract the attention of some of his soldiers. The centurions' helmets are immediately recognizable because they are topped by a big crest of eagle feathers, spread out in an arc that looks like a fan. The reason for this is very simple: it makes it easier for their soldiers to recognize their leaders in battle.

The Psychological Warfare Before the Battle

The Chatti are still far away, but you can already hear the metallic sounds of their armor and weapons. Thousands of men armed to the teeth are marching toward the Romans intent on tearing them apart. It's only natural for the Roman soldiers to be a little apprehensive.

The legion commanders know that this is a very delicate moment: the psychology of combat is fundamental. So, as the centurions keep barking orders to the legionnaires and auxiliaries, the *legatus* suddenly appears on horseback in front of the troops, without his escort (a deliberate move), and begins a short speech. He chooses his words and enunciates them with care, making sure he can be heard all the way to the top of the hill. After praising the great qualities of all the soldiers before him, he asks them for victory. This is the famous *ad locutio*: every general has to give a speech before a battle, to infuse his troops with courage and let them know that he is with them and that he is one of them.

Magus, accustomed to the speeches of his generals, doesn't even listen anymore. But he studies the faces of the general's marshals, the so-called tribunes, who are standing off to the side. He doesn't like them at all. In fact, they are not soldiers but politicians, sent by the Senate or by the equestrian order. They are not part of the army and have very little, if any, military expertise. He knows a lot more about how to conduct a battle than all these men put together. But they are his superiors and he has to obey them.

When the *legatus* is finished, a loud cry goes up from the troops, and they start banging on their shields with their lances. By now the enemy is drawing near, and what he sees is not a large hill but an endless ascent of colored shields. There is a steady, bloodcurdling clamor of lances on shields, as if to say, "Here we are, waiting to rip you limb from limb!"

The psychological warfare that precedes every battle has begun. The Chatti deploy in front of the legion and respond with a choral chant that recounts the exploits of their most valorous hero. The chant is incomprehensible because it is deformed by thousands of voices, reminiscent of the cheers heard in a football stadium. The purpose of the chant is to give them courage and cohesion.

Then they move on to a more woeful war song, meant to instill fear in the enemy. It is another weapon in their arsenal, a missile that strikes deep in the enemy's heart. It's what Tacitus describes with the word *bardito* (from which the Italian word *barrito*, or "trumpet blast," derives): "They make a special effort to emit clashing, strident notes in syncopated rhythm. They raise their shields in front of their mouths to make their voices reverberate louder and darker."

Beyond the theatrics of it all, the result is very sophisticated. The din created by the warriors generates a low-frequency, bass-tone sound wave that stimulates and excites the adversary's involuntary nervous system, which controls instinctive emergency reactions such as panic and flight, provoking an accelerated heartbeat, dilation of the pupils, reduced salivation, and so forth.

Naturally, the Germanic tribesmen don't understand all these physiological details. All they know is that by making this noise they frequently succeed in frightening the enemy and increasing his level of anxiety.

Again according to Tacitus, they understand that according to whether the *bardito* is done well or badly, they can already make some predictions about the outcome of the battle.

This sound wave of death is joined by another, and it too has a psychological effect. The emblems of the Chatti and many other barbarians are wolf or dragon heads with open jaws. They are made of hollow metal (similar, therefore, to a pipe) and finished off with a long tail of very light cloth similar to a wind sock that flutters in the air. These heads are attached to the ends of long poles. When the poles are correctly oriented to the wind they can be made to resonate, exactly like the sound made by blowing into the neck of a bottle. The result is a long howl, like a wolf's. The effect of hundreds or thousands of these instruments is truly alarming.

Killing to Become a Man

The Chatti are one of the toughest Germanic tribes that the Romans fight against. As Tacitus writes, they are physically powerful, extremely determined, clever, and very skilled in battle. They only fight on their feet under the command of leaders chosen by the community whom they obey with great discipline.

To see them described in this way makes us think we are dealing with a group of commandos. But there is another impressive aspect of this people. By now they are close enough that Magnus is able to get a good look at them. He notices that the front line is composed of soldiers with long hair and beards. But not everybody is like that. Why? Tacitus gives us the answer. "As soon as they reach adulthood, the Chatti let their hair and beards grow and only after they have killed a man do they cut them. Standing over the bloody corpse they shave their heads and only then do they believe that they have paid the price of their birth and consider themselves worthy of their country and their parents."

The Battle Is Joined

The Chatti are very close now and they have coalesced into a dense mass that is screaming chants and songs. They are mustering their courage. This is the prelude to the attack and the Romans know it. Thousands of sweaty hands grip the lances; thousands of throats have gone dry.

The mass of Chatti sways back and forth repeatedly. It is truly immense; it covers the entire grassy plain in front of the Romans like an animated forest.

Suddenly the attack is launched. With a howling yell thousands of Germans hurl themselves against the Romans. Swords glisten in the sun, colored shields move rhythmically, long lances point at the Roman front line.

Now the distance between the lines is down to about three to four hundred yards. But the signal for the Romans to attack still has not sounded. The *legatus* is waiting for the right moment. At last he shouts the long-expected order. Like a machine being set in motion, the order is repeated over and over by the commanders of the various units. And the horns, as big as bicycle wheels, are sounded too. They are the walkie-talkies of antiquity. From atop the hill the scorpions and ballistas let fly dozens of long darts. They go buzzing over Magnus's head, sounding like a swarm of angry bees. A few seconds later they fill the air over the barbarians and dive toward the earth. It's a blood bath; dozens of men fall to the ground, leaving holes in the lines of the advancing horde. But the attack doesn't let up. The darts keep on flying, wave after wave. And the Chatti are so compact that nearly every shot hits a target. But the enemy keeps on advancing.

Above the heads of the centurion and his men, the buzzing of the darts is joined by the hissing of arrows; it sounds like the howling and wailing of desperate animals. Every wave passing overhead is answered by more fallen Chatti, struck down by the long arrows. The shots are deadly accurate, thanks in part to the windless day. The Syrian archers are among the most renowned. Their units are easily recognized on the hillside. They have conical helmets, pointed on the top, and long dresses down to the ground.

And that's not all. Now there is a third sound coming down from the sky: the noise of the projectiles sent speeding through the air by the slingshots of the Balearic fighters. They too are part of the legion's auxiliary units. The Romans have always made use of the weapons and techniques of their most insidious enemies, and these slingers are really deadly. Back home on their islands they use their slingshots to hit birds in flight, so hitting an on-charging human being is child's play for them. They are capable of striking the forehead of an adversary as far away as a hundred yards. They are true sharpshooters, and every sling is like a precision rifle shot. It's incredible; they rotate the sling in the air two times and it releases the projectile at a stupefying velocity. When it strikes the adversary's body, it often penetrates deep below the skin, making it very difficult to remove.

The projectiles are the shape and size of an acorn and are made of lead. They are bullets, essentially, made by the very simple process of pouring molten lead into small molds or into a hole made by poking a finger in the sand. Sometimes the soldiers write insults on them or words of scorn for the enemy. One famous phrase was found on a projectile used during the civil wars and conserved in the Civic Museum of Reggio Emilia. A supporter of Marc Antony had engraved his bullet with a very eloquent message for Octavian: PETE CULUM OCTAVIANI—Hit Octavian in the Ass.

Lots of Chatti have fallen, but the horde is still advancing; brute force is the heart of the strategy of many Germanic peoples. A shock wave that overwhelms enemy defenses: that's the spirit of their all-out assault. And then, when the opposing lines come together, it's every man for himself. It's hand-to-hand combat. The Roman tactic is diametrically opposite. The soldiers fight in groups. They win because they are united, fighting "in chorus."

The enemy is near. Magnus orders his four lines of legionnaires to get ready. The soldiers grip their lances, preparing to hurl them. They'll be launched in volleys, starting with the front line, then the second, the third, and finally the fourth, like a lethal wave.

The centurion shouts the signal. The first volley of *pila*, or javelins, sails into the air. Then the second, the third, and the fourth. In the span of just a few seconds, from his sector alone, eighty javelins are hurled into the sky and shower down on the enemy. They bore through bodies and shields. It's a massacre.

The *pilum*, refined by the Romans over the course of generations, is not a normal lance; it's a high-tech weapon. It has a long wooden handle and then, rather than a leaf-shaped point, it has a very long iron rod that ends in a big pointed cone. A ball of iron or bronze positioned in the middle of the lance gives it the necessary mass to increase its power on impact.

The Chatti raise their shields to fend off the javelins, but it's useless. In combat the javelin is the rifle, the Winchester of the age, designed to mow down a charging enemy. If its point strikes the body of a man, the entire *pilum* passes through him. If instead it hits his shield, it may go through (because the point opens a big hole through which the iron rod passes until it strikes the man) or it may stop and crumple. The rod is in fact made of soft iron that bends easily (it even has internal hinges made of wood, designed to snap on impact so that the rod will not be rigid anymore but will hang limply from the handle). It is designed this way so that the barbarian cannot hurl the lance back at the Romans; even worse, he has to throw down his shield, which is now weighed down by the crumpled lance. And a man in combat without a shield is practically dead.

After all the javelins have been launched, each legionnaire pulls out his *gladius,* or short sword. And the lines close ranks to await the enemy, for what one Roman general defined as "a job for a butcher." And we're about to see it. The Chatti have slowed down almost to a standstill to reorganize themselves and fill in the gaps in their formation: they've suffered truly massive losses.

Magnus's century has received the order to move up alongside of the auxiliaries to ward off the attack because the Chatti have spread out and they are incredibly numerous. Now the legionnaires unsheathe their swords. Their sheaths are not on their left as is customary, but on the right so as not to hinder the left arm that is holding the shield. So, in order to pull out the sword the right hand has to rotate on itself. But the legionnaires are used to this and their weapons are ready in an instant.

The Legionnaires' Wall of Shields

Now the enemy is rushing forward against the Roman lines. This is it—impact is imminent.

The legionnaires plant their feet and tighten their grips on shields and weapons. With the auxiliaries on their flank they have formed into a long wall of shields that the horde of Chatti is about to crash into. The collision is tumultuous and savage. It looks like the unstoppable force of a tempest-tossed sea crashing up against the immovable barrier of a sea wall. And the slaughter begins.

The gladius is a special kind of sword, hefty, not very long (about twenty inches or so), with two razor-sharp blades. Its destructive power, therefore, is astonishing. The legionnaires are taught not to hack the enemy by swinging wildly as with a saber, but to stab him with short, rapier-like plunges, because even a wound as shallow as four or five inches is usually lethal. In addition, this method reduces the risk that the gladius will remain stuck in the victim's body, making it easy to pull the sword back out and be ready to fight again.

The legionnaires are experts at this: sudden, silvery flashes shoot out from the sides of their shields striking their adversary with the swiftness of a bite. Some legionnaires purposely aim for the face, because face wounds are more impressive and instill more fear in the enemy army. Others prefer to jerk their sword upward, like a roll-up garage door, and strike the enemy from below.

The centurion Magnus is doing his duty as commander. He fights but at the same time he cheers his men on. "In the belly, Marcus! The belly! Hit him down low!" It's actually an easy blow to strike. The barbarians carry long swords, ideal for cutting strokes; but when they prepare the blow, raising their arm high in the air, they expose their whole side to the legionnaire's short plunge.

For his part, the legionnaire's side is much better protected. He wears a layered cuirass that gives him a lot of mobility despite its thirty-five-pound weight. The legions have a one-size-fits-all cuirass because, thanks to its lacing, the armor can be loosened or tightened to fit the man wearing it.

A surprising thing is that even as the battle is raging the centurions keep on dispensing advice, criticism, and encouragement as if it were a training exercise. They do what a boxer's trainer does from the side of the ring. Only they too are in the ring, in the middle of the fray.

The barbarians doggedly hurl themselves individually against the Roman shields, in accordance with the traditional logic of heroic combat. But the Romans work in teams. While one legionnaire is fighting, the one behind him raises his shield and extends it, tilting it slightly, to protect the neck and the left side of his comrade. And if necessary he slams his shield into the enemy's face. The shield, in fact, also makes for an excellent offensive weapon.

For an instant the centurion sees all white. He has just been dealt a tremendous blow to the helmet. But the protective cross braces on the skull piece have saved him. Without losing his composure he thrusts his gladius at the throat of his adversary, who collapses to the ground. And then again into the side of the adversary's comrade, who was momentarily taken aback on seeing the first man struck down.

Now, however, the Roman front line is getting tired. The centurion, although fighting intensely, notices it out of the corner of his eye and waits for the right moment. As soon as the barbarians drop back to organize a new assault, he shouts the order: *"Mutatio!"*

The soldiers on the front line back up a step and their comrades in the second line take their place. So the front line has been reformed with fresh soldiers, while the barbarians get steadily more tired and less able to think straight.

The centurion observes the middle sector of the Roman lines, where the enemy have concentrated their attack. It holds and gradually repulses the Chatti assault. Horrified, he notices that an auxiliary has just decapitated one of the enemy and is holding the severed head by the hair with his teeth. The auxiliaries are barbarians and it is part of their tradition to cut off the heads of their enemies. The Celts, for example, nail their enemies' heads to the roof beams of their log cabins as if they were hunting trophies; or they display the heads and skulls of their dead enemies at the entrances to their villages. Beyond the borders of the empire, Europe is populated by tribes of headhunters.

The Turning Point

By now the progress of the battle seems clear: the Chatti haven't been able to break through, and now they have lost momentum, not least because of the Romans' relentless "air war" of darts, arrows, and lead projectiles. It is a delicate moment; better, it is the crucial moment.

And the turnaround arrives suddenly. Sensing that the enemy is wavering, the *legatus*, who has been following the battle from the middle of the Roman formation, at the side of his men, gives the order to attack. He knows that at moments like this one, an action of this kind, even though risky, can deliver the decisive blow, the one that sends the enemy running.

The standards are lowered and pointed forward and the horns sound again with the signal for attack. The centurion, sweaty and with blood running out of his helmet from the blow he received, raises his sword and notices the standard of his cohort lowering into position and pointing toward the enemy. Unlike the *legatus*, he has no way of obtaining a bird's-eye view of the battlefield. He is in the middle of the fray, amid shouting, screams of desperation, sweat, and the smell of blood. But he obeys without hesitation and repeats the order to attack. He puffs out his chest and fills his voice with all the power of the blows he has been dealing to the enemy.

Some of the soldiers in the front line look at him for an instant, to figure out if, in the clamor of the battle, they have heard right. The centurion's stance, with his gladius pointing forward, is enough by itself to give them their answer. Following the sharp orders of their centurion, the front line begins moving slowly and then faster and faster. The centurion remains off to the side and makes sure that the line of soldiers advances compactly and in unison, with their shields parallel. The alignment is essential for making sure there are no gaps. But he has to do this while also thinking about how to protect his own life as he advances among the enemy. Luckily, next to him, the *optio*, his second-in-command, checks that no barbarians are waiting in ambush.

The legionnaires proceed, holding their swords horizontal by their handles, a bit like carrying a suitcase. And as they advance they assume a boxer's stance, keeping their left side protected with their shield and their right side ready to thrust with the gladius.

But the barbarians don't move back; they proudly maintain their position. The front line of Roman soldiers is rapidly upon them. Even the *legatus* hears the clash of the shields. For him it is a good sign. The Roman soldiers train every day in hand-to-hand combat, like no other army. Over the years, these legionnaires have acquired the habit of physical combat and an agility in the use of their weapons in tight spaces that the Chatti certainly don't have. And you can tell that from the number of barbarian corpses that are beginning to cover the entire battlefield.

The battle rages in the middle of the plain, thousands of by now exhausted barbarians fight on in desperation. But they won't be moved back. The final blow is dealt by the Roman cavalry, which the *legatus* had kept out of the fray and which now charges down on the enemy's right flank. It's too much. The lines of the already exhausted Chatti totally break down. The horsemen seem like teams of wild dogs furiously assailing their prey. With astounding speed and brutality they pour down on the enemy's right flank, just at the point where they are not prepared to do battle. And the Chatti are overwhelmed, pushing up against each other, trying to find an escape route.

In antiquity, the cavalry is used not so much for killing the enemy with blows from swords and lances but for routing the enemy lines like a steamroller—like a bowling ball crashing into a row of pins. The sudden onslaught of dozens of horses is frightening; you don't know whether to be more careful of the horse or of the horseman who is trying to hit you. So if you are already engaged in frontal combat with an enemy and the cavalry attacks you from the side, you move, you run, and your compact front line dissolves.

Once their lines are broken, the enemy isn't scary anymore; they're disorganized, able to react only as individual soldiers and not as a group, and they become easy prey for war-fighting professionals like the legionnaires. And that's what happens now. Taking advantage of the confusion created by the cavalry, the Roman lines press on and concentrate the attack, breaking through the enemy front. Then the *legatus* orders into the fray the units of the VIII Augusta and the I Minervia, who initiate an encircling maneuver.

The Chatti realize that it's all over. Everywhere they look, all they can see is an extended wall of the legionnaires' red shields, steadily closing in on them from all sides. Even though they still number in the thousands, the barbarians can't maneuver, and they are gradually ripped to pieces by the swords of the legionnaires and their allies, the auxiliaries. The Roman army has the enemy in its fist, like a big apple, and gradually destroys him bite by bite.

Darts from the scorpions and ballistas continue to fall from the sky. They plunge into the Chatti without warning, like bolts of lightning. The warriors hear a brief, loud buzzing sound and then collapse to the ground.

While the more determined among them keep on fighting with conviction, beating back at the Romans, most of the Chatti realize that it makes no sense to stay there, and they withdraw. They are an army in disarray, retreating toward their wagons. The legionnaires don't let up and pursue them, slashing them with their swords. It's a slaughter. The battle rages on into the late afternoon next to the wagons, where the Chatti manage to organize a last valiant defense, using their vehicles as a little fort. Then, just as a fire burns itself out, the Chattis' last faltering flames of war go out. The cavalry chases after the few remaining Chatti, who run off into the forest. It's over.

What to Make of All This?

Victory yells volley back and forth across the battlefield, together with the mottos of the cohorts and legions. But you can also hear the cries of the wounded. The centurion Magnus is still alive. Two legionnaires from his century on the front line are dead and fifteen are wounded. Now he's standing next to his second-in-command, who is sitting on the grass with his legs open wide, his face a mask of pain. He has a long wound on the inside of his thigh that a medic is trying to plug.

To our surprise we notice that here on the battlefield there are doctors moving among the wounded bringing aid. The Roman army is the only one in ancient Europe and the Mediterranean basin to have a permanent medical corps, yet another thing it has in common with modern armies. But it wasn't the only one in the entire ancient world. The ancient Indian treatise *Arthashastra* (350–280 BCE), in fact, described an ambulance service, pulled by horses and elephants, that followed armies into battle.

The medics here have been active throughout the length of the battle. To be sure, they don't have all of the medicines and resources available today, but they know a lot of techniques: they try to stop hemorrhages; they know how to remove arrowheads without damaging arteries; and they are able to amputate limbs with amazing rapidity, cauterizing the wound with hot irons.

The centurion is asked to take off his helmet. He had forgotten about receiving that tremendous blow to the head when he was distracted by giving orders (occupational hazard). Luckily, it's only a flesh wound and the medic applies a poultice made of oils and herbs. Magnus looks at his helmet. The Chatti's downward blow split his fan of red feathers in two, but it didn't manage to go beyond that because of the protective cross braces. So it slid quickly down the whole skullcap, stopping at the metal visor. If it hadn't been for that visor, the barbarian's blade would have cut off the centurion's nose.

If you look at the helmet of a Roman legionnaire, you'll notice that it has protective guards at all the points that could be hit by an enemy sword. It has an ample metal plate that stretches over the shoulders to stop blows aimed at the neck, cheek guards that protect the face, leaving uncovered only the mouth, nose, and eyes. And then a thick visor on the forehead, which runs from one ear to the other, to block hammer blows from a sword or downward strokes from above. For the same reason the helmet's ear holes also have little arc-shaped visors. The resemblance to the antiriot helmets of modern police forces is astounding. And the same goes for their shields and the techniques they use to keep rioters, or enemy soldiers, at bay. The two situations are actually quite similar: on one side, small but well-trained units deployed in a well-ordered formation, and on the other side a mass of people attacking helter-skelter.

Now it's time to start looking for loot. All the soldiers rummage through the dead and wounded bodies, finishing off anyone who protests. The Geneva Convention does not exist. Once again, some auxiliaries pass by, holding by the hair some amputated heads of the Chatti. For them the heads are loot too. The centurion looks at them but doesn't say anything. The habit of taking human trophies will not end here.

Some tied-up prisoners are pushed and shoved into an area where other prisoners have already been rounded up, sitting on the ground, their hands tied behind their backs. Some of them are women. They all have blank looks on their faces. Their lives are going to change forever and they know it. All the Chatti who have been captured alive will be rounded up here. Some of them may be interrogated, but almost certainly the legionnaires have a strong interest in not damaging them: the prisoners are also part of the loot. They'll be sold to slave traders, and the proceeds will be distributed among the legionnaires.

The battlefield has now grown strangely quiet. Thousands of dead bodies lie silently in a misty fog that begins to rise up from the earth, making the scene surreal. Everywhere you look, there are arrows and darts sticking out of the ground, but also swords and banners. They're all pointing in different directions, like gravestones in an abandoned cemetery. And they vanish in the hovering fog.

The centurion walks among the dead bodies. His greaves are covered with blood, his shield marred with cuts and scratches and splattered with blood. It's a vision out of Dante's *Inferno*. The sun is a red ball resting on the horizon, and its rays are caressing for the last time the young men on both sides who up until a few hours ago were full of life and pride. The legionnaire stops; in front of him are two bodies with their arms around each other, almost symbolically. The bodies of a legionnaire and a young barbarian, with long hair and a beard. Evidently, he hadn't yet killed anyone.

It has been said that the clash of two armies is tantamount to a single army committing suicide. Observing this scene of death, where the dead all look so much alike, it's hard to disagree with that assessment. But it's not the right epoch for entertaining such thoughts. Here there is only one principle to be followed: *Mors tua vita mea*; your death is my life.

As he walks along the centurion holds his gladius over the dead bodies of his enemies, its point seeming to sniff them to make sure they are actually dead. Then he bends down over the body of one of the barbarians. He was one of their leaders. He had seen him fighting in the middle of the fray. He was a real brute, a valorous enemy. He slides a ring off the barbarian's finger and a bracelet off his wrist. Then he takes his sword, a nice souvenir to display back at the fort in Mogontiacum.

But up ahead of him, beyond the edge of the forest, the memory of this battle will be totally different and will have markedly different effects. As we're about to see.

Power Rather than Force

We have just seen a legion in combat, the elite soldiers of antiquity, trained with dedication and no concern for the cost. Let's try to get away from the battlefield for a minute. What is the significance of what we have just witnessed and, above all, of this victory?

The answer can be synthesized in just one word, which explains in part the longevity of the Roman Empire: dissuasion. The legionnaires have fought to wipe out a group of barbarians who were not, in all honesty, a real threat to the empire. But their attack on the border did constitute a threat. If it had not been punished and if they had not been eliminated, they would have been imitated by other peoples in other places, and this could have created big problems.

So the strategy of the Romans and their legions can be summed up like this: sow fear. The legions are the atomic weapons of antiquity. But that's not the whole story. A lot of other armies have sowed fear. But the systems, the nations, and the empires that produced them—from Attila to Genghis Khan, from Napoleon to Hitler—disappeared very rapidly compared to the thousand years of Roman rule in the West and another thousand years in Byzantium in the East.

The Romans, in fact, knew how to balance the strategy of power and force in a way that was incredibly effective, allowing their world to survive for a very long time. And the legions were a key element in this strategy of maximizing power and minimizing the use of force. They created a formidable army, an awesome war machine, whose secret was constant training. In short, the message they tried to send their enemies was this: I'm ready, always ready, and very strong. If you challenge me, I'll destroy you. It was a real deterrent. *Si vis pacem para bellum*; if you want peace, prepare for war.

The events of Masada in 73 CE present an illuminating example of this kind of power. The Hebrew revolt, which broke out in the province of Judea, had been put down in blood. Small groups of rebels escaped, taking refuge in a remote province, Masada, where in 66 CE a thousand or so zealots (men, women, and children) barricaded themselves inside an impregnable fortress on the top of a cliff with a fifteen-hundred-foot drop on all sides. Still today, the sight of Masada is striking. It emerges like an iceberg from the infernal plains of the Dead Sea, where the temperature is stifling hot. Yet Vespasian sent an entire legion, the X Fretensis, plus seven thousand support troops. The legion surrounded the "island" of Masada with a long wall and eight camps of legionnaires. You can imagine the logistical difficulties of maintaining thirteen thousand men for months (maybe as long as two years; it's not certain) in the planet's hottest desert, supplying them with all the necessities of life—water, food, firewood. But there's more. A simple siege was not enough. The message had to be clear: we will get you no matter where you go. And so they built a long ramp of sediment, sand, and tree trunks (brought in from who knows where) with a road going up, a huge undertaking, all the way to the base of the walls of the fortress. And then they pushed up the length of the ramp a wooden tower on wheels, eight to ten stories high, outfitted with battering rams. The next morning, when the Romans broke through the wall and entered Masada, the zealots had all committed suicide.

The news spread everywhere, thanks in part to the writings of Flavius Josephus, and it was a warning to all. Whoever tried to rebel in the provinces would be tracked down and wiped out. Sending an entire legion to the desert for months was an enormous expense, especially for the objective of capturing only a thousand people. But the benefit that it would yield would be enormous, both because no one in the empire would dare to rebel (thus sparing other costs) and because it would increase Rome's power. Consequently Rome's enemies would not dare to rebel or attack this stronger empire, their people would accept its rule, and Rome would become even more powerful.

In this regard, Edward Luttwak, a renowned expert on Roman military strategy, has pointed out that every time Rome used its power successfully, it reinforced its dominance. But when it's necessary to use the army—that is, force rather than power—it's a different story. A battle kills a lot of soldiers who have been trained for years, and that is a cost. In other words, force is consumed over time and that makes you weaker. Power, on the other hand, if used well, increases steadily and reduces costs. And this makes a big difference.

Consequently, even though the Romans had the most powerful army in the ancient world, they used it wisely, "surgically," we might say. And they devoted themselves day to day to other kinds of battles, without moving their legions: the battles of dissuasion.

The Secrets Behind the Strength of the Legions

It took at least two years before new recruits were ready to look the enemy in the eye. They followed a long training program in order to become war-fighting professionals. Every legionnaire, therefore, was a costly investment. It's easy to understand then why they were never in the front line.

During imperial Rome, moreover, heroic gestures were discouraged. Heroism belonged more to the Greek world or to the Germanic and Celtic traditions. The response of the Roman general Scipio Africanus to an adversary who had challenged him to engage in individual combat has gone down in history: "My mother made me a general, not a combatant."

But when the Romans decided to fight, they were merciless. They understood that the use of force had a single objective and so it had to be used in the most brutal and quickest way possible in order to achieve peace (for the empire) in the shortest possible time. The Romans could do it that way because they did not have television cameras following their every move and they didn't have to worry about the public being horrified at the sight of dead civilians. They were capable, therefore, of committing crimes against humanity, as they would be defined today, of unprecedented dimensions.

There is one thing we never think about that explains the brutality of the conflicts. In Roman times. Europe and the Mediterranean were still full of forests and woods, large uninhabited areas, and small villages. The entire population of the empire amounted to probably 100 million people. Practically speaking, the total population was twice that of Italy today, in a territory that went from the Mediterranean to northern Europe and Asia. So just a few battles made it possible to conquer vast regions of land or wipe out the enemy for a long time. They were like cup finals to be won in a single game, not a whole championship season. And the Romans had figured out the best system for achieving their objective, with their army of professionals.

But what was it that the legionnaires were defending? Not the emperor or the cities of the empire, but the Roman way of life: from its networks of commerce and finance to its culture and lifestyle. For a great many groups, the empire guaranteed a comfortable life. All the basic needs (food, wine, sex, personal hygiene) were inexpensive. Everyone knew how to read, write, and do arithmetic. There were shows and performances (chariot races, theatrical productions) every day, for free or just about. Compared to the life of the tribes in the forests, they were light years ahead.

Indeed, to the barbarians all of this must have seemed like paradise. That's why they kept hammering away at the border, not to destroy the Roman Empire but to become part of it! That's what the barbarians amassed at the Roman frontier were asking for. They were knocking on the door because they wanted to be let in to enjoy the party.

The Goths, for example, wanted lands that they could settle on, and over time they succeeded; Italy became an Ostrogoth kingdom. The famous sack of Rome was not dictated by the desire to eliminate Roman civilization; on the contrary, it was a vendetta of the Visigoths because the emperor Honorius had refused to give them land. In the end they established themselves in the south of France and Spain. And like them, the Vandals, the Burgundians, the Franks, the Angles, the Saxons, and the Longobards established themselves in various parts of Europe after the fall of the Roman Empire. A fall that was first and foremost an administrative collapse: the mores and customs of daily life remained those of the Romans, with roads, frescoes, baths, horse races, and so on, even though, by now, it was in total decline. All the barbarians that made their way into Europe, in fact, ended up doing just this: civilizing themselves. No more nomadic wandering with wagons and tents, but the comfortable life of a residential building in the city. They changed their ways of dressing and eating in response to and pursuit of the attractions of "western society," in the same way that thousands of people today, in the face of great risks and hardships, cross the Mediterranean or the Mexican-U.S. border. For centuries, therefore, the frontier legions kept the barbarians at bay, with the only system possible: force, and above all the threat to use it at any moment.

But what did all this cost the Roman taxpayer? Edward Luttwak answers the question in these terms: a strategy should be evaluated on the basis of how much security it provides to the collectivity. In the case of Rome, he cites this example: Caligula, who is remembered as a ferocious dictator was actually, according to Luttwak, a first-rate administrator. During his reign the entire empire was protected by twenty-five legions (that is, just over 130,000 legionnaires), plus a similar number of auxiliaries. The total was not much more than 250,000 soldiers. That is a very small number for defending the whole empire (even though in the age of Caligula, Britannia was not yet a part of it). They were all paid decently, fed decently, treated by a medical service and hospitals. The greatest cost was pensions. The army was paid with tax revenues, and all property ownership was recorded in order to levy taxes on it. But the idea that an entire empire, covering three continents, was protected by a number of soldiers that could barely fill two or three football stadiums is truly surprising and unique in antiquity.

And that's not all. With major works of civil and military engineering like Hadrian's Wall or, elsewhere, systems of fences, ditches, and forts, the empire was further able to reduce the number of soldiers deployed in border zones and so reduce expenses as well. (Hadrian's Wall in a certain sense was a soldier-robot that replaced the legionnaires exactly like robots have replaced workers in factories.) The Romans, therefore, had succeeded in finding the way to contain the costs of defending the empire and, along with it, Roman civilization.

Later on, when they adopted a different system of controlling the borders—no longer a line of defense but an open frontier with the defending army divided up and deployed in scattered locations throughout the territory—costs rose at exactly the time when there was less money available, and that's when the decline began.

Night

The battle won, the Roman army is heading back where it came from—but not before building a trophy on the battlefield. After carving a big tree trunk in the form of a Y, the soldiers affix a big helmet, some shields, and some of the enemy's salvaged weapons to it, creating a sort of military totem pole in honor of the victory. After the thanksgiving rituals and ceremonies, the legions turn their backs on the battlefield, leaving behind only the dead bodies of their enemy, on which ravens have already begun to feed.

The centurion Magnus is now back in Mogontiacum. After returning to the barracks, everyone is now on leave. The streets and alleyways resound with the shouts, laughter, and music coming from all the night spots celebrating the victory. While he's passing in front of a tavern, a woman with a big glass of wine in hand puts her arm around his neck, kisses him, and tries to pull him into the bar, but the centurion rebuffs her.

Magnus will not be participating in the celebrations in the city. He has a much more important date, all for himself. Halfway down a big street, he sees the sign of an inn illuminated by the feeble light of an oil lamp: pictured on it is a man climbing a mountain—a mountaineer. It's the sign he was looking for. Just beyond it is an unmarked door. It's the front door of a three-story building in the center of the city.

Magnus opens the door and enters. Immediately, the sounds of the celebrating city are muffled and distant; in the semidarkness he sees a stair leading to the upper floors. Every step he takes is answered by a creaking sound from the wooden stairs. When he gets to the top he sees a light filtering under a door. Here we are. This is the place. With a firm hand he turns the key and opens the door.

On the other side is an elegantly decorated room. Bronze oil lamps in the corners create islands of light that reveal parts of the décor: two folding chairs with leather seats, a marble table, oriental fabrics similar to carpets hanging on one wall, and frescoes all around. The mansard ceiling is high, with naked beams, a modern touch unusual in the Roman era.

On a bedside table there is a sculpture in blue glass; a beautiful stylized dove standing with her wings closed. Her tail is broken—on purpose. The sculpture is actually a bottle of perfume.

In the Roman era, glass blowers are able to create little bottles in the form of long-tailed birds that are true masterpieces. They fill the inside with perfume and then seal the whole thing, fusing the tip of the tail. The woman who wants to use the perfume will have to break off the end of the tail just as is commonly done today with little glass vials. Some of these little bottles have been miraculously preserved intact and are on display today in several museums.

In the back of the room Magnus finally sees the person with whom he has his appointment. She's a noble woman who has a sizzling relationship with the centurion. This room is where they meet for their trysts.

He might have never made it back here. He might already have been cremated, his body reduced to ashes and charred bones, if that blow from the barbarian's sword had hit him just a little harder. This recognition fuels his abandonment to the fragrances and sensations of the night. The morning sun will find Magnus and the woman still locked in embrace.

Milan

~ *Women's Liberation* ~

The Amber Merchant

A small wagon train is making its way through a forest of tall, dark trees. The wind wraps itself around the overhanging foliage and sends it swaying to the rhythm of an unheard tune. The sinuous dance is accompanied by a relentless high-pitched hum, as if all the wolves in this endless forest had decided to howl in unison.

The man driving the last wagon has a tense look on his face. He keeps casting worried glances overhead, both right and left. But then his dark eyes come back down to the level of the tree trunks and scrutinize the forest darkness to see if there's anything moving.

An ambush of Germans is always possible in these parts, because we're traveling south, parallel to the border, which is not far from here. But it's not very likely. This road is constantly patrolled, plus there are small stations with guards and horses placed at short intervals in strategic points.

The man knows that; he's traveled this road many times. But what's making him so anxious is less what might be out there and more what he's carrying in his wagon: lots of amber. This man is an amber merchant. But he's never transported such a precious cargo, a real treasure.

Our sestertius, as you've undoubtedly guessed, now belongs to him. He was given it as change when he bought a new pair of sandals from a shopkeeper in Mogontiacum, who in turn had received it from a centurion who had come in to buy a beautiful pair of embroidered women's sandals. "For my betrothed," he had said.

The amber merchant went into the shop a few minutes later, on his return from a long journey beyond the frontier, during which he had completely worn out his old shoes. But it was worth it; on that journey he had succeeded in acquiring some pieces of amber of a quality and size that he had never seen before.

Why Are the Romans So Wild About Amber?

Amber comes from the Baltic. The local populations gather it on the sea's icy shores. No Romans ever venture there—it's too dangerous. But there is a large network of local small traders and "shippers" who, like so many ants, carry the pieces of amber toward the empire. They use a series of mule trails and back roads that only they know and that together are called the Amber Road. It's the European equivalent of the Silk Road. It is the conduit for millions of sesterces worth of amber, a true stream of red gold, winding its way to the Roman Empire. The destination is Aquileia, a key military outpost of the empire, not far from present-day Trieste, where raw pieces of fossil resin are transformed into masterpieces of art and jewelry.

Amber was not discovered by the Romans; it was already known and highly valued more than six thousand years ago. Even the Mycenaean kings and their women adorned their bodies with amber jewelry, as did the Egyptians, the Greeks, and the Etruscans.

Amber is used to make pendants, necklaces, rings, gaming dice, women's toiletries (jars for colored powders used as makeup, or shell-shaped dishes with brushes for facial creams). Also little statuettes, whose high price was the target of a barb from Pliny the Elder: "A statuette in amber, no matter how small, is more costly than living, and robust, human beings!"

Why is amber so prized? For its color and scarceness, but most of all for its electrostatic properties, which in antiquity must have seemed magical. When rubbed, amber discharges electricity and becomes a magnetic attractant for hair and body hair, a clearly supernatural property. The Greeks called amber *electron*, a term that gave us the word "electricity."

This precious commodity sells so well among the Romans because they are also convinced of its healing powers. Pliny the Elder, the great naturalist who had a long and distinguished military career (probably including at least one battle against the Chatti) and died during the volcanic eruption in Pompeii, confirms this belief. In *Naturalis Historia*, his famous almost encyclopedic naturalistic treatise, he writes: "Still today the peasant women who live beyond the Po use amber objects as jewelry, to beautify themselves, but also for their healing properties. It is believed, in fact, that amber cures tonsillitis and sore throats."

Amber fascinates us still today, mainly because of the insects that it holds captive.

These insects died 45 million years ago, when drops of resin produced by evergreen trees enveloped them in an eternal embrace. We know this thanks to scientific studies carried out by paleontologists. But what was the Romans' explanation for these insects?

It is indeed surprising how accurately Pliny the Elder analyzed the mystery:

Amber is born of the lymph exuded by a genus of the pine tree. . . .
That it is a pine is proved by the smell that amber gives off when it is
rubbed and by the fact that it burns exactly like a resinous torch and
with the same aroma. That amber was liquid in its nascent state is also
proved by some bodies which, when it is held up to the light, can be
discerned inside as ants, mosquitoes, and lizards which became stuck
in it and were then imprisoned when it hardened.

This is the explanation of a rational Roman. Many of his fellow citizens, however, would give you a mythological explanation. The pieces of amber are the tears spilled by the Heliades, the daughters of the sun-god Helios, over the death of their brother Phaëthon, who had used the sun's chariot and then crashed and drowned in the Po. (The Po is the destination point of the Amber Road that departs from the Baltic.)

Our merchant, obviously, couldn't be bothered with these questions. All he's interested in is selling and making deals. And he is very capable. Thanks to a German emissary and some excellent contacts, he has succeeded in obtaining some very rare pieces of raw amber by arranging for them to be "detoured" off the classic amber road and brought to him at a location near the frontier of the empire. And it was worth it. The amber is of the best quality, the variety known as *falernum* because it has the same color as this highly prized wine. It is transparent and reminiscent of cooked honey.

When the Goods Are Human: The Slave Wagons

Now the merchant has only one thing on his mind: get to Italy as soon as possible to sell his precious cargo. And he doesn't like this road through the forest at all. So he has hooked up with a convoy of slave traders, with their wheeled cages crammed with dozens of barbarians. The guards escorting and overseeing the wagons with the human merchandise should be enough to discourage possible attacks.

Let's take a look at these wagons. If we wanted to draw parallels to modern highway vehicles we might put them in the category of tractor-trailers full of livestock that you drive by every now and again. How many times have you asked yourself: what's going to become of those sheep, those cows, those pigs? You can be pretty sure that they don't have much life ahead of them, and that they'll soon end up—in another form—in some supermarket or butcher shop. Then your car accelerates, the truck vanishes behind you, and you forget all about them.

For a Roman it's pretty much the same story. How many times has the average Roman man, woman, or child seen one of these wagons full of human goods pass by their house? Plenty of times. And they've probably entertained themselves for a minute or two in observing them, curious to get a look at the slaves' faces. Then they go back to their daily routine. Slavery is a totally normal part of life. Nobody is scandalized by it. And this is one of the biggest differences between today's world and the Roman Empire.

We approach the convoy of four slave wagons. The first thing that strikes us are the wagons themselves. They creak and rock, turning even the smallest mound or dip in the road into a jostling bounce. Their wheels have no spokes but are full, as they say, and look like round tabletops. Their bars are iron, but on the wagon full of children they're made of wood.

Let's take a look at the occupants. They are Germans. Their hair is filthy and disheveled, especially the women's. But they look like they couldn't care less. Their bodies are half naked, dirty. Even the few clothes they do have are torn and grungy. They've been on the road for days now, and nobody has thought to wash them. They are merely living cargo, nothing more. And then there's the smell. That may be the dominant sensation: the wagons give off an acrid, pungent stench. Not only have the slaves not washed for days, but once the caravan starts up in the morning there is no stopping for bodily needs, which are done in the wagon.

Our eyes naturally seek out those of the slaves. But they all have their backs to the bars, as though they wanted to shut themselves off from the world. Some are standing and others are sitting down. Nobody is talking. They're all looking at the ground, overwhelmed by a fate that has suddenly transformed them from free men and women into objects. And they know that from now on their lives will be full of suffering.

Especially striking is the silence of the children. We go over to their wagon, the smallest. Nobody is crying or whining. They too have used up all their tears. One of them is lying on the floor in the back, motionless. That little body lying in that position, with nobody helping him, sums up all the inhumanity of slavery. It is a lacerating pain that pierces your heart. It may be the most horrible sight that we have seen on our journey. It's as though the future has been extinguished; not only that child's but all of humankind's.

The men, women, and children proceed in silence toward their fate. We can't help but think of other convoys in this same region almost two thousand years later that will make the same journey in reverse, on train tracks, with human cargo destined for extermination.

The Slave Trader

We will never get used to this sight. But how can it be that Romans abide the trade in human beings? Actually, the one person who is hated by the Romans is the *mango*, or slave trader. Slave traders can become immeasurably wealthy, as we can now see. The door opens on a wood-covered wagon, similar to a trailer, and out comes the *mango*, who shoots a glance at the little wagon train. Through the open door we get a glimpse of a small traveling apartment, with a fur-covered bed, on which is sitting a blond-haired girl, undoubtedly a slave.

The man has beady, ruthless eyes, a long nose, and thin lips. He has the prominent belly of someone who eats a lot, if not well, and some rings that betray the prosperity of his business. He never stops working. He's often on the frontier, where he takes delivery of the goods from his German correspondents, who capture people from other tribes and then sell them to him. Or else he follows the legions on their police actions along the border or during invasions. It's not only captured enemy soldiers that he fills his wagons with but also women and children kidnapped during military raids on villages across the border. And when there are no big military operations in progress, he has other sources for his supply of slaves: he sends his collaborators into cities to round up children abandoned by their parents. Every urban center has a place where such children are left at night or in the early morning hours—a temple, a column on a street corner, a garbage dump. Why do these parents abandon their children? Because they are unable to keep them, or don't want to. They are too poor and their family is already numerous; or they are children born to prostitutes. Or they are children of good families who are undesirable because they are thought to be the offspring of infidelity or simply not the right sex. Their owners often put them to work begging for alms, after breaking one of their arms or maiming them—a very common practice to make them better earners.

Then there are citizens of Rome who are sequestered—that is, free citizens who are suddenly disappeared, perhaps while they are away on business—in order to augment the slave market. We will have the occasion to discover this aspect of the trade later in our journey, in another part of the empire.

Entering Italy

Several days later, the convoy has crossed the Alps and is about to descend into the Po River valley. They have come through the mountains, through high-altitude passes where it's freezing cold and snowy. But in the Roman era nobody climbs to the top: mountain climbing is an alien concept. High altitudes are considered hostile environments, dangerous and extreme—a little like the ocean depths are considered today. Except for the occasional hunter of wild goats or chamois, nobody ventures up to the peaks. It's amazing to think that up there on the glaciers, in another part of the Alps, lies the mummy of Otzi the Iceman, the Similaun man who lived in prehistoric times, waiting to be discovered, with his ax, bow, arrows, and clothes. Just think that in the Roman era he has already been there among the glaciers for thirty-five thousand years—longer than the time that separates us from the Egyptian pharaoh Ramses II. But another two thousand years will go by before his remains will be found and studied.

By now the wagon train has left the mountain passes. Although the barbarian captives are used to extreme weather, three slaves have already died from the cold, hunger, and atrocious living conditions in the wagons. Others have sores on their ankles and necks from the iron rings and collars that are used to keep them from escaping.

The *mango* has taken out his rage for his lost profits on his servants by brutally beating them, knowing full well they are not to blame for the deaths. A certain number of slaves are always lost on every journey.

Now, however, that they have just begun their descent, there is one more obstacle to overcome: customs.

Getting Through Roman Customs: Tricks and Checks

Roman customs stations are placed at strategic points throughout the empire, not only on its external borders as might be expected, but also between one province and another. Any kind of merchandise that enters a Roman province must be taxed even if it comes from inside Roman territory. You can imagine the long lines with the customs officers looking for any pretext at all to increase revenues. And that's what's happening now. The convoy has been stopped for hours.

The law is very simple: anything that is used for the journey is not taxed. So, wagons, oxen, mules, horses, baggage filled with clothes, plus anything that is for *usum proprium*—personal use—such as rings, personal jewelry, documents, or a pocket sundial, are tax-exempt. For everything else duty must be paid. Absolutely everything. A pair of brothers driving a small wagon are arguing with the customs officer who wants to tax the urn containing their father's ashes, which they are taking home to be buried in the family tomb. Even a dead body is taxed. It remains to be established how much the person is worth. And that is precisely what they are arguing about now.

The first thing you are asked by the customs officers, called *portitores*, is to provide a list of the goods you are carrying, the so-called *professio*.

The taxes applied are actually quite reasonable, from about 2 percent of the value of the goods to a maximum of 5 percent.

For luxury goods it's altogether different. Silk, precious stones, and prized fabrics are taxed at 25 percent. Our amber merchant is going to have to hand over a sizable sum. But he has, as they say, budgeted for it, because he is a man of the world: he has made it understood that he would like to speak privately with the chief customs officer. As soon as the officer climbed into his little covered wagon, the merchant paid him a handsome sum in gold coins for the amber that had been checked up to that point, and then he put a nice big chunk of amber into the officer's hand, by way of suggesting that the check should end there. "To make a beautiful piece of jewelry for your wife," he told him. Obviously, the largest and most valuable pieces of amber are on the bottom, well hidden, and have gone unnoticed by the officers, who have so far checked only the pieces of average quality that have been placed out in the open by the merchant.

Actually, it's all a sham. The customs officers know full well that if they kept on checking, the more valuable pieces would pop into view, but this way everybody is happy: officially, the officer in charge has made the merchant pay a handsome sum for the customs duty (and there's even enough for a sizable tip to split with his colleagues). For his part, the merchant knows that he has only paid a part of the taxes due, for a sizable savings. Finally, the customs officer's young wife will have a lovely chiseled jewel.

To tell the truth, it's not the first time that the two have met, and there has always been this tacit agreement between them not to finish the baggage check. It seems as though nothing has changed in two thousand years.

The officer in charge gets down off the wagon and gives the order to his subordinates to affix to the *professio* with a seal, the permission for the merchant to leave. They understand right away and signal to the little wagon to leave the convoy and continue on its way.

Immediately afterward, one of the customs officers shouts for joy. At the bottom of one of the bags of a mule driver he has discovered some beautiful silver plates. It's clear that the mule driver was trying to take advantage of his humble appearance in order to smuggle in some luxury goods. Are they stolen? Is he doing it on behalf of his master who is trying to avoid paying customs duty? We don't know the answer. All we know is that in this case the customs officer's instinct has paid off. Years of experience enable them to understand that some apparently humble and anonymous travelers can be the source of surprises and satisfaction. And they have learned how to pick them out.

Now what's going to happen? The law is simple: all the goods will be seized. But the violator will be allowed to buy back the seized goods at a price, naturally, established by the customs officers. Which means at least double the value of the items in question.

Hiding the Slaves

The situation of the slave wagons is much different. The *mango* is walking up and down nervously, pressing the customs officers to hurry because his goods are perishable in the cold. But this accomplishes nothing except to accentuate the meticulousness of the checks. Annoyed by his brusque, arrogant tone, they start rummaging through everything, even his personal baggage, in search of undeclared items. They even start searching the escort guards and all the personnel of the wagon train.

The *mango* is not worried about their checking. He's clean. He knows they're not going to find anything. Actually, he's cheating on another matter. The death of those slaves has reduced his take at the market, so he's trying to pass off two of the survivors as members of his family. One of them is the blond girl that we got a glimpse of on the bed in the wagon. The other is a little girl with the blank stare. He's dressed them in decent clothes and has them sitting in the front of the wagon, next to him. He's pretending they're his wife and daughter.

He has chosen them because they are his most prized goods, and they'll get him a very good price in the market; they are young and beautiful. And then because he can count on their silence. The first is terrorized and totally dominated by the *mango,* who has threatened her with death. The second never speaks. It's a trick that has worked in the past. But it's risky.

Roman law on this issue is clear. Lionel Casson, a noted expert on travel in antiquity, stated that if someone smuggled a slave through customs, pretending that the slave was a member of his family, and the slave revealed his true identity, that slave would be freed immediately, never to be a slave again.

The customs chief looks at the blonde and the little girl . . . and he gets suspicious. It's normal that a wealthy slave trader should have a good-looking wife and a daughter. But the story doesn't add up because of one detail. When he goes inside the wagon he sees only one bed. It's already small for one person; imagine for a couple. And where does the little girl sleep? There's no room, even on the floor.

He realizes that something's amiss. He observes the two of them sitting on the driver's box and he's struck by the blank stare of the little girl. It's a look that you don't forget. The customs chief has understood everything. Yes, but how to free her? She has to be the one to say she is a slave.

He gets an idea. He takes off his helmet and walks over to the little girl. He smiles at her and starts humming softly a lullaby in the Germanic language. It's one that his wife (the young woman who is going to receive the amber jewel) sings to their newborn daughter. The woman he married is a *liberta*, a freed slave. She comes from Germany too. It's hard to say, though, if she comes from a tribe close to the little girl's. The German populations are so numerous and their dialects and customs are very diverse. But the languages have a common source. Perhaps it will work to get the little girl to talk.

The customs chief looks the little girl in the eye and starts singing the first verse, but nothing happens. He intones the second . . . nothing. He tries to sing the third, whispering it into the little girl's ear. Gradually, she hugs him with her little arms. Now her eyes have begun to sparkle. And she calls out the name of her mother.

Like a daughter adrift on the current, her fate has suddenly changed again. The customs chief takes her into his arms and then holds out his hand and drags the young "wife" into the customs office too. The *mango* tries to stop them and rushes after them, cursing and threatening, but he clams up when two more officers, who had been looking on at the scene, pull out their swords and hold them against his chest and throat. The *mango* holds up his hands and backs up all the way to the wagon. He's understood that the game is over.

Liberation

The wagon train is issued a formal order to stop and pull over onto the side of the road to let the other wagons through. The wife of the customs chief is called. When she comes into her husband's office she finds the little girl with dark blue eyes and ruffled blond hair wrapped in a blanket.

All it takes is a few words of affection from the woman in her native language and the little girl comes running toward her, looking for refuge in the folds of her long skirt. It doesn't take much to get her to say that the *mango* is not her father and that the blond girl is not her mother. It's harder to get the older girl, still paralyzed by fear, to talk. But this time, too, the wife of the customs chief, and the language the two women share, gradually break the ice. They were both captured in the heart of Germany by "people hunters" from their same tribe, who then sold them to this slave trader.

After consulting his colleagues, the customs chief goes to the *mango* and officially removes the two slaves from his custody, freeing them on the spot, as prescribed by the law. The man can't believe what's happening to him and turns red with anger, but he can't react. After paying his customs duty he orders the column of wagons to get back on the road.

Rocking and creaking and jostling their way along, the wheeled cages set off again for the plains of the Po Valley. Behind the bars nobody moves. They are all waiting to find out what fate has in store for them at the first slave market, which by now is not far off—just a few days hence. And so the wagon train, with its fated cargo, creaks on down the road, turns around the bend, and disappears. Watching it all the way are the deep blue eyes of the little girl who is clutching the skirts of her new mother. Yes, the customs chief concludes, his family has added a new member today.

What Milan Was Like in Those Days

The amber merchant has finally made it to the Po Valley. He could have gone to Aquileia, which has a flourishing amber market, but he has decided to come this way because he has some excellent customers here for his pieces of raw amber. They are one of the best-known families in an old city called Mediolanum, that is, Milan.

The dimensions of Milan in the Roman era are certainly not what they are today. In Trajan's time, the site of the future Sforza Castle, now in the heart of the city, was still outside the walls, in the countryside. Nevertheless, Mediolanum is a very important city on the checkerboard of imperial Rome. It was a useful behind-the-lines military base during the campaigns of Julius Caesar, and later on Augustus built a long defensive perimeter wall around the city.

Its size? If you were to measure the area of present-day Milan's cathedral square and multiply it by a factor of 6 or 7, the result would be the area enclosed by the city's republican walls. So Mediolanum is not immense, but it has everything: a forum, baths, a nice theater. It even has a long arena for horse and chariot races inside the perimeter of the city. This is unusual for a Roman city; generally, the races are held outside the walls. On the other hand, the stadium—the amphitheater where gladiator fights are held—is outside the walls. So the Milanese have to go out through one of the city gates if they want to see the show.

Mediolanum is a Romanized version of a Celtic name. In fact, Milan was founded seven centuries ago by a Celtic tribe called the Insubres.

According to some scholars, the name Mediolanum derives from its location in the middle of an extensive network of roads. And right from the start, its center corresponded more or less to the center of the current city, including the cathedral square. Back then, obviously, there was no dome-top statue of the Blessed Mother. In her place, however, the city already had another outstanding sacred female figure, inside an important temple. She was Belisama, the goddess of the arts and of the professions related to fire. Polybius, the Greek historian who lived about two hundred years before the birth of Christ, compares her to Minerva. In her temple, the cathedral of the Celtic age, were kept the venerated battle flags of the Insubric Gauls, known as the "unmovables."

For those arriving here after many days of traveling, Mediolanum has a familiar profile: a long line of low walls, surmounted at regular intervals by towers. The plumes of smoke rising up behind the old defensive wall are the signs of a city rich with life; something that is not at all displeasing to the amber merchant, tired from this long journey and yearning for a nice bath. He quickens the pace of his wagon until it becomes a mere speck in the distance, soon to be swallowed up by one of the city gates.

Mediolanum's Upscale Trendy Atmosphere

Here we are on the streets of Milan, in the neighborhood of the theater (the future opera house La Scala will be built just a few blocks from where we are now). Our sestertius has changed hands again. Now it's inside the purse of one of the members of the wealthy Milanese family called on by the amber merchant. There were quite a few of them sitting around the table when he displayed his precious collection of samples. Already at that moment, however, he no longer had the sestertius. He had paid one of the family's slaves to keep an eye on his wagon parked at the entrance to the city, and that was all it took for the sestertius to enter into someone else's possession. Now it is in the purse of one of the daughters of the wealthy Milanese man who has bought some pieces of amber to have them made into jewelry.

She is a beautiful woman, tall and thin. Her black hair is wrapped in a complicated chignon on the nape of her neck and arranged in a pharaonic hairpiece that towers over her forehead, forming a tall structure reminiscent of a papal tiara. It was made out of a light wooden frame covered with black hair brought from Asia; a true Roman-era hair extension.

The most notable feature, however, is her clothing, excellently tailored and certainly very costly. Nobody else on the street has such precious garments; today we would call them designer clothes.

She's with another woman, her friend, who is also from the same social class, as demonstrated by her similar dress. Her shoes are made of decorated and perfumed leather (the Romans knew how to tan leather so that it had a very pleasing smell, an idea that no one seems to have taken up today). The two women are wearing extremely fine tunics that wrap their bodies seductively. Bright red ribbons, crossing between their breasts and around their waists, highlight their youthful feminine charms. It is evident that the two women belong to the cream of Mediolanum society, as we can also intuit from the two elegantly dressed bodyguard-slaves who follow close behind them.

If the men who pass them on the street admire them primarily for their attractive physiques, the other women who spy them from windows or from the back rooms of shops where they work focus on the quality of their clothes. And theirs are looks of envy. What they admire most is the *palla*, the shawl that the merchant's daughter is wearing around her shoulders. It's made from the finest silk. Acquiring silk of this quality is very difficult, and only the wealthy can do it. As we will discover later in our journey, it comes from very distant places, beyond the Roman Empire, directly from China. And it has come all this way thanks to an extensive chain of merchants who have crossed distant sun-baked deserts, snow-capped mountain ranges, and vast tropical oceans. Given its rarity, this garment should be in a museum, not here in the middle of the street.

One cannot help but be impressed by the women's free and easy manner, their infectious laughter, the way they stop to examine and then purchase the veils on display in a shop or the jewels of an artisan on the corner of the street. And they pay for them with a nonchalance and a sense of security that betray their affluence. They know it and they take pleasure in it: they are the ones who manage their money, not their husbands or their brothers.

To us today it seems like an all too familiar scene, one that can be observed every day on the elegant streets of modern Milan or any other big city. But how normal is a scene like this one in the era of Trajan? We are accustomed, in fact, to thinking about the rigid rules that regulated women's behavior in the Roman era. These two women, on the other hand, don't fit that scheme at all. Is their independence a rule or an exception?

An Emancipated Woman

Actually, such carefree behavior is the result of a long process of emancipation for Roman women that gradually evolved over recent generations. Much has changed since the archaic era, when the wife sat in silence on a stool while her husband, stretched out on a triclinium, enjoyed the banquet with his invited guests.

Now Roman women are allowed by law to manage their inheritances and family money without intrusion by their husbands or brothers. They can stretch out on couches to eat at banquets, go to the baths and—horror of horrors—drink just like men, thus provoking the ire of some misogynist authors. Juvenal was particularly venomous in his judgments of independent women who, in his view, were too free. In his *Satires VI* he writes of some women: "She drinks and then vomits like a snake that has fallen into a cask. And her husband, totally nauseated, squeezes his eyes shut, struggling to keep down his bile."

During the empire, female independence actually reached levels that were comparable to those of Western society today. It's astounding to see how many resemblances there are to this aspect of social life in our own time, even regarding relationships between couples. Consider divorce, for example. It is by no means a contemporary phenomenon, and in Roman times it was very common. It was absolutely normal, for example, to meet men and women who were divorced not once but several times. Getting a divorce was so easy that many women had several husbands over the course of their lives. And because there was always a dowry involved, the stories got as involved as the plot of a soap opera. Let's take a closer look at this twenty-first-century world from two thousand years ago.

Lots of Divorces . . . and No Children

The two women continue walking down the street until they are joined by a handsome man. Well-dressed, with an engaging manner and a captivating smile, he takes the black-haired woman under his arm and walks along with her and her friend. This man is her new fiancé.

After years of marriage to an older man, the black-haired woman has "exacted" a divorce and found a new companion, whom she now wants to marry. He is indeed younger and more vigorous than her former husband, but in the eyes of many he is a dowry hunter. He has only recently been divorced as well, and he's been on the lookout for a good match.

Dowry hunters were very common in Roman society and they prowled like sharks in search of prey, to the point that even Martial (I,10) mentions them.

> Gemellus wants to marry Maronilla;
> he desires it, he urges her, he implores her, and sends her gifts.
> Is she so beautiful?
> Nay, no creature is more disgusting.
> What then is the bait and charm in her?
> Her cough.

By cough he obviously means poor health, an illness that will probably take her to her grave so that Gemellus, the dowry hunter, will inherit all of Maronilla's estate.

The trio vanishes at the end of the street, laughing and talking in loud voices, still followed by the two silent shadow-slaves. As we have said, such a group is not at all a rarity in Roman society, and even less of a rarity is the fact that none of the three has any children. They don't want them.

Nobody has children and everybody gets divorced. Why? It's a phenomenon whose roots go far back. In the time of the republic, Roman marriage was always favorable to the husbands and not to their wives. In the *cum manu* marriage, the hand (*manus*) or legal control of the woman passed from the father to the husband. Hence the tradition of the man asking his future father-in-law for the hand of his daughter. The decision to marry was not up to the woman, but to her father. A Roman woman in this type of marriage could not decide to leave her husband. She was under his *patria potestas*, his absolute power, as were their children, slaves, and servants. The husband, on the other hand, could repudiate his wife for any reason whatsoever, even the most banal.

Gradually, with the end of the republic, this form of matrimony disappeared, to be replaced by marriage *sine manu*, in which power over the woman remained with her family of origin. This meant that the wife could also repudiate her husband at any time. And if the woman came from a wealthy family while the man did not, he might find himself from one day to the next without the means to support himself. This change gave Roman women an immense power and a remarkable independence from their husbands. Under the Roman Empire the Senate approved a law that allowed women to control and manage all the money and property they inherited from their fathers. Previously, her husband and brothers managed her inherited property. This also greatly liberated Roman women. With the fall of the republic, therefore, women became economically independent and had the same rights as men in marriage.

To get a divorce it was sufficient for one of the two to pronounce certain phrases in the presence of witnesses and the divorce was effective instantly—a much faster procedure than what we have today. Divorce became so simple that it spread like wildfire. And society was hit by an "outright epidemic of conjugal separations," in the words of Jérôme Carcopino, a French historian and one of the most renowned experts on ancient Rome.

Indeed, if we look at a list of the "big names" of ancient Rome, we discover that many of them were parties to multiple divorces, something that the history books seldom mention. Here are a few:

- After four divorces, Sulla married for a fifth time, in his old age: a young woman who was also divorced.

- Julius Caesar was divorced once.
- Cato Uticensis, commonly known as Cato the Younger, divorced his wife, Marcia. She remarried, and her second husband died, making her very wealthy. Subsequently, Cato remarried Marcia, primarily for her money.
- After thirty years of marriage and several children, Cicero repudiated his wife, Terenzia, in order to marry Publilia, who was much younger and very rich. Terenzia didn't take it too hard, however: she remarried twice.

Underlying all these matters of the heart, as you have no doubt guessed, was very often a healthy sum of money, partially because, in cases of divorce, the woman could take back all of her dowry except for those assets that a judge held should justly remain with her husband for the care of their children or as an indemnity.

Free to Have Multiple Husbands

So, in the imperial age and under the reign of Trajan, a wealthy woman has considerable social power: she is financially independent, legally authorized to manage her own property, and in the end capable of keeping her husband (even a famous one) on a leash, especially if he married her for her money. It is no coincidence, then, that women often decide to do as the men do and marry more than once.

For the first time in history, they marry by choice, for love, for convenience, but not by imposition, as it used to be for their foremothers. In the necropolis discovered in the Vatican, there is the case of a woman, Julia Threpte, who lined up the funeral altars of her two husbands. For her first husband she built an altar of very high quality, a sign of her love. For the second, she settled for a much smaller altar, with a curt and dismissive epitaph. (Who knows how the third husband must have felt, if indeed she had a third.)

In describing this society, which in certain respects seems almost more advanced than our own, in *De Beneficiis* Seneca wrote: "No woman need blush to break off her marriage since the most illustrious ladies have adopted the practice of reckoning the year not by the names of the consuls but by those of their husbands."

With a bit of sarcasm, in his *Daily Life in Ancient Rome* Jérôme Carcopino described the changing status of Roman women from the republic to the empire this way:

> Then, the woman was strictly subjected to the authority of her lord and master; now she is his equal, his rival, if not his *imperatrix*. Then, husband and wife had all things in common; now their property is almost entirely separate. Then, she took pride in her own fertility; now, she fears it. Then, she was faithful; now, she is capricious and depraved. Divorces then were rare, now they follow so close on one another's heels that, as Martial says, marriage has become merely a form of legalized adultery." (1940; 100. Translated by Emily Overend Lorimer)

The Declining Birth Rate

Another feature of this period is the declining birth rate, which accompanied women's liberation. For generations, Roman society has been plagued by chronically declining births, identical to what Western societies are experiencing today.

In our case, the cause has been attributed to the rise in the marriage age and the increased difficulty for the wife to become pregnant, but also to the high cost of living that makes it hard to maintain a large family. And then there is influence of the consumer lifestyle, in which money is invested more in the quality of life than in children (contrary to our grandparents, who considered children an economic investment for the future, a sort of pension plan). And what are the reasons for the low birth rate in the Roman era?

We're not sure. Several hypotheses have been advanced, such as widespread poisoning from the lead contained in wine, though that is not very credible for an entire population. Or perhaps merely a deliberate refusal to have children on the part of Roman women (of the upper classes), in order to maintain both a lifestyle free from the restraints of maternity and a young, seductive body not debilitated by repeated pregnancies, which, as we shall see, were also quite risky. To be sure, in the social pinwheel of marriages and divorces, children might seem like a cumbersome burden.

All of these explanations, however, are difficult to reconcile with the emphasis placed on fertility and motherhood in this age. The reasons for the declining birth rate are not clear, but the issue was real. As Carcopino has shown, the funeral stelae in honor of the deceased erected by, for lack of children, his or her freed slaves, are amazingly numerous.

Naturally, the empire has its antidotes. To make up for the shortage of children, the practice of adoption becomes more and more popular among the upper classes. So in their old age, a lot of wealthy people adopt already mature adults in order to continue their "line."

And to compensate for the low birth rate, the practice of manumitting slaves, either while the master is still living or by testament, gives new blood to Roman society, which by nature is multiethnic (but monocultural—that is essential).

The Profile of the Emancipated Roman Woman

But what sort of people are these women who are so liberated for their time? If we were able to invite them to our homes for dinner, what kind of guests would they be? Certainly, many centuries lie between us, but there may still be a way to find out. If we read between the lines of Juvenal's caricatures of Roman women, we may be able to design their profile.

What we discover is a woman who is extraordinarily forthright, witty, intelligent, capable of conversing at table on all subjects, from poetry to international politics: a woman who is informed, who strives to understand her time, and who, above all, speaks her mind. That's why men are so frightened (and critical) of her.

In the sixth of his *Satires*, Juvenal writes that women have stopped embroidering, playing the lyre, and reading aloud. Now they have a passion for politics, keep themselves informed about the news arriving from all over the empire, avidly seek out information about trials going on in the courts, about rumors going around the city and high society gossip, "weighing the gravity of the dangers threatening the king of Armenia or of Parthia; with noisy effrontery they expound their theories and their plans to generals clad in field uniform…while their husbands silently look on," as Carcopino says.

Roman women, in other words, open themselves up to society, leave their homes without bothering anymore to cover themselves in their mental and social burkas. They walk on the streets, go to the theater, to the Colosseum, to the circuses to cheer on their favorite driver in the chariot races. And they go to the baths, where they undress and take baths together with men, something that was inconceivable in the archaic period.

They are modern women, real women, even when it comes to sex. Why should only men be allowed to enjoy the pleasures of life now that women have economic independence and are able to divorce whenever they want to? Now that they are so free, say some observers, in many cases women have become nothing more than housemates of their husbands. Perhaps, but at that very moment the husband is amusing himself with a concubine in another room of the house, something totally legitimate and accepted in Roman society. And so? So maybe the lives of these women can be summed up in two words: *vivere vitam*, live life.

But how many women participated in this liberation? A lot, as we have said, but not everyone. It's accurate to say that this revolution in social customs involved primarily the wealthy classes in the major cities. Elsewhere, among the poor and in places removed from high society, the old rules still governed the family.

Naturally, the information that come down to us about the situation of women were for the most part written by men. It would be interesting to know what the women themselves would have said.

Getting Married at Age Ten

The trio, the two women and the young man, have just gone around the corner. As they were walking by, they didn't notice the young woman walking in the opposite direction, hugging the wall. From her clothes we can tell that she is of humble origin. She walks with her head down, wrapped in a *palla* much more modest than that of the women she has just passed. She's following a man, staying six feet or so behind him. Her husband is walking ahead of her without deigning to say a word to her. He is much older than she; he could easily be her father. What kind of world does this woman live in? It's as though the Roman woman were a coin: on one side there's the portrait of the emancipated woman, whom we have just described; on the other, there's the traditional one. Two faces of the same society.

Life isn't easy for these women who are tied to tradition. Under Trajan, as in all eras of the empire, their childhood is very short. At a very young age, they are pledged in matrimony to their husbands—sometimes at around thirteen, sometimes less, even as young as ten.

In such cases, however, detailed agreements between the parties prohibit the new spouse from having sexual relations with his child wife. This tradition will be a constant in the Roman world and will also continue in the Byzantine Empire (though, sadly, there is ample evidence that many men did not respect this obligation).

This horrible practice of making girls marry at such a young age, even before puberty, before they are capable of procreating (a custom still today widely practiced in many third-world countries, especially Islamic ones), may be shocking for those of us who are accustomed to women marrying much later—often at an age when Roman women were already long dead.

Why are they made to marry so young? There are a lot of reasons, but essentially because they have to bear a lot of children, knowing that many of their offspring will die and that they themselves will have short lives. Very short.

Infant mortality in the Roman era is extremely high, 20 percent or even higher. That's what emerges from a study of the Isola Sacra necropolis near Portus in Ostia, which has provided one of the largest Roman samples ever examined (two thousand deceased, of whom eight hundred still had a complete skeleton). The researchers estimated an infant mortality rate on the order of 40 percent within the first year of life. So every Roman couple knows that they must have a lot of children if they want to be certain that at least some will survive. The law also points in the this direction. The first emperor of Rome, Augustus, responding to a dramatic demographic decline, established that in order to benefit from certain economic subsidies and tax incentives a Roman woman had to have given birth to at least three children (and a freed slave at least four).

Even if she wanted to, this would not be easy for a Roman woman. And she is certainly not helped by the chronic difficulty in having children that, as we have seen, seemed to be spreading in Roman society. Anxiety about the ability to procreate among women tied to the traditional principles of archaic Rome is visible in all those sanctuaries related to feminine fertility (usually connected to water or some fountain with miraculous powers) and in the votive offerings found by archaeologists. One can sense the social pressure that these women were subjected to.

Sometimes poor nutrition, which was very widespread at the time, was the cause of infertility. But women didn't know it and there was not very much they could do about it.

Childbirth: Russian Roulette

In the absence of the medical knowledge and hygienic practices that we have today, bringing a child into the world in this era was a heroic enterprise. A Roman woman was a thousand times more likely to die during childbirth than an Italian woman today. The data speak volumes: today in Italy, one woman in ten thousand dies in childbirth; in the Roman era (as indicated by several estimates) the ratio was one woman in ten. Real Russian roulette.

Complications that kill women in labor, such as placenta previa, which prevents the baby from exiting the uterus and causes massive hemorrhaging, anomalous positions of the baby, and so forth, are usually resolvable today. To all of this must be added lethal infections that arise in the days following the birth. If we consider all of these risks, as well as the fact that women give birth many times over the course of their lives, it is no wonder that few of them reach advanced age or survive their husbands.

A grave stone found in Salona, near Split on the coast of Croatia, is quite eloquent. Under the name of a slave woman, it reads: "She suffered for four days to give birth, but she did not give birth and her life ended. This stone placed here by Giusto, her companion in slavery."

If giving birth was comparable to going to war, the rest of life for many Roman women was just as hard. Alongside the emancipated women who, as we have seen, have attained a relationship of parity with men, there is a multitude of women whose lives are determined by others.

A little girl marries because it is so decided by her father. At a young age she is promised to a much older man, not infrequently an old friend of her father's. The age difference between them can be thirty years or more. It is not unusual for the wedding date to be set for when the girl turns fourteen (the minimum age as established by law). But even before that she may be sent to live in the house of her future husband. Needless to say, in this case (and in all cases of arranged marriage) women do not marry their husbands for love.

And then what happens? Roman law and morality dictate very precise behavior for women: absolute fidelity to their husbands and unobtrusiveness in public—like the girl who is walking behind her husband. Now he has entered the front door leading to their small apartment on the third floor of a nondescript building. She follows him and enters her "prison."

Renting a City Car in the Roman Era

It's dawn. A young woman and her gigantic servant are hurrying down the main street of the city. It is semideserted. Passersby are few and far between. In the middle of the street two dogs are fighting over a bone thrown there last night from a tavern at closing time. The young woman covers her head with her long shawl to keep out the cold. Her servant, on the other hand, doesn't feel cold; all he's wearing is a tunic that reveals glimpses of his powerful chest. He's a kindly looking German, whose hair and beard are prematurely gray. He is effortlessly carrying two enormous bags filled with everything necessary for their journey. The young woman is leaving for a short trip accompanied by her servant.

So, what do you take with you when you leave on a trip in the Roman era? This same question has been asked by Lionel Casson, the author of a monumental study on the subject. Here is what the Romans preferred to put in their baggage:

The bulkiest items are kitchen implements, because during the journey the traveler will cook for himself. Then there are toiletries, a blanket, a towel, some changes of underwear, comfortable sandals and heavy shoes for rain and snow, and, naturally, a hat for the rain or sun, depending on the season. Beyond that, the traveler has to bring along the appropriate clothing for the regions he will be traveling through: a light cloak (*lacerna*) for warm weather, a long wool cloak with a hood for cold weather (the *birrus*, identical to the Arab burnoose), the Roman poncho (*paenula*) for the rain, etc. The traveler must also not forget to put in his bags gifts for the person he intends to visit or who will be offering him hospitality. And a few other items. Actually, except when they travel with their own wagon, Romans travel light.

And what about money? Roman travelers hide it in purses tied to their belt or in little leather bags tied around their neck and kept under their tunic, just like travelers do today. (Next time you're in an airport just look at the extra thin pouches and purses on sale at the duty-free shop.) Along with their money they put in any other items of value.

Women, naturally, are advised not to wear jewelry in plain sight: rings, earrings, bracelets, and necklaces are to be kept hidden. Some women put them in the lining of their *strophium*, or girdle, and some sew them inside the folds of their clothes, as the young woman who has our sestertius has done.

But that's not enough. Travelers have to prepare another kind of baggage: their psychological baggage. Romans have a strong belief in omens. They are messages to be taken seriously, even if they are brief. And so, like the Neapolitan cabala, every sign has a precise meaning and constitutes a true traffic light for the departure. Here are a few of them.

> Green light if you dream of a clear sky with stars, or the goddess Aphrodite, or the god Mercury, protector of travelers.
> Donkeys and mules are good signs too; they mean your trip will be safe, but slow!
> Yellow light if a gazelle shows up in your dream. You have to take into account its state of health. If it's up and running, the trip will go fine. If it has a limp or is lying down, it could be a bad omen.
> Red light if you dream of a wild boar (violent thunder storms), an owl (storms and bandits along the road), or a quail (you'll be the victim of a scam or robbed by brigands). Dreams of Dionysus or Castor and Pollux are also bad signs.
> Finally, a good sign: if in your dream you see a statue of the gods that appears to be moving you can take heart because the gods are with you.

We'll have another occasion to return to these premonitory signs when we embark on a sailing ship at Ostia to cross the Mediterranean, because there we will discover some other superstitions connected with travel.

As they make their way along the nearby streets, the two travelers meet up with small groups of people heading out of the city: lines of servants carrying packages, bags, and purses. They are followed by their master, who has to leave on a trip. Since it is prohibited to use wagons in the city after dawn, many people have their own slaves or porter-slaves carry their baggage to their vehicles waiting for them at the city gates. In some cases they have themselves carried there too. One fat woman is stretched out languidly on a litter transported with a certain amount of strain by four slaves. Luckily, she doesn't have far to go.

When they get to the city gates, the young woman and her slave head in the direction of some stables that are already open. They stop to read the prices on some signs and then go inside. These stables are the ancient equivalent of Avis and Hertz, where you come when you need to rent a wagon. As soon as they are inside, the clerk, a Greek slave, shows them the available vehicles.

There is a small *birota*, that is, a two-wheeled cart for two people at the most. Or there's an *essedum*, bigger and more elegant. We could compare the first to a small compact and the second to a luxury convertible. The Greek recites the names of some well-known personalities in the city who have rented these vehicles recently (which may or may not be true).

Some other possibilities are a *raeda*, a four-wheeled open wagon, and a *carruca*, similar but with a canvas cover (identical to the covered wagons of the Wild West), the equivalent of a seven-seater minivan for a big family. Some *carruca* models are even outfitted so you can sleep in them, the campers of the Roman era.

For the larger vehicles, however, in addition to the driver you also need someone on the ground who holds the horses by their bridles and walks beside them. Do you know the technical name for this unlucky fellow? *Cursor,* a term that we use today in reference to the little pointer that flashes when you write on a computer.

The young woman chooses a wagon at the back of the stable: a two-seater, a *covinnus*. It's small and easy to drive; we could think of it as a Roman-era city car, the equivalent of a Smart car, and you see a lot of them on the roads of the empire. But this one is designed for use outside the city and not for use in urban traffic. Indeed, the urban centers of many cities are actually large pedestrian malls because, as we have said, during the day the circulation of carts and wagons is prohibited.

Having negotiated the price and paid the rental fee for the wagon, the two climb on board. The slave will be doing the driving. The horses nod their heads and then set off. As soon as the *covinnus* is outside the city gate, the slave gives the horses a brisk lashing and they break into a trot. Through their dark, wind-tossed manes the young woman can see the unpaved road stretching out toward the horizon. She smiles. The journey has begun.

Traffic on Roman Highways

The two travelers pass by a small wagon train. It's a rich man's convoy. Apart from the enormous number of bags, the wagons also carry what amounts to an apartment to be assembled every evening. The wealthy, in fact, don't sleep in wayside inns. Instead they carry everything they need with them. The slaves will set up a big tent with chairs, tables, a comfortable bed, carpets, etc. Naturally, they also have pots and pans and food to cook (in addition to the food they'll purchase along the way). The whole thing is reminiscent of today's luxury safaris, where, after riding around all day guided by a ranger in an off-road vehicle, the tourist comes back to the camp for a sit-down dinner served by waiters in livery and then sleeps in a big tent replete with a bed, tables, and even a shower and toilet.

They go by another traveler, a lawyer, stretched out on a litter. He's reading the text of the closing argument he is going to give in the next town. He gestures and speaks out loud. The eight slaves carrying him on their shoulders don't seem to be paying any attention to his jabbering. People like him, who prefer using a litter to a wagon, do so for just one reason: the smooth ride. Of course the journey takes a lot more time. But who's in a hurry? In Roman times, contrary to today, there's no need to run. It's not out of the question, however, that at the first postal station, he'll replace the slaves with two mules attached to a shaft.

Who does one see on the highways of the Roman Empire? The travelers are decidedly different from the ones we see on our modern highways. Romans travel for different reasons than we do. There are very few tourists, and there are no reentry traffic jams after long weekends. The vast majority of travelers are people who have to travel for work, government workers most of all. There is a constant movement of all kinds of state employees: from public officials to tax collectors and couriers, all the way up to the heads of imperial power, such as provincial governors. Their entourages, composed of advisers, assistants, soldiers, assorted employees and slaves, are impressive mostly for their dimensions. They almost give you the impression that they are the emperors.

But when the emperor really is on the road, it is an event. Everything comes to a standstill, just as when we close roads to traffic for a cycling competition or a road race. An emperor on the move is a real parade, comparable to what happens on Independence Day in the United States or Bastille Day in France. Everybody lines up on the side of the road to get a look at the most powerful man in the world.

There is only one parade that's longer than the emperor's and that one you never want to run into: the legion. A legion on the march, with thousands of soldiers, all the supply wagons, and the wagons carrying the disassembled war machines, can keep you blocked for hours. And if your luck is so bad that you run into an entire army, best to pull off the road and pitch your tent. You won't be going anywhere for several days. And it really happened, when Trajan decided to invade Dacia and called up large numbers of legions. Try to imagine the congestion on the roads, the curiosity and the fear of the inhabitants of the small towns in the provinces at the sight of that constant stream of soldiers and vehicles. And the profit turned by merchants and shopkeepers providing for the needs of thousands of men on the march.

But there are some analogies with the modern era. There are vehicles comparable to our tractor-trailers (slow wagons pulled by oxen), our utility vehicles (wagons and carts), our buses (coaches), our motorcycles (men on horseback), our bicycles (people on mules), and finally, lots of people on foot. Walking was the most common means of transport throughout antiquity.

One curious detail concerns the horses. They were much smaller than the horses we know today, not much bigger than ponies. So it seems appropriate to think of them as the motorcycles of the time because of their size and maneuverability. In the cities there were no horses like the ones tied up in front of the saloons in westerns. A Roman would have thought they were giants, not to mention hard to handle and lacking in endurance, and with limbs and joints more vulnerable to rough terrain.

Another interesting fact is that you don't see many horses on the road. They were used primarily for war, the postal service, and hunting. Moreover, most people couldn't afford the expense of buying and maintaining them. So there were many more mules on the road than horses. And people who traveled on foot also hitchhiked. Most of the time they got rides on farmers' wagons. It was slow, boring, and annoying for people with sensitive ears; the squeaking and creaking were unbearable.

At mile 9 on the journey from Mediolanum some red tile roofs come into view. In the modern era this area will be the site of the town of Melegnano, and it is highly likely that the original nucleus of the town was formed by these very houses. Now it is a *mutatio*, an imperial postal station.

Our two travelers stop and get down off the cart. The slave gets some water for the horses and checks their shoes. The woman goes into the courtyard in the middle of the houses.

We could compare a *mutatio* to a roadside service area with gas pumps and a mechanic as well as a restaurant. There are stables where you can change tired horses (thus the name *mutatio,* or "change") and get fresh ones (in other words, fill your tank with gas). There are stable boys, veterinarians, horseshoers, artisans who can repair broken wagons (in all respects, the equivalent of a mechanic's garage). And, just as on a modern highway, you can get something to eat. There are fully outfitted kitchens preparing a full menu of simple and inexpensive meals, from lamb and pork to ricotta cheese and hot focaccia.

There are almost always some taverns that spring up nearby, replete with beds and prostitutes. The people who stop there, however, generally don't sleep there. Just like we do at our service areas, they get a light snack, change horses, and then get back on the road. In the course of a day's journey, you'll come across one or two *mutationes* along the way before the sun goes down. And then, as if by magic, before nightfall a big motel will appear on the side of the road. The Romans call it a *mansio*. The distance between one way station and the next is never more than twenty-five to thirty miles, or the average length of a day's journey. Here, travelers can eat and sleep, change horses, and have a nice bath: the *mansiones* almost always have small bath complexes. Not only that, they will even offer a free change of clothes for postilions and couriers (in case they're soaked with rain or splattered with mud).

To make travel safer, police stations, called *stationes*, will be added over the years, with guards to keep watch on the roads. Finally, in some areas, there were checkpoints every mile or so manned by a sentinel.

But not all travelers can take advantage of the service areas and the way stations; at least not without paying. Free access to these traveler assistance stations is reserved for public officials, that is, for those who are traveling on behalf of the government, like couriers carrying official messages. Each time they stop to change horses or go to the baths, couriers have to present a special letter (*diploma*) displaying their credentials and authorization to use the services.

This is the system of the so-called *cursus publicus*, instituted by Augustus primarily to carry government mail (not that of private citizens) throughout the empire. The couriers (*speculatores*) can thus change horses quickly and get some sleep before getting back on the road. A winning idea, especially considering that the postal service did not get any faster than this until the invention of the locomotive. In Egypt, for example, it took only six hours to cover the same distance and there were four deliveries per day.

Private travelers are not allowed to use these services and have to rely on inns and taverns. Naturally, many powerful people would like to have a *diploma* at their disposal to travel comfortably, but one has to have authorization from the emperor. A lot of people pull strings to get one. Others officially request that the emperor make an exception for them. One such example is Pliny the Younger, the governor of Bithynia, a province in Asia Minor, who in 111 CE (just a few years before the era that we are exploring) asked this favor of Trajan, who responded: "My Lord, until now I have not granted a *diploma* to anyone. . . . However, my wife has learned of the death of your grandfather. Since you wished to rush to the side of your aunt, it seemed excessive to me to deny you the *diploma*."

Naturally, there was a great deal of abuse by big shots, with bribes and even sales of diplomas (in theory, a crime punishable by death). Today we might compare it to an authorization to use an official car and driver for private purposes. There are even some cases where public officials are known to have blatantly disregarded the rules, trying to requisition the horses assigned to the *mansiones* (they had as many as forty mounts, including both horses and mules) or demanding that their friends or relatives be given lodging in their rooms.

As the young woman and her slave are leaving the *mutatio* in their fast, light cart to head back toward the road, they happen upon a man on horseback approaching at a gallop. He comes into the courtyard and jumps down off his horse in a rush. He is an imperial courier (*speculator*). The stationmaster can tell it's an emergency from the worried look on the courier's face. The courier is a young lad with freckles; his cheeks are red from the strain of the long ride. He pulls out a *diploma* from a leather tube he keeps around his neck and hands it still rolled up to the stationmaster, asking for his fastest horse. The man immediately orders that the stable's best horse be prepared and purely for formality unrolls the document, without even reading it. Then he looks the young man in the eye: "Everything all right?" He is drinking avidly from a pitcher, and rivulets of water are streaming down his chest. The stationmaster's wife has offered him the water and she urges him to drink slowly. She has a maternal smile. He reminds her of her sons who are now enlisted in a legion stationed in the north, the XXII Primigenia. The parents heard about the battle on the frontier from another courier who rode through here some days ago. Then nothing more. The couriers are not supposed to give out any information, but inevitably some of the news of a big victory against the barbarians leaks out. The lad, a little excited, declares that commendations and promotions are on the way for everyone involved, and that the document he is carrying is on its way north, to Mogontiacum, to the commandant of the legion.

The stationmaster smiles, puts a hand on the boy's shoulder, and offers him a nice canteen of wine. "Take this and use it well, but only when you've finished galloping!" A little intimidated, the young man thanks him and then bites ravenously into a ricotta cheese focaccia that the stationmaster's wife has prepared for him. He doesn't have time to finish it. His horse is ready, already saddled. He jumps up into the saddle without using the stool that the stable boy had put in place for him. Then he turns, smiles, and waves to the man and his wife. In an instant he is already outside the gate in a cloud of dust.

The average speed of a Roman courier (literally a pony express) is 7 kilometers (4.2 miles) per hour, including stops to change horses. This means about 70 kilometers (42 miles) per day, compared to 20 to 30 kilometers (12 to 18 miles) for those who travel on foot and 40 to 50 kilometers (25 to 30 miles) for those going by wagon. Lionel Casson has calculated that a courier can make it from Rome to Bari in seven days, to Constantinople in twenty-five, to Antioch (Syria) in forty, and to Alexandria in fifty-five days.

Actually, when they "floor it" couriers can triple their average speed and cover up to 210 kilometers (125 miles) in just one day, maybe riding through the night. They do it with the system that we have seen, with breathless rides and rests that seem more like pit stops. So in 69 CE, when the mutiny of the legions stationed in Mainz, Germany (where the XXII Primigenia is now), occurred, it took only eight or nine days for the news to reach Rome.

REGGIO EMILIA

~ *Humor, Seduction, and Adultery* ~

Scenes from a Wedding

After a long journey the young woman spent the night in an inn in Placentia (Piacenza). Then she got back on the road early the next morning in time to get to Fidentia (Fidenza) for her best friend's wedding.

It was a beautiful ceremony, the bride in a splendid saffron shawl and her face partly covered by a lovely orange veil, so bright it looked like a flame (that's why it's called *flammeum*), and crowned by a myrtle wreath.

The groom was even more attractive than usual. Maybe it was because of the special occasion or the reflected beauty of the bride, her friend, a truly unique woman. For the entire ceremony she couldn't take her eyes off them. She didn't miss a word of the ritual. Sure, when it came time to sacrifice the bull, she closed her eyes, but when he examined the animal's entrails the haruspex smiled so spontaneously, giving a verdict so sincere and positive for the couple that everyone was surprised by his optimism. At most weddings, the outlook is usually not so uniformly positive. And knowing the newlyweds as she does, she's sure their glowing prospects are truly deserved.

Afterward, there was a huge banquet with lots of guests that lasted into the night, even though the wind created some trouble for those in attendance. And then she too had to do her part.

When everyone got up from their places and the nuptial procession headed off toward the home of the groom, it was she, the best friend of the bride, who accompanied her to the conjugal bed, where the newly-wed husband was waiting for her with a smile brimming with desire. Shortly thereafter, he would take off her cloak and loosen the triple knot of her tunic. As everyone was on their way out to leave the couple alone, she took a last look before going out and saw them kissing passionately. She closed the door and, smiling, let out a long sigh before joining the others.

As everyone is leaving with torches and lamps, we decide to linger. The evening air is cool, and all the stars are out, regaling us with their flickering light. Our thoughts return to our last look at the newlyweds. Do the Romans kiss the same way we do?

Roman Kisses

The Romans have names for three different kinds of kisses. There's the *basium*, that is, the classic affectionate kiss of lovers. It's sweet and full of feeling. All you have to do is look at some statues like the ones that were discovered in Trier, which show some couples kissing: like pairs of high school sweethearts they tilt their faces to the right. Then there's the *osculum*, the respectful kiss, the one you give your relatives. Last comes the *savium*, the especially erotic kiss expressive of lust that is given during sexual relations.

If you find this way of distinguishing the various kinds of kisses surprising, stop for a minute and take a better look at the world around you and you'll see that today, when it comes to different kinds of kisses, we have many more.

Italians give friends and family two symbolic kisses (cheek to cheek) when they meet again after a long time, and they give only one to people they see intimately on a daily basis (the husband who kisses his wife before going to work, for example). In other countries, however, the kisses are often more than one: in Holland, France, and many other European countries three kisses are standard, but sometimes even four or five, depending on the local custom.

Then if you consider kissing the hand, and in Russia, until recently, the custom of a kiss on the lips between men, you can see that the Romans, if faced with these modern habits, would feel very confused. The Roman world of kissing was actually simpler than ours.

There is one curiosity with regard to the Roman kiss. It has been said that initially the *osculum*, the more discreet kiss, had an investigative purpose. The husband used it to check if his wife had been drinking wine, and all the men in the family, if they wished, could do the same to check the breath of the women in the family. It was a sort of cross-verification to ensure the family's good reputation.

With respect to the widespread practice of kissing in the Roman world, we have also discovered a surprise: the Romans may have been the first in history to outlaw kissing. Almost two thousand years ago, the emperor Tiberius ordered the prohibition of kissing in public. The reason? To combat an epidemic of herpes (*labialis*). Even with his almost total absence of scientific knowledge in this field of medicine, Tiberius was right: that is exactly how the contagion spreads. We don't know, however, how much his order was respected, especially over time. Kisses really can't be outlawed.

Reggio Emilia: Roman Jokes

It's now a few days later. Our sestertius, used by the young woman to pay the bill at the inn where she stayed, has now arrived here in Regium Lepidi, present-day Reggio Emilia, about thirty miles away, carried by another lodger at the inn. Now he's with a friend outside a *popina*.

The two men are happy to rest their feet after a long walk through the fields in the countryside around Reggio. For a few seconds they don't speak, enjoying the shade of a tall plane tree, sitting on simple wooden stools, and a light breeze that feels like a cool caress on their cheeks.

Then, having gotten situated, one of them turns to the innkeeper:

"Two reds, and lighten them up with a splash of water; but not watered down, eh!"

As we have already had occasion to note, wine in the days of the empire has such a high level of alcohol that it's normal to add a little water. Nearly everywhere, and for generations now, innkeepers often go too far, watering down the "nectar of the gods" to increase their profits.

But in a place not far from here it's just the opposite. To hear Martial tell it, the city of Ravenna has so little drinking water that it costs as much as wine! As one of our two friends immediately remarks: "In Ravenna a sly innkeeper gave me an unexpected treat; I asked for wine with a splash of water and he gave it to me neat!" and he bursts out laughing.

The other man shoots back: "Yeah, water is so expensive there I'd rather have a cistern of water than a vineyard. I could make a lot more money selling the water!"

These simple wisecracks, sharp, spoken in Latin with a thick local accent, were recorded by Martial in Book III of his *Epigrams* (56–57). The poet lived in this area for a while.

Having a good laugh after a hard day's work is a common practice in these parts, and that won't change over the centuries. Downing a healthy glass or two with friends, accompanying the wine with a few jokes and funny stories, is more than a habit. It's human nature. But what kinds of funny stories make the rounds in antiquity? What's their sense of humor like? Did the Romans have their equivalent of modern Italy's carabinieri stories or America's blonde jokes? The answer is yes!

We know some of the jokes that were told in Roman times thanks above all to the *Philogelos or Laughter-Lover*, a humorous collection of 265 jokes written in Greek, compiled probably in the fifth century CE.

It is organized just like any modern book of jokes, in categories: funny stories about the inhabitants of certain cities thought to be a little on the dull side (Cuma, Sidon, Abdera, etc.); some stock figures with typical character defects displayed in daily life: the grump, the miser, the coward, the wise guy, the jealous friend, the guy with bad breath, and so on.

But there is one character who figures in almost half of the stories: the egghead, the obsessive-compulsive intellectual with his head in the clouds. We might call him a know-it-all who doesn't quite get it. The jokes about him are as common in Roman times as carabinieri jokes are in Italy today, or Aggie jokes in Texas, or Newfie jokes in Canada.

But keep this in mind: a sense of humor isn't fixed; it changes with the times. To make you laugh, a joke has to be as fresh as a good piece of fruit, tied to the historical moment; otherwise it's not funny anymore. (You might have noticed that your grandfather's jokes usually go over like a lead balloon.) So, although some of the humor has lost its edge over the centuries, it's surprising to find that some of the jokes handed down to us from antiquity can still make us chuckle.

A guy goes to the doctor and says: "Doc, when I wake up I feel dizzy for half an hour and then I get over it and everything's okay. What's your advice?"

The doctor: "Wake up half an hour later!"

A guy from Abdera sees a eunuch go by with a woman on his arm and asks his friend if the woman is the eunuch's wife. When the friend tells him a eunuch can't have a wife, he exclaims: "So, she must be his daughter!"

An egghead runs into a friend of his and says, "They told me you had died!" His friend responds, "But can't you see I'm alive and well?!" And the egghead: "Yeah, but the person who told me is a lot more reliable than you are!"

During a voyage at sea, a terrible storm breaks out and when an egghead sees his slaves crying in fright, he yells out to them: "Don't cry. In my will I've given you your freedom!"

A barb for the greedy: "A cheapskate made out his will and named himself as his only heir!"

On bad breath: A guy whose breath smelled like the plague runs into a doctor and says to him, "Doc, take a look in my mouth. I'm afraid my palate has dropped down." He opens his mouth wide and the doctor yells, "Your palate hasn't dropped down; your ass has come up."

On the inhabitants of Cuma, now part of the city of Pozzuoli, near Naples: A guy from Cuma is riding his donkey near a vegetable garden. Seeing the branch of a fig tree, full of ripe figs, hanging over the street, he stands up on his donkey and grabs it. But the donkey runs off, leaving him hanging from the tree. The custodian of the vegetable garden asks him what he's doing up there, and the Cuman says, "I fell off my donkey."

A Cuman's father dies in Alexandria, Egypt, and he gives his body to the embalmers. A long time goes by and he sees that they still haven't embalmed the body, so he asks them to give it back. The guy in charge, who has dozens of bodies in storage, asks him for a distinguishing characteristic of his father. And the Cuman answers: "He used to cough a lot."

"Take my wife, please!": A misogynist whose wife has just died is walking in her funeral procession. A passerby asks him: "Who is it that's gone on to a better life?" And he says, "I have, now that I got rid of her."

Modena: A Seducer on the Attack

A soldier is sitting in a tavern having a good time. He's an officer in the cavalry, and when he hears a certain joke he bursts into uncontrollable laughter. The joke has a deep meaning for him; he has never wanted to get married. On the contrary, he's an unrepentant bachelor. He doesn't have a wife but probably has more than a couple of children scattered about here and there. Today, we would call him a gigolo with all the traits of an accomplished ladies' man.

Let's face it, it runs in the family. His grandfather is best remembered not so much for his numerous liaisons that make him a Casanova of antiquity but for his acrobatic love techniques. And yet, in all likelihood, you've never even heard of him. His name is Quintus Petillius Cerialis. In 60 CE, during Nero's reign, he was in Britain commanding the IX Hispana legion when the revolution led by Boudicca broke out. Cerialis tried to round up all the soldiers he needed to defend the city of Camulodunum (Colchester). Despite their heroic resistance, however, his outnumbered troops were quickly overwhelmed. He barely escaped being killed himself.

But Cerialis didn't always get the worst of it in battle; on the contrary, when Vespasian came to power, he sent Cerialis to Germany in command of another legion and there he found himself again right in the middle of a furious revolt, this time by the Batavians on the empire's northern border. He succeeded in defeating his adversaries (he fought together with the XXII Primigenia, which we got to know in the chapter on Germany) and he was awarded all possible honors by Emperor Vespasian, who was his brother-in-law.

It was in that very war that a number of amorous (and quite lucky) mishaps took place. One night, the Roman camp was attacked by the barbarians. But Cerialis wasn't there. As luck would have it, at the time he was otherwise engaged with a Roman noblewoman at a villa not far from the camp. He arrived at the battlefield half-naked.

And that's not all. On another night, after Cerialis had taken his newly built fleet of ships up the Rhine to reach an advance post of Roman soldiers, some barbarian commandos in smaller vessels untied the mooring lines of his flagship and silently dragged it away with them without anybody noticing. Then, when they burst inside to kill Cerialis they were met with a surprise: he wasn't there. He was elsewhere, spending the night in the company of a genteel local lady . . . and he had to make his way through enemy lines to get back to his men, under siege.

The next year, Cerialis was appointed governor of Britain and had to fight against still another enemy, the Brigantes of northern England. But he didn't lose his amorous habits and started up a "diplomatic" relationship with the Brigantes' former queen, Cartimandua, a sort of Cleopatra of the north—a charismatic woman with a strong character.

Cerialis finished his career in Rome, where he was twice appointed consul and entered into the highest spheres of court under Domitian. Tacitus describes him as more of an impetuous soldier than a reflective general, accustomed to taking it to the limit every time. His ascendancy over his men was reinforced by his simple and direct manner of speaking and his granite-like loyalty. And his strong, decisive, and loyal character must also have been what made him so attractive to women.

How to Seduce Someone at a Banquet

Our coin has now passed into the hands of this handsome officer with the penetrating eyes who finds himself stretched out on a triclinium bed at a banquet. He is one of the invited guests of an important fabric merchant. Judging from his place in the triclinium he is not one of the most important guests. There is, in fact, a precise code at the places to recline that immediately expresses the hierarchy of those in attendance. The host, obviously, is in the center.

Between one course and the next, between a poem and a brief dance, the conversation has touched on a lot of subjects: from the abundance of the harvest, to the latest news from the Orient, to memories of travels in the provinces with their strange local customs. The young officer has chimed in politely, but he's quiet right now because he's concentrating on another exchange. For some time now he has been flirting with the wife of the master of the house, who is lying next to him. It's a very risky activity, but that's exactly why he finds it so arousing, not least because the mistress of the house, considerably younger than her *dominus*, seems to be playing right along. She's shapely, with deep brown eyes and gorgeous red curls cascading down her shoulders like sinuous grapevines.

The young officer is just putting into practice what Ovid advises in these cases, a veritable Ten Commandments of seduction, specifically for banquets. Here is what the great poet, who lived about a hundred years ago, advises in Book I of his *Ars Amatoria*, a three-volume work. (Translated by A.S. Kline)

Stay close to her so that it will be easy to "speak many secret things, with hidden words she'll feel were spoken for her alone." Or, make tenderly flattering comments to her so "she will understand that she is your mistress." And stare "in her eyes with eyes confessing fire."

Then the poet turns bold, advising to take first the cup from which the woman has just drunk and drink from it at the same point, placing your lips exactly where she had placed hers, in a sort of deferred kiss.

Be the first to snatch the cup that touched her lips,
And where she drank from, that is where you drink.

This is courtship as hot pursuit, first with glances and words, then with kisses from afar, and finally with touching, public but discreet and hidden.

And whatever food her fingers touch, take that,
and as you take it, touch hers with your hand.

And what about the husband? It's embarrassing how Ovid suggests charming him with flattery and hypocrisy.

Let it be your wish besides to please the girl's husband:
It'll be more useful to you to make friends.

He even offers little stratagems. At Roman banquets, in fact, it was a custom to have a drawing to select the name of the "king of the feast," that is, the person in charge of deciding on the quality of the wine to be served and the number of cups to be drunk over the course of the evening. Ovid advises passing the scepter to the master of the house if you should win, and assenting to all of his pronouncements.

> If you cast lots for drinking, give him the better draw:
> give him the garland you were crowned with.
> Though he's below you or beside you, let him always be served first:
> Don't hesitate to second whatever he says.

But has Ovid no sense of guilt at all? No, and he says so quite openly, even if for hypocrisy's sake he lets it be understood that it can't be avoided.

> It's a safe and well-trodden path to deceive in a friend's name,
> though it's a safe and well-trodden path, it's a crime.

All of this is exactly what our officer is doing now, to the letter. His hands touch hers fleetingly but often, their eyes remain still in long and longing gazes, their pupils dilating. And then? Here's what Ovid advises:

> Then when the table's cleared, the guests are free,
> the throng will give you access to her and her room.
> Join the crowd, and softly approach her,
> let fingers brush her thigh, and foot touch foot.

At this point, everything is clear between the two and, according to Ovid, at the first opportunity the man must speak to the woman directly.

> Now is the time to speak to her: boorish modesty
> fly far from here.

This is where the seducer's dirty work begins: according to the poet, the weapons of seduction are flattery and false promises, and in this the seducer (Roman or modern) must be skillful and pitiless.

Ovid has more to say, but we can stop here. Our officer has now managed to go off alone with the young wife for a few minutes while the master of the house is taking his guests to see the beautiful horses he is training for the races. We don't want to intrude on their intimacy. But what would happen if they were to be discovered?

What Was the Risk for Adulterers?

For centuries the Romans considered adultery to be a one-way offense: sexual relations between a married woman and a male who was not a member of the family. A man is free to have relations outside the marriage, even with the family's female slaves, while the woman must be totally faithful.

Until the time of Augustus, a betrayed husband could do justice himself by killing his wife (who was subject to his authority as *pater familias*), while her lover risked either death or more probably castration. Then came Augustus, who tried to combat extramarital relations (which must have been extremely commonplace) within a more general framework of returning to the sound principles that had made Rome great, as well as combating the alarming drop in the birth rate and the increase in divorces.

The Julian law on the punishment of adultery, *Lex Julia de Adulteriis Coercendis*, promulgated by Augustus in 18 CE, clearly established how adulterers were to be judged. And it remained in effect, with few changes, for the life of the empire. The essential point is that the law inserted itself between husband and wife: adultery was no longer a family affair but a public crime.

The law required the husband of the adulteress to repudiate her and sue for divorce. Within sixty days of the divorce decree the ex-husband could request that criminal proceeding be initiated before a jury. Once that time elapsed, the right of action passed to the father of the adulteress; and if that additional time elapsed anyone could propose the accusation, as long as he was a citizen of Rome.

The Prescribed Penalties

A convicted adulteress lost half of her dowry, a third of her property, and was relegated to exile on an island (*ad insulam*): in the case of Julia the elder, Augustus' daughter, the chosen place was the island of Pandataria (now Ventotene).

Beyond that, the law provided that a woman found guilty of adultery could not contract other marriages, nor wear the stole reserved for matrons. Instead she had to wear the brown toga that was usually the distinguishing dress of prostitutes. The law laid down penalties (though much lighter) for adulterous husbands, who, in the event the adultery resulted in divorce, had to return his wife's dowry. And the lover of the adulterous woman? Heavy penalties were provided for him too. He was sent to another island, and half of his property was confiscated.

But the law also provided for more severe penalties. It established that it was legal to kill the two adulterers, in a sort of crime of honor. They could be eliminated by the father (adoptive or natural) of the woman or of her husband. But some rules had to be respected.

The father of the adulteress could kill her and her lover only if he caught them in the act (in the paternal home or the home of the husband). But he had to kill them both! If he killed only one of the two it was considered homicide.

The husband, on the other hand, was not allowed to kill his adulterous wife (because she was "under the authority" of her father), but he could kill her lover provided he was of low social extraction and had been caught in the act in the husband's home.

Once the betrayal was discovered (with or without bloodshed), the husband was obliged by law to repudiate his wife in order to avoid being accused of pandering (*lenocinio*), or "inducement to and exploitation of prostitution" (as it is called in Italy today), and he had to notify the magistrate within three days of the betrayal and, where applicable, the killing of the adulterer.

How often was this law applied? Very rarely. The number of people publicly tried and convicted of adultery was very low. Practically speaking, the law against adultery was a legacy from an earlier time, so much so that just a few decades before Trajan came to power the law had nearly been forgotten and Domitian was forced to solemnly renew its principles. When the Roman Empire fell, however, in all the Germanic kingdoms that sprang up to replace it, the archaic practice of the private vendetta once again became the normal practice.

Despite its relatively primitive provisions, Augustus's law nevertheless contains an important aspect: for the first time the law also punished the man. Moreover, the convicted woman was removed from the cruel revenge of her husband.

Under Septimius Severus the law's sanctions became more severe (the risk was no longer exile but death); however, cases of adultery diminished in number thanks also to the ease of obtaining a divorce, as we have seen.

But how common was adultery in the Roman era? According to Jens-Uwe Krause, who teaches ancient history at the Ludwig Maximilians University in Munich, then as now people gossiped a lot, especially in the smaller cities and towns of the empire where everybody knew one another and it was difficult to keep a betrayal secret. So there were plenty of cases that ended up in court and, from reading the authors of the late imperial period, it appears that attending a trial in the Forum of a woman accused of adultery with her slave was so frequent that it was no longer news. Cassius Dio declared that over the course of his consulate adultery complaints were so numerous (three thousand) that because of the scarcity of judicial personnel (this certainly sounds familiar), the great majority of the cases never made it to trial. And that's probably the way it was all over in the empire. Consequently, only a few truly outrageous cases were prosecuted.

Who Did Women Cheat With?

So, while husbands enjoyed full freedom to engage in extramarital sexual relationships, who did their wives go to bed with? The most readily available lovers were their slaves. They were in the home, within easy reach, and above all they were obligated to keep quiet. Then there were men like the strapping descendant of Cerialis.

Why is the wife of the host so attentive to the young officer she has just met? Certainly because of his manner and his appearance. But also because in ancient Rome a woman has very few opportunities to make outside contacts. She'll never be able to form a circle of friends and acquaintances outside the home, so she must go looking for lovers from her husband's circle of friends or work associates. From this perspective, it's not immediately clear if the young man, for all his amorous skills and abilities, is the hunter or the hunted.

RIMINI

~ *A Delicate Operation* ~

The Domus of the Surgeon Eutyches

The officer leaves the villa while the other guests continue singing and reciting verses together with their host. By now they have lost count of the cups of wine they've drunk. And our officer has lost count of the number of women he's seduced. All he knows is that tonight he has added one more.

A slave has prepared his horse for him. He has even brushed him down. The officer is impressed by this unrequested service and he puts a hand in his purse. His manicured fingers pull out our sestertius and give it to the slave. Then he climbs up on his horse and vanishes into the night.

The slave's robust fingers grasp the coin like the jaws of a predator and swallow it up, sliding it down into the palm of his hand. His grip is strong. It's a rugged hand, the hand of a man who is used to working the land, its skin tough as leather, with wide, thick fingernails. In an instant our sestertius has entered a new world, the world of a slave who tomorrow will be involved in a delicate mission. His name is Lusius.

The Checkerboard of Civilization

The creaking and groaning of the small wagon moving across the terrain sounds like an old work song, keeping the travelers company. Nobody is talking; the conversation died out hours ago, like a used-up candle. On board this small, four-wheeled vehicle, pulled by two mules, are a man and woman with their ailing son, sleeping serenely for now in his mother's arms, undisturbed by the constant jolts. Driving the wagon are two slaves; one of them is Lusius, certainly his master's favorite servant, his jack-of-all-trades. Before we learn more about the parents' journey, let's consider for a moment the unusual landscape we are now crossing.

Both sides of the road are lined by a series of fields of identical size and appearance, arranged one after the other with surgical precision. If we were to do a flyover and gaze down at this place from above, the scene before us would be truly surprising: in place of pristine nature, with its forests, lakes, and rivers, there stretches out before us an immense checkerboard of identical cultivated fields. A checkerboard whose internal divisions are rigidly geometrical, reminiscent of a shopping mall parking lot. It's a landscape that we are accustomed to seeing and that seems very much out of place in an era so distant from our own.

All of this is the result of a precise subdivision of the territory conquered by the legions that has been carried out by the Roman administration for the benefit of its new settlers. It is the so-called centuriation of the countryside, a land use policy that has been implemented in various parts of the empire.

The land has been subdivided into one hundred large squares of fifty hectares each. But the Romans would use another term; they would say that the squares were composed of two hundred *iugera* (yokes) each, the term taking its name from the piece of farm equipment that is used to join two oxen. A *iugerum* is the area that a yoke of oxen are able to plow in a day, about 22,500 square feet. As always, the Romans are very practical. In the mountains, where the land is harder to plow, the yoke is smaller (a detail to keep in mind if you want to buy some land in those parts).

Why is the subdivision process called *centuriation*? What does the number 100 have to do with it? We might say it's a play on words. Each of these large squares is called a *centuria* because it contains approximately one hundred areas of two yokes each. Elsewhere, on lands assigned with less than full ownership rights, instead of squares the divisions are rectangles (*strigae* or *scamna,* depending on their orientation), but these are minor variations of the same system.

This checkerboard of land is crisscrossed by a uniform grid of larger and smaller roads, proper *decumani* (running east-west), and *cardines* (running north-south), just as in Roman cities. The end result is an extremely well-ordered subdivision, parceled into lots that the Roman state assigns to new settlers and that cannot be divided without the express authorization of the Senate. It is a new, unprecedented way of exploiting the natural landscape. Indeed, in many areas of the Roman Empire, centuriation redesigned nature in a way that had never been seen before. And this countryside of the future Italian region of Emilia Romagna is a prime example: the geometric fields that radiate out on both sides of the Via Emilia represent the Roman mentality that spread throughout the empire like seeping water, reshaping even the natural lay of the land.

Right now the wagon is passing some men with strange wooden instruments who are verifying the alignment of boundary stones and stakes, probably for a border dispute. Historical documents demonstrate that such disputes were frequent. It was quite common for boundary stones to be moved, allowing the culprits to steal a long slice of a neighbor's field.

Here, the surveyors' work is not all that difficult. The dispute will be resolved quickly. It is truly impressive to see such a precise grid of fields in such ancient times, when there are no computers, or aerial photographs, or lasers. How do they do it? Everything has been calculated using simple but effective instruments such as the *groma*, which you often see reproduced in books or displayed in museums. It looks a little like the skeleton of a small beach umbrella, only instead of spokes it has horizontal wooden crossbars with plumb lines hanging down from the end of each arm. It works like a rifle scope and makes it possible to plant border stones with great precision. All you have to do is line up two plumb lines of the *groma* with a stake planted in a field, even at a considerable distance. The virtual line that joins these three reference points will be traced on the terrain and it will be as straight as a laser beam.

Amazingly, this subdivision of the fields is still visible today. When you fly over a part of Emilia Romagna, for example, it looks like you're flying over an immense patchwork quilt. In his famous memoir of the 1930s, *Christ Stopped at Eboli*, Carlo Levi writes about trains crossing the "mathematical countryside of Romagna." The ancient centuriation is evident even in the names of many of the small towns in present-day Emilia Romagna: Cento, Nonantola (from *nonaginta*, ninety), Ducenta, etc.

Underlying this surgical subdivision of the terrain is a precise Roman strategy of conquest. Veteran legionnaires are assigned a piece of land, a form of severance pay, where they can live with their families. In this fashion, generations of retired soldiers, together with ordinary citizens, colonized territories conquered by the legions, expanding Roman civilization.

These new settlements were insurance. They functioned as outposts on the borders to warn of imminent invasions, but first and foremost they exported "Romanness" to barbarian territories, absorbing the local populations into the economic and cultural orbit of Rome. Just as a piece of uncultivated land can become a field of grain, the newly settled barbarian lands were transformed into the living fabric of the empire.

Journey of Hope

The child's cry suddenly interrupts the silence in the wagon. The little boy is wailing, his face contorted with pain. His mother tries futilely to calm him. He puts his little hands on his head and thrusts his face amid the folds of his mother's dress in search of maternal comfort. He's four years old, five at the most, and the right side of his head is bigger than the left. He suffers from hydrocephaly (water on the brain), but what makes his situation so desperate is the tumor that is causing it; a tumor that has developed slowly, making his brain asymmetrical. His skull has been forced to adapt to the greater volume on the right side, gradually becoming deformed as the boy has grown.

But the immediate problem is the violent headaches caused by the pressure that continues to build inside his cranium. It's a real torture that has become almost constant in recent days, even waking him from a deep sleep. His parents have tried everything to cure his illness, from medicines prepared by physicians to improbable remedies suggested by conjure women specializing in incantations and magic spells. They have even appealed to the goddess Carna, often called upon by mothers and caregivers to ward off the *striges*, nocturnal birds— tawny owls, snow owls, and other nocturnal predators—which in ancient times were thought to be the equivalent of our vampires. It was believed that they entered houses under cover of darkness to suck the blood of babies and nourish themselves on their flesh and internal organs. The boy's parents performed the ritual to drive away the birds. After scoring the door to the boy's room three times with a branch of a strawberry bush, they sprayed the threshold with purifying water while holding in their hands the entrails of a young sow to offer to the *striges* in place of those of their son. Finally, they hung a branch of a hawthorn bush on the window frame in his bedroom.

But nothing worked.

Now the only solution is an expert surgeon. They have been told that the surgeon will have to make a hole in his skull to let out the "evil" that is pressing up against it on the inside. But it's not easy to find a surgeon who is skilled and reliable, and the cost of the operation is very high. Or rather, for this family, the cost is unimaginable. They belong to the lowest rung of Roman society: farm slaves. They are part of the community of slaves of a large farm near Bologna. Yet now they are on their way to one of the best surgeons available who operates in Ariminum (present-day Rimini). How is this possible? Who helped them pay for it?

They are the beneficiaries of a small miracle. Their master, moved by their dramatic situation, has provided for this journey of hope, paying for it all out of his own pocket: the journey, the operation, and the surgeon's fee. Why did he do it? Maybe he was just living up to his role as master and father of his community of slaves, honoring the duties that were incumbent upon him in the Roman system as *paterfamilias*.

But maybe there is also another reason that runs counter to our clichés about the master-slave relationship. It is simply not the case that all masters were violent and inhumane. Masters often had relationships of mutual respect with their slaves, and in some cases friendship and even love. That's the reason why so many slaves were freed, or why sometimes the master-slave relationship blossomed into matrimony.

The little boy vents his pain in tears and screams. He's drenched in sweat. The wagon stops. His father and mother both try to reassure him, caressing him and holding him in their arms. During this unplanned stop, Lusius jumps down from the wagon to take a look around. Fate has determined that they have stopped right in the area of a small temple dedicated to healing. There must be a spring in the vicinity because we are in the middle of nowhere. The temple is reminiscent of those little churches or chapels that are sometimes seen by the side of the road here in Europe; in many cases they are the descendants of pagan temples that were built on the same spot. Indeed, sacred places often "change costumes," but their role remains the same.

The slave approaches the temple and climbs the stairs. There's nobody there. The walls, however, are covered with votive offerings. Anatomical parts and bodily organs made from clay, stone, or wood (elsewhere, in more important temples, they might be made out of copper, silver, or gold): heads, eyes, breasts, arms, legs, feet, fingers, hands, ears, intestines, and even genitals. These votive offerings (*donari*) have been brought here by people who want to ask for a blessing or who have received one and have been healed. You see a lot of them today in archaeological museums.

Lusius, exactly like museum visitors today, observes each offering, surprised by the variety of illnesses represented. Here's a votive offering with two ears made of stone and an inscription explaining that the Gaul Cuzius wishes to thank the gods for restoring his hearing. Nearby there's a terra-cotta arm with some circular reliefs about half an inch in diameter. In all likelihood they represent psoriasis, a disease already known by the time of the Egyptians. Now his gaze turns to the clay head of a woman. She has clumps of hair rooted in her scalp only in a few places on her head. Lusius has never seen a disease like this. Today we know it is alopecia areata, a disease that causes hair loss in specific points of the scalp but not in others. Lusius is even more surprised by the problems related to the genitals. Here's an incredibly oversized scrotum and, not far away, a penis, with another smaller one beside it. His eyes bulge out of their sockets.

It must be said that these votive offerings are a testimony to the Romans' relationship to the various illnesses represented. Since there was very little medical knowledge in Roman times, they faced disease by turning simultaneously to two types of medicine: "sacred" medicine directed to the gods, as demonstrated by this temple, and "scientific" medicine, as demonstrated by the wagon on its journey to the surgeon. Actually, this is still true even today. All you have to do is go into a church or a shrine anywhere in Italy and you will see the same votive offerings, usually in the form of silver-plated legs, eyes, or internal organs.

The principle divinities that people turned to for intervention were Minerva, Carna, Mephite (the goddess associated with poisonous gases rising up from the ground), and Febris. Then there was a real dynasty of healing divinities: Apollo the physician, his son Aesculapius, and Aesculapius's daughter, Salus, the goddess of health.

To placate the gods when an epidemic broke out, the Senate ordered the performance of rituals such as the lectisternium, a propitiatory banquet arranged in solemn fashion with the only guests at the table being statues or images of the divinities, the gods on triclinia and the goddesses on chairs, in accordance with the strict etiquette of archaic Rome.

And it doesn't end there. There are also specific feast days to ask the divinities for protection from illness and disease. December 21, for example, is the date of the *divalia vel Angeronalia*—the feast of the *Angeronalia*—dedicated to the goddess Angerona, whose name sounds familiar to us because it derives from *angor* (angst, anguish), which corresponds to the sense of suffocation associated with angina. The goddess Angerona, in fact, cured heart disease.

Lusius is now looking at a pair of gladiators in combat. They are pictured on a little lead mold representing a Thracian and a Murmillo fighting each other with helmets and shields decorated with marine figures. What is it doing here? Probably a wounded gladiator wanted to thank the gods for healing his wound.

The slave is startled by a thin, bony hand that reaches out and grabs onto his arm. It belongs to one of the custodians of the temple. The priest is not present. He's gone to bury the surplus votive offerings in a sacred hole (a periodic cleanup, necessary in all ancient temples, which has rewarded archaeologists with huge collections of votive offerings).

In the priest's absence, oversight of the temple has been left in the hands of this half-blind slave. He's thin and bald, with a long beard and a very few misshapen teeth; one of his eyes is so clouded it's almost white, giving him a sinister look. Frightened, Lusius makes a quick getaway and climbs back up on the wagon.

Traveling to Rimini in the Roman Era

The wagon is now moving onto a long, white bridge. The underlying water sends back a perfect reflection of its five arches, creating a beautiful visual effect of five different-sized circles. This bridge is one of the attractions of the city of Ariminum. It was commissioned by Augustus and completed under Tiberius, and it is a true masterwork, built so well that it will survive more than two thousand years of history (including an attempt by the retreating Nazis to blow it up during World War II). Today, it is still a precious artery for automobile traffic.

Modern-day Rimini is an enormously popular beach resort, yet most of its millions of Italian and European visitors never stop to consider that it was once the land of barbarians. We are accustomed to thinking that the barbarians lived very far from Rome, in the forests of Germany or perhaps in the arid regions of North Africa (the name of the Berber people comes from the Greek word for barbarian, *barbaros*), or still farther off in the deserts of the Middle East. At the beginning of its history, however, Rome had to fight the barbarians right at home on the Italian peninsula. Some generations back (until 268 BCE) the region of Romagna that we have just crossed on board this little wagon was a foreign land, inhabited by strong tribes of Gauls. In its war of conquest to the north, the Senate of Rome decided to send six thousand soldiers to found a new city, a colony in the middle of Gallic territory, as a stronghold to support Roman expansion in the Po River valley. In reality, the members of the expedition were farmers as much as they were soldiers—settlers as much as combatants—and they came from Lazio and Campania accompanied by their families. They decided to build the new city at the mouth of a river, the Ariminus (the present-day Marecchia), and so they called the city Ariminum.

Having gone through the checkpoint at the entrance to the city, the wagon is proceeding toward its center. The noise of the wheels has changed; the road surface is no longer the gravel of the Via Emilia, the long consular road on which they crossed the countryside. In Rimini the road is paved and the wheels feel the resistance of the hard stone, sending it up the spines of the passengers. At regular intervals some small noises can be heard as the wheels roll over the gaps between the paving stones. It's the Roman equivalent of the rhythmic sound a train makes when its wheels move from one track to another.

The wagon is now heading down one of the main streets, with porticoes on either side, under which are located a never-ending line of shops and stores. Lusius observes every detail: three men chatting, leaning against one of the columns of the portico; a class of schoolchildren sitting on the ground, under a canopy, listening to their teacher with his unmistakable stick slicing the air; an old blind man with his hand on the shoulder of a young boy, his slave, who helps him make his way through the people and the merchandise displayed on the sidewalk (the equivalent of a seeing-eye dog); two boys using little stones to play at marbles.

He smiles at the futile struggle of a fat man trying to unhook a straw-covered amphora hanging from the door frame of a shop. The worried shopkeeper runs over to help him, but it's too late. The customer's massive body has already set off a domino effect on a series of amphoras placed on the ground, which are now rolling out into the street.

Lusius is surprised by the geometry of the streets. They intersect at right angles, and the houses are just as orderly. He has never seen such a city before. He has always lived on the plantation and has only a vague childhood memory of the serpentine streets of his birthplace. The son of slaves, he was sold at birth by his parents' master to his current owner. The rule is simple: the children of a slave couple belong to their master, who can sell them at his pleasure, exactly as we do with the puppies and kittens of our pet dog or cat. In this era, a segment of society not only has no possessions; they can't even raise their own children.

Slaves have a very limited view of the world. Their living conditions make it difficult for them to get to know what lies beyond the house and the neighborhood where they work. And slaves who live on farms in the middle of the countryside are tantamount to exiles, more often than not born, living, and dying in the same place without ever leaving it. Naturally, this is not always the case. A lot of slaves are sold, move from one place to another, or from time to time are sent to work in different places by order of their masters. A special category of slaves consists of those who have won the trust of their master and who act on his behalf in doing errands, making purchases, transporting goods, visiting his various properties, and so forth. This is exactly the case with Lusius, but he has never been sent on such a distant mission as this. Even though today an automobile would cover the distance from Reggio Emilia to Rimini in less than an hour, for him the wagon's journey is a real trip abroad.

Now his eyes meet those of a young woman sitting on a wooden bench. From the way she's dressed, she doesn't seem to be a slave. Maybe she's a *liberta* or a Roman woman, in which case he certainly shouldn't be staring at her like this. But instinct doesn't respect social conventions. She stares back at him and offers a daring smile. As though hypnotized, the blue eyes of the young slave don't leave hers for an instant. Just as he is about to say something to her, the wagon goes around the corner and the sea comes into view at the end of the street, and he is hypnotized anew. The slave has never seen the sea before, and he can't take his eyes off it, his mouth half open and his blond curls blowing in the wind. Some rectangular sails dot the horizon. He has heard so much talk about it in the stories of his fellow slaves and now there it is, just yards away, but he can't go touch it. He's a slave and he has to obey orders. A hand lands brusquely on his shoulder. It's the father of the sick child, wanting to know the way to the surgeon's house.

The young slave has a flash of intuition. He jumps down off the wagon and goes over to the girl who had left him spellbound. He approaches her with his eyes cast down in a sign of respect. He knows he's risking a lot if he behaves wrongly. But he also knows that their gazes have established something between them. The girl is surprised to see him approaching, even though she had been hoping it would happen. And she fixes him with her eyes, dark and luminous and framed by dark hair with copper highlights. She's wearing a strange metallic pendant that glistens in the sunlight. He asks her if she knows the house of the famous surgeon, and she smiles, showing brilliant white teeth that stand out against her Mediterranean olive complexion. She offers to accompany them. The slave is walking beside her now. He's holding the horse's bridle in his hand and is leading the wagon on foot. He can't help noticing the girl's body, which with every step sways sinuously under her tunic. She's Venus in person, he thinks to himself.

On the way, their hands brush up against each other several times, hidden by the crowd. He explains to her why they are here and she listens in silence, time and again casting a compassionate glance toward the child in the arms of his mother.

Now the group is walking through the Forum, which is a pedestrian zone. The wagon has been left in a nearby street, watched by the slave-coachman.

The forum is crowded. It's a little like walking through a train station at rush hour: well-dressed men chatting, teenage ne'er-do-wells jostling and scuffling, fathers with their children. One thing is unmistakable: there are more men than women. That's the way it is in the forum and on the streets of all the cities in the empire. Despite the emancipation achieved by women in this second century CE, the world beyond the walls of the home is still dominated by men.

They have now arrived in the center of the forum, at the point where the main streets of the city, the *decumanus* and the *cardo*, intersect. Lusius notices a pillar with a statue on top. There are others in the piazza, but this one is special. It's a statue of Julius Caesar. He hears the voice of a young lad who is guiding some out-of-town visitors: on this spot in 49 BCE Caesar addressed his troops after crossing the Rubicon, ready to march on Rome. This pillar still exists today, and there is always someone ready to tell its story to visiting tourists.

Crossing the piazza of the forum our group has several encounters with litters carrying aristocratic men and women with vitreous gazes, stretched out in affected poses. When a litter passes by the intense perfume of the mistress combines with the pungent odor of the sweat of the slaves who are carrying the litter. The mixture creates an indescribably odorous wake, the "exhaust fumes" of this ancient means of transport.

Almost like an opening theater curtain, a passing litter reveals to us an unusual scene: a group of old men in togas is gathered in front of a milky-white wall. They remind us a little of travelers checking the arrival and departure times in our train stations. Actually, however, they are reading edicts and announcements that the city administration has written for citizens on this glowing white wall. Similar walls can be found in all the cities of the empire. When the announcements are out of date and more room is needed for new ones, the administration has the wall whitewashed. And it is the Latin word for this white hue (*albus*) that gave us the official name for this type of wall: *album*. Yes, the word we currently use to indicate a collection of photographs, souvenirs, figures, even recorded songs, has its origins in the Roman piazzas of two thousand years ago. Over time, in fact, the word album became a generic term for any surface on which to write or leave accounts or recollections, right down to our own time.

Entering the Surgeon's House

Now our little group has turned down a side street, passing in front of a *popina*. The unmistakable smell of grilled sausage wafts out of the tavern. It's a real temptation for them all, but they don't have time to lose. The black-eyed girl advances quickly, making her way through the people huddled around the marble-topped counter from whose round openings issue forth liters of wine and big ladles of seasoned olives. Some of the people notice the bundle that the woman is carrying with the little feet sticking out, and they immediately understand and step to the side. They all know that the famous surgeon lives at the end of the street and scenes like this one are a daily occurrence.

It's not hard to figure out which house is the surgeon's. The masonry benches on either side of it are occupied by a small silent crowd waiting for an appointment. When the group gets to the big green door with two bronze rings, Lusius stops for a moment and looks for his master's letter of introduction, a sheet of papyrus bearing the seal of his personal ring. But the black-eyed girl beats him to it. She knows one of the slaves of the house who is in charge of the administration of this clinic. Meeting her really was a nice piece of luck. In just a few seconds, one side of the double door opens and a smiling face looks out. It's a young man with a clean tunic and a gentle manner. All it takes is a few words and the group is inside the door.

It's an odd house. It doesn't have the typical layout of the *domus* from an earlier time, which can be seen today in Pompeii. With the passing decades, housing in Roman cities had to come to terms with a problem that we know very well today: the lack of space. The empire's prosperity has increased the population of its cities, creating a boom in the demand for housing. Consequently, square footage in all the cities of Italy and throughout the empire has become too precious and costly to be wasted on nonfunctional spaces. In order to increase the number of rooms, the elegant *domus* has been refitted with partitions, walls, and upper floors, completely transforming its original layout.

So the *atria* with their pools of water have disappeared and been re-placed by rooms and hallways. Those beautiful interior gardens that we are used to seeing in films and drawings, with their perfumed essences, fountains, and colonnades, have been downsized and transformed into simple courtyards overlooked by the floors above. And very often a re-habbed *domus* is divided into two or more independent houses. This house is an example: half of it has become a medical clinic.

Now our little group is going down a long corridor leading to the waiting room. They all feel they are in a place imbued with solemnity. The corridor is dark, dimly lit by a single multiflame oil lamp in the middle of the ceiling. And there's a strong smell of incense, as in temples. Why do they burn incense in this house? The reason is simple: incense has mild antiseptic properties, and it is traditionally indicated for all those places with a high concentration of people in need of treatment: temples, shrines, and, obviously, medical clinics.

While Lusius speaks with his "colleague" from the administration, showing him the letter of introduction, the family of the little sick boy takes a place on the wooden bench in the waiting room. All around them are other patients waiting to be seen. The room is a perfect microcosm of the illnesses of the era.

A Toothache in Ancient Rome

It should be pointed out that in this era, and in general in the first few centuries after Christ, there is still not a precise distinction between physicians and surgeons. A good doctor has to be able to perform surgical operations and also prepare medicines like a pharmacist. There is a definition of the physician-surgeon that can help us understand the conditions in which surgery was performed. It was written by Aulus Cornelius Celsus, who lived two thousand years ago under Augustus and Tiberius, and who was the author of *De Medicina*, a very interesting treatise on medicine:

> Now a surgeon should be youthful or at any rate nearer youth than age; with a strong and steady hand which never trembles, and ready to use the left hand as well as the right; with vision sharp and clear, and spirit undaunted; filled with pity, so that he wishes to cure his patient, yet is not moved by his cries, to go too fast, or cut less than is necessary; but he does everything just as if the cries of pain cause him no emotion. (Loeb Classical Library, 1935. Translated by W.G. Spencer)

Would you enter an operating room, today, knowing that the surgeon won't pay any attention to your screams of pain? (A great invention, anesthesia.)

Two white-haired men are sitting opposite the sick boy's family; one of the two has a conspicuous bandage that passes under his chin, goes up over his cheeks and finishes in a nice big knot on the top of his head. He looks like an Easter egg wrapped in a ribbon with a bow on top. With the palm of his hand he tries to protect his cheek, swollen from a painful toothache. The he turns to his friend and asks him, garbling his words:

"Are you sure we were right to come here instead of going to the other doctor, Dialus?"

His friend tries to encourage him with a wisecrack: "We sure were. A while ago Dialus was a doctor; now he's an undertaker. He does the same things now as an undertaker as he did when he was a doctor!" And then he proclaims: *Aegrescit medendo*, which means, loosely translated, "The cure is worse than the disease."

Indeed, by and large medical practitioners are not very popular for a lot of reasons. Their remedies are much less effective than modern ones and their knowledge of the pathologies they treat is still very rudimentary compared to today. Besides that, there are a lot of charlatans who take advantage of people's trust, inventing false therapies and miracle cures.

As if to underline the popular prejudice about doctors, a female voice cuts through the silence in the waiting room. She's launching into a tirade about another doctor by the name of Simmacus: "I was sick. Then Simmacus came to see me accompanied by a hundred of his disciples. Two hundred cold hands touched me all over. Before that I didn't have a fever. Now, thanks to Simmacus, I do."

What will happen to the patient with the toothache? He has come to the clinic of a renowned doctor but he could just as easily have gone to the barber down the street. As their second job, barbers also pull teeth. With methods that are rather less than refined, as you might imagine. But will things really be all that different here? What the patient with the toothache still doesn't know is that when it's his turn he'll have to undergo a real torture. There are lots of instruments used by Roman dentists to pull teeth, and the most feared is certainly the dental pincer, or *forfex*. Then, as often happens during the operation, if the crown of the tooth snaps and the root remains stuck in the jawbone, the doctor will have to use another pincer, even more awful, whose name says it all, *rhizagra*, from the Greek, meaning "root grabber"!

All this for what is probably a cavity. And the treatment for cavities truly makes one appreciate how far dentistry has come. In the Roman era it is believed that cavities are caused by a mysterious gnawing worm, capable of boring through enamel as it would through an apple. It is a very ancient theory that goes back at least to the Babylonians and will last well beyond the time of the Romans.

The first step in the cavity cure consists in eliminating irritating foods and applying medicines and mouthwashes composed of opium, incense, pepper, and henbane. A relative of the potato and the tomato, henbane has an anesthetic effect and is also a potent hallucinogen. But it is also a very dangerous plant. Its leaves and especially its tiny black seeds are extremely poisonous. Shakespeare mentions henbane in describing the death of Hamlet's father. So treating a toothache is no joke, and the patient can only hope that no mistakes were made in preparing the medicine. That explains why people often turn to the great luminaries of the medical profession rather than trusting their fate to the practitioner down the street.

The next step in the treatment is to plug the hole in the tooth with grains of pepper or ivy berries. If—as is certainly more than likely—the remedy doesn't work, the hole is filled with an infusion of oregano and arsenic in olive oil and closed with wax. But some practitioners don't stop there. A certain Rufus of Ephesus has the habit of making fillings from a mixture of alum crystals, myrrh, cumin, black pepper, and vinegar. A real high-tech hodge-podge of the ancient world.

How well do these remedies work? We don't have any scientific records, but it is highly likely that they were not very effective in treating the pain. Toothache suffers could fight it with wine and infusions of catnip (the same herb that domestic cats like to rub against). But in most cases, inevitably, the affected tooth has to be pulled. As a result, Roman-era smiles are quite striking by our standards, and are quite likely to be missing several teeth. But nobody pays much heed. That's just the way things are in this era.

The surprising thing—but not all that surprising when you think about it—is that cavities and dental problems often affect the wealthy more than the poor. A diet rich in sugars and carbohydrates, typical of those who lead a life of ease, devastates the mouth much more than a low-sugar diet. To be sure, a poor person who doesn't get enough to eat ends up losing his teeth from malnutrition. Nevertheless, studies of tombs in rural areas near Rome have uncovered this paradox: in many cases the teeth of slaves are more intact than those of their masters.

And what does one do when one loses a tooth? One of the remedies for filling a gap in a smile is to replace the missing tooth with a false one made from an animal's tooth, usually oxen or calves. The animal teeth are filed so they can be adapted perfectly to the patient's mouth. Interestingly, as early as the fifth century before Christ the Etruscans were able to make dental bridges from gold leaf. They were hooked onto healthy teeth and contained false teeth to be used as prostheses. But this is a technique that did not go over very well in the Roman era.

One last chilling fact. Reading Celsus one learns about an inhumane (at least in our view) technique for treating an abscess or a gum problem: apply a red-hot piece of iron directly to the affected tissue. This might just be the treatment that the man with the toothache is contemplating right now: he is staring into the void.

Cataract Problems? Here's the Solution

A woman and her husband are sitting beside him. She has a complex hairdo of braids rolled up behind her head, fixed by a hairpin made of bone inserted horizontally like a bolt lock. Her husband, meanwhile, is staring at the ceiling and chewing on a special kind of gum made from a mixture of juniper berries and portulaca. This chewing gum of antiquity is actually a remedy for halitosis, thanks to the fresh and penetrating aroma of juniper. It's the ancestor of those herbal lozenges that you often see advertised today, the ones that are so strong that as soon as you put them in your mouth they take your breath away.

But it's his wife who has the serious problem. She can no longer see out of one eye. The eyewashes that she was prescribed and has used over the past few months have accomplished nothing. She's got one in her hand right now. Roman eye washes are not liquid like ours. They come in the form of a small stick, made of hardened pasty mixtures that have to be diluted, preferably with mother's milk. One of the stranger ingredients is *castoreum*, which has soothing effects; it is made from a genital secretion of the European beaver. Would you put something like that in your eye? Probably not. But in Roman times it was thought to be a panacea.

In many cases these eyewash sticks are marked with the seal of the doctor who made them, partly as a form of publicity but mostly as a way of avoiding counterfeiting (even back then, fake medicines were in circulation). Sometimes the seal includes, besides the name of its creator, the name of the active ingredient and the instructions for use.

Roman doctors are able to carry out delicate surgical operations on the eyes: in this case the removal of a cataract. The woman will be made to sit against the light, in a lower position with respect to the surgeon, with an assistant standing behind her to hold her head still. Then, with the utmost care, the doctor will insert a needle between the cornea and the choroid membrane and with a slow movement he will guide the cataract downward.

Yes, perhaps it's best we stop here.

Also because some strange sounds can be heard coming from another room. They sound like groans, slowly rising in a crescendo to a final strangled shriek. Some of the doctor's slaves look at each other and smile. The patient in treatment has a decidedly special problem: she's a woman suffering from hysteria. The word *hysteria* derives from a Greek term *hystéra,* meaning "uterus." So it's no coincidence that today we use the terms hysteroscopy, hysterectomy, hysterosalpingogram, etc., for examinations or operations on the uterus. In fact, physicians in ancient times believed that hysteria struck those women whose sexual energy, not being liberated, had accumulated to a debilitating overabundance. Women at risk, therefore, included widows, spinsters, and all women who did not have regular sexual activity. As early as the first century CE the prescribed treatment for hysteria was a clitoral orgasm. The affected women went to the doctor, who used his own hands to induce a "paroxysm." This practice was still widespread up to the end of the nineteenth century.

Here's the Doctor

It's finally time for the doctor to see the sick boy and his parents. One of the doctor's slaves comes to call them. They jump up and quicken their step to keep up with the slave. The door to the doctor's office opens. They hesitate in the doorway, knowing they must now face one of the most difficult chapters in their lives. It's the father who goes in first, followed by his wife who is holding the little patient. They get to the center of the room and stop.

The doctor almost seems to be ignoring them. He's sitting behind his desk writing a prescription for a patient on a wax tablet. The floor is decorated in a beautiful mosaic pattern depicting wild animals on the run—a panther, some birds, a gazelle, and a lion—arranged in a circle around a mythological figure: Orpheus. This is not a coincidence. According to mythology, Orpheus with his scepter could tame wild animals and vanquish death. A good image to inspire trust in the doctor's patients. On one side of the doctor's office is a door to another room, a *cubiculum*, where a bed is illuminated by the dim light of an oil lamp. This room serves as a day hospital for the doctor's patients. Here too the floor mosaic is truly elegant.

The mother's eyes scrutinize every corner of the room. The walls are painted with frames and decorations, and they have a long red strip on the bottom that goes all the way around the room. There's not much furniture. Besides the desk, there's a chest, a shelf lined with texts and treatises for consultation, in the form of thick scrolls of papyrus. The mother's eyes pause to examine a long low table: a slave has already laid out the surgical instruments for the operation. They look like instruments of torture.

The father feels the light touch of something wet on his sandal and toes. It's the caress of a rag soaked with vinegar that a slave is using to clean the floor of the traces of blood left from the last operation . . .

The doctor stands up. He's a handsome man in his forties, black hair with just a touch of gray, regular features, and nicely shaped fleshy lips. His big black eyes are striking, as is his gaze, attractive and charming, perhaps because of the crow's feet at the corners of his eyes. His features and his accent betray the identity of his homeland: Greece.

He knows the master of the slave family very well; he's been to his farm-villa many times. And he also owes a great debt to the man for once having resolved some problems for the doctor, thanks to a high-level intervention. So the operation will be performed gratis. He listens in silence to the parents' account of their son's illness. The little boy observes him, still clinging to his mother. He's not afraid; instinctively he sees the doctor as a friend. And he's right. He is the only one who can save him. The doctor observes the boy sympathetically as well. His head is tilted slightly to the side and he's smiling.

The doctor's warmly reassuring and plainly Mediterranean countenance communicate a very interesting context for this scene. At the beginning of Rome's history, the figure of the physician did not exist. It was the *paterfamilias* who took care of his loved ones and his slaves with prescriptions and wisdom handed down from father to son. It wasn't until the conquest of Greece that Rome came to know the figure of the professional physician. Greek physicians came from the most famous medical schools of the time: Ephesus, Smyrna, Antioch. The eastern Mediterranean of those days was the equivalent of the United States today, with its research centers, universities, and great institutions of knowledge, such as the celebrated library of Alexandria, Egypt.

And so, initially at least, the physicians circulating in Rome were essentially slaves of Greek origin (evidently much appreciated because their market price was considerably higher than the average). In a very short time these slaves were freed and in their new status as *liberti* they were permitted to start their own private practices.

Interestingly, Romans were not well suited for the medical profession in part because, according to the Roman code of values, a citizen could not profit from saving his neighbor, at least not through manual labor per se. In his *De Officiis,* Cicero declared that a cultivated Roman could know medicine but not practice it. A Roman would view this as we today would view a priest presenting the faithful with a bill after every Mass or confession.

It was Julius Caesar who really understood the value of these professional practitioners. In 46 BCE he granted free physicians the right to Roman citizenship, thus legitimizing their role in society. Under Trajan, doctors are by now well-known figures. Yet, despite the passing of generations, the medical profession continues to remain in Greek hands. In fact, based on the inscriptions discovered by archaeologists on tombstones and the like, 90 percent of physicians are still of Greek or Middle Eastern origin. And a hundred years later, in the third century CE, this would still be true of three-quarters of physicians.

In the era of Trajan there is a new trend among wealthy Romans, one that we might compare to the modern idea of the personal trainer. This is the figure of the *medicus amicus*, a sort of listener and adviser regarding the physical and psychological ailments of the Roman patrician class. For the less well-off there is a sort of local public health service, with the number of doctors (called *archiatri*) varying from five to ten, depending on the size of the city. Appointments to the office, salaries, and certain benefits were established through imperial approval.

Naturally, there is also criminal liability for doctors in cases of egregious malpractice, as set forth in the *Lex Aquilia* of 286 BCE and the *Lex Cornelia de Sicaris et Veneficis*, which punished poisoning but also the prescription, sale, and purchase of poisonous substances.

The doctor asks the parents to sit down and speaks to them in reassuring tones. He imagines their pain and anguish and tries to comfort them, without, however, letting them perceive the difficulty of the operation. While he is explaining to them how the operation will proceed, the boy is given a glass of a very sweet liquid containing some ingredients that will numb his senses almost to the point of making him lose consciousness—an early form of anesthesia.

The mother, meanwhile, can't take her eyes off the instruments lined up on the table. There must be thirty, maybe more. Actually, they are only a part of a vaster arsenal of instruments, at least a hundred and fifty or so, scattered about the doctor's office, some in their cylindrical metal cases (identical to the cases in which we keep our glass-and-mercury thermometers), others placed in wooden boxes or rolls of leather. She doesn't know it, but those instruments are suitable for almost all the operations described in the ancient texts and allow us to gauge the surgeon's ability in many fields, from dentistry to ophthalmology, from urology to orthopedics.

Which instruments will he be using? He has a vast array to choose from. There are a lot of bistouries, or surgical knives, with a common handle in the form of an elongated leaf. We count no less than ten types of interchangeable blades, differing in shape and size, from one made for precise incisions to broader ones for cutting through muscles.

The Romans' knowledge of anatomy and their surgical techniques are surprisingly well developed, and we can see just how modern they are by some of the doctor's tools. There is, for example, a surgical knife used for opening the spinal column. There's a selection of pliers for extracting teeth, which we imagine will be used on the man with the toothache. They're shiny, made of bronze or steel, each one a little masterpiece produced by specialized artisans under the guidance of the doctor.

Some of the pliers are used for another type of extraction, for removing splinters or arrows from bodies. We notice some peculiar-looking pliers that remind us of the tongs that bakers use to take pies and cakes from their display windows but they obviously have another use. They have two serrated valves on the ends similar to the jaws of a crocodile. They are used to grab onto the tonsils at the bottom of the oral cavity. They clamp shut and with a quick twist and a yank the tonsils are stripped clean. Still others are used for closing blood vessels or for sewing a wound. There is no lack of instruments for risky operations, such as an S-shaped tube for the removal of calculi from the bladder through the urethra, and even a ceramic hot-water bottle, in the shape of a foot, to be filled with hot or cold liquids, for the treatment of arthrosis, arthritis, and inflammations. A surgeon today would have no difficulty recognizing instruments almost identical to his own.

The little boy is now lying on the operating table, dazed by the effect of the mixture he was given to drink. Total anesthesia doesn't exist in this era, only analgesic substances that lower the body's capacity to feel pain. Those derived from opium, already known to the Romans, are the most effective, along with beverages with a high alcohol content.

Now the doctor examines the boy's head. The area where the incision will be made has been totally shaved. With the utmost solemnity, the surgeon takes a scalpel in hand. It has a lance-shaped handle and an extremely sharp blade. He holds it as though it were a pen and presses it delicately against the boy's soft skin. The boy's father closes his eyes. The mother squeezes hers shut in a grimace of pain. Because of the special nature of the operation they have been given permission to remain in the doctor's office, but they are standing off to the side. Around the table, in addition to the surgeon, are two slave assistants, one of whom is holding the boy's head still. The blade cuts; almost immediately a rivulet of blood comes streaming out. The boy tries to move but the hands that are holding him (and the liquid he has drunk) do not allow him to defend himself. With remarkable quickness, the scalpel outlines a window of flesh. Rapid cutting movements separate it from the underlying bone. When it is completely detached from the bone, the skin is folded to the side, like the page of a book. The blood is abundant because the scalp contains a lot of blood vessels. A dab with a cloth and a water rinse clean the area, leaving the skull in plain view. Now it's time to cut through the bone.

Among the many instruments spread out on the table ready for use are some drills with very sophisticated serrated bits, to be put in motion with a rotating brace. But as we're not dealing with the thicker skull of an adult, the surgeon must proceed with even more caution.

His hand glides slowly over the instruments on the table and stops on a chisel. This one will do fine. He picks it up and with the utmost care he holds it against the bone, above the temple. He starts to dig a small groove, as though he were creasing the bone, with a technique known as "progressive abrasion." He proceeds delicately, putting into practice a principle that Galen will expound on several decades from now in his treatise *De metodo medendi*, namely that when a surgeon operates on very thin skulls, a simple section is much safer than drilling. The father is dumbstruck.

The surgeon's manual dexterity is truly amazing. In almost no time at all he has managed to open a "hatch" about two inches in diameter in the little boy's skull. He drops the chisel and hammer into a small bucket of water that one of his assistants promptly takes away. (This is how surgical instruments are cleaned and "sterilized" in the Roman era.)

Now, with another instrument, the surgeon pries up the disk of bone to be removed. Gradually, the disk is lifted away and we can see the first of the meninges that protect the brain. We can also glimpse the almost imperceptible throbbing of the outermost blood vessels. Holding an oil lamp up close, the surgeon's assistant makes it possible for him to smooth and clean the edge of the hole so it will not damage the meninges. This window will become a safety valve to relieve the pressure that has been exerted on the brain by the growing tumor. If the boy survives, the bone will gradually grow back until it recovers the hole. But will he survive?

In his heart the surgeon knows that he has not resolved the problem; he's only relieved the pain. In this era, a tumor has no cure.

The incision is closed by folding over the flap of skin and sewing it back into place. Some historical documents point to the use of bone splints to hold pieces of skin together. For suturing, Galen advised using thin threads of animal intestines. Another material that was sometimes used was Celtic linen. The growth of scar tissue was fostered by the application of compresses and poultices made from medicinal herbs.

The surgeon picks up a clay bottle labeled with the Greek word *chamaedrys* and tips it until a dense liquid comes oozing out. He rubs it on the incision. It is an extract of the germander plant, used in ancient times to treat traumatic lesions and heal abscesses and ulcers. Even today it is used as a cleansing wash for the mouth and nostrils and to counteract the spread of gangrene.

The operation ends with a strange ritual. This doctor is indeed one of the best, but he's not able to save everyone. Many deaths are not explainable. It's no coincidence, then, that this doctor surrounds himself in his office with amulets, good-luck charms, and objects that invoke the protection of the gods. In particular, there is a small bronze hand associated with the cult of Jupiter Dolichenus, the divinity that presided over the success of military organization. A serpent wraps around its wrist and thumb, and a pine cone covers the index finger. This hand is fixed to the end of a wooden rod as though it were a sort of scepter, and the doctor, reciting sacred incantations in Greek, waves it over the boy's wound. Then he looks over at the father, smiles, and half closes his eyes, letting him know that everything has gone well.

He gestures that the boy can be taken off the table. The father and one of the surgeon's assistants carefully lift the body of the little patient and carry him into the other room, his legs dangling like those of a marionette.

Discovering the Sea

Will the boy live? We hope so, but we'll never know for sure. Our journey is about to start up again, following our coin.

Archaeologists did actually find the skeleton of a five- or six-year-old boy, who lived at the beginning of the second century CE, the son of slaves (or freed slaves) who worked in the country. He had a brain tumor that deformed his skull, and on that side of his head there was an opening made by a surgeon. The boy survived the operation and must not have suffered anymore from the painful headaches that required the operation. But he didn't live long. Unfortunately, the tumor brought his short life to an end a month and a half later. Now his skull and his little remains are conserved in the Museum of the History of Medicine at the Universitá La Sapienza in Rome. This little boy found by the archaeologists lived in Fidene, on the outskirts of Rome.

After the operation the family needs some time before they can start their journey home. Mother, father, and son have found hospitality at the home of one of their master's clients, who has given them a room in his house just two blocks away from the doctor's office. The boy has to remain totally at rest for a few days before getting on the wagon to go back home. The Greek doctor has come to see him several times, bringing compresses and medicines, changing his bandages, checking the wound. Even though he's used to seeing the pain and suffering of his patients every day, he has developed a sincere affection for this little boy, so hard hit by the misfortunes of life, who smiles at him every time, especially when he brings him a present.

During this rest period, Lusius has had the chance to realize two of his dreams: discovering the sea and falling into the embrace of Venus. The young girl who led them to the doctor's house took him down to the beach, right to where the waves come lapping over the sand. The slave smiled, hesitated, and then, smiling again, touched the water and waded in. He looked out at the vast expanse of the sea, its color gradually changing as the eye moves away from shore, and the power of the waves. He had never seen so much water and didn't think it was even possible. And he couldn't resist. He took off his tunic and dove in, shouting with joy, being careful to stay where his feet could touch bottom because obviously he didn't know how to swim.

The beach in Rimini in Roman times is radically different from the beach we know today: the coast is farther back, but above all it's uninhabited. There's no tourism so there are no beach umbrellas, no cabins, no bars, no entertainers, and, obviously, no lifeguards or Nordic vacationers. The beach is a simple border, a no-man's-land between two worlds, as arid and inhospitable as a desert. And that's the way it's treated: nobody even thinks of spreading out a beach towel, lying in the sun, going for a swim, or spending their holidays here. The only people you see are some occasional fishermen taking a walk or kids playing in the waves. The sea and the beach have no part in Roman amusements.

Later that evening, when the stars had filled the sky, Lusius and the girl stretched out behind an abandoned boat, far away from everything and everyone. The sand and the stars caressed their bodies locked in a long embrace. On the morning of their departure, Lusius paid his bill at the modest inn where he had stayed. And that's where our sestertius changed hands again. It ended up in the locked wooden drawer of the innkeeper, mixing in with lots of other sesterces.

But it wasn't long before its journey started up again. From the same inn, two rooms away from the slave's room, a well-dressed, well-built man with a severe look on his face came striding out onto the street. His head held rigidly straight, his movements measured and brusque, he walked with a military mien, his sandals making short metallic bursts with every step. There's no doubt he's wearing *caligae*, replete with metal cleats on the soles. Indeed this man is a soldier, a Batavian who's part of an escort detail for Caius Nonius Cepanius, a famous military commander under Trajan and later under Hadrian. He has been with him for years, following him throughout the entire military campaign in Dacia. And he is still following him now that he's in command of a select cavalry unit.

When he paid his bill he was given the coin as change. He looked at it for a second, smiling at the image of the emperor, then stuck it in the purse hidden under his belt, mounted his horse, and headed for the south gate of the city of Rimini. Riding under the big Arch of Augustus he passed by two lovers embraced in a fond farewell. He didn't recognize Lusius and he kept right on going, leaving as he has always done: at a gallop. He turned into a dot on the horizon on the Via Flaminia, heading south.

THE TIBER

~ *Coming into Rome by Water* ~

The landscape opening up before our eyes is divided by the deep green expanse of a large river. It winds its way slowly and sinuously across the plain, bending this way and that like an enormous snake on the prowl. Lines of tall trees rise up along its banks, the first line of an army of giant plants that climbs the hills and mountains of the surrounding country-side, cloaking them in its thick green mantle as far as the eye can see.

It is amazing to see this dominance of nature in the Roman Empire and in general in the ancient world. We have already noted it several times on our journey, but one can't help but be continually struck by it. Humanity, with our roads and marble cities, so important in our history books, is actually a small exception in this ocean of green and wildlife, dominated by forests, mountains, waterfalls, lakes, and, of course, rivers.

But this is no ordinary river. It is a waterway that plays a fundamental role in the history of civilization, as the Tigris and Euphrates in Mesopotamia, the Nile in Egypt, and the Yellow River and the Yangtze in China have done. This is the Tiber.

The Tiber is closely tied to the birth of Rome, both in myth and in history. Legend has it that the basket carrying the newborn babes, Romulus and Remus, floated down this river. The basket then ran aground on one of its banks, where a she-wolf discovered the two infant brothers and raised them in a cave on the Palatine Hill. Recently, in the process of making underground soundings with a special drill, archaeologists discovered a beautiful cavern topped by a round vault. A video camera lowered into the cave revealed ceilings covered with stucco and colorful mosaics. Andrea Carandini of the University of Rome, who for many years has conducted important excavations on the Palatine bringing to light Rome's most ancient roots, believes that this cave could well be the actual Lupercal, a place long venerated by the ancient Romans, convinced that it was the mythical grotto of Romulus and Remus.

Apart from the legend, the Tiber really did play an important role in the origins of Rome. Its shores, in fact, were the meeting place for the populations from the north and south of Latium, with their different languages and cultures: Etruscans, Latins, Sabines, and, before them, pre-historic groups and communities. They sold livestock, traded agricultural products and handcrafted goods, and purchased metal tools and instruments. And merchants from the Tyrrhenian Sea sailed up the river in pursuit of their commercial activities. Salt was one product that followed that very route.

All of this happened not just anywhere on the banks of the Tiber but in one precise location: Tiber Island. The island marked the ideal place for crossing the river, a bit like a stepping-stone in the middle of a stream or puddle. In the beginning, people crossed the river on simple boats before the Sublician Bridge established a stable connection between the banks and became a stimulus for communication and commerce.

On the eastern bank were the famous seven hills, later to be named Aventine, Capitoline, Caelian, Esquiline, Palatine, Quirinal, and Viminal. They constituted an excellent point of control (and command) over the entire area. Some of them were even quite steep and therefore easily defended. It's no wonder that they were occupied from the dawn of time by villages of wood cabins (as demonstrated by the postholes that supported the cabins and numerous objects discovered by archaeologists).

At the foot of these hills were extensive flatlands, which, probably from the earliest times, were a kind of primitive forum. The flatlands were ideal for commercial exchanges, but they were also the place where agreements were negotiated and marriages arranged. The main items traded in these forums were salt, livestock, and foodstuffs. Centuries later, in imperial Rome, there continued to exist two important markets: the Boarian Forum (for the sale of meat and livestock) and the Olitorian Forum (for the sale of fruit and vegetables). The history of Rome has never really been interrupted.

Our heads are teeming with these thoughts as we continue on our journey. Observing the lazy progress of the Tiber through the plains of this silent, uncultivated natural landscape, Rome, with its frenetic life, noisy streets, and crowded markets, seems very far off. Yet the capital city of the Roman Empire is extremely close, no more than fifty miles from here. And a sign of its nearness appears right before our eyes. It's a small city, the most important in this area: Ocriculum.

Immense fortunes have been accumulated here ever since the days of the republic. And entire classes of merchants have developed true dynasties of commerce here, amassing enormous wealth.

So what made Ocriculum so rich? This city flourished because it was built at a strategic point for the commercial exchanges taking place here between Rome and Umbria and the Sabine Hills. It is located at the point of contact between the Via Flaminia and the Tiber, two important arteries for the transport of goods. And that's why it has become much more of a cardinal point for the economy than Assisium (Assisi), Iguvium (Gubbio), and Spoletum (Spoleto), which are all a little farther north. In the modern era, this situation will be turned on its head. Its strategic vantage point for trade having disappeared, Ocriculum will turn into an almost unknown small town (Otricoli; now called Orte), while the other three towns will become popular destinations on the international tourism circuit.

Ocriculum rises above a bend in the Tiber, and its port hosts an intense traffic of cargo ships and barges that come and go, loaded with goods. A number of boats are tied up now at the dock in single file. We can hear a background hum of voices from which emerge occasional shouts or curses to be drowned out in turn by the shrieking sound of pulleys and winches. The tether lines of the boats at the dock stretch and contract with the ebb and flow of the current, emitting a long, sad sound, like a cello.

Our attention is attracted by a dog barking and wagging its tail. It's standing on an enormous stack of wood on a barge that has just released its tether lines and is now being rapidly dragged by the current toward

Rome. The huge mass of logs, blocks, and bundles of sticks slides by majestically behind the moored boats, almost as though it were a mountain of wood slipping into the landscape. Its load will be used not so much for making tables, floorboards, or roof beams but for heat—a particular kind of heat: the heat of the baths. The baths of Caracalla alone (and there is no doubt that the same was true for Trajan's baths) consumed no less than ten tons of wood per day. It has been calculated that the basements of the baths of Caracalla were able to hold two thousand tons of wood, enough to last about seven months. And they were only one of the eleven large bath complexes in the capital, leaving aside the eight hundred smaller facilities. Rome consumed immense quantities of wood every day, for the most disparate purposes. The demand for wood to feed Rome, and all the great cities of the empire, led to the clear-cutting of entire forests in Europe and many areas of the Mediterranean, with the resulting disappearance of species of animals and plants and the destruction of local ecosystems. In sum, the Romans were the forerunners of something that is still going on today: the intensive deforestation of vast areas of the planet. What we are doing to the tropical forests and in other parts of the world, the Romans did to what was then the known world. Then as now, the wood was transported by ship, not only in the Mediterranean but also on the rivers of the empire. Such is the case here, in Ocriculum, where barges go by overflowing with timber cut in the forests around Mount Fumaiolo, where the Tiber has its source and where there is an important center of lumber production.

A curiosity: the huge barge that has just left the dock will probably never come back here. It's not worth the effort to pull it upriver against the current—it's too big. The solution is simple and ingenious: since it's made of wood, it will be dismantled and sold by weight, just like its cargo.

By now, the barking of the dog on top of the stack of wood has grown faint, to be drowned out by the background chatter and noise of the port. The barge is on its way.

The barges are destroyed upon arrival at their destination, but what about the others: do they come back here? If going down to Rome is easy—you just go with the flow—how do you get back upriver? There is no choice but to resort to towage, pulling the boats from the shore with long ropes. Here in Ocriculum they use oxen to pull boats against the current, a practice that remained in use in Italy until the beginning of the twentieth century, as documented in photographs from that time. But elsewhere the Romans use slaves (something that still happens today in China along the Shennong River, not with slaves but with teams of porters). The slaves pull the boats with the strength of their legs, the ropes wrapped around their torsos. They advance bent forward, like someone walking against a gale-force wind. It's a very common scene along all the rivers of the Roman Empire. This means that wherever towage is used there are footpaths and roads on the riverbanks where the trees are cut down to allow clear passage, a detail often overlooked when we think of Roman-era landscapes.

From a dock we see a young man jump onto a boat with a nifty move. He's wearing a yellow-orange tunic with a purse hanging from the belt that swings back and forth as he walks. Our sestertius is inside his purse. He's had it with him since yesterday evening, when he won a game of dice with the soldier we saw leaving Ariminum on horseback. All it took to change the fate of our sestertius was a double six.

The young man takes off his cloak and turns to the helmsman: "Take it away, Fulvius! We're on our way."

Two slaves release the tether lines, push the boat away from the dock, and jump aboard. It doesn't take long for the hull to be snatched by the current and swept along like a dead leaf. The helmsman steers the boat with a sure hand, looking at the horizon. The river is clear. The voyage will be smooth. Destination: Rome.

The Center of the World

The fishing line tightens, vibrates, and seems to want to cut the water, swinging violently back and forth; the fish has been hooked! The boy skillfully pulls on the rod, bent into an arc by the weight of the fish. There it is, flashing silver, as it glides along just below the surface of the greenish yellow water. Yes, when it gets to Rome the Tiber no longer has the deep green color that distinguishes it in the countryside. Instead, it's full of sediment, carried by the waters of the Aniene River that joins it just north of the city. The locals refer to it as the "blond Tiber." Gradually, carefully, the boy lures the fish toward the shore and pulls it up onto the grass. It's a nice catch! As he fiddles with it, trying to remove the hook (identical to the ones we use), a boat loaded with amphoras of olive oil passes by behind him. It is the boat we saw leaving Ocriculum with the young man in the yellow-orange tunic aboard. Three days have gone by and he's now standing on the bow, intently looking out at the river as it stretches out before him.

The view of Rome from the Tiber, glowing in the early-morning sun, is something that you never hear described in the age of Trajan. At first glance it reminds us of the Ganges, in India, where it passes by the holy city of Benares (today, Varanasi). On the left bank, there is a stone stairway that comes down almost into the water, where it meets a small dock. There are no cranes or containers, naturally, but numerous small groups of people, dressed in colorful tunics, talking among themselves. It is the first small port area in the city, used to facilitate the transport of goods to the narrow streets. Some boats are moored side by side, like the gondolas in Venice. They are unloading goods to be delivered to small shops that, already at this early hour, are receiving their first customers.

Now our boat lines up with one of the many arches supporting a large bridge. It's not the first bridge we've passed: the boat has already gone under the Milvian Bridge, about four miles upriver. This one was built by Nero, so he could have easier access to the gardens and portico of Agrippina, his mother. But to us, in modern times, it means something more, because it connects Rome to the area that is now the Vatican. In Trajan's time there were no basilicas; it was just a rural area with few buildings. There is a circus (that is, a race track), perhaps a bit decrepit by now, where Nero made martyrs of early Christians, accusing them of setting fire to Rome. This is also where Saint Peter died in 64 CE; his tomb was located, along with those of thousands of other people, in a vast necropolis that grew up alongside the road leading to the bridge. The Christian faithful built a small shrine in his honor where they come in groups to venerate him. Later, Saint Peter's Basilica will be built on the site of this shrine. Passing under the bridge, we can already see a fair amount of pedestrian traffic. The rush hour has begun.

After the bridge, the Tiber makes the first of its two large bends in the city of Rome. It's surprising to see that the riverbanks are not well maintained; for the entire length of the river's course through the city there are almost no retaining walls to prevent floods, such as we see today, but only fields that come down to the water's edge, some patches of bamboo, or small beach areas made of silt and tufts of grass. As a result, when the

Tiber overflows its banks it often provokes disastrous floods. According to Titus Livius, the popular classes of the city are so used to floods they even consider them "divine messengers." It is believed, in fact, that the most serious floods are harbingers of some tragic event, a natural disaster or a catastrophe that will upset the life of Rome. To get an idea of the frequency of the floods and the quantity of sediment that they bring into the city, keep in mind that in the span of a century and a half, the sacred monument of the Ara Pacis, the altar of peace built by Augustus in an open area, will be surrounded by accumulated sediment so high that a flight of stairs will have to be built to assure access to it.

Despite a series of imperial measures designed to control the river, the poor maintenance of the Tiber's banks makes it look like a river in today's third world. The banks are littered with broken amphoras, animal skeletons, and all kinds of trash. The shore is dotted with small wooden docks where we can see little boys dive into the water and come up smiling. A little farther off, glowing white herons and egrets punctuate the shore line, perched on beached tree trunks. Next to them lie old boats, broken up and abandoned. Sticking out of the water are the ribbed hulls of two other smaller boats that the Tiber is gradually devouring. Naturally, there are also boats that are still intact, pulled up onto the shore and arranged in a line. They are white with blue and red decorations. At this very moment, one of them is moving away from the shore, propelled by oars. Aboard there are three people and some well-secured sacks. They agilely avoid a decomposing animal carcass, being pecked at by crows.

It's a vision that doesn't fit well with the pomp and splendor of the capital of the empire. It's as though we were coming into the city through the service entrance, the one that films always portray as looking out onto narrow streets full of accumulated trash. But all you have to do is raise your eyes a little to see that you are in a special place. Just a few steps beyond this no-man's-land is an uninterrupted line of buildings and palaces as formidable as a row of legionnaires' shields. The line begins where the level of the land becomes a few yards higher. And some of them are multistory buildings, like the ones that can be seen today, for example, along the Arno, near the Ponte Vecchio in Florence. They are *insulae* that on one side overlook the streets of Rome and on the other the Tiber. Gazing at these buildings as you're going down the Tiber you see a streaming checkerboard of windows that open onto peeling plaster walls, balconies, drying laundry, and above all, scenes from everyday life. It's a little like moving slowly through a city on a train and catching glimpses of kitchens and dining rooms, with people eating or watching TV.

Here, too, you can see snapshots of life: an old man leaning out a window, eating a focaccia; a young man putting on a red tunic. A little farther on, a woman just out of bed opens the shutters and pushes them back against the walls of the building, stretching out her arms. All she's wearing is a very light tunic. Then she sees us and covers herself instinctively, shooting us a withering glance. Two windows later, a man empties his chamberpot from the fourth floor.

Now we're coming up to the area of Piazza Navona, where the river bends around the marshy plain of the Field of Mars before heading straight for Tiber Island. By now, we can see buildings of a certain architectural importance. Passing before our eyes are colonnades, statues, and porticoes, with people coming and going inside, already busy doing errands. Beyond this first line of buildings, we get a glimpse of the rest of Rome, with the roofs of its buildings and temples and, standing high above the early-morning mist, the majestic mass of the temple of Jupiter atop the Capitoline Hill.

By now we are coming into the heart of the city. History is all around us, its great names included. We glide under the great arches of another bridge, built by Agrippa, son-in-law of Augustus, who also built the Pantheon.

Ahead is Tiber Island. As we pass to the side of it, we notice its distinct profile. The Romans have exploited its oblong shape to construct the form of a ship, using blocks of *peperino*, volcanic tuff, faced with travertine marble. The entire island has been turned into a monument, with an obelisk in the middle symbolizing the mainmast. They have portrayed the hull, planked with wood and decorated with portrayals of, for example, Aesculapius and his snake. The whole thing is painted to look like a real ship, and from far away, in the morning mist, its mass looks like a trireme galley anchored in the middle of the river.

For four hundred years it has been home to the Temple of Aesculapius, the Greek god of medicine and healing. In the third century BCE the city was struck by a grave pestilence and a delegation was sent to Epidaurus, in Greece, to obtain a statue of the god. While the delegation was waiting to be received, a snake, the incarnation of the god, came slithering out of the temple, climbed up onto the Roman ship and, when the ship arrived back in Rome, slid down into the Tiber and swam to Tiber Island. For the Romans it was a message from the gods. They built the temple here in honor of Aesculapius and the plague came to an end. Its location had another, very practical, benefit: those who were sick or in need of healing were drawn away from the city, and the risk of spreading an epidemic was reduced. The Tiber, in other words, creates a natural cordon sanitaire.

The island is connected to the two opposite banks by two bridges, Fabricius and Cestius, under which we are now passing. And right after them comes our destination: a long dock on the left bank of the Tiber. This is where the main warehouses of Rome, the *horrea*, are concentrated. They remind us of the great industrial complexes of modern automobile factories. They cover an enormous surface area and appear to the eye as an endless line of long roofs. Their arcades, facing the river, look like so many open mouths. We might call them the famished mouths of Rome, a true demographic monster, a Hydra not of a thousand heads but of a thousand mouths, constantly needing to be fed.

Even at a distance the view is striking: endless lines of slaves stream up and down the diagonal ramps leading to the shore from the ships docked on the Tiber, carrying goods of every imaginable size and description, swallowed up by the open jaws of the *horrea*. The whole operation is coordinated and organized as though it were an enormous anthill.

Some of the goods come from the farthest corners of the empire. From this vantage point, one gets the sense that the entire empire revolves around Rome, that its unifying mission is to feed, defend, and increase the power of this city.

ROME

~ *The Center of the World* ~

A Walk Through the Backstreets of the City

We are walking around Rome with the young man in the yellow-orange tunic who has just disembarked. Looking through the papers that he had to sign, we've discovered that his name is Aulus Cocceius Hilarus. After delivering the olive oil and the routine formalities, he has an errand to run for his sister before heading back to Ocriculum. As you can easily imagine, anyone who comes to Rome is almost always asked by friends and relatives to buy something that's hard to find in the provinces. Rome has everything.

Hilarus has to find some spices and a perfume, so he heads off on his trek through the city streets on the lookout for, to start with, a *taberna unguentaria*, or perfume shop. A custodian at the entrance to the *horrea* had given him directions to a neighborhood where he'll find a wide selection and reasonable prices.

Like all visitors to the city, Hilarus follows the main streets to avoid getting lost in the labyrinth of alleyways that he doesn't know very well. The first thing that strikes him is the number of people out on the streets. In Ocriculum you never see such crowds except on holidays. But here it's a normal part of everyday life. There are so many people that he spends more time trying to avoid running into someone than he does looking at the sights of the city around him. The main street is starting to get so crowded that he can't even see its stone-block pavement. Thousands of faces pass before his eyes, most of them slaves but also well-dressed lawyers on their way to the Forum with their clients and women with their husbands or escorted by a slave out for a round of shopping.

This crowd on the street is a two-story affair, like a building: the ground floor is occupied by ordinary people, while the upper level is occupied by VIPs, who pass by stretched out on their litters. And there are a lot of them going by in both directions, almost like gondolas on the Grand Canal in Venice. When two litters pass each other, their occupants observe one another at a distance, and then at the moment of passage they turn the other way. Some even pull the curtain closed—an obvious sign of their superiority.

Hilarus is forced to step to the side to let a litter pass; the slave that precedes it, acting as a path breaker through the crowd, pushes aside anyone who doesn't get out of the way. To keep from getting run over, the young man steps up onto the sidewalk under the portico and takes advantage of his raised position to take a look at the person in the litter: a double-chinned matron wrapped in expensive clothes and looking bored. He views her passage much the way a modern pedestrian might view the billboard on the side of a passing bus.

Hilarus decides to continue on under the porticoes, which flank almost all the main streets of Rome. They are supported by brick columns and pillars covered by a coat of plaster that has a red strip running along the bottom, the same strip that runs along the base of all the buildings. The columns themselves are quite dirty, covered in handprints and graffiti, the flaking plaster exposing the brickwork. His gaze falls on a line of graffiti: "Lovers are like bees; their lives are sweet as honey." He smiles; it's funny to see this romantic sentiment in such a chaotic place. He leans his shoulder against the column and decides to take a minute to observe the human river flowing by him on the street.

The Postman Always Rings Twice . . . If He Comes!

He sees a postman go by. He's a *tabellarius* by the name of Primus and he's desperately trying to find the right address. In imperial Rome there are no numbers on the buildings. So how does he go about finding the right place to deliver the mail? We see that he's carrying a small wax tablet, a sort of ancient GPS, with directions based on the various monuments in the area. To get a sense of what's written on it we can refer to a postman's itinerary immortalized by Martial in his *Epigrams* (I, LXX):

> Go, my book, and pay my respects for me: you are ordered to go, dutiful volume, to the splendid halls of Proculus. Do you ask the way? I will tell you. You will go along by the temple of Castor, near that of ancient Vesta, and that goddess's virgin home. Thence you will pass to the majestic Palatine edifice on the sacred hill, where glitters many a statue of the supreme ruler of the empire. And let not the ray-adorned mass of the Colossus detain you, a work which is proud of surpassing that of Rhodes. But turn aside by the way where the temple of the wine-bibbing Bacchus rises, and where the couch of Cybele stands adorned with. pictures of the Corybantes. Immediately on the left is the dwelling with its splendid facade, and the halls of the lofty mansion which you are to approach.

These directions start out from the Forum, the "zero point" of Rome, where the temple of Castor and Pollux is located. They lead past the brilliant white temple of the Vestal Virgins and up the Via Sacra (which still exists today) to the enormous statue of Nero with its crown decorated with rays of sunlight (which supposedly rivals the Colossus of Rhodes; later it will be moved by Hadrian close to the Colosseum, giving the stadium its name). They go around other temples and monuments that no longer exist but were then situated on the Palatine near the Arch of Titus, finally leading to their destination.

Like today's taxi drivers, the *tabellarii* of Roman times probably knew the city very well, so they didn't really need such long and detailed explanations. Nevertheless, Martial shows us that even then the city's major monuments and temples were the "lighthouses" that people used to orient themselves, whether they were *tabellarii* or just ordinary citizens.

Who Are These People on the Streets?

Hilarus's gaze falls first and foremost on the people who are moving slowly or standing still, as they're easier to observe. Here comes a street vendor offering loaves of bread to prospective customers, swinging his basket back and forth in the crowd. Then a snake charmer passes, surrounded by a group of onlookers, one of whom is a wide-eyed little boy. The boy doesn't know that the snake's teeth have been pulled, nor does he know that the charmer's secret is not in the music but in the clump of colorful feathers attached to the end of the musical instrument that the charmer waves back and forth in front of the snake, distracting it.

The charmer's tune is gradually drowned out by the gravelly voice of a street cook who is carrying some smoking-hot sausages on a couple of hotplates. He is a perfect forerunner of the hot dog vendors that you see today on the streets of New York.

Now comes the grocer's delivery boy, a bundle on his shoulder. He's making his round of deliveries and knows he'll have to climb a lot of stairs. The Roman *insulae* don't have elevators. Lucky for him, the wealthy live on the lower floors, so only rarely will he have to go all the way up to the top floor. But the number of trips and the number of steps he'll have to climb is so great that by the end of the day he'll be exhausted.

Among the people off to the side of the street, Hilarus notices a man who is standing guard outside a shop and another who is probably a street poet waiting for some customers—those who would pay for a simple composition to court the object of their affections or flatter the powerful man they are on their way to supplicate. Street poets like this one, always anxious to make a little cash, will also write letters for the illiterate, who are actually not nearly as numerous in Roman society as they will be in the Middle Ages and subsequent eras, all the way to the Industrial Age.

Another representative of the arts makes his way slowly through the crowd. He is an actor who is talking with an impresario lying languidly on a litter. Actors are looked down on in Roman society; they're barely one step up from prostitutes. But this actor is an exception; even the impresario has stopped his litter in order to listen to him. The actor's name is Numerius Quinctius and he is extremely popular, a sort of George Clooney of the age. From his name we understand that he is a freed slave of the important Quincti family. Both he and his wife are freed slaves; her name is, naturally, Primilla Quinctia: it is a Roman tradition that freed slaves take the surname of their former masters.

All these men and women, from Primus the postman to the actor and his wife, lived during the era of Trajan, as we know from writings on daily life by Martial and others and from the testimony of tombstones. The same is true for the person that Hilarus hears talking behind him. He turns around and sees two men sitting in a *popina*. They are old friends:

> Julius, you're the dearest of all my friends, if promises made, if old oaths sworn long ago still have value, your sixtieth year is approaching, the days you have left to live are not many. You're wrong to put off what perhaps one day will be denied you: your past is all that belongs to you. What awaits you is a chain of pain and fatigue. All joys are fleeting, they don't stay with you. Hold on to them, the joys, with your hands, both of them, and even when they are held so tight they can often fall from your heart. Believe me, the wise man does not say: "I shall live." To live tomorrow is to live too late: you must live today. . . .

Hilarus smiles. In this city of so many opportunities, a similar philosophy of life guides the behavior of hundreds of thousands of people. In the age of Trajan it is the mentality of the majority of Romans throughout the empire. We will have occasion to come back to this idea: for the Romans, today is everything. After death there is nothing more.

Heading Down an Alleyway

Hilarus resumes his walking. When he comes to a big statue of Mater Matuta, the goddess of the morning, whose gaze dominates the street, he turns down a narrow alleyway. All of a sudden the sunlight vanishes, and it's cooler. Indeed, the light doesn't penetrate here and it seems to Hilarus that the houses are going to crush him any minute now; they're so close together. Often the backstreets of Rome are not straight, and this one is no exception. It bends right and then left, according to the way the buildings are fitted together.

The pavement is packed earth, with rivulets of foul-smelling water. At times the stench is so strong it's unbearable, especially when he passes a pile of accumulated garbage, which forces him to hold his nose. Hilarus encounters small groups of people or lone men and women from all levels of society. Although the street itself is shabby, it is part of the daily route of poor people, rich people, and slaves. To be sure, a litter would have a tough time getting through here, if for no other reason than the assault on the master's nostrils. This too is Rome.

The alleyway opens onto a street. Finally! It's a bit wider, with shops lined up on either side. The air is breathable, and Hilarus is hit by the pleasant smell of grilled fish. There's a nice aroma, coming from above. He stops and looks up: some white smoke is wafting upward from a second-floor window. Higher up, beyond the smoke, is an impressive scene. The *insulae* are really tall buildings. Between one building and the next there are networks of cables and ropes, many of them hung with tunics and various items of clothing put out to dry by Roman housekeepers.

He looks intently at the walls of the buildings. The lower parts are made of solid brick, but the higher the floor, the shoddier the material, as revealed by the plaster facing, also of very poor quality, that has peeled, flaked, and fallen off over the years. Like a drawing in an anatomy book, the skin covering the body of the buildings has been removed, revealing its skeleton and muscles. Above the bricks, the walls are made of a shoddy clay-based paste applied to a grid of thatched branches and crushed stone. You can see the wood beams very clearly, making evident the dimensions of the various floors and rooms. It's as though we were looking at the medieval houses of Normandy, with their skeleton of beams on which the hammer blows of the carpenters are still visible.

The windows have no glass panes—too costly. They open and close with wooden shutters, like the doors on a cabinet. In a lot of cases you can see what look like closets hanging on the outside walls of the house. Actually, these are small covered balconies (a classic violation of the building code, we'd call it today), which make it possible to enlarge a miniscule apartment by adding on a small block of airspace. This is where the braziers used for cooking are installed, with windows or grates for ventilation. Other, smaller closets, elegantly decorated, are used as masks to protect windows. In this way, the inhabitants can look out at the street without being seen.

These buildings are not all the same. Some are lower, while others thrust upward, thanks to little superstructures like towers, or extra stories built in different periods. These upper "frontiers" of housing aren't made of brick or clay, but of tile and wood. The walls are topped by overhanging cornices, with a long series of little clay vaults between one flat tile and the next. This is the realm of the poorest of the poor. When seen from below, Rome is a series of superimposed cities, every level stratified with different materials, different people, and different mentalities. The rich live on the lowest level and as you go up the poverty rises. It's like putting together in the same building the life of ease of a wealthy neighborhood and the misery of the poorest slum.

Shopping on the Backstreets of Ancient Rome

Hilarus continues his walk down the street, passing by a series of stores and shops stocked with all kinds of goods. There is an endless line of them. How to find the perfume shop? There are so many people that stopping each time to see what's on display is a chore. It's like being in a Middle Eastern souk. So he does exactly what we do when we're in a hurry—he looks at the signs.

Indeed, every shop has its own sign. They are smaller than ours today, about the size of a suitcase, and usually they are fixed on the wall above the entrance, but many are hung like flags, pointing out into the street so they can be seen by people approaching from either end. These signs are made of wood, marble, or terra-cotta panels. They are almost always carved in relief, and, in the absence of neon lighting, they are painted in gaudy colors.

Hilarus reviews the signs on the various shops. Here we have five pigs' legs all in a row, identical to our cured hams. Evidently it's a butcher shop.

Next to it, a sign with a goat. Here they sell dairy products: cheeses and milk. On the walls you can see little hanging baskets with ricotta cheeses wrapped in fig leaves.

A little farther on, three straw-bottom amphoras indicate a winery.

And then there's a sign for a tavern, at the intersection with a side street: you can read the menu on display, just like today in the restaurants of historic city centers. The sign reads: ABEMUS IN CENA: PULLUM, PISCEM, PERNAM, PAONEM, BENATORES ("For dinner we have: chicken, fish, ham, peacock, game"). Well, if there's peacock on the menu it's a very refined cuisine. The owner has also added a symbol of warm hospitality: a heart.

Beyond the tavern is a fabric shop. Hilarus can see some cushions hanging from one corner and prized fabrics hanging like towels from bronze rods attached to the ceiling. A man is examining a set of samples in the hands of the proprietor while his wife is sitting on a bench waiting.

Then he comes to the shop of a jeweler with glass paste necklaces and an assortment of rings. The proprietor is talking with a customer about the price of a nice gold bracelet in the form of a snake. There are other jewelry shops nearby; evidently they're grouped together for security reasons.

After passing some other stores, he comes to a wine shop with the proprietor sitting at the counter and a lot of amphoras lined up behind him. But the counter is unusual: it's so high it almost seems like a balcony. His curiosity piqued, Hilarus stops to take a look. He's never seen wine sold this way. The proprietor is a wine distributor. A customer goes up to the counter carrying his own amphora, asks for a certain type of wine, and pays in advance. Then he puts the open amphora in a niche and holds it upright with his hands. The proprietor pours the desired wine into a funnel-shaped sink that is built into the niche. This way the customer gets a quick fill-up and goes on his way. There are at least three pairs of niches, perhaps for different wines.

In a nearby shop a butcher is pounding a piece of meat with powerful cutting blows. In our time, butchers prepare different cuts of meat on a countertop, but this one sets the pieces to be cut on a sort of strange stool, made from a wood log supported by three legs. In some countries, such as Egypt, it's possible to see the same scene today, as if time has stood still. All around the butcher, the quartered pieces and some accompanying flies are hanging from hooks and nails. His wife is sitting in the back of the shop, with her hair rolled up in a triple turn of false braids to create a chignon. Her elegance and serenity are striking compared to the violence of her husband. But actually her job is much different than his; she's in charge of the bookkeeping and she's checking the credits and debits in the book of accounts.

Finally, Hilarus spies the perfumer's shop. On the sign we read his name: Sextus Aparronius Justinus. And as soon as Hilarus steps inside the doorway he is overwhelmed by sweet fragrances. The perfumer comes over to him with a smile: "May I help you?"

Rome, Already a City of the Arts in the Age of Empire

Hilarus had to sniff a lot of terra-cotta jars before he found the right fragrance for his sister. He got a few extra jars of it; not too many, because in this era perfumes don't last very long and their scent decays rapidly.

As you might imagine, there were some women in the shop; some men came in, too, to purchase some personal items. If you think cosmetics use by men is a modern trend, you're mistaken. Back in the Roman era lots of men were in the habit of anointing themselves with perfumes and creams. And it wasn't unusual for a man's toilette to last quite a long time. Professor Romolo Augusto Staccioli has observed that many men "competed with one another in showing off their use of the most extravagant fragrances and spent hours in the barber shop having themselves perfumed." He goes on to inform us that at banquets and in public places, such as at the circus or the amphitheater, there was a generous distribution of scented substances, sometimes even sprayed on the seats, to cover the smell of blood and death coming from the arena where gladiators, condemned criminals, and animals had been killed.

When Hilarus paid for the perfume, our sestertius changed hands once again. But it didn't remain in the shop of the perfumer Sextus Aparronius Justinus for very long. Shortly after Hilarus's exit an elegant, wealthy Roman comes in, his affluence transmitted by his stature and appearance: tall, robust, white hair, black eyebrows, blue eyes, and a forthright, confident gaze. His prominent, aquiline nose accentuates the nobility of his countenance. He is accompanied by his slaves and *clientes*, or people who have come to ask for favors. He receives many requests a day; he is a prominent citizen.

He thanks the perfumer for his purchase and, looking at our sestertius, which he has been given as change, reveals to us his philosophy of life: *homo sine pecunia est imago mortis*—a man without money is the image of death. It is a phrase that is frighteningly real in Roman society, where the only thing that counts is social status and people are judged according to the rank their wealth has allowed them to attain.

Then, with the same elegance with which he entered, he picks up his perfume in its dove-shaped glass container, makes his way out the door with his retinue of slaves and "clients," and climbs into his litter. Direction: the Portico of Octavia, where he is going to meet his wife and surprise her with a gift of perfume.

The Portico of Octavia is an isolated place, removed from the crowded streets, an ideal place to go for a peaceful stroll. With its many bronze Greek statues, it's a veritable museum. Incidentally, by Trajan's time ancient Rome is already a center of art, with its own museums and many dedicated visitors.

This is but one of the many faces of Rome. At the time it would have been considered the ancient counterpart of New York for its tall buildings, Amsterdam for its red-light districts, Calcutta for its neighborhoods of destitute poor, Rio de Janeiro for its festivals and enormous stadiums (the Colosseum and the Circus Maximus, equivalents of the Maracanã), but also Paris for its great museums. No city today brings together all of these characteristics.

To be sure, it might seem odd to think of ancient Rome as a center of the arts. What objects of ancient art can be put on display in a place that is itself part of the ancient world?

First and foremost, the art of Greece.

Initially, Rome was a "cold" city, with no artistic masterpieces to speak of. Everything changed with the onset of expansion and the wars of conquest, especially the Punic Wars. As underlined by Lionel Casson, after the conquest of Syracuse a lot of Greek statues and paintings were taken to Rome by General Marcellus and distributed in various points of the city. It was like opening a dam. For the next 150 years, as Rome expanded its empire to the territories of Greece and what is now Turkey, large numbers of masterpieces of every kind were brought to the city: hundreds of bronze statues at a time, works of the greatest sculptors of the past.

On the occasion of the conquest of the Greek city of Ambracia, for example, 285 bronze statues and more than 230 marble ones were brought to Rome. After his victory over King Perseus, Aemilius Paulus brought back so many masterpieces that his victory parade lasted an entire day. Then came Corinth.

Picture these Greek cities with their shrines and temples totally plundered. Witnesses from the time spoke of empty foundations, with holes where statues had once been anchored to the floor. Throughout the course of antiquity, the Middle Ages, and the Renaissance that was the price of defeat. Everyone knew it.

Today we would call it looting. To this day many countries are still confronting the issues of these spoils of war. How does a country decide to give back what by now has become part of its own cultural heritage? Italy has been very sensible in this regard. It has returned the immense obelisk of Axum to Ethiopia, a fragment of the friezes of the Parthenon to Greece, and even a Roman (!) statue of Venus to Libya, to cite just a few of the examples that have made the news. This is an approach that we hope will continue to be adopted around the world as a remedy for the plundering, thefts and "illegitimate appropriations" of the past.

The City's Museums

Two thousand years ago these concepts were unknown. An enormous number of ships, therefore, had transported to Rome a true treasure trove of art, plundering the Greek world. Sea voyages were highly risky in those times, and storms at sea constituted a sort of "anti-seacraft" battery that sunk many of the transport ships. The statues that sometimes re-emerge today from the bottom of the Mediterranean, like the Riace bronzes, for example, are often from the classical period. And who knows how many more are still down there, buried under a layer of fine sand or at a depth too deep to be salvaged. We trust that future archaeological techniques will be able to identify them, recover them, and bring them to museums where they can be admired.

In the Roman era these works were displayed in temples and public places, but during the republic there was a kind of mania among wealthy Romans for collecting art works in their private homes. The villas of powerful families had special rooms and spaces used exclusively for the display of paintings and statues—true private museums.

We know that Cicero was one of these collectors. And Verres, the governor of Sicily whom Cicero took to court for his opprobrious thefts (winning the case), was capable of obtaining works of art through extortion (like the famous *Eros of Thespiea* by Praxiteles, separated from its owner for a paltry sum) or by confiscating them or, even worse, by paying hoodlums to steal them.

With the advent of the empire things changed. Greek art was returned to public places thanks to Julius Caesar and Augustus, who inspired all the subsequent empires to do the same over the next two hundred years. Rome became an open-air museum.

The most famous pieces on display were masterworks by Praxiteles, Polyclitus, Lysippus, Myron, Apelles, Zeuxis, and Scopas. They would have been admired in the main "museums" of the city, actually places where people gathered for a variety of reasons: for the pleasure of taking a stroll, as in the Portico of Octavia (where they could admire Praxiteles' *Eros of Thespiae* or the twenty-five bronze statues by Lysippus of *Alexander's Squadron*), or for sporting events, as at the Circus Maximus (where one could view Myron's *Hercules*). Those who attended religious rituals might find themselves in the company of great masterpieces: the famous paintings of Apelles, for example, were in the Temple of Diana and the Temple of Divine Julius (Caesar). Even people who went to the baths passed by immortal works such as the statue of *Apoxyomenos* by Lysippus at the baths of Agrippa. Finally, lots of other artworks were conserved on the Capitoline (Praxiteles' *Kairos* and *Tyche*, and Lysippus's *Hercules*, etc.)

This brief list, which does not include theaters and other gathering places, shows us that Rome was not just the administrative, economic, and military capital of the empire, but that it had also become the world capital of art. It is saddening to think of how many of its masterpieces would be destroyed over the years by natural disasters, like the big fire that occurred during Nero's reign, or because of the simple need to recycle the bronze for other purposes, as happened during the Middle Ages.

Rome was not only home to art museums; there were also objects and collections on view that could be defined as archaeological-historical and naturalistic. We could admire the sword of Julius Caesar in the Temple of Mars Ultor (later stolen, as often happens in many modern museums). In the Temple of Jupiter, we could see the dagger that killed Nero, and in another temple, the skin of a huge snake killed by legionnaires in proconsular Africa (Tunisia) during the first Punic War. Moving on to the Capitoline Hill, we could admire a spectacular block of crystal weighing a hundred pounds.

These collections alone (to which we could add others of jewelry and precious stones—Caesar alone had six different collections put on display in the Temple of Venus Genetrix) allow us to see that the Romans took pleasure in nurturing the mind with culture, something that is often overlooked when we restrict our view of ancient Rome to the pleasures of banquets and the killing of gladiators in the Colosseum.

Rome—just like any other city, ancient or modern—has its public face, made up of monuments, temples and shrines, and landmarks. But what of the private lives that unfold all around them? All of the locations we are visiting also have a place, naturally, in a different sort of geography of the city; for example, the geography of courtship. The walls and silent blueprints of the buildings discovered by archaeologists in Rome can't tell us the best place in ancient Rome to look at the sunset, or where to go to meet eligible women or men. The Latin poets, on the other hand, are good sources for that kind of thing. Especially Ovid, who in his *Ars Amatoria* points out the best places to go looking for love!

According to him, the capital of the empire is full of beautiful women.

> Your Rome's as many girls as Gargara's sheaves,
> as Methymna's grapes, as fishes in the sea,
> as birds in the hidden branches, stars in the sky:
> Venus, Aeneas's mother, haunts his city...
> If it's young girls you want, thousands will please you.
> You'll be forced to be unsure of your desires:
> if you delight greatly in older wiser years,
> here too, believe me, there's an even greater crowd.

Ovid's encouraging words seem to indicate a certain availability of Roman women, especially mature ones. We'll never know for sure how much any of this corresponds to reality. But the striking thing is the precision of his "geographical" advice. Ovid suggests, in fact, to go searching under the Portico of Pompey, and also under those of Livia and Apollo, where works of art could be found. Art and quiet are much loved by women in a chaotic city like Rome. Caesar's Forum, next to the Temple of Venus, near the fountain, is another perfect place, to hear Ovid tell it. To this list he also adds a temple of an Egyptian cult, the Temple of Isis. Why? According to Ovid, because it was frequented by women who went there above all to pray for fertility. Quite a cynical choice for a Latin lover...

And then there's the theater. The poet considers the theaters true "hunting preserves" for prowling swain.

But hunt for them, especially, at the tiered theatre:
that place is the most fruitful for your needs.
There you'll find one to love, or one you can play with,
one to be with just once, or one you might wish to keep.

Ovid could certainly never be accused of feminism; nor could most of society in the ancient world. In Ovid's view, women went to the theater in large numbers, theaters being one of the social spaces in ancient Rome. He claims that they certainly went there to view performances but also to be looked at.

As ants return home often in long processions,
carrying their favorite food in their mouths . . .
so our fashionable ladies crowd to the famous shows:
my choice is often constrained by such richness.
They come to see, they come to be seen as well:
the place is fatal to chaste modesty.

But the circus, where one goes for chariot races, is perhaps the place that offers the most opportunities for finding romance, because there's a crowd, there's confusion, you don't have to transmit messages back and forth with your eyes as at the theater. You can even sit right next to a woman or man, and things are much more direct.

At this point, Ovid gives a series of suggestions on how to land a woman at the Circus Maximus. Today we may laugh at their artifice, but they are valuable and interesting because they describe for us the concerns and habits of people in a bygone world. Here is a brief list compiled from his work.

- Take advantage of the most highly promoted races, with the most famous horses. The Circus is jammed and this offers a series of advantages and opportunities. And there's no need to rely on nods or secret hand signals.
- It's essential to be quick to sit next to the woman you want to court.
- Sit as close to her as possible, taking advantage of the narrow seats, and try to make physical contact; it helps the approach.

- Find an excuse to start up a conversation (the words of the arena's announcer always provide some excellent prompts).
- Figure out which stable or horse the girl is rooting for so you can second her and rejoice with her.
- Be a very attentive cavalier: plump up her cushion, cool her with makeshift fans when it's hot, procure a wooden stool to put under her feet, or be careful that the person sitting behind her doesn't press their knees against her back.
- Find a thousand excuses to manage to caress her or touch her in some way. For example, use your fingers to shake the lap of her dress to remove any dust (real or imagined) raised by the chariots.
- With the excuse of not wanting to dirty the edge of her tunic or let her mantle drag on the ground, lift up one side of it. If the girl doesn't object you'll have a chance to look at her legs!

In other words, any excuse will do, or, as Ovid himself points out, "the little things are all it takes to win over light hearts."

Naturally, we'll take it upon ourselves to add, courtship works only when the other party wants to be courted: the man merely appears to be the hunter; in reality it's the woman who lets herself be captured and who captures in turn.

Free Bread for (Just About) Everybody

Our coin has changed hands. Now it's in the purse of a man, one of the *clientes* of the *dominus*. He received it as a *sportula*, a donation from his powerful lord. The *dominus* hands something out, whether food or money, to his *clientes* every morning.

Let's follow this man on the streets of Rome. He looks to be about twenty-five. His name is Marcus; we hear a barber call him by that name as he passes the shop.

Now he's walking along the wall on the side of the Balbus Theater. Of the three large theaters in Rome, this is the smallest, with a capacity of 7,700 people. But for the Romans it's a little jewel because it's the most beautifully decorated. Everyone will tell you about, for example, the six little columns of onyx, black and shiny, that can be seen on the inside, true masterpieces of nature. And of sculpture, given the fragility of the stone.

But this man is not the least bit interested in the theater; he keeps on walking at a fast pace. We notice that he's carrying an empty sack in one hand. What is it for? And where is he going? Let's try to find out.

On the corner at the end of the street, a beggar sprawled on the ground raises his hand as Marcus passes. The beggar hasn't chosen that spot by chance. He had to fight to get it because it's a strategic point for begging. Actually, we hadn't noticed until now, but the street is lined with beggars, sitting on the ground and leaning against the walls. Desperate people, some of them seem to be nothing more than a pile of rags. Among them are women with small children. Their faces are dirty and their cheeks hollow. These people are hungry. But the man doesn't even deign to look at them. There are always so many of them when he comes here; he can't help all of them.

Having gone through the entrance, he comes into a large square, where a small crowd has gathered. There must be more than a hundred people, all of them carrying a sack like his. They're all lined up single file, as if they are outside the box office for some big event. Indeed, the head of the line is under the portico of a large building. We don't know what's inside.

Our man gets in line too. We try to figure out who the people are in front of him. But they're all so different; they don't seem to have anything in common, apart from the empty sack. There are old men and young men, blond and dark-haired, curly-haired and straight, skinny and fat . . . a real sample of the male inhabitants of Rome. All right, they do have something in common—they are all men. So perhaps this has to do with some administrative procedure from which women are excluded. Many of the men are holding cards made out of wood or lead.

Let's review what we've seen: an empty sack, everyone in line, a card, and a lot of diverse men outside . . . . That's it: this must be the place where the free distribution of grain is held, the so-called *frumentatio*! Indeed, not much time passes before we see an old man coming down the stairs with some difficulty, carrying a full sack, with the help of his nephew. Every so often some grains spill out of a hole in the cloth, unleashing a furious fight among the poor as soon as the two men emerge onto the street.

How to Satisfy (Just About) Everybody's Needs

This is one of Rome's many surprises. Every month there is a free distribution of about five *modii* of grain, seventy-five to eighty pounds (a *modius* is about fifteen to sixteen pounds). But not everyone has the right to receive the dole. One has to be listed on the official registry of recipients, which excludes women and children. The requirements are simple: you have to be a citizen of Rome residing in Rome. At that point you are part of the *accipientes*, the beneficiaries of these free distributions. You get a card made of wood or lead on which are inscribed not only your name but also the number of the arch where the grain will be distributed and the established day. It's an effective system for dividing up the army of people, 200,000 strong, who have a right to these free distributions. Every day, in fact, 150 men show up in front of each arch.

These numbers make your head spin, and they require an extraordinarily efficient administrative and organizational structure. This structure is the *annona,* or food administration board, which guarantees the citizens of Rome the satisfaction of one of their primary needs: their daily supply of bread. At its head is a prefect (*praefectus annonae*) who supervises the whole operation: he is a proper minister of grain. It's not an easy job. He not only has to distribute the grain, he first has to procure it from throughout the empire, organize its shipment to Rome, and store it in special warehouses from which it will be distributed.

This is how it all started, in the early centuries of the republic. The grain was supplied by the regions near Rome and shipped to the city. In the beginning the distributions were not free, but, a little like what happens today with oil, there were strategic reserves set up in the city to be used in case of famine or to lower the retail price of bread whenever it got too high.

At first, the grain was sold at a subsidized price, much lower than the market price, and finally in 58 BC, with the approval of the *Lex Claudia Frumentaria,* it was decided that grain would be distributed for free to all citizens of Rome (especially to the less well-off), except for members of the Senate who, being for the most part big landowners, certainly didn't need it, and the members of the equestrian order, the very wealthy entrepreneurs of the time. This meant that each year Rome distributed grain to three hundred thousand people (later reduced to two hundred thousand).

The line of people moves forward, albeit slowly. The men of the *annona* are very well-organized. In the meantime the men in line chat, laugh, or try to mooch a free dinner (this is one of the preferred activities on the streets of Rome). We instead make a few calculations, which lead us to ask a question. If the number of people fed is two hundred thousand, that amounts to eighty-four thousand tons of grain per year. Where do they come by all that grain? On our way here, coming down the Tiber, we didn't notice any immense fields of grain around Rome. Or in the rest of Italy.

The "Oil Wells" of the Roman Empire

The answer is simple: they bring it in from the areas of the empire that produce it in large quantities, such as Sicily, Sardinia, Spain, North Africa, and above all, Egypt. Together these areas manage to provide much more grain than required, up to two hundred thousand tons per year.

In particular, North Africa and Egypt are the breadbaskets of the empire. The historian Flavius Josephus, who lived in the age of Trajan, claimed that Africa alone (that is, present-day Tunisia) would have been able to feed Rome for eight months if necessary, and Egypt four. Taken together, in other words, they could satisfy Rome's grain demand for an entire year. And this helps us understand their strategic importance for Rome.

They are, in effect, Rome's "Saudi Arabia." In the absence of industrial technologies and machines, bread is the indispensable fuel that powered the minds and muscles of the empire, from administrators to artisans to soldiers. (Interestingly, a loaf of bread in the days of the empire provided up to twice the calories of our modern equivalents.)

To continue with the oil analogy, the Roman era, like today, had its "tankers": large ships for the transport of grain that set sail on the Mediterranean as soon as weather conditions permitted. (Because of the threat of storms at sea, navigation was interrupted every year from November to the beginning of March.)

When, with the onset of spring, the sails of these big ships appear on the horizon, the news travels immediately to Rome and spreads among its inhabitants, who burst into celebration. With year-round access to fresh food in our supermarkets, it's hard for us to fully appreciate this aspect of Roman life.

And the Roman era also has its "supertankers": they are immense ships, supersized for antiquity, with a capacity to transport enormous quantities of grain. We may meet up with some of them during our journey through the empire. They are so huge that when they get to Italy they can't tie up at the docks; they have to anchor offshore and transship their precious cargo onto smaller vessels.

The sacks of grain arrive first at the port of Trajan, next to Ostia, then travel up the Tiber against the current, on ships suited to fluvial navigation (*naves caudicariae*), pulled by bulls or slaves. These boats carry the grain to a series of docks, right under the Aventine, where the grain is unloaded and stored in gigantic warehouses (*horrea*), some of which are several stories tall. Inside them are stored all the foodstuffs, not only grain, to be distributed to the populace. Everything is overseen with great care by the *horreari*.

But how do the Romans convince the provinces to "give" two hundred thousand tons of grain each year to the inhabitants of Rome? Simple: this is one of the taxes that the provinces have to pay. And they pay it in goods rather than money. They are direct taxes generally or rents for public or imperial agricultural land.

The interesting fact, as revealed by Professor Elio Lo Cascio of Frederick II University in Naples, is that this is the way a considerable part of the city's population is fed (not everyone: slaves, freed slaves, and foreigners are excluded). When all is said and done, the system satisfies the basic needs of a head of family and, perhaps, another family member (his wife or a child), allowing them to use their own money to purchase other necessary items or more food. In this way, one of the wheels of the economy is kept turning. And it's not a small wheel, seeing that Rome is the biggest city in the empire and in all of antiquity.

So now it's finally our turn. Marcus shows his card to an employee of the annona, sitting at a table. The atmosphere is very relaxed. As he's copying down the information he chats with his colleagues who are distributing the grain, telling them about his brother-in-law's faux pas last night at dinner. Everybody laughs. But when it comes time to actually hand over the grain, silence fills the room, and the man in charge of the delivery measures out with precision the *modii* to be supplied. The *modius* is a wood or iron bucket that hold about fifteen or sixteen pounds of grain. To guarantee that nobody in the administration cheats by using buckets that are just a little smaller, the bucket has an iron cross on the top. Anyone who wants to can measure the arms of the cross and verify that the bucket is the right size.

There is something almost artistic about this ritual. Every time the slave pours the grain into the *modius*, right up to the brim. Naturally, a small mound is created that the man in charge has to level off, removing the excess grain with a sort of T-shaped shovel, called a *rutellum*. His rotating movements recall those of a pastry chef spreading the icing on the cake or perhaps the moves of someone making a crêpe, spreading the batter on the hot griddle.

In just a few minutes Marcus's sack is full and he is on his way, saying farewell to everyone. For this month his bread is guaranteed.

The Praetorian

The next morning, Marcus enters a shop; he needs a new tunic and is trying some on for size. They look like so many T-shirts that go down to his knees. They are produced in a series of workshops where workers and slaves are employed—somewhere between the shop of a real craftsman and a semi-industrial factory. Marcus tries several of them with the help of the shop owner, always willing to adjust the fabric where it bulges. He chooses a simple one, without colored strips or decorations, similar to the clothes worn by most of the inhabitants of Rome. It's made of raw flax and when he pulls it over his head he can feel it scratching his skin. It will take a while for it to soften. He pays 15 sesterces for it (about $40) and leaves, heading down the street illuminated by a beam of morning sun. Our sestertius has changed hands again. Now it's deep in the darkness of the shop's cash box, mixed in with a lot of other coins, each with its own history, each with a lot of stories and curiosities to be told that nobody will ever know.

It's not long, however, before our sestertius is back on its journey, thanks to another customer who has come to purchase some *subligaria*, Roman underwear that look like soft loincloths that loop around the waist and pass between the legs.

The next morning, the sestertius is in the hand of its new owner, who is turning it nervously. The man's name is Caius Proculeius Rufus. His family hails from Spain, from Asturica Augusta (present-day Astorga), to be exact. Having finished a training period, he is about to start his new job. He's dressed like a soldier, but he is not a legionnaire who will be sent to defend the far-flung corners of the empire. On the contrary, he is part of the corps that must defend its heart. He is a praetorian. And today is his first day of service in the emperor's palace, on the Palatine.

The praetorians are not universally loved, and certainly not by their comrades-in-arms the legionnaires, who guard the frontiers. The reason is simple. They do not serve in some forgotten backwater of the empire, but in the world's liveliest and most entertaining city, Rome. They do not risk getting killed every day by some raving barbarian. They don't suffer the cold, in a foreign land, far from home. Yet their salaries are higher than those of the legionnaires (who receive barely 100 sesterces per month, around $225). Their period of service is shorter (sixteen years rather than twenty-five), they get greater benefits on leaving the service, have more opportunities for promotion, and if a new emperor comes to power (and has to ingratiate himself with this "elite personal guard") they receive attractive cash bonuses. There is plenty of reason for their battle-scarred colleagues to look upon the praetorians with disdain and jealousy, if not downright hatred. And the same goes for the populace, which does not love them, even if they respect them for their power. In reality, the praetorians are very powerful on the political level, first and foremost because they are often involved in the intrigues that accompany an emperor's fall from power or his successor's rise to the throne.

This doesn't mean that they are never involved in combat. When the emperor goes on a campaign, the praetorians go with him. But not all of them. Of the ten cohorts stationed in Rome, a small portion stays behind to guard the imperial palaces and properties. Our new praetorian belongs to this last group.

The man reported for duty at dawn and his colleagues made him wait in a small service room, at the guard post, where he is pacing back and forth nervously. He has to wait for the change of shift before he can go in. The rules here are followed to the letter.

He hears some approaching footsteps. The door opens and, standing tall against the sunlight, a praetorian in full uniform presents himself. He is our man's direct superior. This praetorian has just commanded the change of the guard and his sparkling helmet, with gold decorations and a mane of bright white ostrich feathers, make him seem even taller. Actually, the praetorians resemble modern Italy's cuirassiers—the elite guard of the President of the Republic: tall, with a uniform that is strikingly elegant. Their colors are as pure as the driven snow: their tunics are white, not red like those of the legionnaires, and so is their *subarmalis vestis*— those large, flat dangling strips that form a kind of skirt on the statues of Roman condottieri. Actually, they are the end pieces of a short-sleeved, padded, leather battle vest to be worn under their armor, which sticks out at the bottom with that skirt. The padding protects the praetorians' bodies from being chafed by the metal of their armor, and the vest blunts the effects of blows received in battle.

In short, the praetorians' white uniform symbolizes purity. Naturally the weapons they use are old favorites: a gladius, a dagger, a lance, and a shield emblazoned with their symbol, a scorpion. Why the scorpion? Given their reputation for courtly intrigue, the choice of a poisonous animal seems ill-advised. In reality, it is meant to recall the important reorganization of the praetorian guard implemented by Tiberius, in the month of June, under the constellation of Scorpio.

After the obligatory formal presentations, the superior removes all his parade armor, hangs it in a cabinet in the guard post, and accompanies the freshly enlisted recruit on his first tour of the emperor's palace.

Thanks to this new keeper of the sestertius we are now able to explore the palace of the Roman emperors. It really is the place where the most powerful men of antiquity lived and reigned: the Roman-era equivalent of the White House. As we follow them, we wonder about the place where the palace is located: why of all the hills of Rome did they choose to put it on the Palatine?

The Palatine, Where It All Started

The Palatine is certainly one of the most important hills in the history of Rome. We've all heard of it. Why is it so important?

According to the legend, Romulus and Remus were raised by a she-wolf in a cave right here on the Palatine. And it was also on this hill that Romulus is said to have founded Rome in 753 BCE, subsequently killing Remus. But apart from the legend, one fact is certain. Archaeologists have discovered holes that were dug here for the poles that supported some incredibly ancient cabins. The Palatine has been inhabited from as early as the eighth century BCE. Certainly not by Romulus and Remus, but by people of the Iron Age.

They chose to live on this hill because from the top (and from the top of the nearby Aventine Hill) they could dominate the only traversable point of the Tiber, a ford near Tiber Island. A strategic position, therefore, for the economy as well. The first market areas of Rome, as we have seen, grew up at the foot of the Palatine and Capitoline Hills: the Boarian Forum for livestock and the Olitorian Forum for vegetables.

So the Romans were not wrong to imagine that the place where Rome was founded, the place where their power originated, was on the Palatine Hill. But they imagined it in a mythical way. Before Romulus and Remus, as the story goes, the hill was inhabited by some Greeks who were supposed to have met Hercules and, later, Aeneas. On this hill, then, as chance would have it, were the most noble ingredients for the birth of Rome.

When the city began to grow, the hill was home to the people who mattered—the patrician families, the senators. They had sumptuous houses with mosaics, frescoes, colonnades, and internal gardens. Almost all of the most famous inhabitants of Rome lived here, from Cicero to Catullus to Marc Antony, and many, many others.

And one day, here on this hill, the future Augustus was born. When he became an adult he decided to live here. It's incredible, but two thousand years later the house of Augustus and that of his wife, Livia, adjacent to it, are still visible and open to the public. Inside, you can still see the frescoes with their vivid colors—fiery reds, deep blues, and bright greens. It is astonishing to think about all the times Augustus must have gazed with his own eyes at these very same frescoes, absorbed in who knows what thoughts.

And you can still see his "cubicle," a small room with painstakingly restored pictures and decorations. This is where Augustus meditated, wrote, and relaxed. Its simplicity surprises us: the most powerful man in the empire did not surround himself with luxury. His simplicity was certainly a lesson for everyone in the Roman era.

But Augustus's successors were not equally modest. Over the span of a century the Palatine changed its face radically, to the point that it became one gigantic, grandiose royal palace that was home to a long series of emperors.

Still today, if you walk up the side of the Roman Forum, leaving behind you the throngs of tourists, you find yourself suddenly immersed in the silence of the greenery among the imposing ruins of the emperors' palaces. It's lovely to sit here and read, or simply to stop and think. You are sitting in one of the central places of history. This is the birthplace of our way of thinking, of living; the birthplace of our modern world.

The Palace of the Roman Emperors

The two praetorians are standing in front of a huge building, full of multicolored marble, columns, and statues. It's about the size of a cathedral. Yet it's only the beginning of the imperial palace.

This extraordinary structure was built by the emperor Domitian toward the end of the first century CE (Tiberius had already begun construction but on a smaller project). Domitian's architect, Rabirius, came up with a winning idea: divide the palace in two: a public area, where the emperor worked, and a private area, where he lived and rested. Both parts, obviously, were overflowing with luxury.

For our visit we'll follow the two soldiers who have just slipped under a colonnade. The first stop is a praetorian guard post, a room identified today as the *larario* (a room dedicated to the cult of the household divinities, the *lari*), but actually a sort of small barracks whose back wall is covered with lances and swords ready for use. It's a completely furnished armory. This is the room that controls the entrance to the palace.

The two soldiers each put on a toga. It's obligatory attire in the palace, just like a jacket and tie are worn in the presidential palace, the Senate, or the Parliament today. Then the superior opens a door and invites the new recruit to enter first. He does it with a smile because he knows the effect it will have on the young soldier, just twenty years old. The youngster goes through the doorway and is struck dumb. He's just entered the Royal Hall, the great throne room where the emperor holds audiences. His gaze wanders through the expanse of the awesome space, the same sensation we might feel today on entering Saint Peter's Basilica for the first time. It's a breathtakingly tall space, all lined with precious marble.

To the side, all around him, the young praetorian runs his eyes up and down a beautiful series of columns faced with *pavonazzetto* marble (characterized by irregular veins of dark red, with blue and yellow tints), and walls covered with polychrome marbles. All around are niches with statues in black basalt. He immediately recognizes two of the figures, Hercules and Apollo (they will be rediscovered in the eighteenth century and are now on display in the Museum of Archaeology in Parma). It is a solemn space, emitting a breathtaking grandiosity. Instinctively, the young man lifts his gaze upward. A second series of columns runs all around the perimeter with arches faced in multicolored marble panels. And higher still is a series of large windows through which wide beams of sunlight stream silently down to rest on the pavement.

The ceiling, which is probably more than seventy feet high, is coffered and supported by an orderly forest of trusses. From down here on the floor it's hard to tell, but it seems to be made of gilded wood and it is an amazing masterwork, sculpted by the most skilled artisans of the age.

The lad moves further into the room. He is stunned. This room is nearly 130 feet long and almost 100 feet wide. Now he's looking down at the floor: it is a huge checkerboard made of marble squares, as big as dining-room tables, each of which has a green or pink disc in the center, or a square of red marble. It seems almost like the formation of a legion made of marble.

The young praetorian has come to a halt on an island of light created by one of the windows. His body seems to be wrapped in a luminous aura that stands out against the semidarkness of the niches all around him. In front of him is a semicircular apse with a marble platform. On the top sits the throne of Emperor Trajan. So here is where the most powerful man in the world sits and commands. It is here that he dispenses justice. The young man is petrified.

The throne has not been used for a while because Trajan is far away from here, busy with the wars against the Parthians, Rome's Asiatic enemies. But when he is in Rome it is in this very room that he holds his audiences and meets with ambassadors. If Rome is the heart of the empire, this is the heart of Rome, and therefore of everything. Chills run down our spines when we think of how much history has taken place here, how many decisions were made right here. Decisions that are now the subject matter of our history books.

This great hall is not only an architectural masterpiece; it is an instrument of politics. It was made to look like this so as to transmit, on first glance, the power and wealth of the empire. For almost three hundred years, awestruck by the dimensions and the sumptuousness of the spaces, foreign delegations will be received here by emperors.

The two soldiers continue on their tour.

A door opens and a large courtyard appears, surrounded by columns of antique yellow marble. A large square pool nearly fills the entire surface area of the courtyard. In the center of it a fountain gushes and all around it there emerges, at the water line, a marble labyrinth in the shape of an octagon, for aquatic special effects.

Naturally, during the tour the superior explains to the new praetorian his duties, the palace rules, the changes of the guard, and so forth, but the lad is distracted. Beyond the pool more doors open up. It's the emperor's dining room, identical to the great hall in form, marbles, and decorations, but a bit smaller. This triclinium room, also called the Coenatio Iovis, changes temperature according to the seasons. Under the polychrome marble floor there are empty spaces where hot air is forced through in winter, like at the baths. In the summer, on the other hand, the room is cooled by two nymphaea or grotto-like niches with fountains and water spouts that open out onto the room on both sides. Trajan eats stretched out inside a large semicircular niche set on a raised platform.

The young praetorian's visit continues in the private area where the emperor lives. This second part of the palace (Domus Augustiana), which forms a single block with the part we have just visited (Domus Flavia), develops on two stories, exploiting a depression of the Palatine. The floor of the lower level is forty feet below the floor of the upper level, or about four stories of a normal building. It is a truly immense living area.

The two praetorians cross rooms with extraordinarily high ceilings, where the only sound is the reverberation of their own footsteps. In other, smaller rooms, all they can hear is the sound of water spouting from small fountains. Along their itinerary they are surrounded by an endless collection of busts, marbles, and Greek statues. It may be one of the most beautiful exhibitions of ancient art ever seen. But we'll never be able to see it . . . it has all been plundered over the centuries. The masterpieces encountered by the two praetorians, from frescoes to sculpture, are too numerous to count, but we do make note of a couple. Most surprising is a large pool surrounded by an elegant colonnade. At the center there is an island with a small temple dedicated to Minerva. This idea will be copied by Hadrian in his fabulous villa in Tivoli.

The two praetorians discover the second wonder upon opening a large door: suddenly they are in a small Eden. It's a garden, 500 feet long and 150 feet wide. Looking down on it from above, the young praetorian sees trees, aromatic bushes, geometric flowerbeds, and then fountains and works of art. But also birds, turtle doves and peacocks. Running all around the perimeter is a two-story colonnade. It's easy to imagine the emperor taking a stroll here, or meditating, or delighting in the company of a personal friend.

Some slaves are silently working in the garden. Even though the emperor and empress are not in residence, everything is kept in order and cleaned on a daily basis in case the imperial couple should return without warning. They even put fresh flowers in the vases on the tables in the various rooms every day.

The young soldier has seen very few members of the house staff going through the rooms. Where are the servants? His superior shows him a descending staircase. In no time they have descended to the "technical" sector of the palace. It's a network of tunnels used by slaves, servants with tools and equipment, carts, and so on, but also by praetorians—all so as not to disturb the upper floors. (Again, Hadrian will use the same system in his villa in Tivoli.)

The absence of the imperial couple has made it possible to conduct this relaxed visit of the palace and grounds. If they had been present, with all their guards and commitments, our visit would have followed a much different pace. The two praetorians have even been granted free access to the emperor's baths, whose water is supplied by a branch of the Claudius aqueduct.

Their last stop is spectacular. As the sun is setting, the two soldiers come out onto a balcony that overlooks the Circus Maximus.

When Trajan stands on this balcony, with all of Rome around him and the red disk of the sun bowing before him, it must truly seem like he has the whole world at his feet.

CIRCUS MAXIMUS

~ *The Secrets of Ben Hur* ~

The next evening the praetorian Caius Proculeius Rufus goes to celebrate his new, challenging post with some friends. When the bill comes the praetorian pays for everyone. And one of the coins he uses to pay is our sestertius. So, as it leaves behind the laughter of the partiers, our coin begins a new adventure. But it doesn't go very far. At a nearby table a man with an absent look and a pointed beard is seated alone. He's the one who receives our sestertius in his change. Where will it take us now?

A Fast-Paced Jaunt Through the Backstreets of Rome

The outstretched arm of the statue of Augustus seems to point to some far-off place in the pitch black night. Some drops of water hang suspended on the underside of the gilt-bronze limb. Indeed, it rained in Rome tonight, as we can tell from the wet roofs and from the drops that are still dripping down from the top floors of the *insulae*. Dawn is still a ways off, and the air is cold and humid; the few passersby, wrapped up in capes and mantles, scurry along, hugging the walls of the buildings as though they were shadows. They try to avoid the big puddles that have formed on the narrow streets, skirting around the edges or jumping over them.

Yes, in this city the puddle problem seems like it will never go away. The main streets, well paved with slabs of stone and modeled in a convex, "donkey's back" shape to make the rain water run off to the sides, are often forced to surrender to extemporaneous dams of city trash—broken baskets, rotten fruit, rags—that create long lakes along the borders of the sidewalks. The shopkeepers and residents constantly complain, but the administration has too many problems to deal with; and actually, all it takes is a broom to put things back in order. On the back and side streets, however, there is no solution. They are unpaved, and when it rains they are best avoided because they turn into quagmires.

Our coin is now in the hands of the tall, thin man with the pointed beard who was sitting alone last night at the table next to the praetorian and his friends. From the way he's dressed he doesn't look to be wealthy. His cape is a hodgepodge of patches and mendings. And his cream-colored tunic is worn and frayed in a number of places. Yet he doesn't look like a slave, or a poor person either. There's something strange about this man. He's walking at a brisk pace as though he were late for an appointment. He frequently steps into small puddles, the dirty water seeping into his sandals and squishing out in muddy spurts between his sandal straps and toes. But it doesn't seem to bother him. He's preoccupied with something, an anxiety that you can read on his face. What can it be? Why is he walking so fast?

After turning a corner the man darts suddenly into the entryway to a building, just in time to avoid a big wagon passing by on the street that misses him by a hair. It came out of nowhere.

It's part of a fleet of wagons that drives through the city every night to resupply the stores and shops. During the day, as we have noted, the wagons are not allowed to circulate. There's always traffic, but in daylight it's the human kind. Walking on the main streets of ancient Rome, then, is the equivalent of walking today through a crowded Métro station at rush hour. You're always getting bumped into; it's impossible to walk in a straight line; you have to swerve to avoid slaves, obese men, gaggles of chattering women, litters. At night, on the other hand, the streets are nearly empty, but as we've just seen, they can also be dangerous.

The man has had a good scare; he was too absorbed in his thoughts, and the wagon driver had even accelerated at the intersection, yelling a curse at him after the near miss. But there's no use getting upset with this road hog: people like him are violent and irascible. Now he's vanished in the darkness, going through another intersection with a long shout of defiance. He drives at a breakneck pace because if he doesn't get out of the city before dawn, he risks having to pay a big fine and maybe even having his vehicle impounded.

Our man breathes a sigh of relief and resumes his walk. If he had been run over, nobody would have come to his aid. Nobody would have stopped the wagon. At dawn he would have been just another dead man on the streets of Rome: killed in a robbery or a drunken brawl, fallen in a pitched battle between the poor and the desperate, or massacred by a band of young thugs, or a victim of hunger or cold. Night in Rome is like night on the savannah: there are lots of predators waiting to strike.

Now dawn is brightening the sky and the man has almost arrived at his destination. We're about to discover what is making him so anxious.

He's slowed his pace. The farther he goes down the street, the more people there are around him, almost as though he were moving through a galaxy of human beings. They are all on the move; it's a crowd that is all heading toward the same destination, at the end of the street. It's an unusual scene, almost biblical.

The sides of the street are no longer like the ones he walked down to get here. Not at all: dawn has not broken yet, but all the shops on the street are already open, as indicated by the lighted oil lamps bobbing up and down above their entrances. They form a long chain of points of light all the way down to the end of the street.

A lot of *popinae* have already opened for business. In the dim light of the oil lamps hanging from the ceiling, the man sees their customers leaning on the counters, biting into grilled sausages or focaccia buns dipped in honey. A waitress pours some steaming liquid into some terra-cotta mugs. Given the hour, coffee pops immediately into our minds, but it is completely unknown in Roman times.

Actually, in 117 CE, coffee, which will one day become a worldwide symbol of the Italian lifestyle, served as espresso or cappuccino, is still growing wild on the high plateaus of Ethiopia. It will take another fifteen hundred years before it arrives on the streets of Rome. In fact, the year 1615 is the official date of its arrival in Europe, thanks to Venetian merchants, although by then it has already been a beverage in the Islamic world and Yemen for over two hundred years. A curiosity: the word *coffee* synthesizes its entire history. It derives from the Turkish *kahve,* which in turn comes from the Arabic *qahwa,* which indicated a bitter beverage obtained from the seeds of the coffee plant, with such an energizing effect as to be considered a medicine.

The woman has finished filling the terra-cotta mugs, which four men are now lifting to their lips. The contents are so scalding hot that they screw up their eyebrows from pain as they take little sips in silence. If it's not coffee that they're drinking, what is it? We walk closer and can smell the answer: it's wine. Served diluted with boiling water, it is reminiscent of *vin brulé.* None of us today would habitually drink boiling hot wine, especially not first thing in the morning or seasoned with spices that totally change its taste. No doubt about it, the wine of ancient Rome is markedly different than ours today. We have seen that repeatedly on this long journey of ours through the empire.

But there's no time to stop here. Our man is overtaking everyone he encounters and is heading deeper and deeper into the growing crowd, provoking some protests here and there. The odors in this pressed-together mass of people are indescribable. Clothing is imbued with the smells and whiffs of the last places each person has been before coming here. And so there is the smell of oil lamps, grilled sausage, horse, burnt wood, undigested onion, rain-soaked fabric. . . . And then there is also the stench of unwashed skin and sweat. Nobody has gone to the baths yet today.

Everyone is pushing to get through the crowd, and we raise our eyes to get a better look at their destination. Above the crowd we can see the imposing structure of the Circus Maximus.

Where the Sabines Were Abducted

The immense arcades of the Circus Maximus seem like so many gaping jaws of some voracious monster devouring the people. This monster has eyes that make his bite even more frightening: a host of large square windows that open out from the structure's two upper levels.

In the blue predawn light, the colors haven't woken up yet. The whole scene is still very ghostlike. All you can see is the rigid majesty of the arcades of the Circus Maximus, alternating between dark arches and light pilasters for over five hundred yards. We have come up on the curved side of the structure, and before our eyes one whole side of it stretches out, straight, like an enormous government building.

It's unbelievably big. How could such a mammoth structure have been built by men? We are in the heart of antiquity, and this is, and will remain, the biggest and largest-capacity stadium ever built by humans. Not even in the modern era has anything this immense ever been built.

The Circus Maximus is also intimately tied to the history of Rome. This is where the rape of the Sabine women is said to have taken place: According to legend, Romulus, first king of Rome, organized some chariot races and invited the Sabine men with the sole purpose of distracting them, and then abducted their women. Obviously, the story is not true, but the love of chariot races, on the other hand, is. Chariot races were one of Rome's favorite pastimes from the very beginning of its history. In the eyes of the earliest Romans, this long, wide valley running between the Palatine and the Aventine hills, called the Valley Murcia, seemed like a gift from the gods, the ideal setting for their races. All they had to do was lay out the track. But there was a problem: a small body of water ran through the area. The solution was found around 600 BCE by Tarquinius Priscus, the fifth king of Rome, who channeled the stream into a canal and built the first circus for chariot and horse races.

The water from this canal fed a second canal, which ran all around the track, like the moat of a medieval castle. It was ten feet wide and just as deep. Its purpose was to keep the animals from jumping on the spectators. Actually, in the beginning, the Circus Maximus was used for all kinds of spectacles: not only horse races but also for combat between gladiators, combat between men and wild animals, theatrical performances, and so on.

Before the Colosseum and other large entertainment facilities were built, the Circus Maximus was the grand space for mass entertainment in Rome—a concept that has survived into our own age, using the stadiums of our cities to host athletic meets, football games, rock concerts, theatrical productions, political speeches, and so on. It's no wonder, then, that this place was even more important and exciting than the Colosseum. There was always something happening here, with just a few days between one event and the next. It was the real "amusement park" of the capital of the Roman Empire.

And perhaps for this very reason, the Circus Maximus served still another purpose for the rulers and administrators of Rome. You will certainly have heard the expression *panem et circenses,* bread and circuses. It is a celebrated phrase of the poet Juvenal that expressed a very simple concept: "Give the people bread and races in the Circus Maximus and you won't have problems." The strategy of largesse and entertainment effectively created strong popular consensus and distracted public opinion from politics. And the emperors knew it well. So, that enormous structure was an important instrument in maintaining their grip on power.

For all these reasons—popular passion, political strategy, but also as an extraordinary machine for moving money through the economy, as we will see shortly—the Circus Maximus was used continually for centuries, even though it underwent various modifications, restorations, and embellishments. For just how long? Twelve hundred years.

The first chariot race was held in or around 600 BCE and the last in 549 CE, under the Goth king Totila. Can you imagine a stadium used without interruption for twelve hundred years? It would be like going to see a game today in a stadium built by Charlemagne and used without interruption since then.

Even these few bits of data make it easy to understand the special nature of the Circus Maximus. (But that's not what the ancient Romans called it. For them it was simply the Circus.) And that brings us back to the crowd that is gathering under its arcades now in a freezing cold dawn. What is it that drove these people to come here at such an odd hour?

The Underworld of the Circus Maximus

The man we're following slips into one of the arcades of the Circus Maximus. Together the arches form an incredibly long portico, identical to the ones you see in the historic centers of so many European cities. The most surprising thing is that underneath them many shops are already open, with their goods on display. It looks like a very, very long shopping center, a city within the city.

Many shops are selling food to be taken into the stands (olives, bread, cheese, pickled fish) but also cushions, parasols, capes against the cold and rain, etc. Others display goods that have nothing to do with the races: clothes, olive oil, spices, terra-cotta pots and pitchers. There is even someone hammering copper kettles and someone else selling votive statues. We are in the center of Rome and the portico opens out onto one of the busiest streets in the capital. It's only natural, therefore, that it is also the best place to sell goods and do business of all kinds.

Leaning up against an archway, some young women are waiting for customers. They have an oriental look: dark, curly hair, dark complexion, ample hips, and elongated eyes accentuated by heavy makeup. Their veils barely cover the goods they are displaying and selling. Some men, many of whom are along in years, have stopped to talk with them and negotiate the price. They are their first customers of the day.

These Mediterranean women are very much sought after by the men of the capital. Contrary to today, there is no place in the erotic imagination of the Roman man for Nordic women, with blond hair and blue eyes; the ideal of the sensuous woman is the dark-haired woman of the eastern Mediterranean, from Greece, Turkey, Syria, Lebanon, and so on.

A man in his fifties, conservatively but elegantly dressed, observes the scene from the street. His eyes fill with contempt; he makes a grimace of disgust and scribbles something down on some pages already full of notes. Then he nods to his servant to go ahead and open up a path for him in the crowd. His gaze has returned to how it was before, a bit absent with a vein of sadness. He vanishes into the crowd. This man who is apparently so normal and nondescript will go down in history as one of the most famous and biting poets of antiquity. He is Juvenal.

His acidity is renowned, as are his pessimism and his continuous references to past and, in his opinion, happier eras. Women, especially emancipated and liberated women, bear the brunt of his jibes. They, along with homosexuals, are the favorite targets of his *Satires*. A few years from now he'll even launch an attack on the next emperor, Hadrian, for his homosexual relationship with Antinous. It's risky: it is believed that Juvenal was exiled to Egypt by Domitian, disappearing from the scene but leaving us all of his pungent critiques of Roman society.

The scene that he has just witnessed, under the portico of the Circus Maximus, will come to occupy a place in literature. His look of disgust actually gave birth to some phrases, barely sketched out in his improvised notes, that we will later read in this form.

I cannot abide, Quirites, a Rome of Greeks; and yet what fraction
of our dregs comes from Greece? The Syrian Orontes has long since
poured into the Tiber, bringing with it its lingo and its manners, its

flutes and its slanting harp-strings; bringing too the timbrels of the breed, and the trulls who are bidden ply their trade at the Circus. (Satire 3, translated by G. G. Ramsay)

Juvenal complains frequently about this commerce in sex in the vicinity of the Circus Maximus and points his finger at immigrants, especially those who come from Syria. It is curious to note that in the Roman era, too, prostitution so often involves young women from the East forced to live on the streets—in this case, from the east of the Mediterranean.

Betting at the Circus Maximus

The shops don't occupy all the porticoes of the Circus Maximus. Between one shop and another, two passageways open up that lead down to the grandstands. The sequence is visible even today, among the few patches of the Circus's ruins that emerge aboveground. Beyond the shop there is an entrance corridor toward the lower tier, the one reserved for VIPs, followed by an upward-sloped entrance, with stairs leading to the Circus's upper tiers, for the popular classes. And then the sequence is repeated with another shop, another entrance corridor, another set of stairs, and so on.

Our man is in the middle of the crowd. As we too are pushed this way and that we ask ourselves why so many people have crowded into this place before dawn. The reason is simple: entrance is free (or very inexpensive) in the popular sections, where there are no assigned seats. (Nevertheless, some historians maintain that access to events and performances in the Roman era depended on having a *lusoria* card similar to the one used for going to the theater. But in the crowd we're in now nobody seems to have one.) So, prefiguring a modern habit of fans who line up for rock concerts, a lot of people prefer to get there many hours before the show in order to get a good spot with an excellent view. Since there is no system for reserving seats, it's not unusual for people to come to the Circus even a full day before an event.

In other sectors, reserved for the wealthy and celebrities, it's a whole different story; there the seats are assigned. The VIPs will show up considerably later, when the stands are already jam-packed, choosing the right moment for a regal entrance so they can be seen by everyone.

From this perspective, the Circus is the real stage where the people who count in Rome—the wealthy, the patricians, members of the equestrian order, and senators—love to appear and put themselves on display in an atmosphere reminiscent of Oscar night, in a frenzy of smiles, expensive clothes, and jewelry.

Our man, however, doesn't seem the least bit interested in getting a good seat. He steps out of the crowd as it goes up the first steps of the stairway and slips into a shop under the portico. Actually, it's a *popina*. In the entryway he walks by two customers who are already drunk and about to start a fistfight and makes his way at a brisk pace toward a group of people seated around a table off to the side. It's one of the many such groups that can be encountered around the Circus Maximus.

Betting on horse races is such a flourishing business that it would be enough by itself to justify the expense of organizing these races. Perhaps even more of an indicator than the number of spectators, which is already impressive in its own right.

You might imagine such a high volume of betting taking place in big rooms outfitted with blackboards presenting all the information on the day's races: the positions of the contestants, the names of the charioteers, in some cases the names of the horses, with continuous updates. That's what we have been used to seeing for generations now at our racetracks. It's possible that this setup also existed in the Roman era, but archaeologists haven't discovered any evidence confirming the scenario.

The bookmaker is a fat man with very fair skin, green eyes, and thinning blond hair, which he keeps uselessly long on a head that has long since surrendered to baldness. He's holding a double waxed tablet with the names of the charioteers, the distances of the races, and the odds. He's surrounded by intensely attentive faces. Who are the bettors assembled at this table?

Looking at their faces, we see that they are ordinary people. There's a butcher, whose tunic is sprinkled with blood stains (his wife doesn't know he's here—he told her he was going to the wholesaler to order some new deliveries of meat); an employee in the public administration; a short, puny, almost hairless shopkeeper; a soldier on leave; a cutler who's missing a couple of fingers, lost, we imagine, in a work accident; and a slave in search of a big win that will enable him to buy his freedom.

Next to him is a well-dressed man, apparently well-off. His sweaty hands are nervously playing with some coins, ready to be put on the table.

They are people of different social backgrounds, with different personal histories and different faces, but in their eyes they all have the concentrated and rather gloomy gaze of those with a passion for betting; a passion shared by all, rich and poor alike.

Now we can understand the tension that was driving the man whom we have been following, his fast-paced stride, his walking through puddles, his distraction that almost got him run over by a wagon. He's got gambler's fever. The only thing on his mind is this moment, the thrill of placing a bet. There are plenty of Romans who have ruined themselves betting in these squalid places. He is one of them. The patches and repairs on his mantle are actually the scars inflicted by his financial ruin.

The bookmaker clears his throat and goes on with the list of races. When he says the word "Sagitta," our man nearly jumps. In Latin it means "arrow" and sums up quite well the qualities of this horse. It's for this very horse that he's come here today.

Indeed, the Romans talk for days on the streets and in the taverns about the races that are going to be held at the Circus Maximus. They know the names of all the charioteers and all the horses, including their pedigree. No wonder the Christian writer, Saint John Chrysostom, once complained that the inhabitants of his era, fourth-century Rome, could make a complete list of the most famous horses but didn't know the names nor even the number of the apostles.

It's just like what happens today with soccer or football. If you think of the banter and rivalry between coworkers or bar patrons in the days leading up to a match between crosstown rivals (or the days immediately following), you'll have a good idea of the atmosphere surrounding chariot races in the Roman era.

Sagitta is not one of the names that was most heard these past few days on the streets of Rome. Other horses are favored. Sagitta has already had his day in the sun. At one time he was an excellent horse, but for various reasons he never recorded any great victories, just some good placements, so his odds have remained pretty long. Now even more so since he's on the verge of being retired. Nobody believes he's still capable of a big victory.

But that's exactly why the man we have followed all the way here is betting on him. He went to have a look at him when he was training (something that a lot of Roman racing fans do, lining up like hedges along the sides of the private tracks of the various stables), saw how strong he was, and especially the great experience of his charioteer, a mature man with a lot of races behind him and capable of getting every last drop of energy out of his horse. And he asked himself how it was that such an expert charioteer had chosen Sagitta, putting him in his team of four along with three other horses. Does he know something special about this steed? Impulsively, as race day drew closer, our man decided he had to bet on them. And to do it he plunged himself further into debt.

The bettors have accumulated a nice pile of sesterces on the table, regularly recorded as bets. The man we followed is the last to put his down: he pulls out our sestertius together with several silver denarii and three aurei, which shine bright as a lighthouse on a promontory. Then he puts the whole bunch of them on the table. It's all the money he has. The bookmaker looks at the bet; it's rather high, and unusually so for an old warhorse like Sagitta. Sure, if he actually wins, the payoff will be a real fortune, given the odds. But it's practically impossible, considering the champions he'll be racing against. The bookmaker stares at the man with his green eyes—the eyes of a predator with his prey in hand. And with a quick move of his hand he clutches the pile of coins and makes it disappear into the wood box that he carries tied to his belt by a chain. The metallic sound of the coins is drowned out by the sound of the lock snapping shut. Two armed slaves stand on either side of the bookmaker, staring like guard dogs at anyone who approaches.

The bet has been made. Now we just have to wait for the race . . .

The man who placed the bet is given a receipt: a card made of bone with some information etched on it which, together with the odds of the bet, is inscribed on a wax tablet. Then the bookmaker goes on to another race.

So our coin has changed owners once again. Will it come back into the hands of its last possessor together with a lot of others? It all depends on Sagitta.

Our man comes out of the tavern and finally heads toward the grandstand. He has the relaxed air of someone who has done his duty. He goes up the long stone staircase together with the rest of the crowd.

The stairs are so worn from foot traffic that they are smooth and slippery. An old man loses his balance, but he's forcefully held up and helped to climb the stairs, almost carried along by the crowd. Nobody can stop; everybody wants to go up.

The system of zigzagging stairways is extremely efficient. As we can see, the people keep on moving and nobody ever stops. The secret to managing the passage of the crowd, from the street to the stands, is very simple: there is not just one entrance but dozens of them around the whole perimeter. Furthermore, once you've gone through the entrance archways, the Circus Maximus becomes a veritable Swiss cheese, with an endless number of passageways and ramps that divide the flow of the crowd into a thousand streams, allowing it to move quickly. The same system is used in the Colosseum and lots of other structures for mass entertainment.

Amid the rumbling of footsteps and voices, the crowd fills the interior corridors of the first tier of the Circus, then those of the second tier as well. Then the stairways switch to wood and take people up to the highest ring, which is also made of wood. We're almost there. Just a few more steps to climb. And then we come out into the grandstands of the Circus Maximus.

As though in a dream, the rumbling goes silent and the cool outside air envelops the spectators emerging from the entryways one by one. Waiting for them, as soon as they emerge onto the grandstands, is the rising sun, peeking out from behind the distant mountains to the east and warming their faces, still taut from resisting the cold wind of dawn.

The view is glorious. This is the Circus Maximus in all its beauty and majesty. The marble grandstands stretch out toward the horizon like so many rays of stone. It gives the impression of looking out over an enchanted valley, white as snow, arranged in ordered levels. It is a world away from the chaos of the narrow alleyways of the surrounding area, as though someone had dropped onto the city an immense set of white cliffs now being occupied by flocks of spectators. The immediate thought is that a place like this is destined to last forever.

Actually, Trajan has given the Circus Maximus a new look. Under Domitian, a huge fire had destroyed its two long sides, and the emperor had begun to rebuild it, but then he died suddenly. Trajan has finished the job, giving the structure its monumentality and the image that made it famous throughout the empire and down through the ages. Unfortunately, nobody in the modern era has ever known what the Circus really looked like; over the centuries after the fall of Rome it was pillaged and buried in sediment. Luckily, there are mosaics, coins, and even relief sculptures and tombstones that portray it (and that are the basis for these descriptions of this day at the races). Moreover, we also have some descriptions written at the time, left to us by the ancient authors, almost like emotional snapshots of this colossal construction.

The Biggest and Largest-Capacity Stadium in History

Pliny the Younger, a contemporary of Trajan's, summed up all of its splendor in just a few words, calling it the "worthy seat of a world-conquering people." The measurements of this monument speak loud and clear. It's between 650 and 700 yards long and 175 yards wide. Its track occupies a surface area of more than 400,000 square feet, which is twelve times that of the arena floor in the Colosseum. Between the first row at the bottom and last row at the top, the distance is just shy of 40 yards: a long way but not too long for the hoi polloi sitting in the highest seats to be able to pick out, one by one, the "Romans who count" sitting in the first rows. But how many people can it hold?

It's worth lingering on this for a minute because the figures help us to understand the exceptional nature of this manmade structure. Each tier of seats turns around the structure for a total of 1,550 to 1,650 yards. In other words, every row of seats is nearly a mile long. (Better not make a mistake when you're looking for your seat.)

The total capacity of the Circus has always been a subject of heated debate. We don't have any precise figures, but experts like Fik Meijer, professor of ancient history at the University of Amsterdam, have made some calculations.

Each spectator has at his disposal a place no more than 16 inches wide, 20 inches long, and 14 inches high. But we have to consider all of the interruptions in the rows caused by the openings of the entry and exit passages (and there are lots of them), the steps going up and down the grandstands, and then dividing walls and other structures. When all is said and done we arrive at a total capacity of 150,000 spectators.

This is an honest and conservative estimate. Let's say it represents the minimum capacity of the structure. It may be able to hold even greater numbers of people, as would seem to be suggested by Pliny the Elder in his *Naturalis Historia*, where he speaks of 250,000 spectators. In the late classical period, it was even said that as many as 480,000 people could be seated in the stands, but this is probably an exaggeration. In any event, even a capacity of 150,000 people, as estimated by Professor Meijer, is immense, almost double that of the biggest soccer stadiums in Italy: the Meazza in Milan seats a little over 80,000; San Paolo in Naples, 76,000; and the Olympic Stadium in Rome, 73,000.

And it is much greater than the capacity of the biggest stadiums in the contemporary world, from the legendary Maracanã in Rio de Janeiro (originally designed to hold 160,000 spectators but actually with a current capacity of just 95,000 seats), to the Campo Nou in Barcelona (98,000), and the Azteca in Mexico City (101,000).

Even if we consider capacity where many spectators remain standing, packed in like sardines, only very few exceptional structures can come close to the Circus Maximus: the Penn State University football stadium (107,000 seats), the Melbourne cricket stadium (100,000 seats), and the Salt Lake stadium in Kolkata, West Bengal (120,000).

All this demonstrates the exceptional place of the Circus Maximus in history. Today, despite the availability of the most advanced technologies, the highest-quality steel and concrete, the best engineering minds, and the best software, nobody in the world has built something superior to the Circus Maximus.

Perhaps it's because there's no reason to. Those who go to the stadium for a sporting event, a race, or a rock concert, constitute a minority of the population. There is not much use for oversized stadiums. But that is not the case with the chariot races in imperial Rome. The Circus had the capacity to hold, according to the estimates, as many as one-seventh or even one-quarter of the inhabitants of Rome.

We can begin to grasp, therefore, the Roman passion for the races and their importance to society, a concept about which relatively little has been said, convinced as we have been that the Colosseum was the real main attraction. But if we consider the capacity of the Colosseum (a "mere" 50,000 to 70,000), its role and the importance of the gladiators in the Roman mind take on much-reduced dimensions.

Where Does the Marble in the Circus Maximus Come from?

There are still a lot of unoccupied sections, and the white marble dazzles the eyes of anyone looking up and down the rows. In this moment the Circus, in the words of an old chariot-racing fan who has just sat down beside us, is "as naked as Venus taking her bath." In a way, the scene does remind us of the candor and beauty of the marble goddess on display at the baths. And, like Venus, the stadium is gradually dressing itself in the tunics, fabrics, and colors of its spectators.

We'll never know who supplied the marble for all the stairs and all the columns in all the capitols. But we do know where at least one of the marble suppliers for the Circus lived. Archaeologists have identified his house in Lunae (modern-day Luni), a Roman city on the coast of Liguria, near La Spezia. All that's left of this city today are some silent ruins sticking out of the ground in the countryside, visited mostly by foreign tourists. It's a shame because it's a very interesting site, with the remains of an amphitheater, the forum (where recently a small treasure trove of gold coins was discovered, likely hidden before an enemy attack), and the villas of some very wealthy Romans.

The floor of one of these villas is where archaeologists have uncovered a mosaic representing the Circus Maximus, seen from above, with its grandstands and its covering. It is one of the few representations of the Circus that have come down to us from that time, and so it is very useful to scholars as an instrument of research.

The owner of the villa was almost certainly a marble wholesaler (the famous marble quarries, also used by Michelangelo, are not very far from here), and he boasted proudly that he was one of the main suppliers for the Circus—so much so that he had it represented on this mosaic. That's not extraordinary; many wealthy Romans paid homage to the source of their wealth in a mosaic (commerce in wines, animals for the Colosseum, and so on).

To exhibit their power they also liked to commission beautiful mosaics representing some great event or spectacle that they had sponsored as a gift to the community. If, for example, they had organized an important day of combat with gladiators in the arena, they portrayed it replete with the wounded, the dead, and the names of the most famous champions. What looks to us like the scene of a massacre (would you portray on the floor of your living room the images of men stabbing each other, pools of blood, dying combatants and cadavers?) was for them a badge of honor for the family, a gift they had paid out of their own pocket for the city, obviously as a way of winning public support.

So that's the origin of all those beautiful mosaics of gladiators that we see so often in museums. The same thing goes for chariot races. In fact, the description of the race that we are about to see is drawn from mosaics of exactly this type found in several villas, like the one in the hunting villa in Piazza Armerina in Sicily. As strange as it might seem, no complete written description of the races in the Circus Maximus has come down to us. The best evidence we have as to how these famous races were run comes to us from these "photographs in stone" (together with bas-reliefs and decorations on oil lamps, sarcophagi, etc.).

Emperors and Crowds in the Circus Maximus

With the dawning of the brand-new day, the ever more deafening noise of the mob scene in the street has moved into the stands, which are by now filled by a multicolored throng.

It's interesting to recall that it was this very confusion, in the early hours of the morning, that drove more than one emperor into a rage. It is well known that the imperial palaces are located on the Palatine, very close to the entrance arcades of the Circus Maximus, and it's easy to imagine how many emperors were rudely awakened before dawn by the noise, the shouting, and the uproar of the gathering crowds. Their reaction was not always very regal.

The emperor Caligula, for example, got to the point of sending in soldiers to silence and disperse the people to the tune of cudgel blows. The result was a real bloodbath. Under the blows from the billy clubs, or perhaps the crush of the crowd, dozens of men and women were killed, including many members of the equestrian order. Another emperor, Elagabalus, even made use of a system adopted during sieges, the equivalent of tear gas, but much more dangerous. He had the throng pelted with snake-filled amphoras, creating a generalized panic, the result of which was another massacre of spectators, trampled to death.

In the era we're talking about there is no such danger. Trajan is well loved by the people and knows how to make himself so. Instead of taking his place in the *pulvinar*, the grand imperial tribune that rises up like a small temple over the grandstand, well separated from the general public, he prefers to sit among the spectators, exchanging comments with them in Latin with his strong Iberian accent, and the crowd feels that he is one of them. He's not here today; he's far way from Rome, in the east. But the inhabitants of Rome and of the entire empire love him and feel his presence, as though he were a protector of their families and their homes. They perceive him as a kind of universal *paterfamilias*, capable, as he in fact was, of expanding the empire as never before, giving it strength and prosperity.

The Spectacle Begins

By now almost all the seats are occupied. A small fat man is sitting near us, his double chin covered with the bristly stubble of his unshaved beard. He's staring at the tribunes in front of him on the other side of the Circus. He turns toward us and gives us a long look, as if trying to remember where he's seen us before. We begin to talk, and we learn that he is a retired centurion, now a doorman working at an *insula* in the city. Today is his day off. He offers us some wine from his leather canteen.

Our chat is interrupted to make way for two young women who need to get to their seats farther down the row. Their *stolae*, or long tunics, tickle our feet. They smile at us as they go by, and we are enveloped by their perfume, refreshing and inebriating. Just as soon as they sit down, not far from us, two young men start talking to them. And the two women answer. At the start they are a bit aloof, but then they seem curious and open to the advances of the young men.

Since there's no separation between men and women in the grandstand, a lot of young men come here with the sole purpose of checking out the women. None other than Ovid himself suggests this strategy in his celebrated *Ars Amatoria*.

The two boys have already asked the girls which stables they're rooting for, pretending that they are supporters too. They're acting out a script so old that even the doorman looks over at us and smiles, giving us a wink. Back in his day he adopted the same strategy. That's how courtship begins in the Circus Maximus.

Enter, Solemn, the Pompa Circensis

By now the whole Circus is soaking in sunlight, the track has been swept smooth, and a pair of race assistants run to get into position. These are the final touches of an organizational procedure that has gone on for days. Now everything's ready. The crowd is buzzing; for the last several minutes the various factions of fans have been chanting the names of the most famous horses and charioteers along with slogans designed to provoke the ire of the opposing factions. And the crowd laughs. It's amazing how much the whole scene calls to mind the pregame excitement on display in stadiums in our own time.

The start of the race is a true ceremony that follows a very rigid protocol. We could compare it to the opening ceremony of the Olympic Games. The race organizer, in practical terms the man who has financed today's races, will be the first to come around the track at the head of a long procession that will begin a long ways off, as far away as the Capitol. Like a general at the head of his victory parade, he will cross the Forum flanked by a cheering crowd on his way to the Circus Maximus for a prerace glory lap.

We can already hear the sound of ovations reaching us from outside the stadium. At first they were quite distant, but they're getting stronger all the time, a sign that the parade is drawing close.

Suddenly, announced by a blast of trumpets, the parade appears on the track and the 150,000 spectators explode into jubilant applause. The excitement is indescribable; the noise is so loud you can't even think, let alone hear yourself talk. Everyone directs their gaze to the majestic triumphal arch that occupies the center of the curve, sticking out like a mountain amid the stands.

It may seem odd that there's a triumphal arch mounted in the middle of the Circus Maximus. Actually, the arch is part of the theatrical setting for triumphal marches celebrating military victories. Built by Titus, it is one of the cardinal points of the generals' victory parades when they enter Rome. The official parade route calls for them to pass through the

Circus Maximus to be acclaimed by the throng, before continuing on to the Forum and the Capitol, where they render homage to Jupiter. In essence, the military victory parades move in the opposite direction of the parade we are now watching.

The first into view are several young men on horseback. They are the scions of Rome's most famous families. After them, some other young men, on foot. Then, in a pandemonium of acclamation, the charioteers make their entrance driving their four-horse chariots, or quadrigae. Each spectator seeks out his personal favorite, and as soon as he sees him he yells out his name. The crowd is up on its feet and the charioteers salute the crowd with broad, sweeping waves. The ovations go all the way up to the stars and can be heard throughout the city. Hundreds of thousands of Romans, busy with their daily routines, turn their heads in the direction of the Circus. For an instant, almost by magic, the Circus Maximus enters all the houses of the city, all the streets and the minds of all the inhabitants of the capital of the Roman Empire.

This is the so-called *pompa circensis*; the one described by Dionysius of Halicarnassus is identical to the scene we are seeing now.

Two quadrigae follow behind all the athletes involved in the other contests of the day: charioteers who will compete in the youth categories, jockeys on their steeds for the horseraces, even acrobats for the entertainments that will be staged between races. Next are dancers and musicians with lyres and flutes, dressed in purple, and porters carrying statues of divinities and ritual objects in procession.

Finally, welcomed by the jubilant cheers of the crowd, the man who paid for and organized the races comes onto the track, a thin man with white hair, standing tall in his chariot. Actually, it would be more correct to call it his quadriga. Depending on whether there are two, three, or four horses, the name of the chariot changes from biga to triga to quardriga, and so on. They got up as high as a team of ten horses, and even twenty. But these were more for exhibitions than races; it's almost impossible to have a contest with teams that numerous—they're practically uncontrollable.

Race Chariots, Stables, and Champions

The procession advances with a solemn air, making a lap around the track; for the longest time the cheers are deafening. Now the quadrigae are passing in front of us and we can get a good look at the charioteers. What's really amazing are their outfits, if we can call them that; it almost seems like they're going off to war. Each of them has a leather helmet, a chest protector fashioned out of leather strips wrapped around his torso, leg guards, and even a dagger. What do they need all of this for? For survival.

Indeed the danger of being killed in a race is very high. Often the chariots overturn, and the falls are incredibly violent. And there's always the risk of being trampled by the team of four pulling the chariot behind you: sixteen galloping hooves are a real body grinder capable of mutilating even the most robust charioteer.

But the most feared threat is something else: to be dragged by the horses around the entire length of the track. The charioteer doesn't hold the reins in his hands, they're wrapped around his body like a belt, replete with belt loops. This way the charioteer can exploit his full body weight, bending right or left, to give more force to the orders he yells to the horses. It's a little like the skipper on a sailboat leaning out over the edge of the boat.

But this means that if his chariot turns over, the horses will rip him out of his driver's seat and carry him away with them, dragging him who knows how far. He will wind up mutilated and skinned alive. So in that case, it's absolutely essential to cut the leather reins with the dagger that he carries in his chest protector. But will he be able to? Lots of charioteers weren't, and were dragged to their deaths.

The chariots are very different from what we usually imagine. The bigas of the film *Ben Hur* would never have been able to race here. They are too big and heavy, with their high platforms, ideal for the triumphal parades of victorious generals but totally useless in a chariot race. It's the usual Hollywood mistake. It would be as if our descendants, two thousand years from now, came up with the idea that Formula 1 car races were contests between the BMWs and Ferraris that are driven on highways. Sure, they're fast cars, but they have nothing to do with Grand Prix racing, where the cars are light, low, and streamlined, engineered to squeeze out the smallest fraction of a second during the race.

The same can be said for the chariots. Archaeologists have never uncovered a racing chariot. There were very few of them, too light to hold up through the centuries, and even back then they were short-lived; they were dismantled after the races or ended up demolished on the track. Exactly like what happens to Formula 1 race cars, in fact: it will be tough in two thousand years to find one still intact. It's much more likely that future archaeologists will turn up a Ferrari built for highways and city streets. And that's what has happened in classical archaeology; what has been found in Etruscan tombs are the remains of bigae or quadrigae for parades, but never Roman racing chariots.

So what did the racing chariots look like? There's one passing right now in front of where we're sitting. It's quite different from what we'd expect after the depictions in films. The platform is very low, about halfway up the charioteer's thigh; it's made out of a solid wood baluster with a painted and decorated leather protector tied to the front. The wheels are amazingly small; the diameter of a tray and no more. And then they're not located at the center of the chariot but much farther back, almost at the back end, so the chariot leans forward, a trick to keep the center of gravity low and the chariot glued to the ground on the curves.

Just as there are the Formula 1 stables for Ferrari, Williams, McLaren, and Lotus, so there are teams in chariot racing. In the time of Trajan there are four of them, called factions, each one with its specific colors. Or better, they are called by their colors: there is the green team (*prasina*), the red one (*russata*), white (*albata*) and blue (*veneta*). And the charioteers have uniforms the same color as their team, again exactly like Formula 1 drivers.

Another surprising thing is the horses. They are not tall, by any means. Often they are shorter than five feet, and to us they almost seem like ponies. But that's the way it was throughout the ancient world. The horses are small everywhere, even in the legions. They don't tire so easily, and they are more agile on rough terrain.

The most prized horse is the *getulio,* or Numidian Berber horse, from North Africa, probably an ancestor of our Arabian horses. But also much appreciated are the horses from Cappadocia in present-day Turkey, as well as horses from Spain and Sicily. Hanging from their harnesses are glinting good-luck charms made of bronze. One of the most common is a half-moon with the ends pointing down, the *lunula*, a true talisman also used by Roman women.

A "Museum" for a Partition

Now the *pompa circensis* parade is leaving the arena, following the long dividing wall in the middle of the track, the *spina*; it's covered with different kinds of precious marble, especially the green-toned serpentine marble. On top of the wall are statues, small temples, and fountains. But the most surprising thing is an enormous Egyptian obelisk, eighty-five feet high. Built in Egypt by Ramses II, it was brought to Rome under orders from Augustus.

We can also see a lap-counting mechanism for the races; it looks like a canopy with seven statues of gilded pairs of dolphins. The whole thing resembles an enormous skewer of shrimp. After each lap a dolphin will be rotated downward, pouring an enormous amount of water out of its mouth. In this way, the entire arena will be able to keep count of the laps completed and how many are left to run. In future eras, the dolphins will be replaced by seven golden eggs, which, after each lap, will splash down into a tub of water. The contestants have to complete seven laps of the track, running counterclockwise, for a total of almost 5 kilometers, or 3.1 miles. The race is over in a little less than ten minutes.

The parade has vanished behind the starting gates. Now the races are set to begin.

The Great Race

The races have been inflaming the crowd in the Circus for hours. There have been some spectacular accidents and surprising victories. The program calls for some twenty-four races interspersed with feats of athletic skill, acrobatics on horseback (much applauded), and challenges between the winners of different races. In other eras, under Vespasian and Titus, there were as many as forty-eight races, and under Domitian even a hundred, just to demonstrate the Roman passion for horses.

The voice of the announcer is a kind of sing-song introducing the various races. In the meantime a lot of spectators have left their seats to fetch a snack, or they have left the stadium altogether.. But the bet-making man that we followed here hasn't moved. He's glued to his seat, watching every race, waiting nervously for Sagitta to make his entrance. And it's almost time.

Up to now the races have been between bigae and trigae, horses with jockeys, and even a strange contest consisting of a race between quadrigae whose drivers, once over the finish line, jump off the chariot to continue on foot for another few laps. This race, called *pedibus ad quadrigam*, is the ancient equivalent of our triathlon. If you've ever watched a triathlon race or an Ironman contest, with athletes stretched to the limit swimming, riding bikes, and then running for miles and thought you were seeing a bizarre phenomenon of the modern fitness-obsessed world, a *pedibus ad quadrigam* race should be enough to convince you that the triathlon rage is really nothing new. It's the umpteenth resemblance between our world and the world of the ancient Romans: a race that combines a wheeled vehicle and the strength of human legs (although there's no swimming, because in the Roman era, almost nobody knows how to swim).

Our doorman observes the man for a while, taking it all in, and turns toward us shaking his head: "Another gambling addict, eh?"

He doesn't have time to say any more before the millionth trumpet blast sounds and our man jumps to his feet. It's time! The voice of the announcer (there are probably several in various points around the Circus, given its huge size) announces the start of the quadrigae races. It's the moment that all the spectators have been waiting for, and they welcome the news with a deafening racket. A lot of them stand up.

They all turn their eyes toward the far end of the Circus Maximus, to the *caceres*, the starting gates lined up under the arcades of a long, low building.

The race assistants have smoothed the track by dragging heavy leather mats over it. They have outlined the starting lanes with chalk. The holes made by the crashing pieces of demolished chariots have been repaired. The congealed blood of a charioteer still stains the marble facing of the *spina*. Nobody has had time to wash it. By now everyone's attention is concentrated on those wooden gates that will be thrown open at any moment.

Everything's Ready in the Boxes

Right now, behind the gates, the charioteers and their teams of horses are getting ready. It's a different world in there. There is a large open space full of frenetic activity. Stable boys are scurrying to and fro, leading horses by their bridles. Some of the quadrigae are moving into position behind the gate. Others are standing still, waiting expectantly. One of the charioteers is busy putting on his leather helmet, while just beyond him another is listening for the thousandth time as his superior explains the stable's race strategy. Just as in Formula 1 races, various technicians in the box are making their final checks; some of them make sure the bridles and belts are well fastened, others lift up the chariots to spin the wheels and look for wavering or telltale friction.

Two quadrigae approach each other head-on and their horses, stallions, get all riled up, forcing the men into a struggle to pull the two chariots away from each other. The tension of the horses is in contrast to the extreme calm of a lot of other horses that are tied to a long wall. These are the reserve horses.

Every stable, in fact, has to have dozens of horses available for the various races, including some reserves to replace ones that get hurt or injured. And the stables also maintain a small army of servants and assistants ready to repair, replace, or fasten every last part of the quadriga, overseeing the horses and the charioteer to transform all the various parts of the team into a single victory machine.

The *morators* are key figures; these are the stable masters who direct all the operations, caress the horses to keep them calm—even sleep with them. They are easy to recognize in this paddock because they are always right next to the horses, down to the last second: they pick up their legs to check their hooves (a crucial detail because horseshoes haven't been invented yet) or keep a tight hold on the horse's muzzle, whispering reassuring words in its ear. The horses are like their children.

Our attention is drawn to a man covered in gold rings, dressed in a luxurious outfit, and followed by an entourage of attentive lackeys. He's chatting with a charioteer, who is listening with his head bowed and his helmet in hand as a sign of deference. The man with the golden rings is the *dominus factionis*, the boss: every faction has one. We might compare him to the owner of the football team or the F1 racing team. As suggested by Fik Meijer in his book *Chariot Racing in the Roman Empire*, he is a man who is used to managing money (today we would call him a savvy entrepreneur), with powerful economic interests behind him. Besides holding the reins of the stable, he's able to exercise strong influence over the organizer of the races, demanding large sums of money to assure the participation of his team. But this is just one of the many deals that are part of the racing environment, plenty of which are under the table and involve only the charioteer and the men of his staff.

Rules, Fixes, and Secret Agreements

Before the quadrigae even leave the gate, another contest takes place that nobody sees. This is "the fix," the secret deal, the negotiation of an alliance to ensure a victory for one charioteer or one faction . . . or, on the contrary, to make sure one of them *doesn't* win.

All of this is reminiscent of the atmosphere at the Palio in Siena. Here, too, the neighborhoods, or factions, are intensely competitive, and so are their fans. Here, too, secret agreements are worked out and called off at the last minute. And the audience at the Circus knows it. They know that there are sneaky deals and dirty tricks, charioteers that sell out, others that pretend to sell out only to then favor another opponent who offers a higher price. And all of this makes the races even more exciting.

Down on the track, in fact, the charioteers are ruthless. Any kind of dirty tactic is fine: pushing an opponent to make him crash into the wall is not a crime; it's something that everybody is waiting to see. (The notorious "Greek wheel" in the film *Ben Hur*, however, with its hub outfitted with blades that cleave through the wheels of his adversaries, doesn't exist. It's another Hollywood invention.)

In order to prevent disasters from happening even before the race begins, the places at the starting gate are chosen by lottery. Marbles matching the colors of the factions are drawn by chance to decide the order of the chariots at the starting gate.

The Race Begins

This is it. It will be the organizer of today's races, a magistrate, to give the signal to start. When he appears with his violet toga atop a special tribune above the starting gate, the screams of the crowd grow louder and louder. The signal to start will be a white cloth (*mappa*) that will be unfurled and allowed to drop.

Meanwhile, in the starting boxes the roar of the crowd is muffled, just as the sunlight is filtered by the ironwork of the gates, projecting an unusual play of light and shadows onto the horses and charioteers. Every charioteer has his whip held high like a sword, ready to give the horses the first violent blow. Their eyes are fixed on the *morator* in charge of the gate. Getting a good start will depend on his expertise and timing. Beads of sweat pearl up on the foreheads of the charioteers. The horses can feel the tension too, and they puff and rear their heads up, scraping the ground with their hooves.

Several feet above their decorated manes, the magistrate's arm is unbending and the clamor of the crowd pumps up into a crescendo, almost like a drum roll. For an instant everything seems to have become frozen in time.

Then the sudden flash of the white cloth dropping from the magistrate's hand causes the whole Circus to explode. In a fraction of a second, the race assistants throw back the bolts and the gates spring open. Like a sudden breach in the wall of a dam, a wave of blinding sunlight washes over the horses and the charioteers. The men close their eyes, start yelling at the top of their lungs, and cut the air with violent lashes of their whips. The chariots lunge forward and vanish into the light. The arena has swallowed them up.

The crowd sees the horses breaking out of the archways; for a second they look like the flames of an explosion that shoots the colorful chariots out of the gates. The stadium crowd is delirious. Everyone sharpens their gaze to see which team has gotten off to the best start. A good start is essential to making sure the chariot gets to the first curve in a good position. In fact, passing is prohibited at the beginning and you have to maintain your lane in the first phase of the race. Later, anything goes.

Our man who made the bet is on his feet, screaming, cheering on his quadriga from the blue team. Sagitta got off to a good start, but is in the middle, not in the lead. On the first straightaway the red team manages to place two of its chariots in the lead. It's a good down payment on victory because the two chariots will be able to execute a team strategy, but you never can tell. Every faction has three chariots in the race—the main one will be protected by the other two, which will block the passing lanes or try to make the opponents crash.

At this instant twelve quadrigae are hurtling down the straightaway headed into the first curve. It's clear that there won't be room for them all on the curve, but nobody gives way and the crowd can see right away that a collision is inevitable. Our friend the doorman realizes it too and his eyes widen.

When they reach the curve the first two chariots (reds) manage to get the best trajectories amid the screams of the crowd lined up like a thick hedge along the bend.

Immediately after them come three quadrigae that try in vain to pull in close to the wall to make the turn better. On the inside the red one seems to have a good chance, but the green one pushes it up against the wall in an attempt to block his move, and in a last desperate move he cuts in front of him just a few yards from the curve. The horses start pulling away from each other, maybe because they're the first to realize the imminent tragedy. The ones closest to the wall, tight against the barrier, lose their heads and jump at the green chariot. For an instant the two teams of horses are all mixed up: It's all one big tangle from which one of the two chariots suddenly emerges straight up, its rudder snapped. It's the chariot of the red team. The crowd gets a good look at the charioteer clinging desperately to the baluster, his face frozen in a grimace of terror, then, like a ship going down at sea, he disappears into the roiling bodies of the horses.

It's a high-speed collision and the entangled mass of horses and chariots hurls forward on its fatal course. The green charioteer is unable to free himself and his chariot is dragged along diagonally, making a deep groove in the track with its only wheel still in contact with the ground, while the other one, high above, spins in slow motion in the void. Everyone is on their feet, and they all realize that something is about to happen, even the charioteer himself who is desperately trying to cut the reins with his dagger. Then in an instant the wheel on the ground, which is supporting the entire weight of the chariot, snaps in two; the quadriga grinds to a halt, turns over, and starts rolling over itself at an amazing speed. The green charioteer is smashed by his chariot and lies motionless on the ground.

The oncoming quadrigae manage to avoid the accident. None of the charioteers even deign to look at their colleague on the ground. That's one of the risks. All they're thinking about is getting on with the race.

The rest of the chariots all get through the first curve without incident, and they head down the second straightaway. The cheering ratchets up another notch.

We note another curiosity. We expect the charioteers to be standing in their chariots they way we've seen them depicted in films, leaning forward with the reins in hand in the position of someone hanging out over a balcony shaking a sheet. In reality, their position is much farther back, reminiscent of a surfer trying to keep his balance, with one leg forward and one back. The necessity of maneuvering the reins with their bodies forces them into different positions, similar to a boxer moving his head to avoid his adversary's punches.

Now on the straightaway the speed of the chariots approaches a remarkable forty miles an hour. It's no wonder that the wheel hubs overheat. Each team has technicians (*sparsores*) positioned along the straightaway with cone-shaped buckets and amphoras to throw water on the chariot wheels to cool them down . . . and of course they always splash the charioteers, too.

On the curves, the chariots slow down, but their speed always fluctuates between twenty and twenty-five miles per hour. Actually, it's on the curves that the worst accidents happen. Everyone knows it. Now the chariots move into the curve, their wheels sending up little fountain-spurts of sand. All the charioteers lean to the inside, like motorcycle drivers sliding to the side on their saddles.

The small wheels allow for tight curves because they keep the chariot's center of gravity low, but the real secret for taking the curves well are the horses. And we can see that very clearly.

The four horses are not all the same; they have different characteristics. The two horses on the sides (called *funales*) are the chariot's real steering wheel. The innermost horse has to be able to make the curve really tight. The one on the outside is forced to run a greater distance and has to do it perfectly, maintaining its alignment with the others. It takes years of training. Sometimes the steeds come from distant provinces, having been scouted by experts from the various stables for their abilities, exactly like what happens today with baseball players or other athletes from abroad.

Whipping the Eyes of Your Opponent's Horses

A roar from the crowd brings our attention back to the race. Two chariots from the middle of the pack are bumping and pushing each other. One of the two charioteers is even whipping his opponent's horses, which is allowed. The only rule is that you can't whip your opponent himself. Just imagine, the veterinarians who work for the competing teams keep as many as fourteen different creams and lotions just for treating abrasions of the horses' eyes caused by whip lashings.

These horses are trained not to be distracted, but the charioteer who is using his whip has noticed that his opponent's outside horse is nervous, and he keeps on whipping it viciously, until the horse gets out of step with the rest of the team, causing the chariot to lose speed and then go into a swerve just ahead of the curve. Out of control in the most delicate part of the race, the chariot loses its trajectory. In an instant it turns over and all the horses fall or "sit down" on the track, just in time for an oncoming quadriga to bash into them. The chariots coming from behind are forced into a sudden swerve and lose speed.

The charioteer who caused the accident can't resist the temptation, and he turns his head to look back at the chaos he has created. He smiles and shouts in satisfaction as the tangle of horses, chariots, and men disappears behind the curve. But those few seconds of distraction are fatal. Materializing just ahead of him are the ruins of the chariot that crashed at the start of the race. The race assistants haven't managed to remove all the broken pieces. A collision is inevitable. The crowd leaps to its feet and accompanies the moment of impact with a loud roar. The horses manage to jump over the remains of the ruined quadriga, but the chariot slams right into them; the terrorized charioteer clings to the platform. Thousands of spectators look on as the wheels jam and the chariot suddenly stops. The impact is amazing. The chariot snaps in two like a piece of kindling wood. The sound can be heard all the way up to the top of the grandstands. The charioteer flies out of the chariot, ripped from his place by his four steeds who haven't realized what has happened, and, feeling the sudden loss of weight, they lengthen their stride. The charioteer is dragged along the track, raising a billowing cloud of dust. He tries desperately to get a hand on his dagger, but he can't find it. The horses don't stop and every few feet a new wound opens up on his body. His prostrate body gets dragged through the entire straightaway and then on the curve he tumbles in a series of somersaults, losing his helmet, which goes crashing into the wall on the outside. The horses head down the second straightaway and are not stopped by the race assistants from their stable until they come to the ruins of the incident that their charioteer had provoked. As for him, he's not moving anymore; he's out cold.

From one of the side doors (painted to match the colors of the four stables) some men come running out carrying a stretcher. There's no time to try to bring him to, the other quadrigae are coming on fast. They dump him onto the stretcher. His body, covered with blood, doesn't move. As they carry him off, his arm dangles lifelessly over the side of the stretcher. Will he survive? We don't know. One thing is certain: his career is probably over.

What we've learned up to this point is that in the case of a serious accident nobody interrupts the race. The race assistants go out on the track to help the injured and carry off the bodies, but they have to hurry because nobody slows down.

Duel for Victory

The man in charge of the lap counter turns the next-to-last dolphin. There haven't been any other accidents.

The two red chariots are now way out in front, and the pack has broken up. The blue chariot with Sagitta has been running last for most of the race, throwing the bettor into a panic. He has remained seated, in silence, almost petrified. Maybe the bookmaker had called it right: Sagitta is at the end of his career; what can you expect from a horse on the verge of retirement? Now, though, for the last couple of laps, his chariot has been moving up impressively. The blue team's charioteer has been deliberately holding his horses back, and now he loosens up on the reins to unleash their pent-up energy and make his move. It's a tactic that's used a lot in the Circus Maximus. The whole crowd has figured it out and salutes every pass with a loud cheer. Now the blue chariot forces the white one to the outside and passes it, moving steadily closer to the two red chariots in the lead.

A man on horseback comes out of the boxes. He's wearing the colors of the red stable. The rules allow the stables to send in riders (*hortatores*) to keep the charioteer informed about the positions of his opponents, a bit like what happens in cycling with the team cars or, in Formula 1, with the signs displayed in the boxes.

The rider quickly reaches the two red chariots, which have been leading the race since the start. He shouts the stable's orders to them. The blue chariot is coming up fast; they'll have to act together to keep it from taking the lead. Then the rider breaks away and heads back to the box.

By now the blue chariot is right behind the red one that's in second place. Every time it tries to pass, the red one cuts him off. It's a real duel that excites the crowd. When they head into the curve, however, the red chariot makes a mistake. The blue charioteer, in fact, drawing on all his experience accumulated in years of racing, has faked a pass to the outside, forcing his adversary to follow him. Then he suddenly switches to the inside and moves up beside him. The two chariots remain side by side for the whole curve around the *meta*, or turning post. But by the end of the curve the blue chariot is ahead. The crowd goes into an uproar. And our bettor has jumped to his feet, cheering. The doorman smiles and remains unfazed.

Now the race is really up for grabs. The whole Circus is absorbed by the duel, shouting out the names of the two rival stables. The blue charioteer keeps his horses charging and is getting closer and closer to the lead chariot. The red charioteer who's driving it still has a good lead, but he also has the disadvantage of not being able to see his adversary except for quick glances procured at the cost of turning his head. They are both expert drivers, which fuels the enthusiasm of the crowd even more.

A roar follows in the wake of the passing quadrigae. Whole sections of the grandstands jump to their feet, creating an ancient version of the wave. But the crowd never cheers all together. Every time the chariots disappear around the curve, the *spina* hides them from the view of the spectators on the opposite side. For them, it's like a long eclipse. And this, according to the ancient authors, only serves to increase their enthusiasm; when the chariots reemerge around the opposite curve, half of the Circus explodes in a roar, while the other half falls silent.

Drama on the Final Curve

Sagitta is the outside horse of the team of four. At every curve, therefore, he has to run a greater distance than the other horses of the team, but he does it with a power and ease that are truly impressive. His mane, decorated with blue knots and bows, waves like a flag with every stride. The crowd is fascinated by him; he's a beautiful horse, in the fullness of his maturity. With harmonious strides, he leads the quadriga around every curve, putting it into the perfect trajectory for the straightaway. He moves in total unison with the blue charioteer, man and animal bonded together instinctively. The crowd loves come-from-behind victories, and by now almost everyone is cheering for this chariot, which nobody considered before the start of the race.

We're coming down to the wire. The last dolphin has been turned. The waterfall that flows out of its head is colored red to signal the start of the last lap. The two chariots grow closer together as they prepare to confront the next to last curve. The blue chariot again feints a passing move to the outside to draw his opponent out and then move up on the inside. But the red charioteer senses the trick and doesn't fall into the trap. He stays glued to the inside wall and slows down a little, to force the blue charioteer to move out of his trajectory and head straight into the curve. He's a sly old fox too.

But the blue driver has a flash of intuition: to go ahead with the passing move to the outside, taking a much wider route around the curve. Sure, it means covering a greater distance, but his horses still have energy to burn. Suddenly the two quadrigae are neck and neck as they start into the curve. All the spectators are back on their feet again.

Sagitta instinctively realizes what he has to do. He gallops even faster, and forcing himself beyond the limit, he lengthens his stride again to keep in line with the others. For the entire curve the two chariots remain neck and neck. Their wheels touch, the horses bump up against each other. They are so close together that when the two quadrigae come out of the last curve they look like a single chariot with a team of eight horses.

But then comes a bitter surprise. The struggle between the chariots bringing up the rear has caused an accident. Two chariots have overturned; the horses are all mixed up together and they're jumping around like crazy. None of the race assistants down on the track have managed to make it to the scene of the *naufragium*. One of the charioteers (the white) is trying to calm the horses. The other, from the blue stable, is lying on the ground, unconscious. Then he raises his head, shaking it a little. He's coming to his senses. But peering through his sand-filled, painful eyes, he glimpses the two oncoming quadrigae charging toward him. He only has time enough to cover his helmet with his hands. The blue charioteer recognizes his stable-mate and he pulls so hard on the reins that Sagitta almost chokes. But he obeys. The chariot charges past the man on the ground, missing him by a hair.

The red driver, however, has no such scruples. Suddenly he sees some daylight open up in front of him, an unhoped-for opportunity. The crowd watches him snap his whip on the back of his horses and looks on aghast at the tragedy. The fallen charioteer is trampled by the horses. The red chariot bounces over his body and goes on with the race, leaving the man facedown on the track. His fellow driver from the white stable rushes to his aid. He gets down on one knee and pulls him up, removing his helmet. His face is a mask of blood. But he's still alive.

The whole crowd whistles and protests, while the fans of the red stable cheer. Their chariot is back in first place and has opened up a wide lead.

All the fans of the blue stable are shouting out their desperation and our man with the bet is back sitting down with a lost look on his face. The doorman, on the other hand, is on his feet, shouting insults at the red driver.

That's when Sagitta pulls out his master stroke. He lengthens his stride once again, forcing the rest of the team to do the same. In a dramatic charge the blue chariot pulls even with the red. Once they're paired, Sagitta leans a little to the inside, squeezing the opponent against the wall. The blue charioteer immediately catches on to the horse's strategy and follows his lead, pulling the reins to the inside. The maneuver works: the red chariot bangs into the marble wall, the inside wheel running up the side,

"If he keeps that up he'll turn over!" the centurion yells, jubilant. The red chariot brakes to avoid the tragedy, bringing his chariot back into equilibrium. By now the two quadrigae are neck and neck coming down the final stretch.

The two drivers whip the horses savagely, but the sound of the whips is drowned out by the roar exploding from the grandstands. The crowd is on its feet, cheering wildly. Only a few hundred yards to the finish line.

The red driver makes one last try: he whips the horses of the blue chariot. He aims directly for the eyes of the nearest horse: he hits them again and again, but the horse doesn't give in. Sagitta rabidly puts even more force into his stride, dragging the rest of the team and the chariot behind him as they gradually move ahead of their red rival.

The red driver realizes that his victory is slipping away and he starts whipping his opponent with all the strength left in his body. His lashes are powerful, cutting blows that lacerate the skin and score the leather helmet. The whole Circus is up in arms.

Like two streaking meteors, the chariots go whizzing by the imperial tribune. This is it, they're down to the wire. Just a few yards left . . . and here they are, over the finish line. The blue chariot that crosses the line first—not by much, but clearly in the lead. Sagitta might actually have been the first across.

The crowd is delirious. Our man the bettor is beside himself with joy: he thanks the gods one by one and hugs everybody around him, including the centurion, who stands there stiffly and then pushes him away with severity. The Circus Maximus looks to be a single living being, shouting, shaking, waving, and exulting. In some sections of the stands entire groups of fans start punching each other. They're acting just like today's hooligans, confronting each other in violent battles in soccer stadiums. The authorities do what they can to prevent such outbursts but, just like today, it's difficult to control these conflicts, which often degenerate into riots with injuries and even deaths.

The Well-Deserved Prize . . . in Sesterces

Down on the track the atmosphere is very different. The men from the blue stable have come out en masse and are celebrating with their victorious charioteer. The stable masters untie the horses and rub them down. The charioteer takes off his helmet, his face radiant, and looks contemptuously at the red quadriga as it slinks out of the arena, disappearing under the arcades of the starting gate, where he had started out so sure of victory.

The race officials scrupulously record the results of the race, and next to the name of the blue charioteer they write *erupit et vicit,* meaning, in essence, "he won at the wire with a last-second lunge." Every victory has a brief but effective description to be left to posterity in the annals: *successit et vicit* ("after a long time in the back of the pack he overtook the leader to win") or *occupavit et vicit* (jumping to the lead at the start he stayed in first place all the way to the end").

So what happens to the winner now? There aren't any shared podiums; only the winner is celebrated. Second is as good as last, even though he receives a small prize. Now it's time for the winning quadriga to take a victory lap, to receive the applause and ovations of the crowd. The charioteer has won what might be the most satisfying victory of his whole career. And as the winning drivers often do, he takes his lap on the back of his best-performing horse, usually an outside horse. And the choice today, obviously, is Sagitta.

So horse and rider are both out on the track again, and the crowd is throwing flowers and strips of blue cloth, singing victory marches, and chanting the names of both charioteer and steed. Our betting man is crying profusely. He's overwhelmed with emotion. He's now going to pocket a sum the likes of which he has never seen before. Behind the man on horseback some race assistants are already repairing the track for the next race. They fill in the holes, sweep the track smooth with big mats, remove the fragments of broken chariots that might hurt the horses.

Surprisingly, the only study of what the composition of the track surface might have been was the one done for the film *Ben Hur*. It was determined that a packed-earth surface threw up too much dust. After countless tries, they came up with the best possible solution: several layers of gravel, with the roughest layer on the bottom, gradually getting finer and finer up to the top layer of sand. But what was the real track of the Circus Maximus made of? The answer to this little enigma lies some twenty-five feet under the present surface where tourists walk or joggers go for runs. Drilling samples have revealed a bottom layer of big pieces of broken pottery to drain off rainwater that otherwise would have turned the track into a swamp, and then, moving upward, finer and finer layers of crushed pottery. In reality, this layered structure is very reminiscent of the Romans' road-building technique. The track of the Circus was probably inspired by the Romans' experience as road builders.

Now the charioteer on horseback has completed his victory lap, and he stops near the finish line. To his right is the *pulvinar*, where, in the absence of Emperor Trajan, the race organizer will present him with his prize. Amid the acclamation of the crowd, he dismounts from Sagitta and slips into a doorway leading to the stage. When he reappears he approaches the man with the purple toga, who smiles at him.

With a regal manner and solemn gestures he pronounces some ceremonial phrases and offers him the prize: a palm branch and a laurel wreath, which he accepts with his head bowed, sweaty and dusty. Her also receives a hefty prize on the order of tens of thousands of sesterces (between 30,000 and 50,000, or more). If our theoretical exchange rate of $2.50 per sestertius is right, his prize is worth between $75,000 and $125,000! Considering that the races are held at least twice and often four times a month (and probably even more frequently), it's easy to figure out that the charioteers really lived on a whole different planet from ordinary Romans.

Now the charioteer makes his exit amid slaps on the back. And a lot of looks, which leave no room for interpretation, on the part of many of the women in the crowd.

How Much Do Charioteers Make? And Who Are They?

In the Roman era, just like in motorcycle and auto racing today, there are some great champions. Some of their names have come down to us, such as Calpurnianus with his 1,127 wins, and Gaius Appuleius Diocles, who won one-third of his races, coming in first 1,462 times. Their victories brought them vast sums of money. The former earned more than 1 million sesterces, the latter an astonishing 36 million, or about $90 million. An outrageous sum for the time considering that a legionnaire earned the equivalent in sesterces of less than $250 per month.

But exactly who were these champions of the Circus Maximus? What did they look like? We know some of their faces, thanks to some extraordinary renderings on display in a room of the National Roman Museum in Palazzo Massimo in Rome. They are the marble busts of seven famous chariot-racing champions, the equivalents of our Mario Andretti, Michael Schumacher, and Ayrton Senna from Formula 1, or even better, the great champions of horseracing, Bill Shoemaker, Eddie Arcaro, and Laffit Pincay. These busts were rediscovered in a small temple dedicated to Hercules during the excavations for the Trastevere Station in Rome in the nineteenth century. The charioteers themselves commissioned their marble portraits to be displayed in the temple, perhaps to thank Hercules for their victories.

The temple soon became a sort of Hall of Fame of the era, a place where generations could admire the faces of the champions who thrilled the crowds at the Circus Maximus. They lived at different times in the span of the 120 years between Nero and Marcus Aurelius. In their busts some are young and others more mature, evidently some of the handful who reached the end of their career in good health. Some of them have beards in line with fashion at the time of Hadrian. We don't know their names, but we can guess the origins of some of them. One in particular has some features that betray his probable roots in Egypt or the Near East. He was young and very focused on his appearance. It's surprising, in fact, to see the almost maniacal precision of his hairstyle: an infinite series of curls placed in orderly rows. The busts confirm that after chalking up a certain number of victories these charioteers became real stars: rich, celebrated, capricious, and always in line with the latest trends in fashion.

It's tempting to compare them to a lot of the champions in modern sports. Some lived in luxurious villas and could afford all the comforts they wanted, just like the patrician class. So they were envied by the more humble classes but also looked on with contempt by the intellectual and cultivated classes for their crassness and vulgarity.

In reality, the life of a professional charioteer wasn't fit for a citizen of Rome. Racing was considered an activity for social rejects; for the most part they were slaves or men from the poorer rungs of society seeking vindication or freedom (purchased with their winnings). So they were almost always men who were uneducated, often vulgar, blessed with sudden wealth and status. Even though they were sports champions, they couldn't hide their humble origins and were looked down on despite their fame and wealth.

The Circus Empties Out

The crowd streams down the grandstands and out of the stadium. There'll be another day of racing before too long, but it'll be tough for it to be as thrilling as the one they've just seen. Today's race will be talked about for a long time to come. On the streets and in the taverns, as well as at the banquets of the rich or in the Forum, Sagitta's name will be on everyone's lips. The centurion comes down the steps and slips into the corridors, blending into the crowd. He pushes some slow movers out of his way and then, finally, with a look of relief on his face, he stops near a wall and leans his forehead up against it (the wall is black from all the men who have done this same thing before he arrived). What for? Then two people move out of the way and we can see the scene: it's a urinal, one of the many distributed throughout the Circus. It's a kind of vertical canal dug into the wall;

it comes from the floor above and continues down to the floor below. This tells us that the various urinals are arranged in columns and that they're connected. There's no need to flush, a continuous stream of water flows down the whole column to carry away the urine and the foul smell. Off to the side there's a kind of washtub or fountain; we can't see it very well because of the crowd in the corridor, where lots of people are drinking, washing their hands, or splashing some water on their faces.

These are latrines for the popular classes. The wealthy, the senators, and the VIPs sit in their own special sections and naturally their toilets are separate from those of the Circus crowd. They're the same kind that you can see at a lot of archaeological sites: a long stone bench with a row of holes that people sit over. The privacy of modern times doesn't exist, but people use their clothes to conceal their private parts. As for the rest—grimaces, smells, grunts, and other noises—well, it's all in the public domain.

Despite these habits and behaviors that seem rather distant from western society, the circulation of water in a structure as gigantic as the Circus underscores the grandeur of this masterpiece of ancient civil engineering.

We make our way out. Some pigeons fly over our heads, with one wing painted blue. Something invented by the fans to celebrate? No, an unusual system for communicating as quickly as possible who won. It's an idea that was thought up a long time ago by, it seems, a resident of Volterra in Tuscany (a certain Cecina), in order to shorten the anxiety of his fellow citizens who had bet on the race. Instead of waiting a long time to hear the result, they will know in just a couple of hours because of the pigeons. Evidently, this old system is still in vogue under Trajan. We don't know where the pigeons are headed, but one thing is sure: the passion for betting on chariot races is universal throughout the empire.

Whatever happened to our betting man? He's gone to collect his winnings. We see him walking by with a big bag under his arm, which, unbeknownst to us, is full of gold aurei. Another bag, almost the same size, is full of sesterces. For security reasons as well as health reasons, he left the building where the payment was made, by a side door. He practically cleaned out the betting table. Now, incognito, he makes his way through the unknowing crowd, his eyes staring at the ground, obviously in shock. Who knows what he'll do now. How will he spend all his money—on more bets? Or maybe after this win he'll straighten himself out. We'll never know. But we will see how he's going to spend at least one of the coins he won.

Still distracted, he's about to cross an intersection of streets, but he stops to let by a yellow litter with red decorations. While he's waiting a hand grabs his elbow. He immediately turns to defend his money, but there's no need. It's a beggar, a man with hollow cheeks and a beard. His eyes have a gentle look to them, instinctively kind. And above all they're bright and penetrating. The bettor stares at him. He doesn't know why, but he understands that he has to help him. Maybe he feels like he owes a debt to fate, or maybe he sees the beggar as a sign from the gods, a request for an offering in return for the good fortune that some divinity sent his way. He sticks his hand into his bag and pulls out a sestertius. A significant sum for a beggar. He thrusts it into his palm and closes his hand over it with a smile. Then he walks off, vanishing into the crowd.

The beggar opens his hand and looks, amazed to see a beautiful coin with an engraving of Trajan's great victory in Mesopotamia. It's our sestertius changing hands once again. The beggar heads on his way and goes to spend it to buy as much food as possible to allow his destitute family to survive another day.

The Circus Maximus disappears behind the beggar, among the houses and the alleyways, almost like a transatlantic cruise ship tied up at the dock of an ever more distant port. The stage set of power, the pulsing heart of the life of Rome, the driving force behind the financial and economic success of thousands of people, from the stable masters, to the bettors, to the salespeople in the stores—it will go on for generations, the roar of its crowds echoing through the capital of the empire.

The fate of the Circus Maximus will be inevitably tied to the fate of the Eternal City. Its last races will be run more than four hundred years from now under the Goth king Totila, more than a century after the fall of the empire. Then the whole area will become a swamp and the structure will be looted and plundered. Later on, under Charlemagne, water mills will be built to exploit the same stream used by the Romans to wet down the track and cool the hubs of the chariot wheels. In the end, the Circus will be totally stripped of its marble and even its obelisks, which the popes will recycle, moving them to the Piazza del Popolo and the Piazza San Giovanni, in the heart of Rome.

Today the Circus Maximus has gone back to attracting crowds, but for other reasons: rock concerts, speeches, protest demonstrations, victory celebrations (for instance, the celebration of Italy's 2006 World Cup victory). New pages of history silently superimpose themselves over earlier pages, written with the faces of the emperors, the charioteers, and the anonymous crowds of ancient Rome.

OSTIA

~ A Real Tower of Babel ~

Who's the Immigrant: The Romanian or the Roman?

The beggar spent our sestertius in a shop that sells bread, cheese, and other food items. We'll never see him again; he and his family belong to those thousands of anonymous people who live, or rather, survive, on the streets of Rome.

A few minutes later, a slave comes into the same store to buy some bread and other food to eat during the day. Our sestertius is part of his change. He opens the purse that his master had given him for the day's shopping and drops the sestertius in among the other coins. We're back on the road again.

The young slave is walking at a brisk pace. He's whistling because the errand he's been sent on will take him outside the city of Rome, giving him a respite from the heavy load of things he has to take care of every day for his master. He's on his way to Ostia. And he's carrying just a few coins with him, including our sestertius.

Our coin is leaving Rome, where it has been for a long time now. But that's normal, because the city of Rome is the largest marketplace in the world in this era, with almost a million people who buy something every day. Every day. Can you imagine the huge exchange of coins that takes place in twenty-four hours? Our sestertius ran the risk of never leaving Rome again.

But now it's with this young slave with his shaved head. He's not much more than a boy and he comes from Dacia. Today we'd say he was Romanian, but in the age of Trajan this part of Europe has only recently entered into Rome's orbit, by way of one of the empire's most violent wars of conquest, which lasted five years (from 101 to 106 CE). Now it is a province of the empire. This young man was one of the many prisoners taken by the Romans, and he's been here for ten years. A lot of prisoners were put to work in the amphitheaters, to fight against wild beasts or as gladiators, and the citizens of Rome have been able to see the tough stuff that these proud enemies of Rome are made of.

The conquest of Dacia has brought a lot of gold to Rome, fattening the coffers of the empire. But history has forgotten the fate of thousands of men, women, and children torn away from their homeland. At war's end, between deaths and refugees who fled to bordering lands, the population of Dacia was so depleted that Rome had to bring in new colonists.

And where did the new settlers of the future Romania come from? From Italy, southern Germany, and Gaul (France)—exactly the reverse of today's migration pattern.

So many of the present-day inhabitants of Romania (not the Rom, who are originally from northern India and came later) are the descendants of those western Europeans who went there over nineteen centuries ago. Over the course of the generations, their DNA mixed with that of other populations who arrived later; we don't really know how much of their original DNA is still present. But in any case something else has remained. Listen to a Romanian talk and you'll notice immediately how similar his language is to Italian, Spanish, and French. Some dialects of Italian are much harder for Italians to understand than Romanian.

The young man continues along the Via Ostiensis—the road to Ostia. He left Rome early in the morning, just at the right time to see the arrest, during a raid, of the owners of a big bakery in Rome. It's something that will make the news. In these big bakeries grain is milled into flour and then cooked to make bread. Near the bakeries the owners have built some taverns where people can drink, eat, and entertain themselves with prostitutes on the upper floors. But the bakery we're talking about has a dark side. Numerous customers who came there to buy bread or have sex have disappeared. As was discovered later, they were kidnapped and forced into slavery, and made to turn the grindstones of the mill. The owners knew how to choose their victims—they were certainly not people who lived in the neighborhood, but strangers. Who would ever come to look for them there? They were *desaparecidos*, vanished in the chaos of Rome. The scheme turned sour when they tried to kidnap a soldier, who reacted by killing some of the would-be kidnappers. It's a true story handed down to us by the ancient authors. This too is Rome.

How to Mail a Letter in the Roman Era

In modern times it takes about twenty minutes to get to Ostia from Rome, but in ancient times it is quite a long walk. Our slave has done some hitchhiking, taking advantage of the wagon traffic on the Via Ostiensis, one of the busiest roads of the empire. In fact, it is really the port of entry to Rome for anyone arriving in the capital by sea. It's no coincidence that the neighborhoods to the south of Rome that have grown up alongside this important road are inhabited by lots of immigrants.

What is the errand the slave has been sent on? In a certain sense, he has gone to deliver some letters for his master and his master's relatives and friends. In fact, he's carrying a shoulder bag containing numerous pieces of mail.

In the Roman era, as we have seen, there is a very efficient postal service, the *cursus publicus*, which delivers official dispatches and letters anywhere in the empire in a very short time, thanks to couriers on horseback. But ordinary people, including the wealthy, are not allowed to use these government couriers for private correspondence. They have to make their own arrangements.

The simplest way is to take advantage of people you know who are leaving on a journey. So if you've got a friend who's going to visit his son in Lugdunum (Lyon) in Gaul, you give him a letter to take to your aunt who happens to live there, and whom you haven't heard from in ages. One letter from the second century CE reads, "Since I happened upon someone from Cyrene who was coming your way, I felt the need to let you know that I'm safe and sound."

According to Professor Romolo Augusto Staccioli of the University of Rome, sometimes people form a consortium, by turns making one of their slaves available who follows a postal itinerary that's useful for them all, with various stops along the way.

Even though it's an ingenious system, there's a problem: you have to wait until there are enough letters to be delivered to the same destination in order to make the trip worthwhile. And often it takes a long time. As Professor Staccioli points out, Cicero excuses himself for the delay in responding to his brother, Quinto, with a postscript that speaks volumes: "I've had your letter in hand for a number of days, waiting for the availability of the 'postmen.' . . . Then, as soon as one of these couriers appears on the horizon you have to scribble down a letter as fast as possible." Again Cicero: "You've got some strange couriers . . . when they're about to leave, they pester you continuously for letters but when they come back they don't bring you anything. In any event, they'd do me a favor if they gave me two minutes to write, but instead they come in, don't even take off their hat, and tell me their companions are waiting for them downstairs."

So is this young slave carrying bundles of letters sealed in envelopes? Not quite—envelopes don't yet exist. Usually the letter is written on a sheet of papyrus (more rarely parchment, that is, sheep, goat, or calf-skin). But since sheets of papyrus are expensive, letters are usually very brief. They are then rolled or folded so that the writing is on the inside, a cord is tied around it and fixed with a drop of wax, on which the seal is impressed (at the knot or on the loose end of the cord). The seal, a little like the sticky edge of our envelopes, functions as a guarantee that no one has opened it and read it.

It's easy to understand, therefore, why seal rings are so widespread among the Roman population (and in today's museums). They are useful for letters; for signing documents; for closing jewel boxes, larders, and so on.

The address is written on the outside fold of the letter and is usually brief and direct: "To Ausonius from his brother Marcus," for example, because it is assumed that the person who will be delivering the letter has been informed about how to get it there.

For very distant destinations, overseas, there are other ways to send letters. If, for example, you urgently need to send a letter to Alexandria, in Egypt, but you don't know anyone who is planning to go there, you go to the port and look for a ship that is going to that city, entrusting the letter to one of the passengers. It would be like our going to the airport today to ask a passenger to deliver a letter for us. Usually, travelers never refuse to carry a letter for someone. It's a time-honored practice; also, it gives the traveler a contact (the recipient) in the place where he's going, in case he needs some help in resolving a problem.

Ostia: A Real Tower of Babel

The slave finally arrives in Ostia. He jumps off the wagon that has brought him here and bids farewell to his fellow slave, his head also shaved, who continues on his way toward a farm.

Before him is the monumental entrance to Ostia, the Roman Gate, consisting of an enormous white marble arch, fifteen feet wide with two large square masonry towers on the sides. These towers are part of the city's defensive walls, built by Sulla generations ago.

In fact, Ostia is a very old city. Its name comes from *ostium*, or mouth, because of its location. It was founded in the fourth century BCE close to the shore, beside the mouth of the Tiber, near some salt marshes. We don't realize it anymore, but salt, so easy to come by today, was a prized natural resource for thousands of years.

By today's reckoning Ostia might be considered the main airport of ancient Rome. Goods and people bound for Rome from all over the empire arrive here by sea. It is a true economic, cultural, and ethnic funnel directed toward the city. It's interesting to think that today's Leonardo da Vinci International Airport is just a mile and a half north of the site of ancient Ostia. A lot of arriving flights fly right over the ruins as they come in to land. This is one place where past and present really do overlap.

And to dwell for a moment on the airport analogy, just as the faces you see today at the da Vinci airport are of people from all over the world, so it was at the port of Ostia in ancient times. Entering the city and proceeding down the main street, the *decumanus maximus*, our slave encounters all the faces of the empire, faces we would refer to today as German, Spanish, English, French, Macedonian, Greek, Turkish, Syrian, Lebanese, Egyptian, Tunisian, Algerian, Moroccan. . . .

It's an enormous crowd of people, as diverse as can be. It's not the first time the slave has been here, but every time he is struck by the people he encounters. Two blond-haired merchants, their fair skin reddened by sunburn, pass by him talking to each other in an incomprehensible Nordic language, whose sounds originate in their throats and not on their tongues like Latin. Right after them he passes three dark-skinned, curly-haired sailors. Their language is exactly the opposite: the *r*'s rumble in their mouths like so many drumrolls. Their words are drowned out by the rhythmic and metallic approach of a squad of soldiers; the first soldier has red hair and freckles, and with each step he takes you can hear the creaking of all the leather he's wearing. Yes, even the clothing talks and indicates the disparate origins of the passersby. Before the eyes of our slave a veritable parade of fashion passes by with the long, colorful gowns of oriental traders, the plaid pants of the Celts, the ragged tunics of old salt sailors, the loincloths of slaves, and so on.

But the people's origins are also betrayed by odors. For a second our slave comes under the scrutiny of a green-eyed woman wearing a veil. Her gaze is like a whiplash. Those green eyes against her dark skin are clearly those of a woman from the East. Her exotic perfume, sweet, intense, and penetrating, hits the slave like a tidal wave. But it's better that he not return her look: she's the slave and concubine of an oriental merchant, a small man who walks with a pompous strut. In an instant she disappears into the crowd, amid tunics and capes. All you can smell now is the sweat of the stevedores working on the docks.

Our slave has never heard so many different languages spoken at the same time. In this respect, too, Ostia resembles the check-in area of an international airport. It's a true Tower of Babel. Maybe the only one that ever really existed. . . .

As the slave continues down the street, flanked by porticoes with all kinds of shops, we can make a few observations. All of these languages, from the African of Libya to the Germanic of northern Europe, continue to exist and flourish despite Roman domination. Nobody has imposed a language, eliminating local tongues. The Romans are very careful not to erase the traditions and cultures of the peoples making up the empire. Except, of course, those traditions that are against the law or the Roman sense of order.

Consequently, we discover a curiosity: if the mother tongues remain in use in the various provinces this means that wherever you go there are always two languages, the local one and Latin (except in Rome, where Latin is obviously also the mother tongue). Though there were those who spoke it perfectly, Latin being almost everyone's second language, it was often spoken badly! Exactly like what happens today with English: it's used by everyone but spoken with very different accents, pronunciations, and cadences all over the world. And in certain remote areas of the empire the people don't speak Latin at all.

Beyond the local languages, Latin is not the only official language of the empire. There is also another one: Greek. The empire can be summarily divided like this: Latin is spoken from the British Isles to the Adriatic, while from the Adriatic to the Middle East, the dominant language is Greek. Greek is the language of the cultural elite; for this reason all the patrician families make their children learn Greek as well as Latin, and so they tend to be bilingual.

And the same thing is advisable for those who travel frequently in the Mediterranean. If you leave Ostia and go west, you'll have to know how to read, write, and speak Latin; if instead you go east, the language you need to know is Greek.

A Cosmopolitan City

It's clear that, just as there are different nationalities present in Ostia, there are also different religions. Besides the Roman ones, here in Ostia practically all religions of the world are practiced. Archaeologists have uncovered a number of Mithraic sanctuaries, temples where people venerated Mithra, a divinity from Persia (Iran). Excavations have also uncovered a synagogue, the oldest in Europe. There is also evidence that Christianity was practiced here. We know that the Egyptian goddess Isis was worshipped, and we can say with certainty that there was a cult of Cybele, the great mother of Phrygia. She was very popular in Ostia where the Asian population was numerous. We even know the name of a priestess, Metilia Acte, and also her husband, Junius Euhodus, as they are inscribed on their sarcophagi.

All of this tells us that Ostia was an extraordinarily diverse and multiethnic city, where in this phase of the empire different languages and religions cohabited without problems. According to Carlo Pavolini, who has conducted excavations and studied Ostia for many years, "Until the twentieth century there didn't exist anywhere in the world a society as open as Roman society."

But apart from the people passing through, who are the inhabitants of Ostia? Ship owners and outfitters, freed men, slaves, laborers, dockworkers, artisans, shop owners, clerks who work in the offices of the huge warehouses, shippers by both land and sea, firefighters, restaurant owners, proprietors of small inns and hotels, and so on. Ostia could be described as a "little Rome."

Identikit of a Migrant Population

Archaeologists have excavated the tombs of the inhabitants of the nearby town of Porto, in the necropolis at Isola Sacra. They uncovered eight hundred skeletons. In an interview published by *National Geographic*, Luca Bondioli of the Pigorini Museum in Rome, who coordinated the analysis of the skeletons, revealed a very interesting fact: teeth can be considered a sort of black box for human beings since their enamel conserves traces of isotopes of oxygen contained in the water a person drank when his or her teeth were coming in. A comparison of the data from the first and third molars (which begin to grow much later, between the ages of ten and seventeen) indicate that one-third of the people in the necropolis were born in some other part of the empire and came to Ostia in their adolescence, perhaps together with their families. And they lived here until they died. This would mean, according to Bondioli, that immigrants were not only single men but entire families. And since Ostia is almost a suburb of Rome, these eight hundred skeletons studied by Bondioli are also a kind of snapshot of the crowd we would have encountered on the streets of Rome.

At this site archaeologists also discovered the oldest-known amputation: the femur of a man was sawed off right above the knee, and he survived for years afterward. This is yet more proof of the great surgical skills of Roman physicians—amputation was a well-experimented technique not least because it was practiced on the battlefields—and of the tough constitution of people back then. Tough constitutions but not great stature. Analysis of the skeletons show that the average height was four feet, eleven inches for women and five feet, four inches for men. Walking through the crowd in Ostia, most of us would probably have felt very tall.

Our slave goes into a *popina*. He's dying of thirst. While he's waiting to be served he observes four men sitting at a table. They are of modest social status. One in particular surprises him. He doesn't seem to ever open his mouth, as though he were holding something between his teeth.

When he laughs his mouth remains rigid and the slave notices that his front teeth are missing. What happened to him?

The slave doesn't know it, but that man has been struck by a rare congenital disease, called syngnathia. His jawbone remains fused to his cranium, with no articulation, making it impossible for him to open his jaws. To enable him to eat, his front teeth have been extracted, opening up a window in his otherwise locked teeth. Rather than eat, the man drinks and consumes mushy globs of food, like an infant. But his disease is not his life's only misadventure. He's part of the community of workers who work in the salt pans. It's a very tough job.

A vast necropolis of salt workers was identified in modern times not very far from Ostia, after unauthorized excavations had begun to unearth skeletons and objects. Archaeologists from the Archaeological Superintendency of Rome, coordinated by Laura Cianfriglia, brought to light some 270 burials. They are what you might expect to find in a poor community: modest, simple, few or no precious objects (only one-third of them had something like a pitcher or a pair of earrings), but rich in information. There is a beautiful necklace, simple, almost primitive, but touching, found around the neck of a baby boy and propitiatory for the next life: it had animal teeth, rounded fragments of ceramic vases, seashells, amber, and a pendant with the Egyptian divinity Bes; objects perhaps found on the street rather than purchased. The excavations also dug up seventy coins, placed in the mouths of the deceased or next to the body, as an offering for Charon. Among the coins was, imagine this, a sestertius with the image of Trajan. It's green from oxidation and the emperor's head is worn away in the center, at the level of his cheekbones and temples, a sign of long wear owing to constant exchanges, rubbing, and clashes. Another story waiting to be told.

The dead talk to us and tell us about their hard lives through the scientific data that emerge from the ground along with their skeletons. According to Paola Catalano, director of the anthropological section of the Superintendency, many of the skeletons show signs of fractures, damage, and wear and tear to the spinal column. Also clear reactions to prolonged effort and mechanical stress in the areas where tendons and ligaments attach to bones; bone protrusions; traces of chronic inflammation. . . .

It's easy to imagine the daily routine of the workers in the salt pans, with the heavy sacks of salt to carry, the shimmering glare that quickly consumes their eyesight, and the salt that makes even the smallest scratch or cut burn.

In 72 percent of the cases the skeletons are men, and few of them are young. Here, too, the age of death is striking: between twenty and forty for the men, even younger for the women, whom we could define as teenagers; in fact, most of the females buried here died toward the end of their adolescence. They are not slaves or *liberti*; they're poor Romans. And among these skeletons the archaeologists have found the one belonging to this man at the *popina,* afflicted with syngnathia.

The pitcher has finally been served and our slave, with his shaved head, drinks avidly, leaning against the counter. His gaze wanders over the walls of the tavern where all he can see is vulgar drawings and phrases. Then he happens upon a series of portraits that embellish one of the walls.

It's a very well-executed decoration, different from the ones on the other walls. It represents seven wise men, and under each of these so-called philosophers there is a motto that sums up their thought. His curiosity piqued, the slave sharpens his gaze, expecting to discover some illuminating teaching, some philosophical insight, and then he bursts out laughing. He laughs so loud that some of the customers turn to look. They are phrases that were unearthed intact by archaeologists and which synthesize quite nicely the atmosphere of this place: "The ingenious Chilone taught the art of farting without making noise." "Talete advises the constipated to push hard." "A good shit each day keeps the doctor away."

The Great Port of Ostia: The Jugular of Rome

Now the slave is leaving the city. Ostia, contrary to what most people think, is actually only an administrative city. The real port in the imperial age is located about a mile and half north.

Once Rome's dominion began to expand, it didn't take long to realize that the small river port at Ostia was no longer sufficient. There was a constantly growing traffic of cargo ships loaded with foodstuffs and goods for Rome. Ships that transported the famous grain for the capital were too big to come into port, so they anchored offshore and then transshipped their cargo. Or they stopped in Pozzuoli, and from there smaller ships went up the coast to Ostia.

In brief, the capital of the empire needed a bigger port. And so the emperor Claudius began construction of a gigantic port north of Ostia, the port of Claudius. Two semicircular docks were built that "embraced" the sea, creating a basin with an area of 160 acres. It was able to hold as many as two hundred ships.

But the most impressive structure was probably the lighthouse. The engineers brought in an enormous ship, used by Caligula to transport a huge obelisk from Egypt, which is now in Saint Peter's Square. These transport ships were used only once to transport something exceptionally large and then never used again. They were the Roman equivalent of *Saturn V*, the enormous rocket that carried man to the moon. And just as a *Saturn V* rocket is now on display in Houston to be admired by tourists, the same thing happened in the Roman era with one of these gigantic ships, in Pozzuoli. It was pulled up on dry land and left on display as a monument to Roman naval engineering.

At Ostia, the Roman engineers brought Caligula's big ship offshore and sunk it, filling it with concrete. They used it to create an artificial island on which they could mount the lighthouse for the port, which was modeled on the lighthouse in Alexandria.

Today the coastline has advanced about two miles farther out than it was in Roman times. The port of Claudius has been incorporated into the coastal land area and is now part of the da Vinci airport. Some of its features can be seen among the meadows, streets, parking lots, and office buildings. There's also a small museum, with the remains of Roman ships unearthed on the site.

The lighthouse island, this bold feat of engineering, is buried near an intersection not far from one of the airport runways. Hundreds of cars pass it every day, their drivers completely oblivious to the masterwork that lies nearby.

The port of Claudius turned out to be a fiasco. Storms sank ships inside the port and it filled in with sand continually, requiring huge expenditures for repair and maintenance. So Trajan decided to build a new port. And it was a jewel.

It was designed and built by his great architect, the Michelangelo of antiquity: Apollodorus of Damascus. The work lasted twelve years, but in the end everyone admired the project that was so original and innovative for the time. The new harbor, connected to the earlier one but farther inland, had the shape of a perfect hexagon, with over six hundred feet of dock space. It is a structure with an eighty-acre surface area that today, seen from the air, is still striking for its perfection and beauty. Not only does it perform its function perfectly, it also projects a bold and avant-garde image. We might compare it to the glass pyramid that marks the entrance to the Louvre in Paris.

A connecting canal was built between the Tiber and the sea and new warehouses were added. Now our shaved-head slave is passing in front of these immense buildings, which surround the docks of the hexagonal port in perfect order. They too are masterpieces in their own right. To keep the grain from going bad inside the sacks, little pilasters (*suspensurae*) raise the level of the pavement of the various *cellae* about a foot above the ground so air can circulate underneath and protect the sacks from moisture (and animals). Furthermore, the warehouses have small entrances, thick walls, well-sealed doors, little light, and a dry climate.

These warehouses are Rome's strategic reserves; the city couldn't live without them. The grain arrives from Egypt with the good weather. The ships that enter the port are tugged to the dock by a *skapha*, a small boat powered by oars, empty out their holds and then leave again. It is a continuous flow that is interrupted by the harsh winter weather. No ships, in fact, cross the Mediterranean between the months of October and March. Navigation simply stops. So once its great reserves have been accumulated the city goes into hibernation, like a bear that lives on the fat it has built up during the spring and summer. During the winter months the sacks of grain are sent regularly from Ostia to Rome so that there is always bread on the tables of its inhabitants, to prevent uprisings, famine, or even just simple speculation on the price.

On the Tiber there is continuous boat traffic, carrying sacks of grain all year long against the current. The grain is carried on big-bellied boats called *naves caudicariae* (from *caudex*, trunk). As the name implies, they are heavy and not very manageable, and they are used essentially as barges, pulled from the shore by oxen or men. The distance is not great, about fifteen or sixteen miles, but the voyage against the current takes two days.

Now our slave has made it down to the dock. He can't believe his eyes. The view is breathtaking. In the distance, out on the sea, he can see dozens and dozens of ships waiting to come into the harbor to unload their cargo. There are lots of sails unfurled and he can see the shape of the ships, bulging and elegant. The ones farthest away dot the horizon with their silhouettes. It seems to us like we're looking at an ancient version of the Allies landing at Normandy.

The slave observes the activity on the docks; every imaginable kind of good is being unloaded from the ships. As he walks along he sees armies of amphoras and bales of who knows what products, strapped tightly with ropes all around. Some *saccarii*, or porters, are coming out of one ship in single file, carrying sacks of grain, and the boards connecting the bow of the ship to the dock bob up and down rhythmically under the weight of their steps.

In another part of the dock, other stevedores, with the help of special cranes that the Romans call *ciconiae* (storks), are accumulating piles of sealed ceramic goblets, protected with straw. You can see a lot of these in museums; they're red, with stamped decorations. They are the good china of all wealthy families. Once they were the pride of Italy, from the Arezzo area to be exact. Now they make them in the south of Gaul—a little like what happens with our products today, copied in China and sold at lower prices.

In the middle of all this confusion is a young boy about twelve years old, with red hair and freckles, sitting on the dock fishing with his feet dangling over the water. He's already caught two gray mullets, but now he's aiming for octopus. He's using some grapnels just like the ones that are used today.

The shaved-head slave stops. One of the ships is unloading some gigantic birds that he's never seen before: ostriches. A slave holds one of them still as he walks down the boards in precarious equilibrium. They look like two ballet dancers trying out a new step. The ostrich gives a start, rears back its long neck, and slams its beak against the slave's head. Then it wriggles out of his grasp and tries to get away. The slave wraps his arms around it even tighter and the two of them tumble to the ground, in a chaotic batting of wings that raises a cloud of dust. Other slaves immediately arrive on the scene to block the bird. But another man intervenes who beats the slave savagely with his cane: the ostrich is a rare breed, worth a fortune, and he is ruining it. The slave, bleeding from the blows, limps along, accompanying the ostrich toward a crate sitting on a wagon.

Our slave stops to look, amazed, at the stream of animals coming out of this ship. To us it looks like Noah's ark. And it's not the only one. Animals are coming down from two other ships, docked just a little ways off. We can see gazelles and antelopes (with pieces of wood wrapped around the points of their horns to avoid injuries and damage) and an elephant with its legs in chains. Its disembarkation is particularly difficult, with a lot of outstretched chains and servants ready to intervene. There is also a *procurator ad elephantos*, an imperial functionary specialized in the unloading of these animals, who is supervising the operation. He is standing next to the owner of the animals, a *libertus* who has become filthy rich with this commerce.

Next comes a tiger. He's wearing a curious muzzle made of fabric or red leather wrapped around his lower jaw to keep his mouth wide open so he can't bite anyone. It's not easy to get him to walk down the gangway; he digs in his heels, puffs, swings his paws. He's tied with ropes in front and back so he can't use his legs to spring. The men in charge of unloading this beast are experts. But the deep scars that some of them have tell us that theirs is an occupation full of ugly surprises. Scenes like this one remind us of the ones represented in the mosaics at the archaeological site in Piazza Armerina in Sicily. At one point the villa there apparently belonged to an animal trader who commissioned an enormous mosaic representing all the different ways of capturing and transporting animals for the shows in the Colosseum. It is a truly extraordinary site, for all the other mosaics conserved there as well.

Our slave is observing some crates on the bridges of the ships that are waiting to be unloaded. Through the openings on the front he can see yellow eyes, immersed in a thick mane. They are lions. A sudden roar from one of the crates provokes an echo of other roars from the crates nearby. But from one of them there is no sound. The stevedores are pulling out the lifeless body of a lion. On the average, only one in five of the animals survives the voyage. We can understand, then, how the animal trade in the empire is causing a huge global reduction in the number of wild animals. And it's all done in the name of more spectacular killing in the Colosseum.

The Great Roman Globalization

Our slave finally finds a ship leaving for Spain, where his letter is directed. He's not the only one. There are six other slaves like him walking up and down the dock looking for the right ship for their masters' letters. He spies a well-dressed man standing near the ship that's being unloaded. The leather bag sitting beside him indicates that he's a passenger. He must be a high-ranking officer in the imperial administration. With all the caution imposed on him by the difference in their social class, the slave approaches with his head bowed and asks him if he can carry some his master's letters to Gades (Cadiz), where the ship is going. It's a long voyage, well past the Pillars of Hercules. The city is in the south of the Iberian peninsula, on the Atlantic Coast.

The man stares at him for a minute, shoots a glance at his leather bag, and then looks at the slave again. He has blue eyes and a well-sculpted face. The only thing ruining the harmony of his features is a scar on his chin, but it gives him a lot of personality. He smiles and accepts the commission. The slave adds a small purse that his master gave him: a small indemnity. The man weighs it in his hand. And he opens it; there are sesterces inside. He's about to refuse, but the slave, bowing his head repeatedly, has taken his leave and is already too far away to be called back.

As he watches him go away, the man feels a small hand squeeze his. The man turns around and sees the deep black eyes of a little girl: his daughter. His wife is standing behind her, smiling. The man bends down and stares at the little girl, tickling her chin with a finger. Clearly his family has come to say good-bye to him before his departure. Two slaves have accompanied them. The little girl is quite striking, especially for the way she's dressed; she's put on her best clothes for her papa. She's wearing a lovely linen tunic, an amber ring, a splendid gold necklace with some little sapphires, and a small silk shawl. All very beautiful, costly, and elegant, indicative of the affluent status of the family.

But her outfit indicates some other things to us as well. The tunic was woven in Rome, with linen cultivated in Egypt. The amber comes from the Baltic, the sapphires from Sri Lanka, the silk from China. All by herself, this little girl is a symbol of Roman globalization.

We think of it as a typical aspect of modern society, but one need only consider this empire to understand that globalization began thousands of years ago, albeit, obviously, with slightly different characteristics, tied to the era. In all the countries around the Mediterranean, as far as the deserts to the south and east and the frozen plains of northern Europe, a single currency is used, a single body of laws, the same way of life, the same style of urban design. Even a single language (with the addition of Greek in the east). You can order the same wine in Alexandria and in London. People dress according to the same fashion, and as we have seen on the docks of Ostia, you can even find products that have been copied and resold (those sealed ceramic goblets).

Obviously there are also the same drawbacks of today's globalization, like the loss of local traditions, architectural styles, and cultures absorbed by the new way of life. Its lifestyle and level of consumption, multiplied on a vast scale on three continents, resulted in the depletion of many natural resources, from the savage deforestation of entire coastlines for the wood needed to build ships to the disappearance of native flora and fauna, which were sent to patrician gardens or the various amphitheaters scattered throughout the empire. It even led to the extinction of curative medicinal plants such as *laserpicium* (also called *silphium*, a true panacea for lots of illnesses), which used to grow in Cyrenaica. Nobody today has ever seen this plant.

This place, the port of Ostia, is perhaps one of the most powerful engines of globalization. All you have to do is look around at the ships that are loading and unloading every imaginable kind of merchandise. And in an hour one of them is going to pull away from this dock on its way to the westernmost shores of the empire. Our sestertius will be on board.

SPAIN

~ *Rome's Gold* ~

Toward Roman Spain

The ship has sailed for miles and miles, stopping in a number of ports to load and unload goods. Today the trip from Ostia to Gibraltar takes three hours by plane. In the Roman era, it is a seven-day journey by boat.

Let's pause for a moment to consider something. By now, our journey through the empire has made one thing very clear: the sensation we have, as people of the twenty-first century, is that living and traveling in the Roman era happens in slow motion. Journeys and voyages are endless, even to get to places where now we would go for a quick weekend trip. Letters take days, weeks, even months to deliver a piece of news, and just as long to get an answer.

Needless to say, we would all find it difficult to live without our telephones and text messages, not to mention email and social networks. The same goes for heating in the winter, shampoo, showers, washing machines, local anesthesia at the dentist's, shock absorbers on cars and other vehicles, soft leather or Vibram shoe soles, razors that don't cut your face, gas stoves, coffee. . . .

Nevertheless, there is one thing that we absolutely don't feel the need for in the Roman era: the clock. Here, all the daily rhythms of life seem to flow naturally, like it does when you're on vacation. There's even time to think and meditate (if you are wealthy), something increasingly rare in our frenetically paced modern society. Compared to the drumbeat tempo of our lives, antiquity seems like a real paradise. But there's always the other side of the coin.

You can enjoy the relaxed rhythm of daily life, but not for long: life is short, as we have seen. For this a Roman man would truly envy us: today we live about twice as long as he does and three times longer than his wife. And what's more, we arrive at old age looking much younger and healthier; in the Roman era a forty-year-old man had already lost all his teeth and a forty-year-old woman was considered elderly.

All of this comes to mind as we look out at the intense blue of the sea, which stretches out before us as far as the eye can see. A few hours ago we passed the Strait of Gibraltar, which for all the ancients, including the Romans, were known as the Pillars of Hercules: stretching out before us is the immense expanse of the Atlantic Ocean. For the ancients, this was an abyss in every sense of the word: the end of the known world, the point beyond which nobody ever ventures. Fortunately, we are sailing along the coastline; Cadiz should be coming into view very soon.

Suddenly we notice some movement aboard ship. The sailors and the few passengers all look out toward the coast, to our right. Between us and the shore we can see a veritable constellation of small boats, almost forming a ring. At its center the sea is bubbling and frothing. It's a tuna fishery into which the fish are channeled by a maze of nets. The most famous and productive fisheries of antiquity are located right here on these coasts of the Iberian Peninsula.

As told by Oppian of Corycus (known as Anazarbus in Asia Minor, a Roman-era poet who wrote the *Halieutica*, a colossal work of more than 3,500 verses on fish and fishing techniques), every spring an army of tuna arrives here en masse. The fishermen wait for them with lookouts posted on top of a hill. These men are experts, capable of making a rapid calculation of the quantity of tuna and their direction. As soon as they give the alarm, the trap is sprung. The best places to fish are the inlets along the shore, neither too narrow nor too windy. The essential thing is that the coast at that point must be vertical and deep.

As soon as the tuna are sighted the fishermen throw their nets into the water. According to the poet, their arrangement "is similar to that of a city in which there are doors and rooms," a perfect image to explain how the school of tuna gets channeled into what the poet calls the "corridors of death." The flow of tuna is so abundant that the men can't capture them all, and the fishing ends when the fishermen see that their maze of nets can't hold even one more fish. At that point they close the entry doors. "The fishing is excellent and wonderful," the poet concludes.

And then what happens? Part of the fish is eaten locally, but the rest undergoes a preservation treatment. Thanks to the abundant salt deposits in the area, a proper salting industry has developed, as observed by the historian Strabo, allowing the fish meat to be sold even in distant markets.

The fishery that we have been examining also produces another product: *garum*, the legendary sauce that is present at sumptuous banquets throughout the empire. With respect to price, popularity, and demand *garum* is comparable to our balsamic vinegar (though its taste is completely different). How is it made?

The Secrets of Garum

We have now arrived in Cadiz and our sestertius is bouncing around inside the pouch hanging from the belt of our imperial functionary. His name is Marcus Valerius Primis. Since he's on official business for the government he's found free lodging in an inn of the *cursus publicus,* and now he's out on the streets, delivering the letters that were entrusted to him. One of them is addressed to the owner of an establishment that produces *garum*, just outside the city.

It doesn't take long to get there; it's on the coast. From a distance, the functionary can already see some boats transshipping some large tuna, probably the ones caught in the *tonnara* that he saw as his ship was approaching the port, a few hours ago.

He's amazed by the acrid odor of rotten fish that he can smell even before he gets to the factory, from quite far away. It's really unbearable. It's no wonder that the factory has been built outside the city. It is a white stone complex of buildings at the end of an unpaved red clay road. On the last part of the road fish bones are strewn all over the place.

Marcus pronounces the name of the recipient of the letter to the slave guarding the entrance and discovers that it's the name of the owner.

A few seconds later, a pleasingly plump and affable man arrives, and after introducing himself, he takes the letter and kisses it, his eyes looking up to the heavens. It's a letter from his brother, who has finally responded to an earlier one of his.

He reads it in a flash, devouring the lines, and then, happy about the news he's received, asks Marcus if he has ever seen a *garum* plant. Marcus has not, and the owner accompanies him to show him the production process. It's an opportunity for us, too, to see how they make a sauce that's practically worth its weight in gold.

It's a fairly big factory, with its buildings arranged in a horseshoe configuration around a large courtyard. The *garum* is made in the left and right wings, and the middle building, facing the sea is where the fish are brought in to be processed. This particular plant doesn't only make *garum*; it's also where the salting of the fish takes place.

We go through a door to enter the middle building. It is very long and occupied by a series of long stone counters, where a number of slaves are cutting open the fish and cleaning them. The fish get a preliminary salting, inside and out, and then they're sent along to the processing line.

What strikes Marcus, and us, is that the entrails are not discarded but are put into a bucket and taken away, amid hordes of flies. We follow one of the buckets as the owner explains to us how they make *garum*.

There are different methods for the various varieties of the sauce. It's not something you want to talk about at the dinner table, but to make a long story short, the fish guts are put into a container together with a large quantity of salt. They add some very small fish, such as sand smelt—similar to miniscule sardines—or some baby red mullet. Then everything is left to steep for a long time under the sun, with frequent stirring. The heat and the sunlight will decompose the mixture, but the salt will keep it from getting really rotten. At this point, a fine-mesh wicker sieve is lowered into the container and pressed down to the bottom. The dark liquid that filters into the sieve is the most precious part. It will be bottled in little amphoras and served at table: this is *garum*. The sediment that remains on the bottom of the tub or container is a dense substance of lower quality, also served at table, called *allec*.

There are also some variations on this recipe. One calls for mixing together mackerel, anchovies, and other fish, churning them into a mush that is put into amphoras. These are left out in the sun for two or three months, with regular stirring, and then some old wine is added, in a proportion of two to one with respect to the fish mush. Finally, the amphora is closed and put in the cellar. We imagine that when it is opened the liquid will have the unusual taste of fish-flavored wine.

Now the owner takes us into the heart of his plant: the tubs where the *garum* has been left to steep. It looks like something out of Dante's *Inferno*. We see all the tubs arranged in a line, filled to the brim with a dense purple liquid, with fish bones floating on the top. Some slaves are mixing the liquid mush with long sticks. The smell is unbearably acrid; it penetrates our nostrils and sticks to our clothes. Flies are everywhere; it really is a revolting scene. Marcus has an obvious look of disgust on his face.

Yet the owner seems to be perfectly at ease here. And he says to us, raising a finger and pointing it toward some amphoras, that this is where they produce the best variety of *garum*. It's made of tuna entrails, together with the gills, serum, and blood, and salt. The whole mixture is poured into clay containers and left to steep for no more than two months. Then a hole is punched in the container and what flows out is premium-quality *garum* . . . or at least that's what people think.

How can people like such a disgusting brew? Just think, at banquets it is poured, with the greatest ceremony, on meat and a host of other dishes. The taste? When attempts have been made to follow the recipe, the result is a liquid that tastes like very salty anchovy paste. This is the kind of flavor and taste that was loved by the Romans. It's probably the salt that keeps this concoction from becoming toxic. The Romans use it not only as a condiment but also as a preservative, and even as medicine.

Our visit is over. Marcus is on his way back to the city and has filled his lungs with the cool ocean air. He'll never deliver another letter to a place like this. In his arms is a small amphora of *garum* that the plant owner has given him as a present. It is of the highest quality.

Where Does Rome Get Its Gold?

A few days have gone by. Marcus has made his way north, passing through Hispalis (Seville) and Italica (where Trajan was born). The region is called Baetica, from the name of the river Baetis, the present-day Guadalquiver. It will acquire the name Andalusia with the fall of the Roman Empire in the West.

He finally reaches his destination, in the far north, the region that in modern times is called Galicia, in the future province of Gallaecia, on the border between Spain and Portugal. This is where the gold mines are.

In fact, Marcus has been sent here, in his capacity as imperial functionary, to inspect the gold production in these open-pit mines. They are among the largest in the empire and they're located in a true natural Eden.

Marcus got up early this morning, before dawn. The goal of the long march he set out on, escorted by a column of soldiers and some other functionaries, is the top of a steep slope at the edge of a plateau. When they reached the top, the sun came up over the horizon, unveiling the extraordinary landscape of these mines.

All around us broad waves of undulating hills, rounded and smoothed by time, seem to vanish into the distance. Their flanks are adorned by the trembling green foliage of chestnut trees. Here and there natural towers, ravines, and canyons emerge like icebergs, sculpted by the erosion of the high plateau.

Suddenly, this beautiful virgin landscape is interrupted by an apocalyptic vision: at the foot of the slope, where the column of soldiers and functionaries has stopped, an immense lunar landscape opens up for miles around, totally treeless and devoid of life. It looks like the bed of a dried-up lake, but in reality it's more than that. It is a deep wound inflicted on the earth, a gash tearing the flesh of this harmonious landscape.

None of this is the work of the gods. It is the work of man. In this Dantean vision, thousands of microscopic human figures are moving around like so many agitated ants. They have been at work since the first light of dawn. The jumbled sound of shouts and clanking equipment arrives all the way up here. This is our first glimpse of the great gold mines of the empire.

The tall cliff that Marcus is standing on will be made to collapse into the underlying lunar valley, bringing to light the layer of gold that it's covering. The collapse will be provoked by a devastating technique that Pliny the Elder defined as *ruina montium*, literally, "destruction of the mountain." The name says it all.

Everything is just about ready for a new collapse. A few minutes ago the signal was given to evacuate the mines. At a number of points around Marcus, on the top of the cliff, you can see a lot of pits from which the first miners have started coming out in groups of two or three. They're dirty and exhausted; their faces are tense, their eyes wide with fear. It's not yet the moment of demolition, obviously, but they don't know that.

Who are these men and what's beyond that dark opening that descends vertically into the terrain just a short distance away from the edge of the cliff?

In just a few minutes a steady stream of human beings comes out of the mines. One of the miners trips and falls and is trampled by those behind him. They seem crazed. They push and shove each other to speed up the exit along an endless series of wooden stairs that lead them out of that subterranean inferno. Some of them are naked, others are dressed in rags. Their bodies are emaciated, covered with mud, scratches, and cuts. Their cheeks are hollow, and their chins bearded. Their missing teeth accentuate the look of desperation on their faces.

Our first thought is that they must be slaves. But that's not right. Those who work here do so voluntarily; they are free men, inhabitants of the area, often in desperate straits. They are paid minimal salaries, barely enough to survive on.

It's a situation that recalls very much what can be seen today in certain areas of the third world where gold has been discovered, such as Africa and South America. The work is extremely wearing, the conditions shocking, but we're not talking about slaves, at least not officially. And all of them harbor in their hearts the hope of finding that great big nugget that's going to change their lives. Something similar is going on in these Roman mines.

Under Trajan, the mines of Las Médulas are at the height of their production and it has been calculated that no fewer than eight thousand people work here. Their work is subdivided into specific roles and tasks: some dig, some carry material out of the tunnels, some sift. The shifts, needless to say, are brutal.

The last miners are coming out now. They're holding on to some wounded coworkers. One body is carried out unconscious with a gaping head wound from which copious amounts of blood are gushing out. You can see the light color of the brain. Maybe he's already dead. The rumor spreads that there's been a collapse at the bottom of one of the secondary tunnels. There have probably been some fatalities. Such accidents happen frequently in these mines. But the Roman authorities have learned not to lose time over them. They can't interrupt the production of gold for the empire to find out what happened to these miserable laborers. The orders are clear: nobody will go down to search for possible survivors, much less attempt to extract the dead bodies. Work on the demolition is already behind schedule. That's the law of the mine. And these casualties all knew it. Their bodies will go down to the bottom, in a little while, together with the cliff. It won't even be necessary to give them a burial. . . .

How to Pull Down a Mountain

Marcus goes over to the entrance of the mine. He tries to see inside, but he can't see beyond the first few yards; the darkness and the dust seem to want to conceal this place of desperation. But we can go farther, because archaeologists and scholars have unearthed the remains of these tunnels and figured out what happened inside them.

The disembowelment of the high plateau went on for generations with astounding precision. Think about when you cut a piece of cake and you rest the knife on it as a way of estimating the size of each slice. That's exactly what the Roman engineers did. They dug holes in the high plateau at a certain distance from the edge of the slope, determining how much of it to cut. Then the miners dug the inclined tunnels by hand. These tunnels (called *arrugiae*) went down at an angle and, at regular intervals, they split off into other lateral corridors a little more than a yard wide, where a person could barely stand up.

Their tools were very simple: shovels, picks, spades, hammers, and wedges. Imagine the working conditions. They worked in the dark, illuminating the area to be dug with simple oil lamps, and the residual material was put in baskets and dragged outside. There was very little air, lots of dust that filled their lungs, and the heat was suffocating.

And then what happened? How did they manage to pull down whole pieces of the high plateau at one time? Today the only system we use is dynamite. But at the time of the Roman Empire it didn't exist. So the Roman engineers came up with a truly ingenious solution, using a force they knew how to manipulate very well: water.

They succeeded in using water as an explosive. Now we're going to see how.

Everything is ready. Marcus has been staring constantly at a large artificial lake of water, built in a very short time, close to the entrance to the tunnel. It looks like a small mountain lake. White clouds hover silently above it like cotton balls. Hardly anybody knows that to fill it with water it was necessary to build a true masterpiece of hydraulic engineering: an aqueduct almost fifty miles long that captures the water from faraway rivers and brings it all the way here by way of channels called *corrugi* (still partly visible today).

Our attention is attracted by the waving of some colored flags: it's the signal that all personnel and miners have been evacuated from the valley. The mine is empty too (except for the bodies of the dead or dying miners). The men in charge of the dams of the artificial lake are waiting for the signal to begin the operation.

The *procurator metallorum*, who represents the emperor, slowly stands up, with one edge of his toga draped over his forearm. He raises his other arm theatrically. Pronouncing a phrase that refers to the emperor, he lowers it brusquely.

That's the signal. The trumpets blare. And, as though in a relay race of sounds, the shouts and orders follow, all the way up to the decisive one, who yells at the top of his lungs to a group of bare-chested miners, positioned at precise points of the dams, who start hammering with heavy wooden mallets. Suddenly, with a domino effect, the dam opens and lets the immense mass of water that it held back for months go free. Like a wild beast in search of its prey, the water comes spilling out into a specially dug canal and charges toward the main entrance to the tunnels.

Everyone holds his breath. Marcus with his eyes wide open, his colleagues with their mouths agape—even the *procurator metallorum* looks on spellbound by the power of that wave, which is about to plummet into its target. From a distance the eyes of the miners follow the mass of water with trepidation. Now they'll know if their superhuman efforts and the dead victims have served some purpose.

Water Used as Dynamite

The water spews thunderously into the downward-sloping tunnels, the force of the wave shatters the walls, wipes them out like a sand castle. Whole sections of the tunnel collapse. Deep rumbling noises pour out of the tunnel entrance, powerful, almost a cry of pain from the earth as it is broken apart and lacerated. This is the moment when water becomes explosive.

The water compresses the air that's left in the corridors, exactly the way a bicycle pump does when you keep the air hole plugged with a finger. And when the air pressure becomes excessive the corridors explode, blowing away the rock.

Now the earth is shaking under everybody's feet. Marcus and his colleagues look around and then lower their eyes to the ground. They can feel perfectly the shocks from the fragmenting tunnels. A geyser of steam mixed with dust comes spewing out of the main entrance to the tunnel.

A violent roar shakes the air; a gash has opened up in the side of the cliff. Then another one next to it, and still another. There it is, the chain reaction that the engineers and miners were waiting for has been set off. As though some immense water pipes had exploded, the tunnels pour out into the open air the water that was compressing them, creating so many spectacular waterfalls that cascade down into the valley. But that's not enough. The cliff begins to tremble, emitting a sinister, somber noise. And like a giant struck by a mortal blow, it sways back and forth and crumbles to the ground.

"The fractured mountain comes down with a roar and a movement of air that the human mind cannot conceive," Pliny the Elder recounts. An entire portion of the front wall of the high plateau collapses, generating an apocalyptic roar; the shock wave slams into everyone. And in their eyes is written just one thing: fear.

Now a salmon-colored cloud rises up, mixed with water vapor, hiding from our view both the valley and the sky. The sun, as though it were afraid, has momentarily disappeared behind that wall of suspended dust and dirt. Like a silk veil, the dust settles into place on everything: trees, blades of grass, togas, faces. . . .

Rivers of mud and rock continue to pour out of the disemboweled mountainside, spreading out like oil stains on the lunar plain. Over the next few months they'll be channeled into a network of artificial canals, leading them all into large collection basins where the gold will be separated from the sediment with sieves. The rest will be pushed down below, extending the lifeless area of the landscape.

Why Gold Makes the Empire Go Round

So a landscape that looks like it came right out of Dante's inferno is where the lifeblood of the Roman economy gushes forth.

There can be no doubt that these mines are of enormous strategic importance for Rome; they are the equivalent of modern oil wells. Gold has always been important for all civilizations, but it became even more important, essential really, for Rome after Augustus created a monetary system based on a gold coin: the *aureus*.

Just as Europe today has the euro or the United States the dollar, the Roman Empire had the *aureus* and all of its denominations.

We should add that over time things changed, and the gold content of an *aureus* gradually diminished, unhinging and weakening the system, provoking price increases, inflation, and so on. It may seem strange to talk of inflation in Roman times, but in a world that was so much like our own, its problems of economics and finance were also like ours.

So it is interesting to discover still another analogy between Roman society and ours, a resemblance determined by one simple and fundamental rule: in order to make a large-scale economy work it has to have a currency that is strong, stable, and universally accepted. And if you think of how the euro and the dollar are currencies of reference in today's world, well beyond the borders of Europe or the United States, it is easy to imagine the importance of the *aureus* even beyond the borders of the empire.

This is precisely one of the problems for Rome's finances. An enormous quantity of gold coins disappear beyond the frontiers of the empire to pay for all kinds of goods, especially the most costly and precious goods, such as silk. And they don't come back into the system, depriving it of some of its wealth. It is a constant financial hemorrhage.

The case of silk is emblematic. As is well known, silk is produced in China and comes to the west along various routes, the most famous being the Silk Road. But between China and Rome lies the homeland of the Parthians, fierce enemies of Rome, who are the middlemen of the silk trade. So not only do immense quantities of gold leave the empire, diminishing the coffers of the state, but they end up in the hands of its most dangerous enemies to the east. In a very real way, the vanity of Roman high society, of the patricians and their matrons, helps the enemy. As a result, over the course of the centuries, the Roman Senate enacted a number of provisions aimed at limiting the purchase and use of silk.

But they don't appear to have worked.

This constant hemorrhage is not the only problem. Gold is needed to maintain three fundamental mechanisms without which the empire would collapse: the gold coins are needed to pay the legions so that they'll keep the barbarians out, to finance the public administration to make the huge empire more efficient, and to fuel finance and commerce to keep the Roman economy running.

The need to have a continuous supply of gold, in ever-greater quantities, was the impetus behind entire military campaigns of conquest. Making a comparison with our own time, it would be like starting a war to possess and control oil fields, in order to ensure a steady supply. Like what happened in the war in Iraq.

At the time of our journey through the Roman Empire, something very similar in concept has just happened. Trajan has recently conquered Dacia, present-day Romania, which is very rich in gold mines. To be sure, the reasons behind this war were strategic: the elimination of a dangerous enemy on the frontiers of the empire, the Daci, led by their charismatic king, Decebalus. The Romans also wanted to expunge the disgrace of the defeats suffered in those lands by Domitian, which culminated in a peace treaty that was humiliating for the Romans and intolerable for the Roman spirit. But one of the most convincing reasons for going off to war, in the eyes of many present-day historians (and perhaps also in the minds of many imperial financial administrators back then) was Rome's hunger for gold. When he came to power Trajan found the coffers empty, and his conquest of Dacia resolved all of his financial problems. Rome did have to go through a terrible war, which lasted for years and is described in the famous bas-relief on Trajan's column in Rome. But afterward it entered a new golden age of prosperity and wealth, wealth that Hadrian then proceeded to "sit on," presiding over one of the most extraordinary periods in history or Western civilization.

Breaking Coins in Half

Marcus Valerius Primis, our functionary, remained in the area for a few days to gather all the information possible on the gold production of the mines for his superiors. Then he left for his journey home.

This time, however, he didn't leave from Cadiz but from Tarraco (Tarragona), a city located about sixty miles from Barcelona. His itinerary is dictated by more official business in Saragossa. (It's curious to discover that this strange name for a city is nothing but a garbled version, evolved over the centuries, of its Roman name, Caesaraugusta.)

Marcus's journey from Cadiz was a long trip on the *cursus publicus* and, since his food and lodging were free (he was traveling on business of the imperial administration), his expenses were minimal and our sestertius is still with him. But now the two are about to separate.

It all happens in a grocery shop in Tarragona. Marcus is buying some fruit for his voyage home. And when he pays, our sestertius changes owners. The grocer takes it into his hands, sticky from the fruit he's been handling. He glances at it distractedly and passes it along to his wife of the perennial beady-eyed gaze, in charge of the cash box in the back room. All we hear is the clink of the coin as it falls into the wooden box and the sound of the key turning in the lock.

Marcus bids farewell and walks off toward the harbor, with a growing and pressing desire to see his family again. He's been away too long. But by now he's got just a few more days before he'll be home.

The grocer is called by his colleague from the shop next door. He has to make change for a man who has bought some fruit but doesn't have any small change. So he asks his colleague if he can give him two sesterces or some smaller coins for a silver denarius. It's a scene that we are accustomed to seeing all the time in the markets or on the streets of our cities. But here we're going to see something we're not used to.

The mean wife in the back room reopens the cash box with a frown of impatience, choosing the coins carefully with her pointy fingers. They look like the tentacles of a spider grabbing its prey. Then she holds out a handful of small change to her husband, the cold look on her face unchanged.

Her husband hands them over to his colleague with a smile. The colleague thanks him, opens his hand to count the coins, and makes change for his customer. In his open hand, however, we notice something unusual: some of coins are broken. They are sesterces that have been broken in half and mixed together with smaller coins like asses, semisses, and so on. Why are they broken in half? And are they still legal tender?

The practice is odd but there is a logic to it. The farther you get from Rome and the major trade routes, the fewer coins there are in circulation, so small change is harder to come by. In the absence of smaller denominations, sesterces are broken in half and used to make change.

These broken coins in the Roman era remind us of the mini-checks that circulated a lot in Italy in the 1970s for the same reason: there was a shortage of small change. In those years shop owners gave their customers candy, stamps, or telephone tokens as change in a kind of barter system that was surprising for a western country, and we imagine that the same thing happened in the Roman era, with shop owners making change in kind.

Today, if a shopkeeper broke a two-euro coin in half to give you a euro in change, he would be breaking the law. In the Roman era, however, it's perfectly legal. The reason is that today's coins have value for what they represent symbolically (the nation's wealth, its gold deposits, etc.). Roman coins are worth what they weigh, depending on the metal they're made of (gold, silver, bronze, copper). If you were to assess the value of the metals used today to make a one-euro coin, you'd come up with a figure of about 15 cents.

In a lot of museums you can sometimes see these half coins on display without explanation: look out for them the next time. They're usually mistaken for broken coins. In reality, they conceal a world that is seldom described: the world of daily purchases in the remote areas of the empire. Actually, a coin worth half a sestertius exists; it's called the *dupondius*, but it's almost impossible to find in these areas. The practical Roman spirit figured out another solution.

Let's return to our grocers. Tarragona actually has a flourishing market, but every once in a while some of these half coins arrive from the hinterland and the shopkeepers try to get rid of them as soon as they can. Just as the grocer's wife has done now.

The customer pockets his change and leaves, tossing the apple he just bought from hand to hand like a juggler. In his purse, however, along with the broken coin, he also has our sestertius.

This man is the assistant to a haruspex, a priest whose job it is to interpret the will and the messages of the gods—by examining the entrails of sacrificed animals, for example. He is waiting for him on a wagon. Their journey will be a long one and will take us to the land that in modern times is called Provence, in the south of France.

PROVENCE

~ *Beware of Brigands* ~

Arriving in Provence

The haruspex and his assistant have departed in their wagon. The road ahead of them is long. Another haruspex is waiting for them in Vasio Vocontiorum (Vaison-la-Romaine), a city in the north of modern-day Provence, for the building of a big new temple. The sacrifices performed by the haruspices are a must before starting construction.

The city of Arelate (Arles) is one of their stops, and when they arrive there they are greeted by an unusual sight. There is a big bridge across the city's large river, the Rhone, but right now the bridge is out of service. A cargo ship is passing through the city and the bridge is being raised. We're familiar with the scenes of a line of cars waiting for an open draw-bridge to let a river boat go through. This is the ancient equivalent: a line of wagons and pedestrians is waiting for the operation to be completed.

But how do drawbridges work in the Roman era? The part nearest the shore is made of masonry; then it turns to wood and is supported, pontoon-style, by boats (whose bows are pointed in the direction of the current). At the point of contact between the two segments there is a sizable masonry arch. It's not there for beauty; it works exactly like the entrance portal of a castle with a drawbridge. By pulling chains that pass through the two pillars of the arch, it's possible to raise a thirty-foot piece of the wooden segment of the bridge high enough to let a cargo boat pass underneath.

There are actually two of these wooden sections, located on either end of the bridge, so two boats can go through at the same time, thus avoiding logjams. The wooden segments are close to the shore, probably because the current is not as strong and the boats are easier to maneuver.

As the ship is slowly passing under the bridge, some of the bystanders notice the haruspex and greet him deferentially; others muster their courage and go over to ask him for predictions, opinions, interpretations of events and situations in their private lives. For the haruspex it's a constant hassle. Every time they see him it's the same story: they never leave him in peace, just as is the case for celebrities today. . . .

The crack of his assistant's whip puts an end to this little assembly; the bridge has closed again and the flow of vehicles and people resumes.

A few days later, after some other stops along the road, the wagon finally arrives in the city, with our sestertius. On a street in Vasio Vocontiorum it changes hands again, in the purchase of an animal to be sacrificed. The haruspex wants to solicit the council of the gods and his assistant wants, finally, to eat a nice serving of meat. So the sestertius passes into the hands of the seller, who in turn gives it immediately to his master, a wealthy man from the city. He is a man who has just recently entered the political arena.

A New Power Couple

There's nothing better than a honey-filled focaccia dipped in milk to give you the energy you need to start your day. Then if you add to it some reheated meat left over from last night's banquet and a glass of wine. . . . In Roman times, the breakfast of those who are setting on off a journey always packs a heavy dose of calories. Not least because once they're on the road it will be hard to get a good meal before evening. And if something goes wrong and the carriage breaks down they might not eat again until the next day. So it's always best to eat well and plenty and bring something along for the trip.

Our sestertius is now in the pocket of an important, recently appointed functionary, who is about to leave with his wife to go to the inauguration of a big aqueduct that is back in operation after some urgent maintenance. For this public figure any event is an opportunity to be seen. The journey will be long, but it won't be uncomfortable; waiting for the couple, in fact, is a well-appointed carriage.

The two are walking along under the porticoes of Vasio Vocontiorum. Contrary to what we've seen up to now on our journey through the empire, these porticoes slope upward. That's unusual. They even have steps. But here they couldn't have done otherwise: the city is set in a mountainous area. In fact, we are now east of the Rhone, in the foothills of the Alps.

In the modern age this region of the empire will be part of Provence, attracting millions of tourists for its mild climate and its cities rich with Roman ruins, such as Arles, Nîmes, Orange, as well as the extraordinary aqueduct of Pont du Gard. And then there's this locality, which is well worth including in the itinerary.

Vasio Vocontiorum isn't a small town. On the contrary, it covers 175 acres and has 10,000 inhabitants, with houses as big as 24,000 square feet, a sign of widespread wealth. The owner of a gigantic 18,000-plus square foot *domus*, Quintus Domitius (the broken tombstone unearthed in his house, with the inscription "of Apollo with a crown of laurels," does not permit us to know his full name), now has our sestertius.

The porticoes echo with the voices and laughter of the passersby, mixed with the clacking of their sandals. The chatting couple passes many different scenes of daily life: on the ground near some empty baskets two little boys are playing with some bones while a spotted puppy looks on, wagging its tail; a man walks by carrying two buckets of water while a woman walks away from a grocery stand carrying two bags full of purchases. Many of the inhabitants of Vasio have kept the traits of the Voconti Celts who used to inhabit this area. They have hard faces, tempered by life in the country rather than urban ease. On their way to the carriage, Quintus Domitius and his wife receive greetings and compliments from everyone they meet.

Riding in a Carriage

The carriage, called a *carruca*, looks like a wooden pioneer wagon out of the Old West. It has a square cabin, with large windows, four big wheels, and a door at the back. It's thoroughly decorated with pictures and silver plates. All things considered, it's a real Roman-era limousine.

A slave opens the door for them and, as Roman tradition dictates, the man gets in first, followed by the woman. They sit down opposite each other, as in a train compartment: he on a throne of sorts, she on a comfortable chair.

Once the door is closed the crew climbs aboard, on top of the carriage. In addition to the driver there is Quintus's man, seated in the middle of the roof, and a carriage assistant, seated on top of a trunk with his back turned to everybody. He holds a sort of lance with a hook on the end, perhaps used to push aside low-lying branches, or maybe as a weapon—it's not clear. Actually, the whole crew is armed; on journeys like this it's quite routine to have to defend against bandits. The driver is armed too. He's a fat man, rough, completely bald, dressed in leather and a heavy cape.

We notice another curious feature of the carriage: two sharp blades at the height of the manes of the horses. They're shaped like sickles, standing vertically, with their cutting edges pointing forward.

Right here in Vaison-la-Romaine, archaeologists have unearthed a relief sculpted in stone that shows one of these *currucae* complete with sickles. There are four of them, placed at the same height as the driver and the other men sitting on the carriage. Were they for cutting low branches when the carriage passed under a tree? Perhaps. We don't know for sure. But it is intriguing to imagine what other purposes they may have served.

With a shout and a swift crack of the whip, the driver gets the carriage on its way. At the outset the horses struggle to move the heavy carriage, but once it starts moving it all becomes easier. Behind this wagon is another one carrying the personal belongings of Quintus and his wife, plus an escort of a few men on horseback. Passersby look on with curiosity at the procession, trying to peek in to see who's inside. Quintus, as his status requires, ignores everybody and keeps his eyes looking straight ahead.

The big iron-clad wheels cut into the surface of the stone slabs of the city street. In certain places, especially at intersections, the uneven pavement provokes some big bounces but inside the *carruca* the impact is softened by the padded seats.

In a few minutes the travelers leave Vasio behind them, cross a lovely single-arch bridge over a small ravine, and head south.

Looking out from the carriage, we see what Provence was like in the Roman era: a landscape of hills and mountains, forests and uncultivated fields. It's not much different from the way it is today, minus the houses, roads, and trellises. In the Roman era it's nature as far as the eye can see. The cities are human islands in an uncontaminated sea of green.

We pass a slow farmer's wagon, pulled by oxen. You can tell right away from how the farmer is dressed that he's a local and not a Roman. The Celts who have long inhabited this place wear pants, while the Romans only wear skirted tunics.

Every now and again we pass a herd of sheep and a shepherd in his white tunic—a slave from some nearby farm—and the acrid smell of the sheep wafts in through the windows of the carriage.

On other occasions, however, our nostrils are delighted by an intense and pleasant perfume. It may be the lavender that grows wild on the entire Mediterranean coast from Spain to Greece. But in the Roman era there certainly aren't the immense fields of lavender that you can admire (and inhale) today.

On board, the couple has not stopped talking since we left. They've got a lot to discuss: the new office, the work to be done on their house in spring, and the newly acquired slave working as a gardener, who always wears a bandana around his forehead and long hair. Quintus wonders gravely if he might be hiding a tattoo. He intends to find out.

Tattoos in the Roman era were not as we know them today. The barbarian peoples, as we have seen, have a lot of them, some of them quite amazing. The Romans, on the other hand, like the Greeks, consider tattoos (and marking the body in general) something to be ashamed of. They normally call a tattoo a *stigma*, that is, a brand, which says a lot about how they are regarded.

One thing we do know is that when a fugitive slave was recaptured his forehead was branded with three letters, *FUG*, meaning *fugitives,* to indicate that he had already escaped once. Or else an *F*, which stood for *fur*, "thief"; or a *CF* for *cave furem*, "beware of the thief."

It's right that Quintus should be concerned. It often happens that slave traders try to pawn off hard-to-handle individuals by selling them in a group of slaves. They'll have to investigate.

The Carriage Is Ambushed

The carriage has gone over a rise and is starting down the other side. It's right in the middle of a forest; the road is a thin strip inside a tunnel of trees. And this is where the trap is sprung. The driver has a lot of experience, but the darkness of the forest prevents him from seeing until the last minute, at the bottom of the slope, a rope stretched between two trees.

It's been placed at just the right height to hit the men on the roof. But the four vertical blades at the level of the horses' heads do their job. They cut right through the rope with a whiplike sound. On board, Quintus and his wife don't notice a thing; they think it's a lash of the driver's whip.

The driver shouts to his men on the wagon and to the escort behind them. They're all ready for an attack. In fact, at the end of the descent, where the road starts to climb again, there's a tree trunk across the road. They can't go on. The driver brakes just in time. Nine brigands come bounding out of the woods, armed to the teeth with swords, pitchforks, lances, and clubs.

The two men of the escort have been surrounded, the weapons leveled at them, before they have time to react. But where's the third?

The passengers are ordered to get out. Quintus has hidden his gold ring inside a fold of his tunic and he gets out of the carriage first, sizing up the aggressors. His wife is terrified. Her eyes are wide with alarm; she's unable to speak. The boy with the hooked lance is down on the ground. He tried to strike back at the attackers, but a blow from a club has knocked him cold. The driver is sitting on the ground too, dazed, his back against one of the wheels and a deep wound on his head. The men carried off the attack with split-second timing: the place, their technique, the rapidity of their actions make it clear that they've done this before and are familiar with the area.

The irony is that Quintus was elected because he had promised better security on the roads of the province, and now he's face-to-face with the problem.

The Life of a Brigand

Quintus is trying to figure out who his attackers are, but he's never seen them before. From their appearance it's clear that they are poor farmers from the area. A couple of them look like fugitive slaves. Another, armed with a gladius, could be a deserter or a renegade soldier. The social background of these bandits is fairly typical of brigands in the Roman era. They are never professional criminals, but small groups who strike sporadically.

Naturally, there are exceptions. The ancient texts tell of famous gang leaders, such as Bulla Felix, in command of as many as six hundred men, who ran wild all over Italy at the beginning of the third century CE, escaping capture with incredible ease, thanks to an extensive network of informers. According to Dio Cassius, Bulla Felix was so clever he was able to obtain the release of two of his men condemned to death by wild beasts in the arena—by entering the jail and pretending to be a magistrate. When he committed a robbery he took only a part of the valuables and released his victims immediately. The loot was then generously distributed among the band. He quickly became famous as a sort of romantic outlaw of antiquity, a precursor of Robin Hood. His career came to an end when Emperor Septimius Severus himself recalled back to Italy a powerful cavalry squadron that had been engaged in a border war in Britain and sent them to chase him down. To get him they used an infallible tactic that has landed lots of criminals in jail down through the centuries, including some famous Mafiosi: a tactic that can be summed up more or less as: "Cherchez la femme!"

It's a celebrated phrase that, unbeknownst to most people, comes from a novel written in 1854 by Alexandre Dumas: *The Mohicans of Paris.* "There's a woman in every case," says one of the characters, "every time they bring me a report of a crime I say: 'Cherchez la femme.'" And that's what the imperial troops did. They discovered that Bulla Felix had a relationship with the wife of another brigand, and by promising her immunity, they succeeded in capturing him as he was sleeping in a grotto. He ended up in the amphitheater, torn to pieces, alive, by wild beasts.

But Bulla Felix is an exception. In the Roman Empire brigands are usually small bands of men in remote, insecure areas, out to rob whatever personal valuables travelers happen to have with them: clothes, coins, or, if they're lucky, animals. In some cases they attack roadside inns, but they are usually in cahoots with the owner, and it is this capacity to maintain solid bonds with the local community that permits them to exist. If they didn't have the complicity and even the help of the local population they wouldn't survive very long.

Their strategies for thwarting the efforts of the law enforcement authorities are many and varied. According to Professor Jens-Uwe Krause, when they were captured many of them managed quite easily to corrupt those who arrested them. In other cases, the arrest wasn't even made, thanks to the protection of socially powerful people—government functionaries or local big shots—who in turn received a cut of the take.

It's not unusual for brigands to have their base on the agricultural estates of some large landowner who is completely in the dark. The brigands are hired by the steward and are officially on the payroll. Obviously, the steward is fully aware of their criminal activities.

Brigands are often members of the local community with regular jobs, and sometimes they are even wealthy men who only dally in armed robbery—real chameleons who recall the figure of Don Diego de la Vega, officially a large landowner known to the law enforcement authorities as the bandit Zorro.

Typically, these brigands tend not to kill their victims. They might beat them up, but killing is not normally part of their modus operandi. Essentially, their objective is robbery. The biblical parable of the Good Samaritan is actually a good example of a robbery on the roads of the empire: the man who was helped by the Samaritan was not killed by the brigands but only gravely wounded.

Brigands also tend not to employ tactics that are too bold or spectacular for fear of provoking a strong reaction from the authorities, which might threaten their survival. In our case, the brigands have gotten in over their heads; ambushing the convoy of a high government official like Quintus is a mistake. Maybe they weren't expecting to run into someone of such high rank or a carriage of this type. But the trap had already been laid. In any event, now it's too late, which is probably why they went ahead with it. But their attack will not go unanswered. They know that. And Quintus knows it as he tries to figure out who their leader is.

The leader of this band presents himself. He's a tall, thin man with a hooked nose, and he gives the official a defiant look. As soon as Quintus opens his mouth to speak, the brigand stuns him with a punch in the face. His wife embraces him. The brigand reaches out his hand and rips off her necklace. He looks at it and then stares at the woman, tilting his head as if to say, "This isn't worth anything—where did you put your good jewelry?"

One of the bandits comes out of the carriage, carrying a small case. He breaks into a toothless smile: "Here they are," he says.

The brigands have hit the jackpot. The ceremony that the couple was going to attend right at the start of Quintus's political career called for a lot of precious jewels.

The robbery continues. The brigands open luggage, select the most beautiful items of clothing to be resold, and scatter the rest on the ground all around. Then they take turns beating up the members of the escort and carriage crew, aiming to break any resistance and convince them to give up anything they might be hiding. During the robbery and the beatings the two men of the escort often exchange glances. They've got the same unanswered question in their eyes: where is their colleague, the third man of the escort?

The brigands gather up all the arms, the horses, and everything of value. Even our coin falls into the hands of one of the band. The leader puts it in his pants pocket, together with the rings and other jewelry.

As they are using their knives to cut down the silver plates from the side of the *carruca*, one of the thieves lifts his head to listen. He's heard something. Another one stops to listen too. They can hear the sound of horses' hooves in the distance. Somebody's coming. Another victim, with more loot? That's the brigands' first thought. But it's not long before the excited looks on their faces turn to apprehension: there are a lot of horses coming, too many . . .

The brigands instinctively come together in the middle of the road and look at their leader. What do we do?

As the seconds go by the sound of the approaching horses sounds more and more like rolling thunder. The boss realizes that these aren't travelers but soldiers. When he shouts to everybody to run it's too late; a squadron of cavalry gallops into view at the top of the hill. In the midst of the chaos the two men from the escort take advantage of the situation to capture and disarm the brigands closest to them.

In no time at all the cavalry overwhelms the thieves. They try to escape into the woods, but it's not easy with all the loot they're carrying, and then they find themselves at the bottom of a gully with rising slopes on all sides. They had chosen this place to make it harder for their victims to get away, but now it's turning into a trap for them.

They are all rounded up in short order. It's not hard for the soldiers to get the better of them; the brigands are not professionals, they're just ordinary men with wives and children. The only ones that put up a serious fight are the two fugitive slaves and the runaway soldier, who wounds one of the cavalry before being pounced upon by another, who grabs him from behind and cuts his throat with a lightning-fast thrust of his knife. On seeing this scene, one of the brigands puts his hands up and surrenders.

When it's all over three brigands have been killed (the slaves and the runaway soldier) and the others have surrendered. The leader didn't give up until a German cavalry officer, with a square face and beady eyes, stuck a gladius under his chin, showing his white teeth.

But how did the cavalry get there so fast? The alarm was given by the third man from the escort, the one the other two were looking for. Just before the assault by the brigands, he had stopped on the side of the road to urinate, and when he got back on his horse he saw the attack from his position on the top of the hill. He made the smart choice not to throw himself into the melee but to make his escape, silently, before taking off at a gallop. He made it to a *statio*, one of the many small military posts placed along the Roman roads in the most risky areas. From there the alarm was communicated to another bigger *statio* where the cavalry squadron was stationed. But how did they communicate so fast without radio, telephones, or cell phones?

With a system that is also based on electromagnetic waves but on a more basic level: the light waves emitted by fire. The Romans invented a very effective system for communicating alarms, especially along the frontiers: a network of wooden towers placed in strategic locations. In an emergency, the soldiers on lookout lit a big torch or set fire to a large pile of wood already prepared. Whenever a tower spied another lit tower in the distance, it lit its own torch, and so on down the line. With this fire-relay system an alarm could be sent over a long distance in a very short time, reaching the forts in the area who respond to the threat. This was the world's fastest alarm system before the invention of the radio.

The speed of the cavalry's arrival on the scene shows us how effective it was. Actually, there aren't *turmae* of cavalry deployed and ready to be called into action in all the *stationes* of the empire. This squadron had been recalled as part of a planned action against another band of brigands in the same area who specialized in kidnapping. This was a major security problem too, one of the dangers travelers had to be prepared for on their journeys through the empire.

Kidnapping

Plagium is the Roman word for kidnapping and the crime itself, *crimen plagii,* is widespread in the empire. The aim is not to ask for ransom; that can happen, as in the case of Julius Caesar, who was kidnapped when he was young, but it's not the norm.

The real objective of kidnappers is to capture men and boys to sell as slaves. It would be a mistake to think that this kind of kidnapping is something completely removed from our own contemporary lives. It still happens today to lots of young women and girls from the East, who are kidnapped to be sold as sex slaves in the European prostitution market. What's different in the Roman era are the figures. If you think about the huge numbers of slaves circulating in the Roman Empire you soon realize that, between those who die and those who are freed, there is an enormous shortfall in the supply of slaves that needs to be filled every year with tens of thousands of new slaves. According to Professor Krause the shortfall could be as high as half a million people, every twelve months. How to feed this market? In three ways: with wars; with the acquisition of human "goods" abroad (hunted down by man hunters exactly as it was done in Africa right up until recent times), or through kidnapping.

Kidnapping can happen anywhere; no place is sacred. We have seen that even the owners of the big bakeries in Rome kidnap their customers. Other dangerous places for travelers were roadside inns and taverns in the country. Often the innkeepers, in cahoots with the criminals, had their own lodgers kidnapped and then sold into slavery. Toward the end of the empire, even private homes would become targets. In North Africa groups of land pirates attacked isolated houses or small villages, capturing their inhabitants to sell them as slaves.

But it's on the highways that the risk is greatest, and the particular threat here comes from large commercial farms. Large numbers of Roman citizens are captured and put to work on farms. It's a source of real anguish: a father or son disappears on his way to or from work and is never heard from again. One tragic fact: the preferred victims are little boys, because they are easier to kidnap and when they are taken far away they can't explain where they came from.

Commercial farms are the worst places for a slave. They often overwork and underfeed their slave laborers, and provide them miserable living quarters. Not surprisingly, premature death is frequent, which is another reason why large landholders have a constant demand for slaves. Kidnapping is a good way to get them quickly and for free. In fact it was so widespread throughout the period of the empire (and before) that, from Augustus to Hadrian, the emperors ordered unannounced on-site inspections of the slave quarters on the landed estates, in search of kidnapped Roman citizens.

What was the risk for a kidnapper? In the republican era, only a fine, then forced labor (if the kidnapper was from the lower classes) or permanent exile (for the privileged). Under Diocletian the death penalty was introduced. But since the problem persisted, Constantine established particularly brutal death penalties for slaves and *liberti* found guilty of kidnapping: either they were devoured by wild animals in the arena or they were killed by gladiators.

Kidnapping is indeed one of the dark sides of life in the Roman era. It's hard for us today to imagine living with this constant threat. But in the past, anyone who left home had to add it to the list of the dangers to be faced in the outside world.

The stolen goods have been returned to Quintus and his wife. And so our sestertius too has been returned to its owner. It's rare that a coin returns to a previous owner, but in this case it is understandable. Quintus and his wife recover from the shock of the robbery, hosted by a wealthy landowner, at a villa in the vicinity.

The next day, bright and early, they resume their journey. Quintus is determined not to be stopped by this incident, and he does his best to turn the fast-spreading news of the robbery to his advantage. When they arrive at the aqueduct a huge crowd cheers him and asks for news about the attack. But he makes a public sacrifice to Mercury, protector of travelers, wayfarers, physicians, merchants, and, irony of ironies, thieves.

Because of his wing-footed speed, in fact, Mercury is the patron saint of many human activities that are known for their speed: robbery, purchases and sales, profit. . . . Perhaps it's no coincidence that the Latin terms for a merchant and his world are *mercator* and *merx* (commerce). If we then add physicians to the thieves and merchants on the list of Mercury's protectees, we get an idea of what Romans thought of them too. . . .

As Quintus is making his speech, we take a look at the surrounding valley. Before us, stretching over a river, is a true marvel of antiquity: the three-tiered aqueduct that Quintus has come to inaugurate.

If Rome conquered the territories of its empire with its legionnaires, it was with its engineers that it put down its roots. In every newly conquered territory the Romans replicated their own model of urban design. And aqueducts are an essential element of the Roman system: the whole empire is studded with them.

Today very few are still standing. Some still work, like the Acqua Vergine in Rome, a masterpiece of antiquity that gives life to other masterworks in the history of art. Imagine: it supplies water to the Fountain of Trevi, one of the wonders of the city and of the world, and the Barcaccia Fountain by Bernini, at the foot of the Spanish Steps.

If today you want to admire the most spectacular and well-preserved Roman aqueduct you have to come here, to Provence, where Quintus is giving his speech. We're talking about the Pont du Gard. The aqueduct, which crosses over the Gardon River, is truly beautiful and elegant; it has three tiers of arches, one on top of the other. It is so harmonious and light it looks like it's made out of playing cards.

Most Europeans don't know this, but this aqueduct can also be found in their pockets. If you look at a five-euro bill, in fact, you'll see an aqueduct identical to the Pont du Gard. Actually, euro notes are not supposed to represent actual monuments, only architectural styles symbolic of European culture. But when you look at the note it's almost impossible not to think of the Pont du Gard.

It was built in 19 BCE by Agrippa, Augustus's son-in-law, in order to supply the city of Nemausus (the name of a Celtic divinity), the modern-day Nîmes. Its dimensions are colossal. Imagine four football fields just a little narrower than regulation, lined up two by two. These are the proportions of the Pont du Gard. It is 1,215 feet long and 158 feet high. Its most impressive feature is its three tiers of arches: six on the lowest tier (each of which is 82 feet wide), eleven on the middle tier, and some thirty-five on the top tier. Why so many?

Underlying any aesthetic considerations are some precise engineering reasons, aside from the need to distribute weight and lighten the structure. The last series of arches on top, for example, serves to diminish the surface area exposed to the wind; a little like making holes in a sail or a curtain. The arches on the bottom, on the other hand, are 22 feet thick in order to hold up against the current of the river. The fact that the aqueduct is still intact two thousand years later demonstrates the ingenious nature of its design.

The pipe that carried the water runs along the top. Exploring it today, it seems like a long, dark, silent corridor, with shafts of light coming down through the holes in the roof. But in the Roman era you could hear the sound of flowing water. Every day, over 9 million gallons of water passed through it—an enormous amount, a figure so large it's very hard to grasp. So let's take an example. Think of a sixteen-ounce bottle of mineral water. If you had 70 million of them you'd have the amount of water that passed through the aqueduct every day. . . for six consecutive centuries.

Secrets of the Aqueducts

There can be no doubt then that the Nîmes aqueduct is an engineering marvel. Especially when you consider that almost the entire aqueduct is underground and emerges only rarely with these beautiful bridges.

But how did they get the water to flow? With a simple downslope. But not just at any angle: 2.5 centimeters (0.98 inch) every meter (1.09 yards), not a centimeter more and not a centimeter less, over a distance of 50 kilometers (30 miles), from the spring to the city. This was the secret of the aqueducts: no hydraulic systems or pumps. What made it possible for water to reach the cities was just the downslope, that is, the force of gravity.

That's why a lot of aqueducts, rather than running in a straight line, have wide trajectories with curves or bridges, like this one that crosses the Gardon, all for the purpose of maintaining a constant downslope (or sometimes to pass over the lands of some powerful landowner who wanted to profit from the construction: lands were expropriated at market value).

It didn't take very long for the Romans to build an aqueduct. The Nîmes aqueduct, for example, thirty miles long and almost all underground, took just fifteen years. Not long at all if you think of how long it takes to build a new section of highway today. And of course, they built it without bulldozers or backhoes, almost with bare hands. Blocks of stones were lifted and carried by simple cranes made of wood, with big wheels where slaves walked on the inside (identical to hamster wheels): the spinning wheel pulled a rope up or down with the block of stone on the end of it.

We turn to look at Quintus, who is gesticulating as he delivers his speech. In a couple of weeks he and his wife will make their entrance into the amphitheater at Arelate (Arles), to the acclamation of the crowd. They'll take their seats next to the governor of the province, as his guests of honor. And when the moment comes for the executions, after some hunting scenes and entertainment, Quintus will have his justice. Among the convicted criminals sentenced to death who will be brought into the arena will be the boss of the brigands and his men. He'll be limping, and from the tribune of honor it will be possible to see the red wounds on his ankles, inflicted by the stocks. Then a roar will put an end to this unpleasant story.

But we won't be there. Our sestertius is about to change hands again. Toward the end of the inauguration ceremony, as he comes down off the podium to work the crowd, Quintus will lose it. A little boy will glimpse its gleaming reflection in the dust and pick it up. He'll give it to his father, a *garum* merchant who will be leaving for Massalia (Marseilles) tomorrow to oversee the arrival of a ship carrying a load of the precious sauce from Spain. And we'll be there with him, in the harbor, waiting.

We take a last look at the majestic aqueduct stretching across the river valley. Some little boys dive into the water and their shouts reach us all the way up here. A small sailboat passes under the aqueduct. It looks like a white feather afloat on the water, being carried away by the current.

The Fonteius Case

For hours now the *garum* merchant has been on the road in his wagon. It's empty but on the return trip it will be full of amphorettes of sauce to be sold to the local aristocracy, who like to make lavish displays at their banquets. Or at least that's what he hopes, if the ship doesn't sink in the meantime.

The risk of shipwreck is always the biggest unknown for anyone involved in commerce on the seas. But it can be shared with others. The practice of mitigating the risk is fairly widespread: a number of merchants get together and each of them pays a share of the cost of the ship's voyage. That way, their costs are reduced and so is the risk of loss in case of shipwreck (even if the whole cargo is lost).

Speaking of costs, the road the merchant is traveling on, the Domitian Way, was the subject of one of the most famous scandals of the day in the Roman Empire. The road is an artery of commerce and routine traffic in this part of the empire, a sort of interstate highway. Its importance was well known and appreciated by Marcus Fonteius, who lived almost two hundred years before Trajan, at the time of Cicero.

For three years he was the *praetor,* or magistrate, of the province of Narbonese Gaul, with absolute powers that he used widely to enrich himself at the expense of the inhabitants of the region. He diverted to his own pocket huge appropriations intended for road repair, the most famous of which was a project for the Domitian Way.

Marcus Fonteius would routinely issue invoices to the provincial government to pay construction companies for work they hadn't done, or they had done poorly, in exchange for kickbacks. He ordered expropriations and confiscations, forcing a lot of Gauls to borrow money at usurious rates from loan-shark Roman banks, his accomplices. Finally, he arbitrarily imposed heavy taxes on the transport of wine.

In sum, he proved to be a genius of graft and corruption, and we cannot but remark on how current his crimes are, given the wave of political corruption that has washed over Italy in the past twenty years. These practices apparently allowed him to squirrel away some 23 million sesterces. It's hard to say how much that would correspond to today, but an exchange rate of $2.50 for every sesterces would add up to about $58 million. That surely seems like a lot of money today, but for the time it was an incredibly huge sum. The Gauls protested and sent a delegation to Rome led by one of their very charismatic princes, Induciomarus. The corrupt *praetor* was then put on trial.

But Marcus Fonteius made a surprise move. He asked to be defended by Cicero, at age thirty-six the most famous lawyer in Rome, who had gotten the governor of Sicily, Verres, convicted on similar charges. It was like a corrupt politician today arranging to be defended by a former prosecutor.

Cicero accepted. Our historical archives preserve a partial version of his final argument, in which he refers to Fonteius as an "excellent Roman magistrate," "a courageous and innocent Roman citizen whom the judges must defend."

We can almost hear him now. Imagine his powerful voice resonating in the silence, in front of hundreds of people: "Let both the gods and men be my witnesses! No, not even a sestertius was displaced without justification. . . .ʺ

Cicero's line of defense was based on a very simple concept. At bottom, Fonteius had done nothing more than oppress the Gauls, whose grandfathers had cut the throats of Roman soldiers while Verres, the infamous governor of Sicily, had plundered the republic and the Romans who had established themselves in Sicily—a much more serious offense.

Result: Cicero won, and Fonteius was certainly acquitted, because he retired to Naples, where he had bought a house for 130,000 sesterces! No conviction, no exile, not even a fine. Nevertheless, he never held another position as a Roman magistrate.

Traveling miles and miles on various roads, including the Via Aurelia (a network of roads that was crucial to the history of the empire's conquests in Gaul), the *garum* merchant finally arrives in Massalia. He stays there two days, waiting for his ship to come in. Imagine going to the airport today to pick up a friend and having to wait that long. There are so many variables that influence sea travel (climate, delays, and bad omens, as we'll see later on) that one always has to be armed with a good supply of patience.

Finally, the ship arrives, stocked with premium-quality *garum*. And the business deal has been concluded. Aboard the ship is a merchant from Pozzuoli. He's a wholesaler who went personally to Spain to load the ship with various kinds of premium goods: olive oil, wine, salted fish, and obviously *garum*. In the gulf of Naples, where he lives, the rich Romans love to live *la dolce vita,* and top-of-the-line *garum* goes down like water. Naples may be the most fashionable place in the whole empire. And that's where we're headed next.

Eutychius, the small businessman from Gaul, pays for his amphoras of *garum* in coin, and our sestertius is part of the pile. He presents it, jokingly, as a little "investment" by his son, who is looking forward to a career in the world of commerce. The merchant from Pozzuoli, also the father of a young boy, looks him in the eye and smiles. Then he turns, picks up a painted wooden statue of Mercury and offers it to him as a gift of encouragement. He has a crateful of them to sell to shopkeepers. In a seaport like Pozzuoli, full of sailors and traveling Greeks, they sell like focaccia buns.

BAIA

~ *Luxury and Licentiousness* ~

The Gulf of Naples . . . Without Vesuvius

Coming into the Gulf of Naples is always spectacular. With the islands of Ischia and Procida to our left, and Capri and the peninsula of Sorrento to our right, it feels like we're making an entrance onto the stage of a natural theater, welcoming us with a warm embrace.

Driven by the wind, our ship makes its way silently into this embrace. The rich merchant is standing on the bow, his hands resting on the wooden parapet and his eyes closed. He is breathing in the smell of land, his land, as the morning sun warms his face.

Like airplanes circling in the air waiting for their turn to land, there are a lot of sailing ships behind us, headed, like us, toward Pozzuoli. Our ship veers left now, up the coast, where we can see a series of bays and inlets; that's where the port of Pozzuoli is. Instinctively, we turn to our right, looking for Vesuvius. Curiously, however, we don't see the imposing mass of the volcano. Vesuvius doesn't yet exist (at least not as we know it today).

Something that is seldom mentioned is that Pompeii and Herculaneum weren't destroyed by the Vesuvius that we know today, but by a different Vesuvius, which, by exploding and disintegrating, changed its shape. Our Vesuvius came into being after that devastating eruption, growing gradually inside the enclosure of the ruins of the old volcano until it finally reached its current size.

So, during Trajan's reign, Vesuvius is probably still too small to be seen from the gulf, unlike the view depicted on modern postcards. As our ship sails into the gulf, clear traces of the cataclysm can still be seen everywhere, though the vegetation has already begun to reclaim the lunar landscape created by the volcano.

Naples, too, is very different in Trajan's time. It's still a city of modest dimensions, very different from the modern sprawling metropolis. But construction has already begun to invade the coastland all around it. At numerous points, in fact, we can see uninterrupted lines of luxury homes. Among those who owned villas here are Cicero, Julius Caesar, Lucullus, Crassus, and Hortensius. And the emperors came here too, from Augustus to Hadrian, with Tiberius, Claudius, and others in between.

This development of the coast is especially evident in the Gulf of Puteoli (Pozzuoli), which we are entering now. We had never seen anything like it before starting this journey through the empire. This part of the Neapolitan coast has been literally coated with cement by the Romans, in line with the classic dictates of runaway waterfront development. And they themselves admitted it: *voluptas aedificandi,* excess (voluptuous) building, was their way of describing what had happened, especially in Baia. Baia is a resort on the Gulf of Pozzuoli with a high concentration of sumptuous villas, gigantic bath complexes, and public buildings, houses, and hotels. We might call it the Roman Acapulco. This is a place where the Roman nobility and upper classes come for amusement, even in its most extreme forms.

Roman Leisure Is Different from Ours

These villas have their own fish farms and even their own oyster beds (*ostrearia*). And that's no coincidence; the tradition of serving oysters as a delicacy was born right here. The person who came up with the idea was a wealthy Roman who lived in the first century BCE, Caius Sergius Orata, the same man who, as ancient sources inform us, invented the system for heating the water in the bath complexes. As his surname indicates—an *orata* is a sea bream—he was also a fish farmer. By all accounts he was a clever entrepreneur with a nose for business.

Actually, profit seeking is a useful concept for understanding the Romans' way of thinking. In general, their villas are designed not for leisure as we conceive it but as *they* conceive it: a place to rest and relax, but one that must also yield lots of sesterces. So if the villa is in the country, it brings its owner profits from crops, wine, olive oil, and so on. If instead the villa is on the coast it brings him profits from its fish farms and oyster beds.

That should come as no surprise. In the Roman world, money is the fuel that propels people to the upper levels of the social hierarchy.

At Last We Arrive

A trireme war galley passes us on the side, silently, with its oars moving in perfect unison. Even at this distance we can hear the rhythm shouted out by the crew chief. (To set the record straight, contrary to how they are portrayed in films, the oarsmen on Roman galleys are not slaves or captives but free men.) The trireme shoots by us and drives forward like a shark, having left its base in the port of Misenum, just beyond Baia.

When you think about it, this area of what is now the region of Campania brings together a lot of the characteristics of the Roman world: luxury, culture, military force, business. There's Baia, a seaside resort and spa with its villas and amusements. There's Naples, a city of culture, ideal for intellectuals because it was founded by the Greeks and still has well-rooted Greek language and traditions, with competitions for poets and musicians. There's Misenum, the base of one of the imperial fleets. There's Pozzuoli, a commercial city and port.

We're about to dock. The ship passes an enormously long, strange-looking pier that sticks out over 1,100 feet into the gulf. More than a pier, it looks like a bridge with fifteen or more arches that sink down into the water. No ships are tied up alongside it. In reality, it serves to protect the harbor of Pozzuoli from rough seas: it is slightly curved, to make it more resistant to the force of the wind and tides, and its arches permit the current to pass under it and keep the harbor from filling with sand.

Aside from its practical function the pier also hosts some artistic masterpieces. On top of it are two triumphal arches; the first, closer to the coast, has a group of tritons on the top in gilded bronze, the second is crowned by a quadriga driven by Neptune and pulled by seahorses that glisten in the sun. Finally, atop two columns stand Castor and Pollux, protectors of seamen.

Souvenirs of Antiquity

At last we tie up at the dock. Eutychius jumps down off the deck and stretches out one hand to touch the soil. Then he grabs a handful, brings it up to his mouth, and kisses it.

A souvenir vendor looks at him and smiles. Then he goes back to bargaining with a customer. His "shop" is a little wagon, covered by a square umbrella, with a myriad of objects for tourists. Among them are some outstanding blown-glass cruets. He's showing one to his customer. We notice that they have pictured on them, in relief, the main buildings, monuments, and structures that can be seen along the coast, from Pozzuoli to Misenum. These cruets are how we're able to describe today what the coast looked like in the Roman era: in their decorative reliefs you can seen the *ostrearia*, the baths, the imperial palaces, and the long pier with its triumphal arches and columns.

These extremely delicate cruets are conserved in various museums in New York, Prague, Lisbon, Warsaw, Odemira in Portugal, Ampurias in Spain, and Populonia in Italy. They remind us of those little ceramic pitchers with a landscape painted on the side and the inscription "Greetings from . . ." that you see in so many souvenir shops in provincial Italian towns.

What other trinkets do tourists buy in the Roman era? Lionel Casson has drawn up a curious list of souvenirs that have emerged from various archaeological digs and ancient documents. So, from Athens, for example, a statuette of the goddess Athena, comparable to the statuettes of Michelangelo's *David* that are for sale on the streets of Florence. Wealthy tourists, on the other hand, buy full-size copies of famous statues to adorn their villas, just as we now buy prints of famous paintings or photographs to hang in our bedroom or study.

In Afghanistan, archaeologists have unearthed a glass with a scene from the port of Alexandria—a modest souvenir, comparable to a glass snow globe. Who knows how it ended up so far away.

Today, people who visit shrines buy statuettes of saints and the Blessed Mother, and the same thing happened in the Roman era. In Antioch, in the Near East, one could buy Tyche, the goddess of good fortune, in the form of a bottle as big as your hand. From Egypt one could take home some "holy water" from the Nile for rituals dedicated to the cult of Isis, just as people do today with water from Lourdes.

Then there are typical souvenirs from specific tourist destinations. Today, for example, visitors to Japan might bring home the latest in consumer electronics. In the Roman era, visitors to Alexandria know that they'll be able to find, at better prices and in greater variety, Chinese silk and Indonesian or Indian spices like pepper, ginger, camphor, and cinnamon. Another typical gift from India is cotton, while perfumes come from the Orient and incense from the Arabian peninsula. In Syria, on the other hand, people buy rugs, embroidery, and precious blown-glass objects.

Naturally, when they get back home they have to deal with the customs agents at the border.

Eutychius is welcomed by his slaves waiting for him on the dock. They'll take care of the formalities for the goods being transported. He goes through customs like lightning. He knows all the customs agents and is in the habit of bringing them all very nice gifts. That's what he's going to do this time too. He goes through with a simple wave of his hand, while the agents are literally frisking a Syrian merchant who can't stop gesticulating, alternating Greek with his native tongue.

When he arrives home, Eutychius finds his wife comfortably stretched out on a sofa, holding a little puppy. In the Roman era too, rich women have little dogs as pets, as will be seen in the centuries that follow, and they love to have themselves painted holding their dogs in their laps. All of this carries a message: dogs are the symbol of fidelity. Cats, on the other hand, are not often seen around these parts, except in Egypt. (In Europe, the animal that might serve as a substitute for a pet cat is, believe it or not, the weasel.)

Coming Home

After spending a long time in the company of his wife, Eutychius makes a visit to the magnificent baths: he is finally back home. His skin is smooth after his bath and his body is invigorated from the massages. He is light-hearted because he knows he'll be seeing his friends at dinner after his long absence. He walks down the street, together with his trusty slave who walks behind him, silent as his shadow.

We are struck by the last stretch of road leading up to his *domus*. Compared to this morning it looks deserted. You can no longer hear the chatter of the passersby or the hustle and bustle of the shops. There are only a handful of people out and about. The shops have been boarded up, their wooden doors shut behind horizontal bars locked into place. They're painted all different colors—green, brown, blue, depending on the kind of shop—and the colors have been so bleached by the sun they look like the fragments of a faded rainbow. For Eutychius it is a familiar sight; that long line of chipped and peeling shuttered shops makes him think: "I'm home." But where is everyone?

The shops have all been closed for a while now. Except for the tavern keepers, antique dealers, and barbers, nearly all Roman workers stop working at the *hora sexta* (in the summer), or at the *hora septima* (in the winter). At around noon, trumpet blasts resound throughout the Forum (sometimes it's simply a man who gives a shout) and everything stops: it's the signal that the working day is over. It's the equivalent of sirens at a construction site. Deals are concluded, offices don't accept any more customers, political activity is suspended (at least officially, because it continues at the baths and at afternoon encounters between the various potentates).

When Eutychius disappears behind the door to his house, he rediscovers the warm light and familiar smells that he missed while he was away. We follow him. At the end of the entrance corridor he enters the atrium, its central pool reflecting the blue sky. Deep in thought, he stops to look at it. Reflected in the water, among the petals of the flowers set afloat for this evening's dinner, two hazel brown eyes pop into view. Eutychius raises his gaze and sees his son, thin as a rail, with chestnut brown hair and a playful look on his face. Behind him, the slave girl who takes care of him smiles, keeping a discreet distance. For much of the day children don't stay with their mothers but with their nannies. Around his neck the boy is wearing a *praetexta*, a bulging round container inside of which is an amulet to defend him from diseases. He hugs his father in a long, energetic embrace. Then the boy starts to wriggle; he wants to get down, and once he's on the ground he runs off to chase a dog that has been peeping out from behind a doorway. The boy is boisterous. Obviously, the slave girl follows him everywhere.

Eutychius walks through the house to make sure that everything is in order for the banquet. We are struck by the colors of the walls, always bright hues that make the rooms come alive, and the mosaics, which are veritable carpets of stone, with well-defined borders, a cornice all around the perimeter and, in the center, geometric motifs or framed squares depicting leisure activities or mythological figures.

Eutychius stops in front of a mosaic to chat with his personal slave about the details for this evening's dinner. The mosaic shows two ships, one behind the other, with dolphins, fish, and moray eels. Simple though it is (made out of alternating black and white stones) the scene is very evocative because it represents a return from a long voyage. The ship on the right has all its sails unfurled and is still in the open sea, loaded with goods. The one on the left is the same ship on arrival, with its sails rolled up and the sailors running back and forth pulling on the ropes. It is coming into a port with a big lighthouse. Just beyond it, in the water, there is a boat with some oarsmen. Perhaps it's the tugboat that is pulling the ship into port or perhaps it's carrying the crew to the dock; it's hard to tell. What emerges quite clearly, however, is the figure of a man on land thanking the gods for a safe voyage as he places sacrificial food on a little altar. The mosaic was commissioned by Eutychius and it represents his life: always traveling for work, with the blessing of the gods. But it also indicates to its viewers the source of his wealth: commerce. The mosaics in Roman houses often function as advertisements for the prosperity of their owner.

Now we take a look at the furniture. There are no large tables, bookshelves, or bulky credenzas; the furniture tends to remain in the background. The pieces are generally small, essential, so as not to get in the way of the real display of wealth represented by the mosaics on the floor, the frescoes on the walls, or the decorations on the ceiling.

In this room we see a lovely three-legged table with sculptures of feline heads adorning its slender legs. It looks like a delicate spider, motionless, looking out from the corner of the room at the immense mosaic, as though it were its web. A thin glass flower vase creates a splash of color against the black and white stone carpet—a touch of light and class chosen by the mistress of the house.

The other corners of the room are occupied by thin bronze columns that look like the bases of floor lamps without any light bulbs; they are topped by statues of divinities or lighted oil lamps. These are the points of light found in every room of a Roman house.

Now the master of the house is in the *peristylium*, the lovely interior garden surrounded by a colonnade. There are flower beds everywhere, well cared for, and bushes with intense Mediterranean fragrances.

Together with the slave in charge of the garden, Eutychius checks that the central fountain—which features a bronze fawn in midleap, chased by hunting dogs—has been adjusted as he had ordered: the stream of water must be abundant and create a pleasing sound effect when it falls into the pool. It's fundamental to the success of the banquet.

Just beyond them, behind a peacock (this one authentic) a little girl is running to and fro. Eutychius's daughter leaps into her father's arms. . . .

The Secrets of the Mistress of the House

We come to a door and out of curiosity we decide to open it, slowly. Not far beyond the door, in the middle of a room with red walls, we discover the *domina*, sitting down, her hands resting in her lap. Two slave girls are fixing her hair, and spread out on her dressing table are all the objects involved in the operation, even a hot iron, the *calamistrum*, for making curls. The preparation of the mistress of the house for a banquet is not something to be taken lightly. It is a job that has already been underway for a while now, and that will take several hours. The final result will be a luminous countenance: her lips a sensuous tint of red, her eyes outlined by soft hues, and a tumbling cascade of curls that seems to flow down over her forehead. (As we have already had the chance to discover elsewhere on our journey, these curls are fake.)

The *domina* is careful not to color her hair red. Along with black and blond, red is widely used during the Roman era, but there is a problem with it: it's toxic. Roman women know that, but many of them continue to use it until the dye literally burns and ruins their hair. There is a solution: a wig. It's very much in fashion to wear one; all (wealthy) Roman women do so regularly. Any *domina* worth the title has a number of wigs at her disposal: blond, black, chestnut brown, red . . . for all tastes and for all occasions. It's just like dying your hair a different color every morning.

Little ivory boxes and toiletries are scattered all over the table: tiny spatulas, large pins made of bone, amber jars of colored powders. On another little table a slave girl is gathering what's left of the beauty mask that was applied the night before. What are beauty masks made of in the Roman era? A recipe reported by Ovid reveals the secret for us. It seems more like a formula for a magic potion than a list of ingredients for a cosmetic product.

- Steep a pound of ervum [similar to lentils] in the liquid from ten eggs. Then mix it all together with a pound of barley (best if the barley comes from the African colonies).
- Let the paste dry and then grind it up, sprinkling in 3½ tablespoons of deer-antler powder.
- Pass it through a sieve; add to the sifted powder 16 ounces of honey, 3½ tablespoons of mixed spelt and resin, and 12 narcissus bulbs peeled and crushed with a mortar.

The result, according to Ovid, is guaranteed. The woman's skin will be soft, velvety, and smooth "as a mirror."

This recipe, along with the daily bath, is part of the seduction strategy of Roman women. Before the profusion of bath complexes people washed completely only once a week, and only partially on the other days. Roman soaps or detergents were quite harsh, made of soda, lye, or pumice stone, rigorously pure and never mixed with other substances. (According to Pliny the Elder, soap was invented by the Gauls.) Consequently, the use of oils and unguents to protect their skin is very widespread among wealthy Roman women. And perfumes are used abundantly.

We moderns usually spray perfume behind the ears and on the bosom. A Roman woman, but also her man, sprinkles perfume on her nostrils, hair, and clothes. At this evening's banquet the hosts and their guests will be stretched out barefoot on the triclinium beds, so it will probably be a good idea for the guests to perfume their feet as well. . . . For his part, the *dominus* will see to it that the walls are perfumed, as well as the wings of the white doves that will be released into the banquet hall at some point.

Cooking for a Banquet

We close the door and let the *domina* enjoy her privacy. We're distracted by a pleasant smell. We follow its trail, sniffing like hounds, passing through the rooms where slaves are arranging the cushions on the triclinium beds, hanging garlands of flowers, checking the oil lamps. We also get a glimpse of some musicians and dancers who are rehearsing in one of the slave's rooms.

Room by room, the smell reacquires the full spectrum of its scents, and we're finally able to figure out what it is: it's a roast, but the herbs and spices that have been added to it have completely disguised the smell of cooking meat. That's why we didn't realize what it was.

That's one of the big differences between our cooking and the Romans'. There are many, obviously, starting with the cooking equipment. Our gas stove? A masonry counter on which to spread the embers of a wood fire. Our metal pots and pans? Mostly clay pots, but also copper stockpots and kettles. And there's no hood for ventilation, just some grates high up near the ceiling.

Usually the kitchen is a very small room, and the slaves work elbow to elbow to satisfy the demands of the *domus*, but this kitchen is remarkably large; Eutychius evidently has a yen for a well-spread table. The cuisine for tonight is Mediterranean, based on olive oil and some condiments unknown to us, such as *garum*. Cumin, coriander, sesame seeds, ginger, and other spices are commonly used, just as we use pepper, basil, and oregano. Consequently, Roman cooking would taste quite exotic to us, almost Middle Eastern. In addition, the Romans have a tendency to mix opposing tastes, bringing to the dinner tables of the empire the sweet-sour combination that we're used to tasting in the cuisines of the Far East.

The *magirus*, the slave-cook, his eyes red from the smoking firewood, is preparing something special. He's pressing a meat paste into a copper mold similar to the ones we use today for sweet pastry, only it's in the form of an animal. There's another one hanging on the wall; it looks like a hare with its legs spread.

We know that Romans love to prepare surprise dishes to amaze their guests. The recipes of Apicius offer some great examples, like liver and meat served in the form of a fish, or "eggs" that actually have cream of wheat on the inside.

The surprises at a Roman banquet are not limited to the menu. The guests are also entertained with dances and performances. In the rooms farthest from the triclinium a clown is putting on his costume, while a group of musicians is taking its place at the far end of the garden, in the part of the colonnade where the acoustics are better.

Everything's ready; in the triclinium the beds await the arrival of their guests. Silver plates; blown-glass goblets; fine, multicolored, vintage Falernian wine, accompanied by other well-loved wines such as Massicus and Ceacuban, will give the banquet panache and prestige.

Tonight's menu is wild boar, roast dormouse dressed in honey and poppy seeds, snails, flamingo, peacock, moray eel (very popular), and sea bream, from the fish farm. Today we might turn up our noses if we were served farmed fish instead of wild, but for the Romans farm fish are a guarantee of freshness because they come from the *piscinae*, the seaside hatcheries at one of the nearby villas. Seafood is always on the menu at banquets. For the Romans it is a treasure, as we can see in the writings of Pliny the Elder: "The sea is the element that costs the most for the human belly, for its preparation, for its dishes, and for its delicacies."

But there is one dish that will inaugurate the procession of courses that the guests are anxiously waiting to taste: the oysters, also raised here in Baia. Eutychius will have them brought in atop a small mountain of ice, greeted by everyone's approval. And what a combination of tastes when paired with the spicy *garum*!

Silverware plays no part at a Roman banquet. As is well known, the Romans eat with their hands (or with small spoons for soups). In fact, the food is served precut. If it does not arrive from the kitchen already in bite-size pieces, it will be prepared at table by a "slave-knife." Each dinner guest has one assigned to him to tear up the food with skillful movements of the hands.

Eutychius will also present his guests with some small gifts. It's a Roman tradition at the banquets of the wealthy. These gifts are called *xenia* (a term that sums up the rules of hospitality in the world of ancient Greece). Generally speaking they are luxury items, either silver spoons or small amber sculptures.

One last detail: during the banquet, incense will be lighted. To be sure, between the perfumes sprayed on bodies and clothes and the walls of the rooms, the sweat, the food odors, the fragrances of the plants and flowers, a banquet is a real test for the olfactory sense. If, to all that, you add incense—whew! Martial once wrote, criticizing a banquet that was light on food and heavy on fragrances, that he had eaten very little but had been well perfumed, to the point that he felt like a dead man (since the dead were customarily sprinkled with incense and perfumes).

Gold, Emeralds, and Dancers from Cadiz

The first guests have arrived. They will be nine in all, the ideal number for a banquet according to Roman custom.

It's interesting to see how our hosts are dressed. He's wearing a red tunic and a deep blue toga, with elegant gold embroidery along the border. She, on the other hand, has an emerald green tunic with a lot of gold embroidery, which, from far away, makes the tunic look like a starry sky. An elegant embroidered silk *palla* is wrapped around her shoulders and she's about to hand it over to a slave to allow her to display the splendid gold necklace, with pearls and emeralds, that adorns her neck. She's also wearing gold earrings in the shape of small scales, with big white pearls dangling where the pans would be. She is virtually covered in gold jewelry, as befits a wealthy Roman lady; serpent-shaped bracelets glisten on her arms, while her fingers (except for the middle finger which is left bare for superstitious reasons) are bedecked with emeralds and sapphires and gold rings with seals of marine blue glass paste bearing the effigy of an eagle.

Rings are not only worn around the base of the fingers, but also around the other phalanges. This is a typical caprice of Roman women and helps explain why we sometimes find in museums female rings with very small diameters. It's likely that many of them were worn by little girls, while others were meant for the toes of matrons. The wife of Eutychius, for example, has a small and very stylish one engraved with the letters EVT VXI, the abbreviation for *Eutychius Uxori*, literally, "From Eutychius to his wife."

All the guests have finally arrived and the banquet has begun. We notice a bit of movement behind the scenes. One of the slaves has recited some verses in Greek and is relaxing, sitting on a stool, happy that his performance was a big hit with the guests. The clown has now made his entrance, salting his miming act with salacious one-liners. At the other end of the garden, the master's personal slave, in his role as entertainment director, is preparing one of the evening's most intriguing moments. The guests are about to be treated to an exhibition by dancing girls from Cadiz. Their dancing is famous even in the most remote corners of the empire.

The dancers are very beautiful, a real chorus line of antiquity. They have long, flowing black hair, and their tunics are so light and transparent that they leave nothing to the imagination. Looking through the thin veils of their tunics we can see that they all have a colored ribbon around their waist, the ends of which hang down over their hips. We also notice that their bodies are totally hairless, like all Roman women.

At a prearranged signal the orchestra launches into a new style of music that accompanies the dancers' entrance. From their places in the triclinium, the banqueters see them come into view at the end of the garden, split into two lines, and make their way down the long colonnade that surrounds it, half on the right and half on the left. Their bare feet make no sound, their bodies weaving in and out ethereally, between one column and another. The effect is very evocative; their shadows expand to fill the surface of the frescoed walls in the background and flutter like elegant dark veils. In just a few seconds the dancers appear in front of the triclinium and come to a sudden halt, stone still, with their hands joined above their heads. Two musicians come into view on either side of the scene. Each of them is holding a triangular panpipe. As soon as they purse their lips and begin to blow, the whole scene suddenly springs to life. The dancers move their hands and feet to the rhythm of the music. Watching them, we realize that they're playing castanets. They're unlike the ones we're used to—they look like two drinking glasses or goblets, probably wooden. The two dancers on either end, however, have very different castanets, which look like spoons. They have two in each hand and hold them like chopsticks, knocking them together to keep the beat.

The rhythm is hypnotic. Their dance is strikingly reminiscent of the flamenco. (It's no coincidence that it comes from the area of Cadiz, which is part of Andalusia.) The dancers transfix the banqueters with their deep black eyes and their swaying, shaking bodies.

But the dance also has other characteristics, as shown in the rare bas-reliefs and mosaics that portray our dancers. They suggest the sinuous movements of belly dancing and poses that seem to indicate a total loss of control, as though the dancers have fallen into an ecstatic trance. One such scene is portrayed in a sculpture from Vaison-la-Romaine. And if we add a very explicit bas-relief unearthed in Aquincum (Budapest), we can recreate the scene of a dance and see that at times clothes can be a useless impediment: the dancer sculpted here has none.

The women have now removed their tunics and are dancing naked. All they're wearing is the ribbon around their waist, the ends fluttering and undulating like snakes. They make every single part of their bodies move exactly as they want it to, just like a belly dancer. Moving to the beat of the castanets, their bodies surge and roil. The dance couldn't be more erotic, and it ends as it began, with a crescendo of castanets that comes to a sudden halt, as do the bodies of the dancers, once again with their hands joined overhead and their legs crossed. The only things moving are their diaphragms, contracting spasmodically in search of oxygen.

Then, as suddenly as they appeared, the dancers vanish among the colonnades, accompanied by the applause of the banqueters, who immediately return to their table talk.

Luxury and Licentiousness

We exit the house and leave Eutychius with his guests. In a few moments the *comissatio* will begin, a toasting contest. The banquet got started sometime between the *hora nona* and the *hora decima* (around three o'clock in the afternoon) but it will go on for a long time yet: maybe six or eight hours more.

In the meantime the sun has gone down and the first stars have come out. The side streets are dark and deserted, but there are a lot of lighted lamps along the main streets, above the entrances to inns, full of travelers; the taverns, busily transforming themselves into clandestine gaming dens; and the many brothels that, in this seaport city, are working at full rhythm.

Walking along the streets we can hear the noises and the laughter coming from other banquets, beyond the high walls of the *domus*, and the furious shouting of a fight in a tavern that makes us quicken our pace.

When we get down to the harbor we notice that Pozzuoli never sleeps. Under the light of thousands of oil lamps stevedores are unloading all kinds of goods. We can say this with certainty because in the twentieth century some fifteen thousand used oil lamps will be uncovered, arranged in perfect order in several storage areas of the Portus Iulius, the big port built near Pozzuoli in the first century BC, now submerged under the sea.

Perhaps those lamps were used mainly for the unloading operations on the immense grain ships that arrived here. Supplying grain to Rome called for round-the-clock activity; that's why they had to work at night. From here, as we have seen, many ships then continued on to Ostia to unload the grain into the storage warehouses.

Before long we arrive at the shores of Lake Lucrinus, an interior lake alongside the bay of Pozzuoli. A long road, the Via Herculanea, runs between the two like a dam. We lean on one of the parapets to look out at the view. The atmosphere is magnificent, the wind is warm, and there is a full moon up in the sky. This area will continue to be one of the most beautiful parts of the peninsula for centuries to come, thanks to its enchanted atmosphere, although in recent times the building boom has partly suffocated the magic of the place.

In the Roman era the situation was really not all that different, though. As we have said, the whole coast is lined with villas, one next to the other. This part of the Campania region has always been a residential area for the rich—especially the nouveaux riches. In fact, Posillipo, the hilltop suburb of Naples, got its name from the villa of a new entry in the realm of the superrich Publius Vedius Pollio, the son of a family of ex-slaves who built himself a villa so sumptuous (and garish) that it gave its name to the entire hilltop where it was located. He had called it *Pausilypon*, literally "repose from the troubles," in honor of the panoramic view.

That is just one example of the villas that can be admired here. Some are so close to the sea that, according to Lionel Casson, "to go fishing all you have to do is drop a line out the window." Almost all of them over-look the water, with lots of rooms in a line under the porticoes, so that each one enjoys a magnificent view. Some villas have multiple stories of porticoes, one on top of the other.

We continue walking along the road-dam of the Via Herculanea, lulled by the lapping of the waves against the rocks. In the moonlight we catch a glimpse of a ship. It looks like a black shadow on the silvery sea. We can see lighted oil lamps and faces moving back and forth in the lamplight. We can hear voices and the laughter of men and women. . . . It's not just a banquet; there's something more going on.

Indeed, to hear the ancient authors tell it, perversion was rampant be-hind the walls of a lot of residential villas, especially in and around Baia, just a mile up the coast from Lake Lucrinus. It is a popular bath resort, and the lifestyle of the villa owners (or their renters) is shocking, even to the most open-minded Romans. "In Roman times Baia attracted anyone who was out for a good time, and it earned a reputation as a place of both licit and illicit pleasures," writes Lionel Casson. "Respectable representatives of the polite society sailed peacefully on Lake Lucrinus during the day; at night they invited onto their boats women of dubious propriety, went skinny dipping and 'filled the air of the lake with the raucous noise of their singing.'"

The same things were described by Varrone, a contemporary of Cicero. But Varrone added other things, for example, that "nubile young women were common property, old men behaved like young boys, and a lot of boys as though they were girls."

Things must not have changed for generations if, a century later, Seneca echoed Varrone, writing, "Why do I have to see drunks staggering along the beach or be disturbed by the noise of parties held on boats?"

That these coasts are occasions of sin and "contagious" perversion was also the opinion of Martial in Book I of his famous epigrams. Here he describes what happens to a virtuous married woman.

> Laevina, so chaste as to rival even the Sabine women of old, and more austere than even her stern husband, chanced, while entrusting herself sometimes to the waters of the Lucrine lake . . .and while frequently refreshing herself in the baths of Baiae, to fall into flames of love, and, leaving her husband, fled with a young gallant. She arrived a Penelope, she departed a Helen. (Bohn's Classical Library.)

The God Kairòs, or "Seize the Day!"

For many wealthy Romans, then, Baia is a place of extreme amusements. But this desire for pleasure corresponded to a mentality that was fairly widespread before Christianity and the belief in the afterlife. The dominant idea was that earthly life is the only life and therefore the time to enjoy yourself is now. Not necessarily according to the "customs" of Baia but even just in the pleasures of daily life.

Naturally, there are different philosophical currents, not to mention numerous religious ones, so attitudes toward life are varied. That said, there is a widely shared belief in the concept of carpe diem, life is now, enjoy what life has to offer in the moment that you live it. This attitude is what underlies the whole concept of luxury, from the banquets to the villas on the coast, the idea being to possess and experience the best things that time can offer you in the fleeting moment of your life.

Symbolizing this idea is a divinity who is truly unique. His name is Kairòs. He is a god of Greek origins who represents the fleeting moment. He is a youth with wings on his back and feet, representing the velocity of time; he holds a scale with two pans, one of which is pushed lower by one of his hands, as though to say, "This opportunity is available for a limited time only." The other hand holds a razor, on which the entire scale rests. The razor represents the possibility that life is subject to sudden change, as sudden as death. He has a striking hairdo: long hair in front while the nape of his neck is shaved. It's the final statement of this philosophy of life: the fleeting moment must be seized when it approaches, because once it has passed (and you are looking at its back) you can never seize it again. . . .

THE MEDITERRANEAN

~ *Adventure on the Sea* ~

Destination: Carthage

The ship releases its lines. Destination: Carthage. Our sestertius is now traveling on a cargo ship, in the possession of a Greek sailor. How did he get it? In the easiest and quickest way possible: he stole it.

Yesterday he was at the baths and noticed a rich merchant arriving with some customers. He was telling them about a banquet he had hosted at his house the night before and how heavy his head still felt from all the wine he had drunk. Wine, by the way, that he had just brought personally from Gaul. When he heard that, the Greek sailor realized that the man must be quite rich. And he could also see that he was indeed tired and foggy-headed from the excesses of the previous night's banquet. An ideal mark. He waited until the man got into line to enter the baths and with a swift slash of his knife he cut the cords of the purse that was hanging from his belt—a classic move at the baths. But the merchant was certainly not stupid because, despite being very rich, he was only carrying two sesterces. Apparently he was familiar with the dangers in Pozzuoli.

Now the stolen property is in a safe place on the boat, wrapped in a cloth and stuck between two floorboards. Better not to trust one's fellow sailors.

The sailor casts a glance astern. Pozzuoli with its merchants' villas, Baia with its baths, and Lucrinus with its orgies are slowly moving off into the distance. Before the ship felt solid and stable under his feet, but now that the water is getting deeper he can feel the heaving movement of the sea beneath the keel, rising and falling. Already several of the thirty passengers who had come aboard in Pozzuoli are feeling seasick. Traveling by sea in the Roman era is not very comfortable. There are no passenger ships. People wanting or needing to travel must go to the port, find a ship bound for their destination, and ask permission to board. For a price, obviously. But the service on board is terrible: no cabins, no beds, no blankets. You sleep on the deck and bring your own food. The voyages are not long, but they are decidedly uncomfortable.

When given a choice, Romans prefer to have the ground under their feet; they don't trust the sea. To be sure, traveling by sea is much less exhausting, you don't have to march for days on end, but the idea that you might die at any moment in a shipwreck is something the Romans will never quite get used to, contrary to some other much more maritime peoples like the Greeks and the Phoenicians. But sometimes they don't have a choice, because of the length of the journey.

To put things in perspective, a sea voyage from Pozzuoli to Alexandria takes about nine days. That might seem like a lot, seeing as how today the same trip takes just three hours by air. But keep in mind that the distance is about 1,000 nautical miles, or 1,150 miles by land. Traveling the same distance on land would take a Roman at least two months. Our voyage to Carthage, in what is now Tunisia, will be short. It will take a couple of days' sailing at a speed of around six knots (about seven miles an hour) to reach the coast of Africa.

The sailors move back and forth on the ship, which is called, as fate would have it, *Europa*, and has the typical shape of a Roman cargo ship (*navis oneraria*): it's big-bellied, and on the stern it has a curious, enormous curl in the form of a swan with its beak elegantly resting on its neck. All the *onerariae* have this sculpture. The ship has a central mast, with a large square mainsail. Above it is another, smaller sail with a triangular shape, to take advantage of the slightest puff of wind on calm days. The *oneraria* has another mast on the bow, lower down, tilted forward like a knight's lance. This is the bowsprit, which carries another small square sail, ideal for making maneuvers.

The commander gestures to the sailors to pull tighter on some lines to catch the wind better. These ships might be beautiful, but they don't zip along like modern sailboats. They're cargo ships, squat and heavy in the water.

Since the Middle Ages all ships have had a single wheel or helm in the center of the stern, but in antiquity this doesn't yet exist. There is no steering wheel, not even the so-called tiller, the bar used to steer a small sailboat. Instead, there's something quite unusual: two rudders on the stern, one on each side of the hull. They look like two enormous vertical oars sticking down into the water. From his post atop a small tower on the stern, the helmsman regulates them both, using two hands as though he were driving a motorcycle.

The Superstitions of Sailors and Travelers

We follow the sailor as he crosses the ship. He walks by a passenger who's looking out at the receding coastline, reciting prayers in a low voice to invoke the protection of the gods. No one on board makes much of it because it's the normal thing to do: there's nobody here who's not super-stitious. This is the mentality of the ancients in general.

On land, before setting sail, neither the passengers nor the sailors know when the ship is going to leave. Sometimes they will wait several days. Departures are determined by the winds, obviously, but also by the omens.

First of all, certain days in the Roman religious calendar—August 24 and November 8, for example—were considered unlucky, and doing work or making deals was practically forbidden on those days. When an unlucky day, say Friday the 17th, coincided with a day of good wind, it might still be risky to depart. The commander would then sacrifice a bull or a sheep to see what the gods had to say. In the case of a negative response, departure would be postponed.

Even when everything lines up just right (wind, religious clearances, and sacrifices), there are omens to consider. And that is a whole other story. Lionel Casson has compiled a list of some of these bad signs that must be heeded: sneezing on the gangway when boarding (but sneezing to the right during a sacrifice is a good sign), a raven or a magpie perched and squawking on the masts, or the appearance of flotsam and jetsam just before departure. Furthermore, it bodes ill for anyone to curse, dance, or, in good weather, cut their fingernails or hair (which, however, can be thrown into a rough sea to placate the ire of the gods).

And then there are premonitory dreams: a key or turbid water is a clear prohibition to depart. A goat is a symbol of rough seas, a bull or a wild boar means a storm is on the horizon. Owls, barn owls, and sparrow owls indicate the imminent arrival of pirates or a squall. Finally, dreaming of someone being gored signifies a sinking ship.

There are a few good omens, as Casson points out. One of them comes in the form of birds (presumably not ravens or magpies) perching on the ship during the voyage. But perhaps the reason for the scarcity of good omens is obvious: the sea is so unpredictable that favorable signs can quickly be proven wrong. The preponderance of bad omens, on the other hand, may actually be a good thing, because the less often you go to sea, the less you risk your life. The worst-case scenario, obviously, would be a bad omen dreamed out on the high seas, when the ship is already at the mercy of fate.

Our sailor is very superstitious; he walks among the passengers making sure they are all behaving according to the rules.

Below Deck

Our sailor goes down belowdecks, officially to check on the cargo but more likely to make sure his loot (our sestertius, but also money from other petty thefts) is still there. At the center of the ship there is a square opening in the deck with a set of stairs going down. It's a dark space that calls for a lantern. In the dim lamplight the sailor leads the way down through an expanse of sacks, and then amphoras, which are lined up next to one another on several levels: the ones on top are inserted between the necks of the ones below and so on. Down in the hold it's easy to see that the shape of the amphoras, so tapered and elegant, is actually a practical design. The ferrule makes them less fragile at the base. The narrow and streamlined shape allows them to be arranged in narrow rows and on several levels. That explains how some ships manage to pack in as many as ten thousand of them. Finally, placing the handles near the top makes them easier to lower and raise during transshipping and transport operations.

We take a look around. The flank of the ship is solid. How are the boards of the planking held together? With the same system that we now use to attach an extension to a dining room table when there are guests for dinner: mortises and tenons, a precise series of dovetail joints that make the structure solid. These are then reinforced with nails bent three times. Examples of this technique of ship construction and of planking "sewn together" in this way can be seen at the Museum of the Sea and Navigation at the Santa Severa Castle north of Rome, built on the site of the ancient Etruscan port of Pyrgi. It's a small museum, but it's the only one that presents, in a complete way, all the techniques of ancient navigation.

Laboratory tests have indicated that for the keel and the frame the ancients preferred hard, resistant woods like oak or olive; for the tenons and planking, on the other hand, they used woods that were lighter, elastic, and resinous, like pine, fir, or larch.

The museum is also home to the only functioning reconstructed model in Europe of a pump used to suck up water. All the Roman ships were outfitted with them in case of a leak or to eliminate the bilge water that accumulated on the bottom of the ship. The pump consists of wooden disks that are pulled horizontally through a wooden pipe by a crank. It's a simple system but very effective. Passing through the pipe, the disks carry out the water as though they were a line of buckets. The result? The pump is able to eliminate fifty gallons of water per minute. And there were pumps in ancient times that were even bigger.

Isis, Queen of the Seas

We hear some shouting up on deck. Our sailor rushes up the stairs to have a look. The passengers are pointing toward an enormous ship that's approaching. We've been sailing on the open sea for several hours now, and the approaching ship is clearly headed for Ostia. It's part of the famous grain fleet. We can see others sailing behind it, all in line. They set sail several days ago from Alexandria and they're crossing the Mediterranean to feed Rome. They are immense and majestic, with red sails and a curl on the stern fashioned with the head of an animal. In the past, every time a ship this size arrived in Pozzuoli the people ran down to the harbor to see it.

The ship passes by us, and everyone on board is dumbstruck. It's the largest ship that can be seen on the Mediterranean: 180 feet long, more than 42 feet wide, and over 44 feet high from the lowest point of the hold to the deck—taller than a four-story building.

This queen of the seas has an expert crew; earning a place on it is the equivalent of being named to the national sailing team.

On the bow we notice some images of the goddess Isis, and her name is painted on both sides of the hull. Everything about the ship is over-sized: the immense anchor, the capstans, the winches, even the stern cabins. The man at the helm, on the other hand, is exactly the opposite: small, his head half-bald, half-ringed with kinky hair, its white color testifying to his long experience on the sea. This small man's hands are in control of a real giant. To make a comparison to modern ships, it's as though he were in command of an aircraft carrier.

According to some estimates, this ship has the capacity to transport more than a thousand tons of grain! It would be interesting to discover how the sacks are distributed in the hold: in order to keep the ship on an even keel, and to avoid contact with the sides of the ship, which are always wet, they must have come up with some ingenious form of shelving inside the hold.

The sailors on the two ships exchange greetings. The *Isis* zooms by our *oneraria* like a cloud; immense, silent, and without stopping.

The Storm

Night falls; the ship sails on. On board the passengers work out whatever arrangements they can for finding a place to sleep. Some of them have spread large pieces of cloth over themselves for protection from the humidity. Others are curled up in the corners with nothing but a blanket. The sea is as black as pitch. The helmsman, or *gubernator*, has the stars as his only reference point, and he keeps an eye on them, guiding the ship with all of his experience. Our sailor isn't saying anything, but last night he had a scary dream: his fellow seamen have figured it out because they notice that he has lain down to sleep right next to the ship's only lifeboat. Actually, it's a simple rowboat that's only used during maneuvers in the harbor and to go ashore. At most it can hold ten or twelve people pressed up against each other, so it's not nearly big enough for everyone. We take a look around: there are no life jackets, and in Roman times almost no one knows how to swim except for those who live in close contact with the sea, like these sailors. So it's easy to understand Romans' fear when they have to cross a great expanse like the Mediterranean, which can unleash a tempest and transform itself into a killer from one minute to the next. Historical records tell us that of the ships that transport grain to Rome, one in five sinks. And a shipwreck in these times means death: there are no radios or SOS signals; nobody comes to search for you. Moreover, ship traffic is very light compared to modern times. After a shipwreck, anyone who doesn't drown remains at the mercy of the sea and dies of the cold in short order.

At five in the morning we wake up with a start; the sea is raging, the wind is taut, and the waves are slapping against the sides of the ship. Everyone is anxious and worried, and among the passengers there are those who are praying and invoking the gods and those who are crying in desperation. In these situations everyone has to pitch in and do their part, passengers included. The sails are wiped down with linseed oil to keep them from tearing. The sea rises more and more, and when the sun appears on the horizon (an instant before being swallowed up by the black clouds), a full-blown storm has arisen. The ship is tossed from side to side by the swirling sea. The waves are as high as hills and are running like wolves around their helpless prey. Suddenly, a wave washes over the ship and, like an octopus, latches onto some passengers, dragging them away. Luckily, they're able to grab onto some ropes and are held on board by some other passengers.

Cargo sacks and the passengers' baggage are rolling and sliding across the deck, but nobody tries to stop them. No one can think of anything but saving himself. The ship is being hammered furiously. But it hangs on.

The struggle goes on for hours until, toward noon, the sea calms down, like a giant going back to sleep. On board, the damage is tallied. The passengers are exhausted, wet, shivering with cold. They look at each other, teeth chattering. But they're alive. Some of them are swearing that they're going to make the return trip on foot, by way of the Middle East.

Man Overboard

A couple of hours later something is sighted in the water. It looks like a big piece of floating wood. The helmsman directs the ship toward the object, which disappears every now and again amid the waves. As the ship gets nearer, it becomes clear that it is a man overboard, clinging to the boards of a shipwreck.

The problem of getting the man back on deck is not easy to solve; a sailing ship can't put on the brakes like a car. It'll have to throw him a line, and he'll have to grab it and hang on tight so he can be pulled on board. Will he have enough strength to do that after all that time in the water?

The ship moves in closer, the sailors lined up on the bow and along the side of the ship ready to launch the line.

Now the man is right in front of us. The helmsman has done a perfect maneuver, and he lets loose the sails, which start fluttering in the wind. The ship loses speed. The man overboard is now just forty or fifty feet away, and we realize that it's a woman. The first sailor launches a line, but it hits the water out of her reach. The second manages to hit the woman, but the rope gets dragged away by the ongoing ship before she can manage to grab hold of it. It's clear that her muscles are stiff and sluggish from the cold of her long time in the water; hypothermia is slowly sapping the life from her body.

Now it's the third sailor's turn, but his launch is too short. It looks like the woman is done for. It will take a wide maneuver to return to the spot, assuming that once it's been done they'll be able to find her again. It's very easy to lose sight of a floating object among the waves.

Suddenly, another line is launched from the ship. It was launched by a man who we will later learn is a veteran, a legionnaire, recently retired. He tied a long rope onto one of the oars of the lifeboat and threw it with all his might toward the woman, exactly as he had been accustomed to doing for twenty years, heaving his *pilum* at the enemy. The oar is heavier than a javelin, but the woman is not far away; and besides, the launch is perfect. The oar with the rope on the end flies through the air beyond the woman and falls into the water very close by. She finally manages to grab onto it, but she's too weak to lift herself up. It's all she can do to hold on to it. From the ship everyone pulls in unison, and they manage to get her near the side of the ship and, eventually, up on board.

After being fed and warmed, she recounts that she is the only survivor of a ship identical to theirs that had been struck full on by the storm. There were a lot of people on board, sixty or so, plus the crew. She hasn't seen any of them. The others all disappeared in the darkness of the night. Miraculously, she had come across these three boards still solidly fastened together, and she clung to them. Those boards, our sailor points out, are not a good sign. They're part of the planking. It means that the ship was shattered into pieces by the fury of the waves, and now it's at the bottom of the sea. All the other passengers are probably dead, or they will be in another few hours, scattered by the waves. The same thing could have happened to us.

A Million Wrecks Waiting on the Bottom

This gets us thinking. A hypothetical estimate of three shipwrecks per day throughout the Mediterranean (a very conservative figure considering that the interruption of navigation during the winter months did not apply to the coastline navigation of fishing boats and small vessels) means that more than a thousand vessels, big and small, sink every year. If we multiply this number by a thousand years, the duration of the Roman era in the West, we get a total of a million wrecks at the bottom of the sea. Naturally, they're not all Roman ships but also include Carthaginian, Greek, Etruscan, and so on.

If we consider that the Mediterranean was traveled by ships for many centuries before the Romans, we realize that the bottom of the sea is an enormous cemetery, full of stories that we will never know. But it is also the most amazing museum of antiquity on the entire planet. If we think about all the civilizations that grew up along its shores—Minoan, Mycenaean, Greek, Egyptian, Phoenician, Carthaginian, Etruscan, Roman—we soon realize that the sea bottom holds an endless collection of objects, handmade goods, and artistic masterpieces from all those epochs and cultures. They are down there waiting: statues by the great Greek masters, maybe even works by Phidias or Praxiteles. Or maybe even one or more Egyptian obelisks on their way to Rome. Today they are unreachable. But future generations of archaeologists will have means that we can't even imagine for exploring the bottom of the Mediterranean. And they may well discover a forgotten past, without having to excavate it.

It's early afternoon when our sailor sights land off in the distance. We've made it. The port of Carthage awaits us.

AFRICA

~ *An Empire Without Racism* ~

Arriving in Carthage

The faces of the sailors and passengers are hit by a blast of hot African wind. It carries the smell of land, a land different from the one they have just left. This smell doesn't have the aromatic edge of the European coasts. Here you smell the dry, dusty scent of the desert.

Carthage earned its place in history by its rise to power and its spectacular demise. Founded by the Phoenicians and transformed into a Mediterranean superpower by their descendants the Carthaginians, it was demolished during the Punic Wars by the Romans, who in 146 BC razed it down to the last stone and poured salt over it so that nothing of the ancient Carthaginian civilization would survive.

The city that the Romans rebuilt was completely new, even in its urban plan, and had nothing in common with the Punic city. It was a drastic and irreversible turn of the page, among the most memorable in history. One thing, however, has remained: the port, which the ship *Europa* is now entering. The Romans kept it and reused it.

The first section is a large rectangle with a surface area of seventeen and a half acres. We are now moving slowly inside it pulled by a tugboat, consisting of a rowboat powered by six large black men. Like a tracking shot in a film our gaze moves across a line of ships tied up at the docks, unloading their cargos. All around them are images of daily life in the harbor: a line of stevedores carrying sacks on their shoulders; the proprietor of a small navigation company scolding one of his employees; two friends, one of whom has just disembarked, hugging each other affectionately. A man chewing his fingernails, sitting on some sacks tied together with a rope; two slaves, one behind the other, carrying a long pole with an amphora dangling in the middle, looking like hunters carrying a big-game animal. The faces are particularly intriguing. Although Carthage is certainly an international port, there is a predominance of dark skin and curly hair. We are on another continent.

The ship moves past the rectangular basin and enters another area with an unusual configuration: it's perfectly round, with a circular island in the center. All around its perimeter are bays from which the Carthaginian war ships used to emerge. A big round roof concealed the dens of these seagoing predators. Gleaming white, it looked like a structure designed by some modern architect. As many as 220 galleys ready to attack would come swarming out of this marine beehive. In the middle, on the island, was the naval command center.

The Romans kept the structure, but they changed its use from military to commercial. A temple had been built on the island, while the long, narrow bays of the warships have disappeared to make room for warehouses to store goods. All around, an imposing colonnade of African marble surrounds the circular basin of the harbor. It's a magnificent sight; imagine arriving on a sailboat at Saint Peter's Square in Rome, filled with water and surrounded by Bernini's famous colonnade. That's the sensation one has on entering the harbor in Carthage.

We tie up at the dock between two ships, one from Alexandria and the other from Crete. The helmsman and sailors are all assembled on the stern where they're performing a thanksgiving ritual for the ship's safe arrival. The helmsman minces some food over the fire and recites some holy words. This is done on all ships both before departure and upon arrival. Later on, he'll go to a temple to make a votive offering for the ship's escape from the storm. And he won't be the only one to do so.

The faces of those on board are tired but happy. The question now is what to do with the woman they fished out of the sea; she's alone and has no money. So a collection is taken up on board. It doesn't amount to all that much, but it's enough to pay for a place to stay, some food, and maybe a new tunic. Then she'll have to make do on her own.

The last one to give the woman something is our sailor. The helmsman gives him a pat on the back to encourage him. He hands her a few coins. The helmsman knows full well that the coins are not his . . . that's why he's forced him to give them up for a good cause. So, partly out of superstition, partly because of peer pressure, and partly to give thanks for the escape from danger, he offers the woman the stolen coins. Among them is our sestertius. The woman is embarrassed and thanks him timidly. She's still in shock.

The news that she is the only survivor of a shipwreck spreads quickly through the city. The woman, Aelia Sabina, is an uncommon person. She's a musician and a very talented singer, highly regarded in Aquincum (Budapest), the city where she lives. Her long blond hair, light blue eyes, and impressive stature betray her Nordic origins at first glance.

Her gravestone will be found by archaeologists in Aquincum. Reading it, they will discover many details about her life. She started out playing a string instrument (*pulsabat pollice chordas*), perhaps the zither or the ancestor of our guitar. And as she plucked the strings she sang with a lovely voice (*vox ei grata fuit*). She was so talented that she very quickly moved on to another instrument, the water organ, with great success. This instrument was the Roman equivalent of the piano, present at any kind of musical event. It was played in chamber concerts, in the *domus*, for a small group of listeners, as well as in amphitheaters when the gladiators fought, so as to create a sort of soundtrack for the most dramatic moments.

We know something else about Aelia Sabina: she is a former slave, a *liberta*, who will go on to marry her music teacher (but at this time she is still single). It is a nice love story, with a curious note: her future husband, also an organ player, is a legionnaire from the II Adiutrix legion, previously deployed in Britain, then transferred to Aquincum by Trajan, with a small contingent sent to Africa. She was on her way to join him when she was shipwrecked.

Now Aelia Sabina is all alone, in a strange city, in a province she's never been to before, and on a continent that she has only heard talked about. Her fiancé is far away and knows nothing of her plight. What does she do now?

How to Become a Divinity

Fortunately, the news of her shipwreck also reaches the ears of a rather important woman named Sextia. She's tall, slender, with a luminous, charming smile. Her dark complexion and long curly hair reveal her distant Punic origins.

She's a priestess, or more precisely a *flaminica*, a religious devoted exclusively to the cult of a single divinity, as archaeologists learned from her gravestone. Her divinity is somewhat unusual: Augustus. During the imperial age traditional gods like Jove, Mars, and Quirinus were joined by cults devoted to the emperors and their relatives, transformed into gods after their deaths. Imagine a modern head of state, a president or prime minister, being beatified at the moment of death and venerated for generations, replete with his or her own temple and priests, incense, offerings, requests for intervention, and holy days like Christmas and Easter.

In the Roman era, the first emperor, Augustus, and his wife, Livia, considered the "perfect couple" who had ushered in the imperial age, were two such divinities. For decades now they have had temples dedicated just to them in every city of the empire, with *flamines* and *flaminicae* officiating at their ceremonies.

Being a priest or priestess has its advantages. It's an office aspired to by all the members of the local elite because it occupies a position of prestige. It's especially advantageous for women because in an openly male-dominated society it offers them an opportunity to exercise an important public function otherwise reserved to men.

As soon as Sextia learns of Aelia Sabina's plight, she sends her slaves to look for her. It doesn't take them long to find her. When the two women meet face-to-face, all the social barriers between a priestess and a *liberta* are swept away, and they immediately connect.

Sabina is a guest in Sexta's home for a few days, observing her daily routine. Sexta is a very energetic woman engaged in various civic activities, in addition to her religious duties. Most of all, she promotes a lot of initiatives for the benefit of Carthage.

Noblesse Oblige

Here we have the chance to discover an important aspect of Roman society: the philanthropy of the rich toward the city and its inhabitants. The priestess uses her family's money to make gifts to Carthage. Other wealthy families do the same by, for example, financing the restoration of important monuments or donating statues, distributing large amounts of money to the collectivity, organizing quadriga races or gladiator fights, etc.

All of this is part of a precise strategy of self-promotion conducted by the most prestigious families in the city. At times the families even compete to see who can give the most important donation. It's a way of building consensus and acquiring fame in the eyes of the community, and it still happens today.

But unlike today, when there is almost always some economic return for the sponsor, in Roman times the donations were officially grants rather than investments and were only partially intended to add luster to the donor's name. In reality, all wealthy Romans have the ethical duty to invest in the city where they live because it is an important part of everybody's lives, the center of gravity around which all of Roman society orbits. It is not unlike noblesse oblige, the social obligation of the nobility to their local community.

Today it is much more rare, and we call it philanthropy. But in Roman times it is so widespread that most of the great monuments, statues, theaters, and amphitheaters scattered throughout the empire are the fruit of donations made by the wealthy, their names often engraved clearly in the marble. If it hadn't been for this ethical obligation of the wealthy, archaeological sites today would be much more bare.

That showing oneself to be generous was a social duty is also evident in a surprising initiative of Trajan's: he created a system for helping poor children in Italy, especially in rural areas, by ensuring regular donations of money to buy food. It was a form of assistance directed primarily to illegitimate children with little or no means of support, who must have somehow made a big impression on Trajan. Naturally, the program only benefited the children of Roman citizens, not slaves. Nevertheless, it is striking to see such a sensitive and modern attitude toward children in such an ancient society.

Trajan's program is called the Institutio Alimentaria. We know about it thanks to the famous Tabula Alimentaria Trajana, one of the longest inscriptions in bronze that has come down to us from the Roman era, discovered by archaeologists in the little town of Velleia in the province of Piacenza.

Trajan personally withdrew funds from his own holdings and lent them to agricultural landowners in the various municipalities of Italy, charging 5 percent interest to increase the fund and guarantees in the form of mortgages on their lands. The money from the interest was used to buy food for needy children, ensuring a continuous supply over the years.

The Emperor's Color

After several days, the news finally arrives that Aelia Sabina's fiancé has been contacted. The priestess arranges for a wagon to take Aelia to her fiancé, and she will accompany her part of the way. In fact for some time now she has been planning a journey to visit her brother, who lives in Bulla Regia, a city located along the route that Aelia Sabina will be taking.

The next day, the two women and a small accompanying procession leave Carthage early in the morning. They're traveling on a *carruca* similar to the one that we saw in Provence, but lighter, given the climate, and with elegant cushions and colored veils on the inside—a feminine touch by its owner.

After setting out, Aelia Sabina notices something on the road and leans out the window for a better look. Seashells are scattered all along the road, at first just a few, then more and more, until there are piles of them, broken and blanched by the blistering hot sun. The fields along the side of the road look like dump sites for these shells. They are, in fact, the waste from an immense processing plant for the production of purple dye, the color of the Roman Empire.

The purple pigment used to dye prized fabrics is derived from mollusks in the Muricidae family, and particularly from the common murex, *Haustellum brandaris*. The pigment is found in a small sack inside the body. Each mollusk contains no more than a drop of the pigment, hence the necessity of gathering huge quantities of these gastropods, with underwater nets distributed along the coast.

It's a laborious procedure: the body of the mollusk must be removed from the shell by hand and left out in the sun for a few days; if it's too small to open by hand, the shell must be broken into pieces with a grindstone. The mollusks are then boiled in a lead pot. Impurities are eliminated, and what's left is the dye that Pliny the Elder described as "that precious pink color that tends toward black and shines."

Behind every ounce of that pigment lies a massacre of mollusks. That explains why it is so costly and why it is considered a luxury, like the very silk that it colors. More than just a dye, it is a status symbol in itself, as Pliny the Elder explains: "It distinguishes the senator from the man of equestrian rank, it's used to propitiate the gods and lends all garments luster: on triumphal vestments it is mingled with gold. Let us be prepared, then, to forgive this frantic passion for purple."

Calling it a "frantic passion" is not inappropriate because, although the Romans did not discover or invent the system for obtaining the purple dye, it was they who took it to such an industrial level as to eliminate the murex mollusks from entire areas of the Mediterranean. In this way the environmental impact of Roman globalization bears a striking resemblance to our own.

The wagon passes by the front of the processing plant, and the odor of tens of thousands of mollusks left out in the sun to dry is unbearable. The smell of rotten seawater goes on for miles. Perfectly logical, then, that these processing plants are always located downwind from towns and cities.

A Journey in the Economic "Strongbox" of the Empire

During the journey, the procession travels through a North Africa much different from the one we know today. Everything is much greener, reminding us of Spain or southern Italy. But we are in the province of Africa Proconsularis, which includes present-day Tunisia and parts of Algeria and Libya.

Aelia Sabina, rocked by the bumpy ride of the wagon, discovers a whole new world, and so do we. We look out onto dozens of rural farms and villas, expanses of cultivated fields, what amounts to a real granary for the empire, just like Egypt. But it's more than grain. There is also an abundance of fruit trees, figs, vineyards, bean fields, and olive groves.

The journey continues, and just as we would on our own highways, we encounter "tractor trailers," cargo wagons loaded with goods headed toward Rome and the rest of the empire. So we discover that North Africa exports much more than it imports: fabrics, wool, ceramics, plus the timber and marble that are extracted near the coast. Africa is a real cornucopia of riches for the imperial economy.

Our convoy encounters a cargo wagon traveling slowly in the opposite direction. It has wheels without spokes, similar to the tops of round tables, which creak on every turn. We notice some big wooden crates onboard; the base of one of them is stained with blood. All of these crates contain wild animals bound for the Colosseum. It's incredible to think of the tremendous effort required to capture a ferocious beast and transport it to another continent, only to kill it in an instant, in front of a crowd in an amphitheater. Just as suddenly as they appeared, the wagons disappear again around a bend in the road, accompanied by the ear-piercing creaking of its spokeless wheels.

A little later we run into some more "live" cargo: slaves. They are black Africans, undoubtedly captured in a raid in some unknown part of the continent. Each one has his own story about how he got here, but the same destiny is waiting for all of them: the total loss of liberty, perhaps a violent death in some amphitheater or a slower death on a farm. Within a very few years most of those we're seeing now, bound with chains and rings around their necks, will be dead.

Building a City in the Desert

The convoy's arrival in the city of Bulla Regia marks the separation of the two women; the next day Aelia Sabina bids farewell to the priestess. She'll continue on her own, with another wagon at her disposal, to meet her fiancé. She'll have a small escort: here, too, there is a risk of being kidnapped, especially in the less inhabited lands that she'll be crossing. But where is her fiancé, the legionnaire? He's at work on one of the most ambitious projects of the Roman era: building Thamugadi (today's Timgad), a brand-new city in the interior of North Africa.

All of the principal cities of the Mediterranean are located near the coast, if not directly on the shore. So why go to a high plateau, at an altitude of three thousand feet and five days' journey from Carthage, to build this one? There is nothing beyond it; we're on the border of the empire. We might compare it to the founding of Las Vegas, built from nothing in the middle of nowhere. If the objective there was profit, in the case of Thamugadi the goal is different: to conquer foreign populations. But not with arms, as we're about to discover.

Aelia Sabina travels for a long time through an environment scorched by the sun. It's a sun that seems to flatten everything, even sounds. The semidesert landscape is immense but silent. All you can hear is the sound of horses' hooves and wagon wheels, screeching against the road surface of packed earth and gravel. Along the way Aelia Sabina is accompanied by the smell of plants scorched in the heat, an unusual aroma for her, one that makes her lightheaded.

Then one morning she sees something incredible: a city appears out of nowhere, right before her eyes. It's at the center of a slightly undulating high plateau, dominated by the mountain of Aurarius (today, the Aurès mountains). After days of open plains and desert, her eyes suddenly take in markets, a forum, temples, baths, a theater. It looks like a mirage. . . .

Even the men of her escort are visibly excited, and they quicken their pace, arriving at the edge of the city at a gallop. Before they enter, a man steps into the middle of the road to stop them. He's well built, muscular, with short black hair. It's Aelia Sabina's fiancé, who has been waiting for her at the entrance to the city. The wagon stops, and the loving couple reunite in a long and intense embrace, made all the more intense by the thought of what might have happened if our *Europa* hadn't happened upon those few wooden boards, which were Aelia Sabina's last hope for survival.

Let's let them go. They have a lot of things to tell each other. She'll be here for a long time. Her fiancé's unit has been sent to this place to complete the construction of the city, the fruit of the work of other legionnaires, veterans of the Augusta III legion.

As tradition dictates, when legionnaires retire after twenty-five years' service, they receive a "diploma," as well as a piece of land where they can raise a family and live out their old age. The lands are almost always in border areas (sometimes only recently conquered) that are to be colonized, like the land on this high plateau.

These veterans have even been asked to build Thamugadi, and over the course of these long years they've done a magnificent job. The city was begun in 100 CE, and by now it has already acquired its general shape, even if a lot of things are still missing. It occupies a surface area of thirty-six acres and has been built with typical Roman precision. One hundred and twenty city blocks have been laid out in a perfect plan, with main streets (*cardo maximus* and *decumanus maximus*), side streets, public buildings, religious temples—in sum all the principal features of a Roman city. Conceptually, it's a miniature version of Rome. But why all this effort?

An Oasis in the Void

Rome was accustomed to conquering populations with arms and force, which as we have seen were frightfully effective. Here it decided to use a different strategy. Thamugadi is perfect as a city because it is a showcase of the Roman way of life: its aim is to subjugate the populations of the region not with the force of arms but with the attractions of the Roman civilization. Starting with its control over water. In a geographical area where water is scarce, there suddenly appears a city with baths—twenty-seven of them—as well as cisterns and sewer canals that keep disease at bay. Archaeologists have discovered that the entire city can be considered a sort of cistern that gathers in the water from the vicinity, filters it and purifies it with decantation basins, and then sends it on to the baths, houses, and drinking fountains on the corners of the streets. In Thamugadi water is not only present, it flows like a torrent, and all of this is thanks to the hydraulic engineering expertise of the Romans, who dig wells, identify springs, channel their waters with aqueducts, and so on. In Thamugadi, in other words, the Romans have created a vast oasis.

But that is only the first step. Thamugadi is supposed to act as a magnet for the surrounding region, attracting people and integrating them rather than forcing them into submission. It will be the quality of everyday life—good cuisine (with previously unknown and refined foods), baths, and culture—that "conquers" the people.

There is also the economic aspect, the opportunity to become rich, or at least improve one's standard of living. Thamugadi offers everyone, without discrimination, the chance to enter into the Roman orbit, to participate in the life of the empire—something that will not happen in later centuries, when there will almost always be a clear-cut distinction between the conquerors and the conquered.

Integration, then, is the magic word for understanding the thinking behind this city. It is a vision very much ahead of its time.

The Romans had faith in its success, too. Consider the theater. Archaeologists have remarked, in fact, that the theater has 3,500 to 4,000 seats—too many, considering that there were 8,000 to 10,000 inhabitants of the city at the time it was built. So, from the start, the city's designers must have believed that the project was bound to work.

And they were right: the city spread very quickly beyond its boundaries and began to develop suburban neighborhoods, arranged chaotically around the core, expanding from an area of 18 to 125 acres. Now, fifty years after founding the city, the Roman inhabitants are few. Almost the entire population is made up of Numidians from the surrounding area. Everything is in their hands: commerce, the city administration, daily life . . . but they no longer think like Numidians. By now, they think like Romans.

Archaeologists have discovered a graffito in Thamugadi that reveals a lot about the city: *Venari, lavari, ludere, ridere. Hoc est vivere*: Hunt, bathe, play, laugh. That's life. This is certainly one of the benefits of living in Thamugadi. But it would be simplistic to think that it was only amusement that won the consensus of the local people.

When Trajan gave the order to build Thamugadi he also launched a campaign to promote the cultivation of olives in North Africa, a campaign that would be carried on by Hadrian. Those who planted the olive trees knew that, if they also obtained Roman citizenship, they would be eligible for significant tax benefits and would have the opportunity to sell their products throughout the empire. This also helps explain why so many Numidians and inhabitants of Mauritania were open to embracing the Roman way of life.

The result is that many areas of North Africa became covered with olive trees, and olive oil became a major commodity of the area. Beginning in the era of Trajan, oil production intensifies to the point of becoming seriously competitive with that of Italy and the Iberian peninsula, as is demonstrated by the amphoras that archaeologists have found onsite and in shipwrecks from this period. African oils will gradually go on to outperform those produced on the Italian peninsula.

Aelia Sabina's fiancé is sitting at a table, writing a letter to her. She's still asleep, after the long journey and the long night spent with him He wants to leave her a short note that she'll find when she wakes up. Not too far away, at this break of dawn on the African plateau, a colleague of his is waiting for him, leaning against a column of the portico. Both of them have to be present at the morning muster.

A young man approaches, observing him in the act of writing.

"What are you doing?" he asks, pointing at the page.

The legionnaire raises his head and looks him straight in the eye. He sees a husky Numidian with curly hair, looking at him with curiosity.

The legionnaire thinks for a minute and then says, "Tell me something that you know that no one else does."

The young man looks off to the side and then turns back to look at him: "My woman is expecting a baby."

The legionnaire writes this information on a sheet of papyrus. He folds it and says to him, "Go to my colleague over there, and ask him to open this and read it."

The young man takes the papyrus. The comrade-in-arms opens it, reads it, then looks at the young Numdian and says, "Congratulations, so you're going to be a father."

The young man looks at him as if he has just performed magic.

For those who aren't able to, writing must indeed seem like a kind of magic. Scenes like this one were repeated countless times throughout history, in all of those border areas where a literate civilization encounters populations without any form of writing. But in the case of the Roman Empire there's a difference: all you have to do is look at the writings on the walls of Pompeii or displayed on amphoras or, better yet, the words etched on the monuments of Roman cities, to realize that in the empire almost everyone, at least in the cities, knows how to read and write. This had never been the case before, and would not be the case again for many centuries after the fall of the empire. During the Middle Ages and the Renaissance, for example, illiteracy was widespread. In the West, not until the twentieth century would literacy return to Roman levels and beyond.

Leptis Magna, City of Marble

Aelia Sabina found lodging not far from the quarters where her fiancé lives. The first purchases she makes in the city are of makeup; she wants to be able to make herself beautiful for her man. She's bought various powders, small spatulas, and oils, and our sestertius is now in the hands of the shopkeeper who sold them to her.

He's a short man, bald, with kind-looking eyes, always ready to smile and make his customers feel at ease. The day after he sells the makeup to Aelia Sabina, he starts on a journey to Leptis Magna, where he is due to receive a delivery of some perfumes and oriental essences arriving from Alexandria. Our sestertius is back on the sun-scorched road.

The perfumer arrives in Leptis Magna after spending a night in an inn. The city appeals to him; it's very different from Thamugadi, much bigger and more populous, and the air is cool. Leptis Magna is right on the sea, on the coast of present-day Libya, away from the quarries and the sun-parched mountains.

It is also appealing because it is a city of marble, full of masterworks of art. It won't reach its maximum splendor for another century or so, when Septimius Severus, the African emperor who was born right here, will adorn it with new monuments. But it's already a lively city, its white marble streets full of people.

Two boys chase each other through the crowd and knock over a basket on display outside a grocery shop. The owner comes out and tries to run after them, but they're too fast, vanishing in the crowd, darting this way and that like squirrels. We close our eyes, sniffing the air. The perfumes of the women passing by are different from those that we smelled in Germany or Provence. They're more exotic and penetrating, perhaps because we're closer to Alexandria, where the fragrances and oriental essences come from.

The people on the streets of Leptis Magna are shorter than we have seen previously, and they tend to have thick, black, curly hair. Three matrons pass by on the street wrapped in brightly colored tunics in various shades of yellow, pink, red. They have full forms and make no effort to conceal them as is the custom in modern times; on the contrary, they seem satisfied to display them in flashy colors. In this era, the ideal female figure is curvaceous and abundant, especially around the hips.

The perfume seller is walking through the market in Leptis. It's a large square with two buildings at either end that look like round temples. Here, too, we are surrounded by marble. Even the fishmonger stands are outfitted with gleaming white marble tables, their feet elegantly sculpted in the form of dolphins. Their counters are piled with fish for sale. The contrast between the snow-white marble and the rivulets of deep red blood dripping from the fish is striking. Making our way through the crowd we approach a stone pillar, engraved with the various units of measure: the Roman foot, the Egyptian royal cubit, and the Punic cubit. On it we also notice an inscription: Annobal Tapapius Rufus, a name that's half Roman and half Carthaginian. This market, the inscription tells us, was donated to the city by the Tapapi family over a hundred years ago, in 9 CE. They have erected the pillar in accordance with the traditional social obligation to donate monuments (but also, let's face it, to leave something of themselves to history).

The same is true of the Leptis Magna theater. There is an inscription left by a certain Tiberius Claudius Sestius a few years ago (91–92 CE), from which we discover that he, like the Carthaginian priestess Sextia, also serves a cult dedicated to a dead emperor (Vespasian, in this case), who donated to the people the altar and the stage of the theater, because "he loves his homeland, loves to make it more beautiful, loves his fellow citizens, loves social harmony."

The perfume seller is a passionate theatergoer. He could easily have sent his slave to make this long journey, but his love for the theatrical art is so intense that he travels here from the mountains whenever he can, and he never misses a production staged by the leading theater companies.

The theater in Leptis Magna is magnificent. The semicircular arc of its ramped seats looks like the curve of a clam shell, and from the uppermost row of seats you can see the expanse of the Mediterranean. This open-air Roman theater is a perfect union of extremes: the white of the marble with the deep blue of the sea, the hard surface of the seats with the soft texture of the waves. It's a unique place, especially in the late afternoon, when the sun becomes a red disk. Even those who sit here today, two thousand years later, feel the pleasures of the mind combined with the pleasures of the eye.

The theater is rapidly filling up with spectators. They arrive a few at a time. The women are made up and well dressed because, as we discovered with Ovid, in the age of empire the theater is one of the main meeting places in the city. The scent of their oriental essences quickly fills the air. Our perfume salesman is able to tell the social status of the women from the perfume they use. The ones at the top are not always the most tasteful. Now, for example, two rows below us a woman is walking by with an enormous hairdo, in the style of the time. Embedded in her hair, amid fake curls and rolled braids, are jewels that hang and dangle like Christmas tree decorations. She doesn't realize how ridiculous she looks. But nobody would dare tell her: the wealth she inherited when her husband died has made her one of the richest women in the city and one of the most desired and revered. Needless to say, her perfume is excessively strong and pungent. Even our perfumer wrinkles his nose.

We take a look around. The people coming in and gradually taking their seats are quite diverse. Leptis is a port city, and you can see people here from every shore of the Mediterranean. But those here in the theater are not sailors, tourists, or merchants passing through; they're the inhabitants of the city, and they are all Roman.

An Empire Open to All

Those faces help us discover a fundamental mechanism behind the success and the longevity of Rome on three continents: integration.

The short speech below, about the integration of different ethnic groups, in society and in politics, was delivered almost two thousand years ago by Emperor Claudius, but it could have been read in any parliament today.

In 48 CE, Emperor Claudius made prominent Gauls eligible to sit in the Senate together with their Roman colleagues. The Roman senators were opposed to the idea, prompting the emperor's response:

> To what cause must we attribute the downfall of the Spartans and the Athenians, as strong as they were militarily, if not to the fact that they spurned as aliens those whom they had conquered? Foreigners have ruled over us. . . .
>
> By now the Galls have become assimilated to us by custom, culture, blood relations: they also bring us their gold and their wealth, rather than keep them for themselves! Senators, everything that we now con-

sider to be of the oldest antiquity was once new; plebeian magistrates came after patrician, Latin magistrates after plebeian; magistrates from still other Italic peoples after Latin.

In these words we can read not only tolerance but even the desire to welcome and integrate diversity into one's own society. It is truly surprising.

Throughout the Mediterranean, Rome opened its doors to the peoples it conquered, thus creating a multiethnic society. Multiethnic, yes, but with just one official culture: Roman law and Roman administration must not be questioned. Those who do not make sacrifices for the emperor, recognizing his authority and therefore automatically that of the whole Roman world, place themselves against the system and are considered enemies. In his own home, any Roman citizen is free to speak whatever language he wants and practice his religion. But the basic laws and rules of Rome must be accepted; they are the same and undisputable for all. Even the Gauls who became senators no longer paid allegiance to their own tribal laws but to Roman laws. This is a fundamental point for understanding how Rome succeeded in becoming the melting pot of antiquity.

In the field of religion, on the other hand, the Roman attitude is very cautious and respectful, mindful that religious conflict can have serious consequences. In this case too, North Africa offers us an interesting example. The Romans don't impose religion, but they have an intelligent approach that allows local religions, with their preexisting rituals and ceremonies, to continue to exist. All they have to do is make them *appear* to be Roman. A local deity might take a Roman name, for example. The Punic god Baal takes the name Saturn and the goddess Tanit acquires the name Celestial Juno. The religion itself doesn't change; it just undergoes a "restyling" to seem more Roman.

A Black Emperor

Is there discrimination in the Roman Empire? Looking at the racial diversity represented among the people sitting elbow to elbow in the theater in Leptis Magna the answer appears to be no. From the point of view of ethnicity the Roman era may have brought about the greatest integration in history. (People may not be discriminated against on the basis of the color of their skin, but discrimination based on social status or wealth is widespread. And it is fierce. In order to become a senator, for example, one had to possess at least 1 million sesterces and own property.)

Roman society is multiethnic because it integrates, rather than marginalizes, the conquered. Not only are the Romans not racist; they consider ethnic diversity a resource because it is the consequence of social and economic mechanisms that ensure a future for Roman civilization. This is an interesting point.

Since we are here in Leptis, let's take North Africa as an example. The Romans allow the Africans access to wealth, success, and the highest public offices. Obviously, the basic eligibility requirement is that they have become Roman citizens in the meantime.

The chances of becoming emperor are the same for an African as they are for an Italian or a Gaul. And an African actually did. If you ever happen to see a famous painting on wood depicting Septimius Severus with his whole family, you might be surprised by his very dark skin. No one raised an objection about it, nor about the fact that he spoke Latin with a strong African accent. Septimius Severus was one of the greatest emperors of Rome, who defended its frontiers and managed the empire much better than some of his European colleagues.

So, the Roman Empire had the capacity to put an African in its highest office precisely because it was a system that opened its doors to the incorporated and conquered peoples who embraced its culture. The mechanism of integration was so effective that at the end of the century that we are now exploring fully one-third of the members of the Senate of Rome will be of African origin, perhaps thanks to the prosperity and wealth of the region. This is one of Rome's most distinctive qualities compared to empires of recent history, such as the English, French, or Spanish, which did not allow people of conquered lands access to high office. In the Roman Empire, however, something similar happened more than once. Trajan, for example, was the first non-Italic emperor in the history of the empire: he was born in Spain.

Our Sestertius Changes Hands

The perfumer hangs on every line of the theatrical production, revels in the special effects, and applauds along with the thousands of other spectators when the curtain falls. Or rather, when it rises: in the Roman era theater curtains rise out in front of the stage, rolling upward like a screen, thanks to an underground apparatus.

The next day, he goes to the harbor and accepts delivery of his goods. He has no trouble recognizing the ship of his Egyptian counterpart. It has an orange sail and the blue eyes painted on the bow to scare off evil spirits are much bigger than the ones on other ships. But more than anything else it's the Egyptian himself who is easily recognizable. He's as thin as a rail with long curly hair and deep black eyes. His only clothing is a white skirt that leaves in clear view the muscles of his torso, contracting with each step.

When the perfumer pays for the goods our sestertius changes hands, and we are about to set sail once again. Destination: Alexandria.

EGYPT

~ Tourists of the Classical World ~

Sailing to Egypt

The harbor of Leptis Magna gradually disappears behind us. A strange destiny befell this city. It remained prosperous and resplendent for many years, and then, with the development of the first cracks in the empire and the incursions of the Asturians in the fourth century CE, it was rapidly abandoned by the elite and by its inhabitants because of its vulnerability to attack. (Leptis Magna and other cities like it had no walls or defensive structures because they developed during the Roman globalization, which molded them according to the dictates of its commerce and social life.) Once everyone had fled, small groups of primitive tribes from the interior settled in the empty city. Archaeologists would later find arrowheads among the ruins of its monuments, which were turned into hunting grounds. In an unraveling of history, centuries of civilization were pulverized in an atmosphere worthy of a postapocalyptic film. But in the end these groups left too, and Leptis Magna became a ghost town. Imagine the deserted colonnades where the only sound was the howling wind, the theater with winged predators nesting in its niches, the empty shops, the houses with their shutters torn off, the imposing bath complexes, once vibrant, now wrapped in silence. And the splendid mosaics with colorful scenes of life, happy faces and gazes, gradually disappearing under the sand. . . .

The ultimate victor was the desert. It gradually buried everything. In certain points the city was covered by forty feet of sand. But it was the sand that saved the city from being plundered and pillaged. It did not come to light again until the twentieth century, when Italian archaeologists rediscovered its buried splendors. Today Leptis Magna is one of the most beautiful archaeological sites to visit, a veritable "marble Pompeii."

Our ensuing days of sailing pass by peacefully. Our ship makes stops in the cities of Berenice and Appollonia in Cyrenaica; finally, one night the Egyptian merchant points out a low star on the horizon. Only it's not a star; it's one of the seven wonders of the ancient world: the lighthouse of Alexandria.

The Seventh Wonder of the Ancient World

What we're seeing corresponds exactly to the description of Posidippus, a Greek poet who lived in Alexandria in the third century BCE.

> Therefore this tower, in a straight and upright line, appears to cleave the sky from countless furlongs away, during the day, but throughout the night quickly a sailor on the waves will see a great fire blazing from its summit. (Translated by Colin Austin)

On sighting the lighthouse the sailors recite holy words of thanksgiving. The lighthouse is consecrated to the Dioscuri, the twin gods of light, Castor and Pollux. Sighting it is thus a sign of the benevolence of the gods, who are sending us a good omen.

Actually, in more rational terms, it is the result of an ingenious technology of the Alexandrian age, which then was lost in the Middle Ages. The lighthouse is not simply a container of oil set on fire on the top of a tower. In all likelihood, the light is reflected off shiny-smooth concave bronze shields that function as parabolic mirrors, concentrating the beam of light toward the horizon. This makes the light visible at a distance of thirty miles, as reported by the historian Flavius Josephus.

Furthermore, we know from ancient descriptions that the top of the lighthouse is cylindrical, and this would leave us to suppose that the shields rotate around the light source, exactly as they do in a flashing light on the top of a police car or an ambulance. The result is a light beam that "spins" and shines on the entire horizon for almost thirty miles. (Thirty miles is the distance beyond which the curvature of the earth prevents the lighthouse, almost four hundred feet tall, from being seen.)

The next day, at long last, we enter the harbor.

The lighthouse dominates the entrance. It is gleaming white and awe-inspiring. Today, we know what it looked like thanks to a coin minted in Alexandria under various emperors (among them Trajan), as well as to mosaics, oil lamps, and even glass objects discovered in Bagram, Afghanistan.

The tower is divided into three parts. The lowest one is a massive square block almost two hundred feet high, with gilded statues of Tritons blowing into huge seashells at its four corners. The next level is a somewhat narrower octagonal tower. And finally there is the cylindrical tower with a domed roof topped by a gold statue: Helios, the sun god (in the Greek era it was Zeus Soter, that is, Jupiter Savior, or Poseidon).

Because the shore is flat, the tower also serves as a precious reference point for navigators to avoid the sandbars that are waiting in ambush in the vicinity.

Approaching the tower, we notice a vertical line of windows along the walls; a small community made up of maintenance workers, administrative staff, and guards lives inside the tower. At about forty stories high, it is the tallest manmade structure of antiquity, surpassed only by the pyramids of Cheops and Kefren.

The Alexandria lighthouse remained in use longer than any other wonder of the ancient world: built in 208 BCE, it was used for more than 1,300 years. During the Middle Ages, the top level was transformed into a mosque. After that, two consecutive earthquakes, in 1303 and 1323, put an end to its role as a reference point for navigators. Finally, the tower was demolished by Qaitbay, the sultan of Egypt, to build a fortress.

One last detail: the tower was built on an island called Pharos, in front of the port of Alexandria, from which it took its name. This name was then used throughout the Mediterranean to indicate towers with the same function, right up to our own time. As a result, when Italians use their word *faro* ("lighthouse") they are paying homage, without even realizing it, to this wonder of the ancient world.

On the Streets of Alexandria

Entering the port isn't easy. There is just one narrow passage next to the lighthouse, diverted by submerged rocks. Immense walls have been erected around the lighthouse island, and the sea dashing against these and breaking around the piers opposite them renders the passage rough and perilous. Indeed, our ship is battered by the waves, but the men on board are used to it, deftly maneuvering to enter the harbor. Once inside, the waters are exceptionally calm.

There are a lot of ships anchored in the roadstead. We pass between two of them and notice some men overboard, swimming under water and surfacing at regular intervals. Each of them has a rope tied around his waist; the end of the rope is held by other men assisting them from on board the ships. These men go by a curious name: *urinatores* (from the verb *urinare*, meaning "to dive under water").

They are the ancestors of our scuba divers, men with a remarkable capacity to hold their breath, who perform various extremely risky tasks, such as military operations against enemy ships or the recovery of sunken cargo, as seems to be the case here. A ship has sunk in shallow water and the *urinatores*, without any kind of mask or fins, are recovering its cargo of amphoras.

As we are passing through we see one of the divers emerge from the water next to our ship. He is a man with a strong build and a decisive look on his face. He watches us pass and greets us with a luminous smile. Then he takes a few deep breaths and dives again.

Getting past the customs authorities is always a problem, in part because it inevitably involves distributing a few gifts. But in the end our young Egyptian merchant frees himself from the customs red tape and gets all his goods through, mostly amphoras of olive oil from Leptis Magna. After depositing them all in his warehouses he is finally free to go wherever he wants, and he makes his way into the crowded streets of Alexandria.

In just a few minutes we find ourselves once again amid the crowd in a big city. But this is not just any city. Alexandria is the second most important city of the Roman Empire. Founded by Alexander the Great, it has become a true megalopolis of antiquity. And the atmosphere, the chaos on its streets, is identical to Rome's.

But there is something that makes these streets different: the people. Here, you really do see all kinds of people. Not only inhabitants from all over the Mediterranean, but also foreigners, so to speak, from farther afield: Ethiopian, Arab, Indian, and Persian sailors and merchants. Here there are entire neighborhoods inhabited by foreigners.

In a way Alexandria is a door to the empire because of its maritime traffic with India and Africa, and we do get the impression that we're at a crossroads. We encounter faces, clothing, languages of every imaginable kind. Here, for example, is an Indian merchant with very elegant features. Two Nubians go by, silent, tall, and statuesque, wearing white necklaces that stand out against their dark skin. They look like two sharks weaving their way through the crowd. The next passerby is really funny. He's a Middle Eastern merchant, a short, fat man; his fingers are covered in rings and he is wearing an exotic tunic. He gesticulates animatedly with a street vendor. With every move his short arms disappear among the folds of his long, flowing tunic, making the scene truly comic.

The strong odor of spices blasts into our faces. We stop. Off to our right on display in front of a shop we see a series of small colorful mounds. The shopkeeper is next to them, sitting on his heels, waving a straw mat as though it were a fan to keep the flies away from the merchandise.

All around us are numerous shops, selling anything and everything. What strikes us most are the colors: the fabrics especially are incredibly colorful. We reach out a hand to feel them. Some are rough, but one in particular is very soft. It's silk. These streets are the best place in the whole Mediterranean to buy silk from China; there is a wide range to choose from and the quality is excellent.

We stop at a corner, under a portico, and observe a curious scene. A man is standing up, dictating a letter to a scribe, who is sitting on the ground. The man on his feet is named Hilarion; he's a modest manual laborer who has immigrated from the nearby city of Oxyrhynchus, much smaller than Alexandria and afflicted by chronic poverty and widespread illiteracy, a throwback to the past. We walk over closer to them and try to sneak a peek at the letter. It's a missive to his sister whose name is Alis, and who evidently is expecting a child. He writes to her that if the baby is a boy she should keep him, but if it is a girl she'll have to "expose her," that is, abandon her in such a way that someone will take her. This is not an uncommon attitude in rural Egypt, and it confirms for us, once again, how varied the Roman Empire is in its traditions and peoples. This letter will be discovered by archaeologists (but, alas, we'll never know if the baby was a boy or a girl).

Shortly thereafter our attention turns to the foul-mouthed cries of a fishmonger. Her profanity and explicit sexual references pronounced with a thick Spanish accent make her a real character, and not a few people stop to listen to her. Hers is just one of the shows being staged on the streets of the city.

The Prostitute of Alexandria

And what about our sestertius? It is with the young Egyptian merchant who has just turned down a back alley, jumping over a turbid puddle. Everything here is paved in dry, dusty dirt, not marble like in Leptis Magna.

The young man passes a tavern and heads toward an open door. A girl is leaning against the door frame, looking at her fingernails, turning her hand left and right. Her dress is semitransparent, and you can see very clearly her large, dark-nippled breasts. As if that weren't enough, her skirts have long slits to provide a better view of her body. She is displaying her goods, just like the spice dealer that we encountered a little while ago.

The girl's name is Nike (Greek for "victory"), and she's a prostitute, one of fifteen in this brothel. The young man arrives and smiles; he asks only if she is free or busy with another customer. He doesn't even ask how much she charges for her services. Evidently, he's been at sea for quite a while. The girl smiles listlessly and goes into a semidark corridor. The place is humble; the chipped and peeling walls are full of stains and graffiti. This brothel is essentially a long, narrow hallway with a dozen or so rooms on the right and left. There's not much light, it smells of mildew, but what really makes the situation embarrassing are the sounds. Every room is closed off by a curtain, which protects against indiscreet eyes but is absolutely useless against noise.

None of this bothers the young man at all. He puts a hand on the girl's hip and pushes her gently into a room. The pimp, the proprietor of the bordello, nods his approval from the end of the corridor. All you can see is his face emerging from the darkness, illuminated by a glancing ray of light. The simple straw mat atop the masonry bed will be the place where they will consummate the sex act. The man's desire is evident. The girl pulls the curtain closed and undresses. He's already her eighth customer today.

How Girls Become Prostitutes

The prostitutes in bordellos are exploited to the hilt by their pimps. They are usually very young girls, with long curly hair and Middle Eastern features, the most requested by the customers because they're thought to be very sexy.

How does a girl wind up here? The vast majority of prostitutes are slaves or former slaves. Sometimes they are picked up off the streets at a tender age, in the places where parents leave unwanted children (the "exposed"). Or else they are kidnapped, exactly as happens today to many girls from the East. Then they are sold at the slave markets: the largest and best supplied are in Greece, like the one on the island of Delos. The price varies markedly, depending on each case. In his *Epigrams* (VI, 66) Martial writes of a girl from the Suburra district in Rome sold for 600 sesterces (about $1,500), but sometimes the prices are much higher than that. The ancient texts recount that Emperor Heliogabalus bought a gorgeous slave for the astronomical figure of 100,000 sesterces ($250,000). But he was an emperor and could afford it.

If a girl is purchased by a pimp she ends up in a brothel. She usually begins her career around age fourteen, but sometimes even younger. In certain cases, however, if the girl is very beautiful, she can avoid the bordello and become a high-class "escort," working for wealthy clients.

Another sad cause of prostitution is poverty. Often in the poorest levels of society, it is the girl's parents who push her to prostitute herself. Some women choose the work themselves. In most cases these are widows or single women with no families. In reality, the few occupations open to women (handicrafts, jewelry making, weaving, and shopkeeping) don't pay enough to live on, especially for women with children. So for women who lose their husbands or their parents, prostitution is often the only way they can earn a living. But there is a risk: it is not uncommon for these unfortunate women who choose to become prostitutes to end up in the hands of usurers or unscrupulous pimps, who reduce them to a condition of servitude.

Despite these dangers, for many women prostitution still appears as an opportunity, from an economic point of view, compared to a normal job. A brief look at the figures explains why that's true. The fee for sex is 2 or 3 asses. If you consider an average of five customers per day (slave prostitutes have many more) a low-level prostitute in a city like Rome can earn as much as 15 asses per day. If you deduct a third to pay the pimp, the figure drops to 10, which is still more than the 8 asses per day that a weaver earns.

Here, obviously, we are talking about the lowest levels of prostitution. It's possible to earn much higher amounts, though it's difficult to say how much in today's currency. We have been using the following exchange rate for the age of Trajan: 1 sestertius equals $2.50. So sex in the Roman era costs about $1.25 (an as is a quarter of a sestertius). That's very little compared to modern times, but it's also very little for the Romans. That's what they pay for a glass of not very good wine.

And maybe this is another distinctive aspect of Roman society. The basic needs and amusements of the inhabitants of the empire don't cost much: bread (which in Rome is even distributed for free), wine (which can, or actually must, be watered down and for this reason is inexpensive), quadriga races, the baths (a quarter of a sestertius), and even sex are all very economical.

The young Egyptian rearranges his tunic. He smiles at the girl and hands her our sestertius. The woman smiles coldly. An instant later, the young man has already pulled back the curtain and vanished into the street. The girl gets up and goes to wash herself at the end of the corridor. She looks at the sestertius that she has received from the young merchant. She runs her fingertips over its reliefs and inscriptions. She wonders who knows where it comes from and who has held it in their hands. She has no idea of the extraordinary story behind this coin.

Then she goes back to the entrance to the brothel. She doesn't even have time to put her transparent tunic back on before a new customer arrives. A fat man. She looks at the pimp, who nods: the other girls are busy, and so the new customer wants her. The girl smiles again and opens the curtain.

Early the next morning, a man walks into the bordello. He is tall, with salt-and-pepper hair, and compared to the other customers he's very distinguished and polite. He respects the girl and talks to her, even when they're having sex. He contains himself longer than the others, and for the first time the girl sees her customer as a person, not just a faceless consumer like all the others. He's not from Alexandria; he's Greek. The man pays for the service with a denarius, and as his change he receives, among some other coins, our sestertius. He gives the girl a peck on the cheek, smiles at her, and disappears into the alleyway. The girl follows him with her eyes as he goes on his way. She doesn't know, why but she can feel that she's going to remember him for a long time.

Now the Greek is once again on the streets of the city. He's not a sailor or a merchant or a soldier. His ways are more refined. He's a tourist. Tourism did exist in the Roman era, but it was not very common. Usually tourists are intellectuals, sometimes doctors or functionaries traveling for work, but in any case they are people interested in culture, from the more elevated class of society. And, obviously, they have some money to spend. To find these tourists, you have to come to this part of the empire.

Tourism in antiquity is concentrated in the eastern Mediterranean rather than the west. The reason is that the "cities of art" are located in the Hellenic and Egyptian world. Everything west of the Italian peninsula is of little interest. These are the new cities, without history or significant monuments. The east, on the other hand, has everything, from mythology to history.

If we were to make a ranking of Roman tourists' favorite places Greece would be at the top, followed by Asia Minor (today's Turkey) and Egypt. In this era they have the flavor of exotic and faraway places. The most popular itineraries generally lead across Greece to the islands of Delos, Samothrace, and Rhodes, and a few others in the eastern Mediterranean. In Asia Minor, tourists go to Ephesus, or to Cnidus to admire the beautiful Aphrodite sculpted by Praxiteles. But above all they go to Troy (exactly like tourists continue to do today), to see the places where Rome has its most ancient origins, thanks to Aeneas, who abandoned the city in flames to make his way, with a few survivors, to the coasts of Latium, where he gave birth to a lineage that would one day number among its members Julius Caesar. In the Roman era, because of its historical and mythological role, Troy enjoys enormous benefits, not the least of which is a tax exemption bestowed on it for its "patrimony" of the origins of Rome. It is full of visitors and aggressive tour guides.

Nevertheless, the most popular place for all tourists remains the city of Rome. People come to see it from all over the empire. And the city is certainly not lacking in places to visit, as we have seen.

Roman tourists themselves come in for some sharp criticism from Pliny the Younger. He accuses them of making long voyages to the east to discover the great faraway masterpieces while ignoring the ones they have in their own backyard. "We take long journeys on land and sea to see what we do not deign even to look at when it's right here under our nose. . . . We have a predilection for everything that's far away while remaining indifferent to everything that's nearby." This contemporary attitude already existed two thousand years ago.

The Romans completely ignored some areas that are very popular with tourists today, such as Africa and India. In the Roman era they were too far away and the journeys were too dangerous, so they remained destinations more for merchants than for tourists.

The Greek tourist came to the bordello just as he had gone to see the many other attractions of Alexandria. It is part of the package of activities for every visitor. The other sights are the tomb of Alexander the Great, the temple of Serapide, the legendary library . . . and then the nightlife neighborhoods, "downtown Alexandria," and the sex districts (which our Greek tourist has just experienced).

What makes Alexandria extraordinary is the mingling of "dirty money" and culture. Small groups of musicians who play on the streets always attract a crowd. This city full of merchants, prostitutes, and sailors is also a city of music lovers. Historians and the ancient sources tell us that at zither concerts even the most humble and uncultured spectators can recognize and react to the smallest mistakes by the musicians. In this regard, Alexandria is like Parma for opera lyrica, with great experts and passionate critics at every level of society, the most feared of whom have seats in the gallery.

Going Up the Nile

The Greek tourist is part of a group of philosophers that, a few days later, gathers on a large boat to travel up the Nile and visit its extraordinary sights. Already in the Roman era the monuments of ancient Egypt are considered part of antiquity. Pharaoh Ramses II lived 1,300 years before Trajan.

Professor Lionel Casson has revealed many of the details of such a touristic itinerary, so similar to today's that it leaves us dumbfounded. It's actually a very comfortable trip. To be sure, there are no propellers or engines that would make it possible to go upriver against the current, as the big cruise ships do today. But the Roman-era ships exploit another engine: the wind. To go up the Nile they raise their sails and take advantage of the winds that usually blow south, against the current; to go down the Nile, on the other hand, all you have to do is drift.

A dimension that we miss today on these upriver voyages is the quiet, the swishing of the water against the hull, the sound of the sails fluttering in the wind, or the oar banging into the wooden side of the boat or slapping against the surface of the water.

It is with this background noise that the group of tourists sail up the Nile and pass by the amphibious zoo of the cane groves, where rhinos brought from India sit in the water waiting to be captured and sent to Rome, to the Colosseum.

An obligatory stop is Memphis, the departure point for the visit to the pyramids. The Greek philosopher manages to see something that we will never see: the pyramids intact, with the gleam of their smooth facing (visible today only at the top of the pyramid of Kefren).

The little group of philosophers looks on, amused, at the prowess of the boys of the village of Busiri, who in exchange for a small donation climb up the smooth walls of the pyramids at breakneck speed.

But an even more impressive sight is the sacred bull of Apis, the living incarnation of the god Ptah (Osiris), which can be seen in Memphis, in the holy buildings adjacent the temples. Traveling farther upriver to the religious center in the capital city of Fayum, you can admire and make an offering to another sacred animal: the god Sebek, reincarnated in a crocodile.

Fayum is one of the granaries of Egypt and thus of the empire. As we can see from our boat, there are lots of plantations and cultivated fields extending inland. Three women and two boys from the local area come onboard. They'll be joining us for the next part of our journey. They are on their way to a party and are dressed very elegantly.

The new arrivals give us an idea of what the Egyptians were like at the time of the Roman Empire. They don't look at all like the Egyptians we know today, the product of subsequent migrations and miscegenation, with strong Middle Eastern features and often with dark complexions. The Egyptians from Roman times could be mistaken for Greeks today, with their curly hair, light skin, and hazel or green eyes.

The women's hairdos are simple but stylish. Oddly, however, their eyebrows are left long and thick, and in some cases they meet above the nose. The first woman, petite and slender, has her hair arranged in thick, tiny curls. She has a lovely pair of gold balance-shaped earrings with three pearl pendants, and around her neck an elegant neckband made of strips of tiny white pearls. The second has her hair gathered in a bun on the nape of her neck, crowned with a gold chain with a decorated disk in the center. Her garments are purple, wrapped around a body that is slender and sinuous. But the third woman, who looks somewhat older, is a bit more fleshy and more shapely—a real matron. She has a chubby face and a long nose. Her hair, gathered in a bun, frames her face in an elegant mass of curls. Her earrings are striking, made of two big amethyst teardrop pendants that jiggle with every move of her head. Even more impressive is her necklace: a gold neck band adorned with pendant bunches of tiny spheres, also in gold.

The women talk with the two boys, undoubtedly brothers judging by how much they look alike. We discover the matron's name, Aline, but everyone calls her Tanos. She is a genteel lady with a refined way about her. We know that she's the mother of two girls. The five newcomers laugh and joke with each other. Then, upon reaching their destination, after a few miles or so, they bid us a polite farewell and disembark, just barely keeping their balance on the gangway.

Watching them get off the boat, with their long tunics and their shawls, a single image comes to mind: India. If you want to have an idea of how people looked in the Roman era, with their long, flowing robes, think of today's Indian women. Their movements, the drapery of their garments, their perfumes (and even their social castes) render the idea with good approximation.

What we have seen on the boat today can also be seen in several museums. Indeed, these same women live on in modern times, thanks to the extraordinary portraits that they had made, when they were alive, to hang in their homes and which were later applied, when they died, to their mummies. The desert conserved them perfectly, and now they are displayed in various museums around the world (Tanos, the matron, is in Berlin). There are lots of them and today they are referred to collectively as the Fayum portraits. Some of them are so realistic that they look like photographs.

Easier than traveling to a museum, you can admire the portraits at home on the Internet. You'll recognize familiar faces that will give you the feeling that you've already seen them somewhere before: a colleague from the office, a shopkeeper in your neighborhood, a former classmate . . .

But the most impressive aspect of these portraits is their penetrating gazes. They feel somehow still alive, and they represent the people that we would have met here in Egypt, during the time of the Roman Empire.

The Tombs of the Pharaohs

Finally we arrive in Thebes (present-day Luxor). From here the group sets out on a journey to a site that still attracts millions of tourists every year: the tombs of the pharaohs. It may seem surprising, but the tombs were already an attraction in the Roman era. We know that not only from ancient texts, but from the graffiti left on the walls by the Roman tourists.

It can be said that in the ancient world tourism, in both the eastern Mediterranean and Egypt, reached its peak during the Roman Empire, thanks to the *pax*, the peace, that the empire established and maintained. There are no more enemies, there are no more pirates, and so from the first century on it was possible to travel in peace (apart from storms and tempests). This extraordinary period will last until the onset of Arab expansion in the seventh century.

Having crossed the Nile early in the morning, the group of philosophers makes its first stop in the place where two enormous statues stand overlooking the road to the Valley of the Kings and Queens.

The statues are as tall as six-story buildings and they represent one of the most powerful pharaohs, Amenophis III, who ruled around 1400 BCE. But the Romans (and the Greeks before them) are convinced that the statues represent the mythological figure Memnon, son of Aurora and king of the Ethiopians, who arrived in Troy with an army of his own to save the Trojans but was killed by Achilles. The Romans are misled because the statues are faceless. After being partially destroyed in an earthquake, all that's visible is a human figure without a face sitting on a throne. But what convinces the Romans that the statues are the son of Aurora is the sound that one of them makes at dawn, as if he were speaking to his mother.

The group of Greek philosophers stops in front of the two statues. They left in the middle of the night to come here and now, together with some other tourists, they are waiting for the propitious moment. The sky has gone from black to blue and the horizon at their backs is getting brighter and brighter. Finally the sun rises, embracing the mounds covering the tombs of the pharaohs and their queens. Some of the group chat in hushed tones. Then they all fall silent. The moment is near. Like faithful followers in adoration of two strange partially demolished divinities, the group is arranged in a semicircle. Finally, one of the statues emits the sound. It's a sharp tone that sounds almost like the resonance of a string instrument. "A low-intensity hum," the geographer Strabo tells us, or a sound "very much like the resonance of the string of a lyre or a zither," writes the Greek historian Pausanias, who lived in the second century CE. Everyone believes it's the statue speaking. Many, including our philosophers, are skeptical. Strabo was too; he didn't know how to explain the origin of the sound, but he remained very rational and scientific, saying: "whatever logical explanation is easier is more believable than thinking that the sound is emitted by those stones." He also wondered if the sound might be made by some hidden person.

But actually, in all likelihood the sound is drawn from the stone by the change in temperature from the cold of the night to the torrid heat of day. In any case, we will never know the origin of the sound; a restoration of the statues carried out under Septimius Severus silenced the statue forever.

At this point, a lot of the tourists turn back; going on to the tombs means heading into the searing hot ravines of the Valley of the Kings and Queens. But some of them do it, including our little group of Greek philosophers. They visit the tomb of Ramses VI, which they believed to be the tomb of Memnon, and then the tomb of Ramses IV (which will later become a place of Christian worship) and a few others. At the most, they visit three or four, no more.

How do we know all this? Lionel Casson has revealed to us how scholars discovered the habits, and even the names, of many Roman tourists. Several of them, including one murderer, left traces of themselves in the form of graffiti. The tomb of Ramses VI has more than a thousand graffiti. In all, archaeologists have found 1,759 graffiti etched with a chisel of some kind, 300 written with black ink, and 40 with red ink. By reading them and putting them together a lot of details have emerged.

The graffiti make it clear, for example, that tourists did not travel alone but in groups, which were composed of families, imperial functionaries traveling on official business, soldiers, or even groups of intellectuals like our philosophers. The graffiti were left by army officers, lawyers, judges, poets, professors, orators, doctors (there are almost thirty of them), and philosophers. And they came from all over: Italy, Persia, Asia Minor, Greece. Some came from as far away as Marseilles or the Dead Sea, confirming that the fame of the tombs of the pharaohs had spread throughout the empire and beyond.

Since they signed and dated their graffiti, it is possible to determine that the "tourist season" lasted from November to April, when the temperatures are cooler, just like today. This was also the season in which navigation was interrupted, allowing for long excursions into the Egyptian interior.

And what was written in the graffiti? Mainly expressions of awe at the beauty of the tombs and their paintings.

"Unique, unique, unique," one tourist wrote.

"I reproach myself for not having understood the inscriptions," another wrote, after trying to decipher the hieroglyphics.

"I've made my visit," wrote still another.

Some slightly bored visitors began to write other things such as, for example, anagrams of their names: Onipsromse (Sempronios), Onaysisid (Dionysias).

But the graffito that is most striking for its irony and modern sensibility is this one: "But does your mother know you are here?"

Toward the Red Sea

The voyage up the Nile continues to its southernmost point, Aswan, near the first cataract. Our group of philosophers goes just a bit farther south to admire the Temple of Philae. But they don't go beyond that. The Roman presence continues with some frontier outposts, little forts where the atmosphere must've been quite surreal. They are the southernmost military outposts of the empire, oppressed by the scorching sun, overwhelmed by sandstorms, isolated at the extreme edge of civilization. Life in the forts of Egypt is documented in some letters found intact, buried under the sand, just as letters were found near the Vindolanda frontier in the north. The content of the letters can be summed up like this: a third contain military news, a third are requests related to beer, another third are about women. The life of the legionnaires on the frontier is the same, whether it's the icy cold north or the torrid south. . . .

But that's not the only similarity. Recall the homework assignment of the son of the commander of the fort in Vindolanda, rediscovered among the letters that were miraculously conserved. He was supposed to write a phrase by Virgil taken from the *Aeneid* (IX, 473), which his teacher dictated to him.

What's incredible is that the same thing was happening, thousands of miles away, in more or less the same period. From the sands of Fayum, in Hawara, a papyrus emerged with a phrase, also from Virgil's *Aeneid*, written seven times by a pupil. Evidently it was a classic for the school teachers of the time. This time, however, the phrase is different (II, 601): *Non tibi Tyndaridis facies invisa Lacaenae* ("You must not blame the hated beauty of the Spartan Tyndarid"). Whether it was in the frozen north of Scotland or the torrid desert of the Sahara, Virgil had to be learned without errors.

Our group of philosophers is on the way back from their long journey, and they stop again in Thebes for a few days. Then, letting the boat be pulled along by the current, they slowly make their way back to Alexandria. One of the stops along the way is in the small city of Coptos, not far from Thebes, where the path of the Nile makes a wide bend. They stop there for lunch.

The philosophers sit down at the tables of a small inn, under an arbor. The view of the Nile is magnificent, with the sails drifting slowly by. At the table next to theirs, two soldiers are playing dice. The dice are decidedly unusual: they are in the form of a woman stretched out on the ground, resting on her elbows and holding her knees against her chest, with her legs open. The numbers are etched on the various parts of her body. It's a pornographic version of dice that we haven't seen before. (They are on display today at the British Museum, in silver and bronze.)

Our philosopher looks at them and smiles. Then he gets up and goes to a little store nearby to buy a canteen. It's identical to a modern canteen only it's made of clay and is protected by a sleeve made of vegetable fibers. He pays for it with our sestertius. He is given his change by an old man with a nice white beard who smiles at him and wishes him a safe trip. A little later the group of philosophers head back to their boat, discussing concepts and issues that seem to have no solution.

Two days go by, and at the same table where the philosophers once sat, a robust man with a massive head takes a seat. At first glance he looks like a boxer. His short hair is combed to the front, just like Trajan. And when the slender waitress brings him his bill, he smiles, showing his chipped front tooth. The man gets up to go to the store to buy a canteen. And that's when he comes into possession of our sestertius.

The canteen is indispensable to him: he has to travel across the desert. It won't be his only reserve supply of water, obviously, but it will be the one closest at hand. A few minutes later he mounts his camel, with a straw hat on his head and his canteen around his neck. He's part of a convoy of camels, which, in single file, sets out on a long journey on a caravan route. The sun is high in the sky and our sestertius is getting hot.

The caravan track that we're traveling on is one of the roads that take people outside of the Roman Empire: specifically, to India. This man is a merchant from Pozzuoli, and he's transporting some highly sought after merchandise to the Orient: red coral. But it's not going to be easy. It will take them many days to reach the ports of departure on the Red Sea: seven days to Myos Hormos (literally, "the port of mice"), and as many as eleven to get to the one where we are going, Berenice Troglodytica.

In order to consume less water the caravan will journey at night and, as on the sea, it will be guided by the stars. The route will be broken up by stops at wells and checkpoints. All along the route we will encounter watchtowers and forts. It's not possible to travel freely on the caravan track: you must have a pass, pay taxes, and, since for all practical purposes the track itself is a frontier, there is a duty, quite expensive, to be paid on the goods. The frontier has a double purpose: it's a way by which the state collects revenues, but it is also a protectionist measure to curtail the hemorrhage of gold in the form of coins (*aurei*), that leave the empire and never come back.

One morning, after the long journey through the night, the caravan comes to a sacred site called Paneion, where there is a natural spring dedicated to the god Pan. It's a place where all caravans stop and the camels lower themselves down to their knees. On the high rock walls all around it, a lot of merchants have left inscriptions, which we try to read. One bears the name of Lysas, perhaps a *libertus* who, on behalf of his master (Annius Plocamus), managed to go all the way to Ceylon in the first century CE.

There is another one that impresses us: the name Gaius Peticius, written in Greek. Today, Peticius is a noble family name common in the Abruzzo region of Italy. This means that a Roman from Abruzzo must have passed through here. Confirmation of this is found in the archaeological museum in Chieti, which houses the gravestone of a member of the Peticius family, showing an engraving of a camel transporting amphoras. The man exported wine to India.

The port of Berenice is located in an enchanting place. The coast is a desert landscape, the beaches are pure white, and the sea is a spellbinding turquoise. In the modern era these coasts are populated by tourist villages, beach umbrellas, and kite surfers (the famous resort of Hurghada is not far from Myos Hormos). In the Roman era these places are considered as far away as the moon: those who come here feel the sensation of having an immense expanse of desert at their back and an even more immense expanse of water in front of them. For the Romans these are places of death, not amusement.

Looking out at the crystalline water, the fish, and the coral, one can feel the vastness of the Roman Empire. It touches Scandinavia on one end and has coral reefs on the other.

The caravan has unloaded its cargo. Berenice Troglodytica is a flourishing city, the true gateway to the Orient. Just think, every year 120 Roman ships depart from here for India! Proof that contacts and trade between the empire and India are not sporadic, as is commonly thought, but regular and continuous. Quite simply, India and Rome are trading partners.

What does each have to offer the other? A jaunt through the streets of Berenice is enough to give us an idea. To India, the Romans export wine, clothing, red coral, blown glass, and hand-wrought metal objects. From India, the Romans import silk, precious stones such as lapis lazuli, pearls, ivory, essences, and spices, especially pepper. Basically, luxury goods. But peeking into the warehouses we also see other kinds of goods in transit through this port: prized wood, coconuts, incense, and even flowers.

The sun has just set behind us. The sky is slowly turning an ever-darker blue, and the first stars are beginning to appear. We look out at the sea in front of us. It's flat and calm, as though it were slowly dozing off to sleep. Will it be like this tomorrow, too? The ship is ready, the cargo is loaded, and if the omens are good, tomorrow we set sail.

INDIA

~ *Beyond the Borders of the Empire* ~

Passage to India

The ship sets off at the first light of dawn. Conditions on the sea are good and the voyage is proceeding smoothly. The name of the merchant from Pozzuoli is Junius Faustus Florus. He's one of nine Roman merchants on board, each with goods below deck that are ready to make the transoceanic leap. But the crew is not Roman. In this part of the world, the Romans rely on Egyptian sailors, who in turn rely on navigators from Eritrea. Navigating these routes requires a thorough knowledge of the Indian Ocean. The ship will exit the Red Sea on the south end, make its way along the coast of the Arabian Peninsula, and then, like a platform diver, it will take flight, pointing its bow straight into the ocean, where the only thing on the horizon is water. There is a trick to making it all the way to India, and it's all in how you play the winds.

For a long time the Arabs and the Indians guarded their secret jealously, but in the Roman era it is widely known: it's the monsoons. From May to September they blow constantly from the southwest, pushing ships from behind, straight on to India. Then, from November to March, they blow in the opposite direction, from the northeast, bringing the ships back with them. It's like watching a piece of driftwood being carried back and forth by a wave on the shoreline. This climatic inhaling and exhaling takes a long time. Junius Faustus Florus knows that it's going to take him a year to make the round-trip voyage from Pozzuoli.

We'll never know how many ships sank and how many Romans died on these crossings. What we do know is that the ships are big, well-suited to face up to the Indian Ocean: 130 feet long with more than 300 tons of cargo onboard.

After a long and mercifully uneventful journey, our arrival in India happens in the early morning. There's a light haze caused by the tropical humidity, a constant presence in this part of the world. Everyone on board has the tired look and baggy red eyes that come with too little sleep.

We notice the white sand shore, crowned by a thick forest of palm trees. We also see some dark canoes, each dug out of a single piece of wood. They belong to fishermen who set out in the predawn hours, just as they do everywhere else in the world. One of them passes close to our ship, and we get a good look at the dark skin and gleaming white teeth of the people on board, who in turn point to Junius Faustus Florus and his companions. The sight of fair skin around these parts means only one thing: a Roman has arrived.

The big ship remains offshore to avoid running aground on the sandy bottom. Some boats come out from the harbor to tranship the cargo and passengers, and very soon the water around the ship is animated by a chaotic hustle and bustle, replete with shouting and reprimands.

When Junius Faustus Florus goes ashore he is overjoyed to finally plant his feet on dry land. But his head keeps on spinning from land sickness. It's not long before another western gentleman approaches him, making his way through the crowd of Indians surrounding the newly arrived Romans. He greets our man with a big smile, and the two of them hug each other in a fraternal embrace. He's from Pozzuoli too.

In all the Indian ports where their ships dock, the Romans form little communities and set up emporiums along the coast. We are now close to the southern tip of India, on the west coast. The name of this port is Muziris and it appears on the Tabula Peutingeriana, the only map of the Roman Empire that has survived down to the modern era. Actually, what we have is a medieval copy of a lost Roman original. But it is a faithful "photocopy" (the work of monastic amanuenses) that reveals a lot about how Romans used it. It is in the form of one very long sheet stretching out to almost twenty-three feet that was rolled up and kept in a leather tube.

So it was a "travel map" designed to be carried on horseback and unrolled with two hands while sitting in the saddle (one hand scrolling up and the other scrolling down as a projector does with a roll of movie film) until you find the section you are interested in. It uses the same principle as modern electronic navigators for cars: it indicates main roads, rivers, cities, postal stations, and roadside inns while totally neglecting the physical geography. Forests and mountains, for example, are merely sketched or stylized. Conceptually, it looks like a map you might sketch on a scrap of paper to help someone who needs directions. The scale is often out of proportion, but the route is perfectly clear and rich in practical detail (landmarks, number of miles, curves, etc.).

Examining the map, it is surprising to see that the Romans know Sri Lanka and also part of the Indian coast, around its southern point. In the 1940s, English excavations conducted in Arikamedu on India's eastern coast uncovered fragments of ceramics from Arezzo (so-called sealed-earth ceramics) with inscriptions in Latin, and other Roman finds such as oil lamps and glass objects. This would suggest that one or more of the Roman emporiums were located on the east coast of India.

The Tabula Peutingeriana helps us to understand the Romans' idea of India. They knew the Ganges River and indicated the distances on the roads not only in Roman miles (4,854 feet) but also in Indian miles (9,842 feet), which means not only that they had traveled the roads but that they indicated for potential Roman travelers the various stopping points using local measurements so they would be able to get around better.

The most amazing thing to see on the map, near Muziris, is the drawing of a Roman temple with the inscription Templum Augusti, a religious building dedicated to the memory of Augustus. In the middle of India!

On the map are plenty of inscriptions such as *In his locis scorpiones nascuntur* ("In these places scorpions are born") and *In his locis elephanti nascuntur* ("In these places elephants are born"), and so on. Then there are two words, clearly linked to silk, but slightly enigmatic: *seta maior*. In all likelihood they indicate China or a part of it.

The story of the silk trade has always been fascinating. Silk reaches Europe by two routes, land and sea. Along the land route (the legendary Silk Road) the silk is controlled and "filtered" by Rome's most dangerous enemies, the Parthians, inhabitants of present-day Iran and Iraq. On the sea route, Rome's dominance is greater. This route is much more economical because the ships can hold greater quantities than can be transported on the Silk Road. That's why the Romans keep pushing eastward, attempting to reach the "source" of silk, China. According to Lionel Casson, at the end of the second century CE the Romans start trading with the Moluccas, Sumatra, and Java.

The Chinese would not sail on the high seas until centuries later, so it was the Romans who went knocking on their door first. We know the official date of this first encounter: 166 CE, when a Roman ambassador was welcomed by the Yellow Emperor, Huangdi. In all likelihood, this meeting did not involve an official ambassador sent by Marcus Aurelius but simple merchants who, like salmon, had swum against the current of the silk stream all the way back to its point of origin. One piece of evidence for this theory is that, as recorded in the Chinese archives, the gifts that they brought with them were not jewels or gold but ivory, rhinoceros horns, and tortoise shells. These are not gifts worthy of an imperial ambassador. In Lionel Casson's view, the visitors were very probably merchants trying to beat their competition by buying silk directly from China and cutting out the middlemen.

The Return Voyage Toward the Roman Empire

So big commercial battles were fought beyond the borders of the Roman Empire. And traces of this intense economic exchange emerge every now and again through the rediscovery of Roman coins. The farthest flung Roman coin to be unearthed was found in Vietnam, in the Mekong River delta.

In India, at least two thousand gold coins (aurei) and six thousand silver coins (denarii) have been found, to say nothing of smaller coins. It's striking to note that some of these coins have deep cuts in them, made by the Indians to ensure these were made of real gold and were not just brass farthings.

The port of Muziris, also cited by Pliny the Elder and Ptolemy, and known as a center of trade for other ethnic groups and civilizations, has only recently been identified as the little city of Pattanam, where archaeological digs have unearthed Roman coins, innumerable fragments of Italic and Egyptian ceramics, a twenty-foot canoe, and even an ancient brick landing wharf with mooring fixtures.

And that's where we are now. Several months have passed, the winds have changed, and Junius Faustus Florus has just boarded a canoe, headed toward a large merchant ship anchored offshore that will take him back to the Red Sea; from there he'll be able to return to Pozzuoli. The man who is rowing him out to the ship is an Indian, with whom he has struck up a fine friendship and who will act as his contact for future commercial ventures. As he is about to board ship, Junius Faustus Florus turns, embraces his friend, and gives him our sestertius as a sign of his friendship. The evening before, in fact, the man had been curious about the face of Trajan and had asked Junius Faustus Florus to tell him about his "king." The coin is a nice reminder of the Roman from Pozzuoli, a keepsake.

MESOPOTAMIA

~ An Encounter with Emperor Trajan ~

Encounter with the Emperor

Our sestertius is quickly put away inside a box and almost forgotten. But the Indian merchant soon retrieves it to take with him when he is about to depart on a long voyage into the Persian Gulf, to the mouth of the Euphrates. He has heard tell by the Arab merchants with whom he trades that things in Mesopotamia are changing: the dominion of the Parthians is crumbling, and the situation is chaotic. The Romans have conquered the northern part of Mesopotamia and are advancing triumphantly on all fronts. It looks highly probable that they'll conquer the entire area (and eventually, they will). The Indian merchant knows how much the Romans appreciate (and are willing to pay for) the goods he can furnish; he has talked about it at length with Junius Faustus Florus and other Roman merchants. So he decides to take a trip, to make new contacts and start up some new trade relationships. If the Romans do make it all the way into the south, he wants to be among the first to open up the best trade channels. It's a tremendous opportunity that could make him very rich. He has to give it a shot.

So he boards the ship of some Arab merchants he knows, who are on their way back to the Persian Gulf. Our coin is on the move again. The voyage goes by uneventfully, and once the Arab freighter reaches the gulf it heads toward the southernmost part of Mesopotamia, where the waters of the Tigris and the Euphrates come together to create a large wetland area (the tip of today's Iraq). This is the location of the port city of Charax, the meeting point of two worlds, the control center for all the seagoing commercial traffic between Mesopotamia and India. It is such an important city that it operates as an independent kingdom, a sort of Monte Carlo on the Persian Gulf. This is where our merchant decides he's going to wait for the Romans.

He picked the right spot. In just a few months his wish is granted. The situation in Mesopotamia is rapidly coming apart. Trajan is moving through it relentlessly, the announcement of each new victory following on the heels of the last. The emperor is driving forward with the invasion he began a year ago. This year he has transported some preassembled bridges from the shores of the Mediterranean across the desert and used them to cross the Euphrates: a colossal enterprise. His army has conquered cities with famous names like Nineveh and Babylon.

Then his fleet of fifty ships sailed down the Euphrates. It is said that his name and titles were written in gold letters across the sails of the ships in his largest squadron. The ships were then pulled across land, with dollies and other systems, more than eighteen miles from the Euphrates to the Tigris, where they surprised everybody, conquering the city of Seleucia and the capital Ctesiphon. Caught by surprise, the enemy king fled, abandoning the city, his gold throne, and his daughter to the clutches of Trajan.

The Romans won, thanks to their lethally flawless organization; even today dragging bridges and ships across the desert is no easy enterprise. But they also benefited from internal conflicts within the Parthian kingdom. Now Trajan is the absolute master of Mesopotamia. There is evidence that coins were minted bearing the inscription *Parthia Capta* ("Parthia Captured"). The Parthians, bitter enemies of Rome, have now been swept away. Trajan is at the acme of his career as emperor. The empire has reached its maximum geographic extension, and it's all happening right now, in the months between the spring and fall of 116 CE.

Before long, another clamorous piece of news arrives in Charax: the emperor is on his way. The whole city is waiting with trepidation. Until now, only one other Mediterranean emperor had come this far east: Alexander the Great, more than four hundred years ago. He was the one who founded the city, giving it its original name of Alexandria—as always after himself. Now, there's Trajan.

The Roman emperor has arrived. Charax's king, Attambelus, has already made an act of submission, and his realm has now officially become a territory of Rome. The insignia of the Roman Empire are now overlooking the Persian Gulf.

Trajan is traveling the streets of the city toward the harbor. The entire population of the lower part of the city is standing at their windows or lined up on the side of the road to welcome the victor. The first to arrive are the cavalry, soldiers, and legionnaires who take control of the harbor. They face no opposition, but we're still technically in a state of war, and you can't be too careful.

And then, here he is, on horseback, riding in the middle of his personal guard. He's wearing a magnificent suit of armor, gleaming, with decorations that shimmer in rhythm with the gait of his horse. His presence is striking, considering how ordinary he looks. In this part of the world, the people have been accustomed for centuries to seeing all-powerful kings who emphasize in every possible way their detachment from the common people. Trajan is different. He does not adopt the pose of the powerful but behaves like an ordinary man, smiling and raising his hand to greet the crowd. Flowers are thrown before him and the people acclaim him, just as they would for any victor.

The first thing people notice about him is his white hair. Trajan's hair went white many years ago, early for his age. It allows everyone, including the enemy, to recognize him on the battlefield. A few months from now, during a cavalry attack that he himself will command against the city of Hatra, the enemy archers will notice his hoary head and try to hit it. Their arrows come so close that some members of his personal guard are killed. This helps us understand the fiber of the man. He is sixty-two years old and still takes to the battlefield, fights with his head uncovered, leads the attack on horseback, marches, eats, and suffers with his men. That's why he is so loved. But it's also why he looks much older than his years. His face is full of wrinkles, his eyes sunk deep in their sockets.

The Indian merchant, standing at the front of a crowd at the harbor, notices it too. He came down here this morning to see some other Indian merchants off on their way back to Muziris. Theirs may be the last ship to sail before the wind turns against them. The chaos provoked by the arrival of the Roman emperor has kept him stuck at the pier, next to the ship, which has now cast off its lines and is slowly pulling away from the dock.

With a certain amount of apprehension the merchant notes that the emperor's procession is heading his way. He stops just a few yards away and observes the ship as it heads out to sea. The emperor is told that this is the last ship of the season for India and that he has just managed to see it leave.

As the soldiers cordon off a passageway, their weapons drawn, Trajan dismounts and approaches the edge of the pier, surrounded by his bodyguards. Trajan looks out at the gulf, observes the ship with its sails billowing, gliding on the water, and exclaims, "I'm too old to go to India like Alexander the Great!" He says it almost to himself, but loud enough that a lot of those gathered around can hear, and so this thought of his will be transcribed and passed down to us.

The Indian merchant realizes that this is a once-in-a-lifetime occasion and that he has to do something. He doesn't speak Latin, but he has a way of demonstrating that he already has contacts with the Roman world. He pulls out our sestertius and holds it up high, showing it to Trajan's entourage.

The emperor turns around to go back to his horse, but he notices the light reflecting off the coin. His curiosity piqued by seeing a sestertius so far from home, he signals one of the guards with a nod of his head, indicating the merchant. A strong grip strips the sestertius from the merchant's hand and takes it to the emperor. Now Trajan holds it up and studies it, turning it over. He smiles. He remembers well the period when it was minted. Then he squeezes it in his fist and looks out at the sea. We can't know what thoughts are passing through his head, but many historians believe that one of the motives that drove Trajan to come all this way, to these shores so far from Rome between present-day Kuwait and Iran, was economic.

By wiping out the Parthians, who operated as middlemen for all the commerce arriving in the Mediterranean from the Orient, he achieved three objectives: he defeated a fierce enemy; eliminated the enormous costs that the Parthians added on to every product that passed through their hands (revenues that they then used to finance their wars against Rome); and acquired direct control over commercial trade with India,

China, and the Far East. It's exactly like what he accomplished when he invaded Dacia, acquiring the gold mines and wiping out a ferocious enemy.

It seems that after this visit to the harbor in Charax, Trajan went back to Babylon to work out the economic details of this newly acquired direct access to the Orient, establishing, among other things, the tariffs to be imposed on the direct route between Rome and India (and China).

Trajan hands the coin to one of his guards and gets back on his horse. The soldier tosses it to the merchant and he too mounts his horse. The procession moves off, leaving the Indian dazed by the encounter. He'll recount it many times in the future to his children and grandchildren.

Our sestertius, having passed through so many hands by now, from the hands of slaves to those of philosophers, from prostitutes to legionnaires, still has not completed its journey.

Indeed, after making some promising contacts, the Indian merchant, who has a very refined sense for business, leaves behind the sestertius, which is perfectly useless to him in India, not least because of its meager value (in the case of a gold coin, things undoubtedly would have been different). One morning, in a tavern in Charax, he trades a small ivory carving of his home town, to which he adds our sestertius, for a lovely dark metal jewel box, outfitted with a Roman lock.

The hand that takes our coin has killed a lot of people in these past few weeks. It belongs to a centurion, a brave man who will be remembered even in modern times for one of his exploits. Held prisoner in the city of Adenystrae when the Roman troops appeared on the horizon ready to attack it, he managed to free himself and, together with his fellow soldiers, kill the commander of the enemy garrison and open the great doors to the city, allowing the legionnaires to enter and conquer it.

The coin will be going with him back to Babylon. He will see Emperor Trajan offer sacrifices in the great royal palaces—more precisely, in the room where more than four centuries ago Alexander the Great died. And he will be present when news arrives of simultaneous insurrections against the Romans in a number of locations in Mesopotamia and of Trajan's efforts to regain control of the situation. It will be a troubled time, with massacres on both sides. And his hands will be stained anew with blood when cities like Nisibis, Edessa, and Seleucia will be razed to the ground: soldiers, women, old men, and children will be run through with swords and shown no mercy. . . .

The Romans have extended themselves without securing the areas behind the front lines and on the perimeter of the lands that they have conquered. The Parthians have been able to reorganize and their counterattacks are murderous. In the end, Trajan, having defeated the main enemy in a big battle, is not able to control such a vast territory. He'll decide to use diplomacy to resolve what he's not able to resolve with arms because he has too few men and resources. He will appoint a king who is a vassal to Rome, Parthemaspates, to rule the territories of Parthia. And he'll go back home to the Roman Empire. Many historians believe that Trajan plans to come back to Mesopotamia the next year to resolve the problem once and for all.

The letter that he will send to the Senate is eloquent: "This territory is so vast and endless, and the distance that separates it from Rome is so incalculable, that we do not have the reach to govern it. So, instead, we will give the people a king who is subject to Rome."

So our sestertius will be making the return trip with the legions of Rome, by way of long marches in the boundless deserts of the Middle East, before finally reaching the shores of the Mediterranean, this time at Antioch.

Antioch

It's the third largest city of the Roman Empire, located on the banks of the Orontes River just a short distance from the Mediterranean. Unfortunately, it is a city of which almost nothing remains today, apart from some beautiful mosaics. Yet in antiquity it was known as Antioch the Great and Antioch the Beautiful. Julius Caesar raised it to the level of a metropolis and all the emperors enriched it with impressive buildings, including a sumptuous imperial residence. The surviving mosaics that decorated the palaces and the baths show scenes of the city: its streets and palaces, a theater, fountains, piazzas full of crowds, children playing, women walking, porters, street vendors, taverns, and so on. There are also some multistory buildings, just as we are seeing now as we follow the centurion, who after arranging his things in his quarters and a long session at the baths, is now out on leave.

Antioch, however, is a wounded city; it still shows the damage done by a powerful earthquake that struck the city while our sestertius was in India. A third of the city was leveled. It was a tragedy of frightening proportions.

When the quake hit, Antioch was more crowded than usual. In fact, Trajan was quartered there with his troops at the time. The city was full of soldiers, along with large numbers of people who had come from all around to ask for an audience, do business, make diplomatic contacts, or simply catch a glimpse of the emperor. In Book LXVIII of his *Roman History*, the Roman historian Dio Cassius describes the earthquake in such detail that it feels like being present at the cataclysm. It is an account by someone who had no scientific knowledge of earthquakes, as some of his examples show, but even so he manages to describe the dynamics of the quake with remarkable precision.

> First there came, on a sudden, a great bellowing roar, and this was followed by a tremendous quaking. The whole earth was upheaved, and buildings leaped into the air; some were carried aloft only to collapse and be broken in pieces, while others were tossed in all directions as if by the surge of the sea. . . . The crash of grinding and breaking timbers together with tiles and stones was most frightful; and an inconceivable amount of dust arose, so that it was impossible for one to see anything or to speak or hear a word. As for the people, many even who were outside the houses were hurt, being snatched up and tossed violently about and then dashed to the earth as if falling from a cliff; some were maimed and others were killed. Even trees in some cases leaped into the air, roots and all. The number of those who were trapped in the houses and perished was past finding out; for multitudes were killed by the very force of the falling debris, and great numbers were suffocated in the ruins. Those who lay with a part of their body buried under the stones or timbers suffered terribly, being able neither to live any longer nor find an immediate death.
>
> Nevertheless, many even of these were save, as was to be expected in such a countless multitude; yet not all such escaped unscathed. Many lost legs or arms, some had their heads broken, and still others vomited blood; Pedo the consul was one of these, and he died at once. . . . And as Heaven continued the earthquake for several days and nights, the people were in danger and helpless, some of them crushed and perishing under the weight of the buildings pressing upon them,

and others dying of hunger, whenever it so chanced that they were left alive either in a clear space…or in a vaulted colonnade. When at last the evil had subsided, someone who ventured to mount the ruins caught sight of a woman still alive. She was not alone, but had also an infant; and she had survived by feeding both herself and her child with her milk. . . .

Trajan made his way out through the window of the room in which he was staying. Some being, of greater than human stature, had come to him and led him forth, so that he escaped with only a few slight injuries; and as the shocks extended over several days, he lived out of doors in the hippodrome. (Harvard University Press, 1925. Translated by Earnest Cary)

The earthquake coincided with a bloody revolt by the Jews in Antioch. This was later known as the Second Jewish-Roman War. (The first revolt, and probably the most famous, had broken out about fifty years earlier, under Nero, and was put down by Vespasian.) Some have argued that the destruction of the city was seen as one of the signs of the coming of the Messiah. The earthquake had incited the lower classes of the Jewish community, especially in the countryside, to unleash a revolt that caught everyone by surprise, including the Jewish elite.

But further study has shown that there were other reasons for the revolt. First was the burden of the *fiscus judaicus*, a tax imposed by Vespasian on all the Jews in the empire after the destruction of the temple. Another cause for the revolt was the tension between Jews and Greeks, especially in Egypt. The Greeks had managed to convince the Roman authorities to impose discriminatory measures against the Jews, who then felt that they were being treated as second-class citizens. This explains the intensity of the violence of the Jewish rebels against the Greeks. The earthquake was thus interpreted by the more fundamentalist sectors of the Jewish community as a favorable sign for an insurrection and sparked the revolt.

Unspeakable massacres were committed against civilians, Greeks, and Christians; entire cities were destroyed and burned from Cyrenaica (where the revolt began) to Cyprus, Mesopotamia, and Egypt. Thanks to its walls, Alexandria was transformed into a sort of fortress, where people, especially Greeks, took refuge after fleeing the countryside. The city held out and was not conquered. To be sure, Trajan's absence due to his involvement in the war in Mesopotamia encouraged the rebels.

But the Roman repression was fierce and relentless. And it is still going on as we arrive here in Antioch, with a manhunt for the ringleaders being conducted in Egypt and in all the other areas where the rebellion had broken out. The merchant from Pozzuoli, Junius Faustus Florus, arrived back in Egypt at exactly the wrong moment, just when the rebellion was in progress. Maybe he was trapped in Alexandria, or perhaps he boarded a ship and managed to escape just before the rebellion broke out. We'll never know. But the revolt turned into a real groundswell that spread through vast areas of the empire. Even the Jewish communities in Mesopotamia rebelled.

The Jewish rebellion is not the only piece of bad news. During our absence from the empire some other grave events have occurred. Taking advantage of Trajan's military defeats in Mesopotamia and the lack of troops on the frontiers, who had been recalled for the war, many of the border populations have attacked the empire. It happened in Mauritania in western Africa and on the lower Danube. There have even been attacks by some tribes in Britain, in the place where we were not long ago. The situation in the empire right now is not very peaceful. But everyday life goes on as always.

Murder

Our centurion is now walking through a still-intact neighborhood of Antioch. The tall buildings here seem to have suffered less damage than in other parts of the city.

All of a sudden he hears a shout. He looks up and sees what he believes to be a white blanket coming down from the building. In a fraction of a second he realizes that that piece of fabric is a tunic wrapped around a woman gesticulating and screaming. He sees her last terrified look before the crash. The impact is violent, the sound a muted thud.

The centurion, despite having seen death up close many times, remains paralyzed for a second, just like everybody else on the street. Then he rushes over to the lifeless body.

The woman died on impact, her face is relaxed, her hair loose. She looks like she's asleep. Only her fingers and toes move, with their last nervous twitches. The blood starts to flow copiously on the pavement around her head.

Everyone tries to figure out where she fell from. The centurion had noticed a face peeking out of the building as she was falling. Now that face has reappeared for a fraction of a second.

A few minutes later, two armed guards make their way through the crowd of people who are staring at the body with morbid curiosity. Nobody thinks to cover her with a sheet. In this society where death is an everyday event, on the streets and in public buildings, like the big amphitheater in Antioch (where crowds watch people being torn to shreds by wild animals), nobody feels the need. It would be like using a sheet to cover a dead cat or a dead bird on the street.

Led by the centurion, the two guards quickly climb the steps of the building that the woman fell from. They knock repeatedly and then, with the soldier's help, they break the door down. The little apartment (*cenaculum*) is in total disorder. There are signs of a violent altercation. A man who must be her husband appears out of nowhere. He's beside himself and tries to convince us that she slipped while she was hanging the laundry out the window. But three long parallel scratch marks on his cheek tell another story.

In the Roman era, wife murder is a common crime, just as it still is, unfortunately, in our society. In the United States, three women are murdered by their intimate partners every day.

Evidence of the situation in Roman times is readily available in the gravestone epitaphs like this one:

Restitutus Piscines and Prima Restituta to their dear daughter Florenza, who was treacherously thrown into the Tiber by her husband Orpheus. Her brother-in-law December placed this stone. She lived sixteen years.

Meanwhile, back down on the street a huge crowd has gathered. They're all talking about a scandalous crime that happened exactly one hundred years ago, under Tiberius. The man involved was a Roman magistrate, a praetor named Plautius Silvanus, accused by his father-in-law Lucius Apronius of having thrown his wife from a window. There was a trial, eagerly awaited and followed by the populace, held in one of the basilicas of the Forum, in which the accused claimed he was innocent because his wife had voluntarily jumped from the window to commit suicide. The incident, as you can imagine, was the talk of Rome. And public interest in the trial grew to the point that Emperor Tiberius himself had to get involved. He went personally to visit the bedroom where the woman had been killed, where the signs of her desperate struggle were still clearly evident. In view of his elevated social status and in order to avoid the death sentence and safeguard his estate from being confiscated to the disadvantage of his family, Plautius Silvanus was advised to commit suicide.

This case of murder is an opportunity to examine the level of crime in Roman cities. And, more generally, how violent the society was. There are some surprises.

Are Roman Cities Violent?

Let's take Rome as an example. It's the largest city in the empire and therefore it has the greatest security issues—though it must be said that Antioch and Alexandria are not far behind in the rankings of most dangerous cities. But we have more information and more firsthand accounts about Rome.

Walking around Rome at night without first having made a will was the act of a madman, according to the ancients. It must be recalled that Rome was the most populous city in the West until the Industrial Revolution, with about 1 million inhabitants or more. All of its problems were quadrupled compared to other cities, violence included.

Professor Jens-Uwe Krause has studied extensively the varied situations in which crimes were committed in the ancient city of Rome.

Disputes and often violence would often erupt over trivial matters like who had the right-of-way on the street. In a society in which much importance was given to differences in social class and status, it was almost normal that clenched fists, clubs, and rocks would fly at the slightest perceived insult or disrespect. Consequently, most fights took place in public places (to the great amusement of passersby), like the street, the market, or even the baths.

One famous case, cited by Pliny the Younger, involves a member of the equestrian order at the baths who was pushed lightly by a slave who wanted to let his master pass. The man launched an attack not on the slave but on his master, knocking him silly for having offended his dignity by allowing him to be touched by a slave.

Another contributor to violence and crime was alcohol, above all when young men were involved. Fistfights in taverns were very frequent and, going home drunk in the middle of the night they assaulted other people on the street.

The reputation of taverns, public houses, and inns after dark was terrible: the proprietors themselves had bad reputations and their places of business, in addition to hosting customers who were always ready to turn an argument into a brawl, also welcomed lowlifes and characters of ill repute such as murderers, sailors, thieves, and fugitive slaves, at least as Juvenal tells it.

Another danger on the streets of Rome was juvenile gangs. While we generally use this term in reference to unruly kids from the lower classes of society, in Roman times this was not always the case. Often it was exactly the opposite: groups of kids from rich families who went around the city causing trouble. They were the ones who, drunk or sober, broke down the doors of bordellos and gang-raped the prostitutes or other women alone on the streets. They were the ones who stole from shops or assaulted passersby (as Nero and his friends famously did when he was young).

Then there were robberies to worry about. The nighttime streets were the ideal place to commit them, especially against isolated groups or drunkards. And sometime the victims died in the process.

So unlike today, daily violence did not take place on the outskirts of the city or in bad neighborhoods but above all in the center city and in public places. Toward the end of the republic, given the lack of security, a lot of people carried weapons on their person. Knives, daggers, and swords were always at the ready.

As time went on the social situation became more secure. Furthermore, with the founding of the empire, Augustus issued a decree that outlawed the possession of arms, except for hunting or traveling (the *Lex Julia de Vi Publica et Privata*). All of this led to a reduction in the number of weapons in circulation. If we observe, for example, the deaths in the city of Herculanum during the eruption of Vesuvius, of some three hundred bodies unearthed, only one has a weapon: a gladius. He was a soldier, and so he was authorized to carry it. The scarce distribution of arms made it so that in the case of an altercation people used their fists, clubs, and anything they might find within arm's reach, like rocks or stones. With a much lower incidence of fatalities.

The Penalty for Murder

And what of murder? If we look at a case from the fourth century, a death during a fight, we are amazed to find that the law is not equal for everybody, but more equal for some than for others.

Indeed, it depends on the murderer's social status. If he belongs to the lowest class (*humiliores*), the sentence is practically death: *ad metalla*, that is in a mine or a quarry (until death), or *ad gladium* (*damnation in ludum gladiatorum*), that is, in the Colosseum in combat with convicts like himself or in the gladiator training school. If, on the other hand, he comes from the upper class, he gets sent into exile and half of his property is confiscated.

Familial violence is widespread. In fact, the brutality of the *paterfamilias* who inflicts corporal punishment on his slaves and his children is not punished by law, except in exceptional cases. And the same is true when the victim is his wife: beatings with fists, clubs, or whips are very common. According to Professor Krause, toward the end of the Roman Empire most women in the African cities were beaten by their husbands. So it happens that murder makes its way into the family as well. For Roman men who kill their companions or spouses, alcohol or an explosion of anger (over the discovery of adultery or some other offense) is often the cause. For the wife, usually, the story is quite different.

The percentage of women who commit murder would seem to be, from the documents, much lower than the percentage of men. And their techniques are more "refined." Contrary to their husbands, there is no explosion of anger, but rather, premeditation. And the preferred murder weapon is very special: poison.

In republican Rome a series of murders by poison involving more than 150 women made it into the limelight. None other than Cato the Elder stigmatized this poison habit with a famous phrase: every adulteress is a poisoner.

A murder case in Syria toward the end of the Roman Empire reveals many interesting aspects about Roman justice as it pertains to murder.

A man is killed at night in the courtyard of his home. His slaves not only failed to defend him; they hid, allowing his murderers to get away. The inaction of the slaves would indicate that the guilty party was known to the household. (In fact, Professor Kraus has highlighted the fact that in most cases, victims and their killers belong to the same social class.) The heirs of the victim took the case to court, and five of the victim's fellow townspeople were arrested. They remained in prison, expecting to die, without sufficient evidence being brought to convict them.

The first enlightening aspect of this case is that in the Roman era a prison term is not a sentence as it is in our time. Here, it's simple: either you're acquitted or you're condemned to exile, to the beasts in the amphitheater (*ad bestias*), to the gladiators, to the mines, etc. Nobody is sentenced to prison. In Roman eyes, prison is much too soft a form of expiation. It is only a place of transition, of pretrial detention, after which, those found guilty are sent somewhere else.

The second interesting aspect of the Syrian case is how one is brought to court in case of a crime such as theft or homicide. In Roman times there was no organized police force such as we have today, no ancient version of patrol cars that arrive with sirens blaring. To be sure, there are firefighters that, together with the *vicomagistri,* or neighborhood police, patrolled the streets. Augustus did institute urban police stations (*cohortes urbanae),* the equivalent of our precincts, in Rome, but for the control of the streets and apprehension of criminals after a crime there is a sort of widespread do-it-yourself approach. It's the people themselves who separate the parties to a fight, keep an eye on suspicious strangers, and so forth.

There are no police detectives who conduct investigations. Instead the victim's families do this on their own behalf, interrogating slaves and neighbors, gathering evidence, etc. Then they identify a suspect, contact a lawyer, and go directly to court. At this point the mechanism of Roman law is set in motion, with the duel between the prosecution and the defense.

Sometimes a case won't make it to trial because the parties reach an agreement beforehand—the accused to avoid the risk of a heavy sentence, the accuser in order to avoid the expense of a trial and to receive some form of indemnity, for example, money. This happens often in cases of sexual violence against a girl from a poor family on the part of some male member of a wealthy family.

Later on another entity will appear on the scene able to resolve disputes before they get to court: the church. Given their prestigious role in society, the clergy will intercept a lot of disputes, arranging an agreement between the parties or issuing their own religious judgment.

A Culture More Peaceful than Ours?

At this point we can draw some conclusions concerning crime on the streets of Rome and in the cities of the empire, giving the lie to a lot of myths.

The first is that, as Professor Krause has demonstrated, there does not exist a criminal class in Roman society. There does not exist, that is, the figure of the "professional criminal," in the style of Al Capone or Tony Soprano. And even where something similar does exist (for example, brigands), it's still more the exception than the rule.

Those who commit crimes do so out of "extemporaneous" necessity. It may be an artisan or a small shop owner who, motivated by need, grabs an opportunity that happens to present itself, and then returns to his occupation. Or it could be someone temporarily adopting a criminal role for some special reason (for example, a slave who has been ordered to commit a crime). In short, in Rome there are no organized bands or criminal associations, such as the Mafia or the camorra. Roman criminals generally act as individuals or with the help of a friend or relative.

The second conclusion is that although Roman society has considerable physical violence (beatings of slaves, wives, children, etc.), there are many fewer weapons in circulation than we have today. Therefore, contrary to what is commonly thought, fights, armed robberies, and assaults are much less bloody than their modern counterparts.

The third conclusion is that, given how often they make use of the courts to resolve problems, we can see that Romans tend not to take justice into their own hands by using violence, and that they have faith in the judicial system. Even if, as we must recall, the system is not equal for all because it privileges and protects the upper classes, ordinary people go to court rather than take justice into their own hands.

Because of this widespread faith in the law and the judicial system, resorting to long-lived feuds and family vendettas, while extremely frequent in the Middle Ages, is unknown in Roman society. In the Middle Ages and the Renaissance, whoever felt their honor had been offended drew their sword, whereas a Roman (for matters more serious than the frequent public scuffles) went to court. And for an ancient and essentially "peasant" society, as Rome was, this is something extraordinary.

EPHESUS

~ *Marble for the Empire* ~

The Centurion's Private War

The centurion goes into a tavern to get a bite to eat. The place is full of people, mostly men. The entrance of an armed man turns the heads of more than one customer. There seems to be a certain diffidence toward the soldiers that have been going around town since Trajan's return from Mesopotamia. But it's only a matter of time; it won't be long before the townspeople are used to their presence again.

The centurion sits off to the side at a small empty table and orders a focaccia, olives, and some pickled fish. Sure, he's eating alone, but it's a meal the he enjoys down to the last bite. At the end, as he sits there sipping his wine, he closes his eyes and thinks back to his time in prison in that far-off city in Mesopotamia. He wouldn't be here had it not been for a chain of unlikely events: The Roman troops' assault on the city. The moment when the Parthian enemy forces went running in all directions onto the defensive walls to get ready for the attack. And then when the prison guard ran out to get into position on the wall, fumbling with his helmet as he ran out, forgetting his keys on the table, so close to the peephole of the cell. . . . Breaking apart the wood board that functioned as a bed was an instinctive reaction, and fishing the keys through the peephole was child's play. And then opening the door, freeing his comrades-in-arms and racing up the stairs, knocking the enemy soldiers cold and taking their weapons. The centurion relives the moment when he threw open the door to the room of the enemy commander, just as that man was putting on his armor, with the assistance of his attendants. All the adrenalin he felt at that instant resurges through his body. He had turned into a fury, an animal. With lightning-fast thrusts his sword pierced the flesh of all their bodies and finally, when he plunged it into the commander's side, that corpulent man with his black beard and his ever-sweaty bald pate, he felt compensated for all the beatings he had suffered in prison. His wine glass held fast in midair, the visual memory of those moments passes before his eyes: the breathless sprint toward the gates of the city as the battle was raging; opening them; the agitated, almost ferocious faces of the first Roman soldiers who burst through them. A gentle touch delicately lowers his hand. It's the hand of the waitress; her gaze is sweet but determined. The centurion has to pay his bill and free up the table. Some other customers are waiting. The centurion takes another couple of seconds to break out of his daydream; his breathing is labored and he bats his eyes repeatedly. Then he pulls out a coin and stands up, forces an embarrassed smile, and walks out. His leg muscles are all stiff. The war is still pulsing through his veins. He's a victim of what will later be dubbed post-traumatic stress syndrome. Who knows how many other legionnaires back from the campaign in Mesopotamia have to deal with these same problems, like veterans of the wars in Vietnam and Iraq. We'll never know. To be sure, the esprit de corps, the sense of fraternity that binds the legionnaires, helps a lot, allowing each of them to unload their pent-up emotions onto the others. To engage, in other words, in group therapy.

The coin, meanwhile, is picked up by the waitress. She carries it to the innkeeper, at the cash box. It remains there for just a few minutes, time for the new customers sitting at what had been the centurion's table to have their meal. When they pay, our sestertius is part of their change.

The Death of the Emperor

The sestertius is picked up by a man with a friendly way about him, salt-and-pepper hair, a captivating smile, with wrinkles on the sides of his mouth. His name is Alexis and he sells marble. He's here together with a colleague, thin and curly-haired. It's their last meal here in Antioch.

Their ship is leaving in a little while and everything has gone fine, from their dreams, to the divine signals, to the sacrifices. They've got the gods' permission to depart.

A couple of hours later they're on the big merchant ship, which sets its sails and starts to pull away from the dock. They take off their fancy clothes. Sailing in the nude is normal, especially in these warm climes. Nice clothes aren't needed on board; they'd just get ruined. Same for their shoes; they're both wearing *caligae*. When they take them off we notice their feet are striped, covered in tan lines from the thin leather strips that wrap their feet.

While at sea, ships have to be careful about false lighthouses. Farmers, fishermen, or shepherds quite often light bonfires, deceiving the ships out at sea when darkness falls that there is a port nearby. The fire setters purposely choose a place where a ship could run aground so they can attack it, steal its cargo, and rob its passengers. These attacks on the maritime wagon train became incredibly frequent, to the point that Emperor Hadrian, and even more so his successor, Antoninus Pius, promulgated very severe laws and punishments against it. Under Antoninus Pius, if the raid was carried out in a violent way and the cargo was valuable, those responsible were sentenced to clubbing and sent into exile for three years, if they were free citizens and well-off. If instead they were poor they were sentenced to three years hard labor. If they were slaves they were sent directly to the mines.

Alexis, a marble dealer, is lying down on the stern under a curtain stretched out to create a bit of shade. Rocked by the movement of the ship, he observes the luminous reflections of the waves on the hull; they look like the flames of a hearth and give the impression that the ship is sailing on a bed of fire. Then he gradually closes his eyes and falls asleep. Off to his right, the coast of the land that we now know as Turkey glides by.

He is awakened by excited voices and the agitation of the crew. They are all pointing at a large group of ships moored in a roadstead in the port of Selinus (Gazipasa). It's the emperor's fleet. What's it doing here in such an anonymous place? There are no sanctuaries or palaces. The coast is bare, except for some hills covered with forests and silent beaches where the turtles come to deposit their eggs. Why is Trajan here? Everyone on board is asking the same question, but nobody has an answer.

Actually, there is a real drama going on. Trajan is dying. In Antioch, after returning from Mesopotamia, he had a stroke that left him semiparalyzed. He turned over the control of operations to an excellent commander, Hadrian, the future emperor. Then he took the imperial yacht, together with the empress Plotina, to return to Rome and enjoy a well-deserved triumph in the capital. But on the way back his condition grew worse, and it became necessary to enter the closest port and take him to shore.

For a lot of people, this comes as no surprise. Lately, the emperor's health has been deteriorating visibly. An extraordinary bronze bust of Emperor Trajan, on display in the forum of Ankyra (present-day Ankara) and unearthed by archaeologists, shows him in what are perhaps his last weeks of life. He is unrecognizable—much different from the statues and portraits that represent him on coins (including ours). His face is drawn, there are circles under his eyes, the bones of his hollow cheeks are sticking out, his nose is prominent and lacking the harmonious look of his younger years. His skin is sagging and his forehead wrinkled. These are sure signs of age, of someone who has faced the rain, the wind, and the desert storms elbow to elbow with legionnaires forty years younger than him. But his sixty-two years are not worn well. He has lots of physical problems and has made too many demands on his body. It is almost certain that what gave out in the end was his heart: without adequate medicine, someone who had already suffered a stroke simply didn't make it.

According to Julian Bennett, a British archaeologist and an expert on Hadrian, there is also the possibility that he was done in by a violent infection contracted in Mesopotamia. Indeed, according to the ancient historian Flavius Eutropius, Trajan suffered internal hemorrhaging. One of his closest and most trusted attendants, M. Ulpius Phaedimus, died just three days later at the tender age of twenty-eight; this may be another indication of an infection that dealt the final blow to an already debilitated organism.

Trajan never clearly indicated a successor. He is thought to have adopted Hadrian on his deathbed, clearing his road to the imperial throne. But there is some doubt about this. For a long time the dominant hypothesis was that Trajan's wife, Empress Plotina, organized the succession, letting everyone believe that Trajan had announced it on his deathbed. We'll never really know.

The inlet and the port of Selinus disappear from view, along with the imperial fleet. After the ritual ceremonies, the emperor's body will be cremated here, and the gold urn containing his ashes will be carried by his ship to Rome, to be placed in the base of Trajan's Column, in the heart of the city. Trajan, even though he is dead, will have his triumph: a grand parade will be organized that will carry his effigy through the streets of Rome.

And so the *optimus princeps* has died; he who has led us to make a unique journey through the Roman Empire at its high point, by making it wealthier, more extensive, more powerful, and more feared than ever.

As an emperor he was different from all of his predecessors. Indeed, he was the first provincial to serve as emperor (even if Emperor Claudius, a native of Lyon, was not properly speaking Italic, Trajan came from Spain), with a surprisingly global and modern vision of the empire. His most striking quality was his personality. He was a soldier who had come up through the ranks, accustomed to hard work and discipline. And, above all, he was a humble man, capable of sitting in the midst of the crowd at the Circus Maximus and eating rations together with his soldiers. He was even able to use his personal fortune to help needy children.

Dante will evoke his heroism and selflessness in Canticle X of the *Purgatorio*. But the common people will remember him for centuries as a just man, the best of the emperors, the *optimus princeps*.

The Marbles of Ephesus

Hadrian will eliminate nearly all of the key players in Trajan's entourage (of which he himself was also a member). He'll destroy the central military command, ordering the best generals to be killed or removed. Even Apollodorus of Damascus will meet his death; he was Trajan's architect, a true Michelangelo of his age, designer of the bridge over the Danube, Trajan's Forum in Rome, and Trajan's grandiose and strikingly original column.

But above all, Hadrian will renounce almost all of Trajan's conquests in Mesopotamia, provoking Dio Cassius to write: "Thus it came about that the Romans in conquering Armenia, most of Mesopotamia, and the Parthians had undergone their hardships and dangers all for naught." (*Roman History*, Book LXVIII, Translated by Earnest Cary.)

This brings us to the following consideration: our coin was able to return to the empire thanks to that brief interval in which Rome extended its borders to look out onto the world of Asia. Otherwise it probably would have remained in India, perhaps to be found later by archaeologists.

As history is turning a page, the ship of Alexis, the marble merchant, continues on its route toward Ephesus. It arrives there after a few days of smooth sailing. After taking care of the formalities of docking and customs, Alexis and another marble merchant go ashore. They walk along chatting together through one of the most prosperous and beautiful cities in all of antiquity. Even in the modern era the ruins of Ephesus are jaw-dropping. With its incorporation into the Roman Empire the city has reached its apogee. Its harbor and its position on the Mediterranean make it a city of prime importance.

As we accompany the two merchants we notice that Ephesus is blessed with prosperity: its streets are paved with pure marble. The city has over two hundred thousand inhabitants, an endless expanse of red tile roofs, arches, temples, an agora, and scores of public buildings.

We cross its expansive forum, next to which rises an enormous basilica, over 650 feet long, divided into three naves. As we're passing by, the sound of voices coming from inside attracts our attention. We look in the entrance and are presented with scenes of public life, with toga-clad men wheeling and dealing. In the Roman era, a basilica is not a church but a building that functions as a courthouse, merchants' lodge, and trade center. It's one of the central points of the city.

We go back to walking amid the crowds. It feels like we're inside a beehive. All around us are temples and public buildings of breathtaking beauty. We pass the temple dedicated to the emperor Domitian, and it reminds us of another curious aspect of Roman cities: the importance of a Roman city is also measured by the number of temples in which emperors are venerated as deities.

It's not easy to build a temple in honor of an emperor. You have to have his consent and then beat the competition from other cities. All of it is handled by lawyers with inside connections. One of them has left a plaque here in Ephesus that reports his exploits. It says that he made several trips to Rome to see the emperor, then he followed him to Britain, Germany, France, Bithynia, and even Syria before crowning his obstinacy with success. We can certainly imagine his gifts of diplomacy, cleverness, and flattery. But he must also have been a real pain in the neck. . . .

Another Wonder of the Ancient World

We get jostled by a group of pilgrims who pass us and keep right on going without turning to look. They're from Egypt and they're on their way to the outskirts of the city, toward the temple of Artemis, one of the seven wonders of the ancient world. That's right, our sestertius is leading us to discover another of these wonders. Why was it built here? It's a very curious story, one that takes us back in time.

Three thousand years ago a primitive cult existed here, probably related to a freshwater spring, which would have been a rarity this close to the coast. It was said to be the work of a goddess who offered asylum to the needy.

Very early on this goddess was identified as Artemis, the Greek goddess with a multitude of breasts; or, according to another version, the testicles of sacrificed bulls strung on the image of the goddess as offerings; or—still another hypothesis—bees' eggs. Her virginity was the symbol of the invulnerability of the refuge that she offered to the persecuted. So it became a protected area and safe haven for anyone seeking political asylum. Its territory was sacred and inviolable.

Over time the offerings to the goddess steadily became more precious and brought Ephesus enormous riches; this led to the birth of one of the most awesome constructions of the ancient world. In about 550 BC, Croesus, who will later succeed his father on the throne of Lydia, asked a wealthy Ephesian for a loan of 1,000 gold coins to allow him to engage mercenaries and go to war, and vowed to Artemis that if he should become king he would build her a temple of unheard-of beauty. He kept his word. The last version of the temple was a massive structure with some 127 columns. Each of the columns was embellished at its base with bronze reliefs and rested on huge blocks of marble.

At some point this wonder was damaged. It is said that it was burned by a madman, Erostratus, who wanted to go down in history, which he succeeded in doing. But it is more likely that the building was struck by lightning, destroying the roof, which was made of wood. The temple was eventually rebuilt, in the form that Alexis and his fellow merchant are seeing in their walk through the city.

Today, all that's left of this ancient wonder is a single column, which emerges from the marsh. But it provides us with an interesting piece of information: it seems that the idea of building the temple in a marsh was the innovation of its architect, Chersiphron, to reduce the impact of earthquakes, which were very frequent in this area.

As we are entering the sumptuous city baths, the voices of Alexis and his colleague are drowned out by the buzzing of the crowd that reverberates throughout the complex. While the two men are inside, we decide to wait for them among the colonnades to observe the passersby. They belong to every nationality and social class. There are ordinary people, but also public figures, who arrive with their retinue of lackeys and supplicants.

It's amazing to recall how many famous figures are tied to this city. Ephesus is the birthplace of the famous philosopher Heraclitus, who expounded on the mutability of things: *panta rhei*, everything flows. And famous visitors to the city included Cicero, Julius Caesar, Marc Antony, and Cleopatra.

Marc Antony (then the governor of the Roman provinces in the east) decided to live in Ephesus and had Cleopatra join him there. As everyone knows, she was a fascinating woman and also very clever. She came to Ephesus not only to be with her lover but also to murder her sister Arsinoë, whom she saw as a threat to her power and who had taken refuge in the neutral territory of the Temple of Artemis. With help from Marc Antony, Cleopatra had her taken out of the temple and killed. Never before had the temple been violated so blatantly.

Once out of the marble halls of the baths, the two merchants stop to greet a sumptuously dressed man who is revered by everyone but who has a sinister reputation. He is the organizer and coordinator of the gladiator fights in Ephesus. He is filthy rich, lives in total luxury, and leads a life punctuated by gala festivities and banquets, like the one he is holding this evening to which Alexis and his colleague have been invited. In a few hours they will be at his magnificent villa, amid perfumed servants and noble women wrapped in exquisitely fine silk robes flaunting their gaudy jewelry.

The Inferno of the Quarries

The next day, bright and early and still a bit hung over, the two merchants are back on board their ship, on their way to a marble quarry. In the area around Ephesus there are at least forty quarries, including the famous one at Teos (present-day Siğacik), where two special varieties of marble are extracted: black "African" and black-and-ash-gray "Africanato." What we're about to see is a radically different world, the antechamber of hell.

The quarry is behind a spur of rock, where the road ends. But we can already sense its presence, announced by the loud hammering of the slaves at work. After going around the spur, the two men reach the guard post at the entrance to the quarry, where they're stopped by a man with a long beard and a clump of hair on his forehead, surrounded by baldness. He's armed and asks to see their credentials. Then, having examined their passes, he lets them go in.

Alexis is ill at ease; he'll never get used to these scenes. Dozens, maybe hundreds, of slaves are at work, some in the shade of the rock wall, some in the glaring sun, which has already started beating down on the rock. An injured slave passes right next to him, assisted by two others who are leading him to the guardhouse; he has a sliver of stone stuck in his eye and is only half-conscious.

The work here is extremely dangerous and knows no pause. It's a real assembly line. The first step to extracting the marble is to dig grooves in the rock with simple hammers and chisels. That's the most debilitating part. Then wooden wedges are stuck into the grooves and water is poured over them. The wood gradually swells up and splits the rock at the selected spot, breaking off enormous blocks weighing five or six tons each. These are then moved by means of wooden levers or small cranes. It is heartbreaking to imagine little boys working here, emaciated and without a future. It's inhuman. This epoch harbors so many wonders but also so much cruelty.

One little boy wipes his dripping nose with the back of his hand and then runs off to get some water to give to an elderly slave. A guard yells at him, picks up a stone and throws it at him, just missing. The kid is more agile than the guard's meanness. In places like this, relations between guards and slaves are atrocious; that perverse psychological mechanism that causes some people to take pleasure in dominating others and seeing them suffer often turns the guards into outright sadists.

Alexis and his colleague have come to take delivery of some bases and capitals that they had ordered. They walk by an area where a line of slaves is pounding away at the rock with picks, making deep grooves. For the past twenty years or so the Roman quarries have been implementing a technological innovation that has improved their productivity: they have designed and manufactured a heavier pick to penetrate deeper into the hard marble. By using this tool and working in a line, the slaves work more efficiently and the blocks are rough-hewn to be finished later on. The big innovation, in fact, lies in not waiting for specific orders, but in "preshaping" columns, capitals, and sarcophagi without finishing them. They are made in serial fashion, warehoused, and then sent out to various places in the empire where workshops of chiselers finish them to the taste of the buyers. It's a sort of preindustrial serial production, not technologically but certainly conceptually. Consider, for example, that sarcophagi are carved with one side twice as thick as the other; in the workshops of the destination city, chiselers will "extract" the cover from the thick side, to the sound of hammer blows.

The two merchants are attracted by a curious wooden structure that makes a tremendous noise. They walk over to it. At first glance it seems to be a simple waterwheel, turned by a torrent, as can be seen in a lot of mills. But this is different, thanks to a mechanism of cogwheels reminiscent of the machines designed by Leonardo da Vinci. The movement of the wheel powers a saw that gradually cuts through a block of marble. We are dumbfounded. It's a stonecutting machine. So the ancients were perfectly capable of building such a machine and saving on manpower; there is just one slave overseeing the work of the machine (which in this way becomes the "slave's slave"). Could this technology have been developed on a large scale?

There are some examples of this kind of automation in the Roman era, as in Barbégal, in France, where a system of waterwheels powered a series of mills, setting in motion a sort of ski lift to which some sleds were attached that continuously resupplied the mills with sacks of wheat. This automated system for cutting marble was found sculpted, with a certain pride, on the sarcophagus (a marble sarcophagus, obviously) of a man who lived right here in Ephesus. But a Roman might object: "Why auto-mate? We have slaves that do the same work at no cost." Perhaps that was all it took to impede the spread of technologies that, as indicated by ar-chaeological discoveries, were certainly within the Romans' capabilities.

The items ordered by the two merchants are ready: thirty-eight Co-rinthian columns with leaves already outlined but still to be finished. It won't take long to load them onto their boat, just a few hours, time to be passed under the arbor of a little nearby inn where buyers usually spend the night. At the inn, while the merchant who's holding our sestertius waits, chatting and drinking wine, his colleague entertains himself with the waitress, taking her to a room upstairs. It's expected that all the wait-resses and female owners of taverns and inns are available for sex, just like prostitutes.

Shipwreck

The ship was loaded quickly. The capitals are arranged like glasses upside down on the column bases. By positioning these marble "couples" one next to the other the hold is filled in no time. When they head out to sea, the ship is weighed down by all that marble, and it moves slowly through the water, heading north along the coast.

It's dusk by now and the sea is beginning to rise. Black clouds hide the stars, and the sea gradually swells higher and higher. It's impossible to go on: with the darkness closing in and the sea swelling constantly, it would be madness to continue. So they seek shelter from a long tract of coast between two promontories.

But it's not enough; the wind and waves are pushing them toward the coast. The sails have been taken down, and a man from the crew keeps plunging a sounding line into the water—that is, a rope with a lead weight on the end used to determine the depth of the water.

Another sailor is turning the crank of the bilge pump, sucking out the water that got into the hold when the waves washed over the deck. The ship is coming dangerously close to shore. In the semidarkness, Alexis and the other merchant can see clearly the white caps of the waves break-ing against the shoreline.

A member of the crew immediately throws over the anchor in an at-tempt to keep the ship from drifting into shore. But it's useless; with the stern turned toward land and the bow toward the sea, the ship, like a rider in some aquatic rodeo, straddles the waves that the sea sends up against it.

Then comes the final blow; the keel bumps against something, maybe a rock on the sea bottom. The ship pivots on that point and rolls on its side, pushed by the waves. Inside the hold the cargo is shoved out of position, causing the ship to lose its equilibrium.

Alexis gasps in horror as the ship leans more and more without stopping. The blow from the wave must have opened a hole in the side of the ship, because it feels like it's about to tip over in the sea. Copious amounts of water come streaming out of the bilge pump. It's as though an artery has burst open inside the ship.

It's too late for any more maneuvers; by now the water is over the bridge and flowing all over the ship. When it gets to the big opening that leads down to the hold it pours inside thunderously. It's the end: every man for himself. The ship sinks with determination, heading for the bottom like a knife.

Now Alexis and all the men are in the water. It's all happening in the dark. There was no need to jump; they were swept along by water that washed over the deck. The men are at the mercy of the tumultuous waves and the current. Fortunately, they're all able to save themselves; the beach is very close.

The ship sits down on the bottom, which gathers it in softly. Over the coming decades the hull will disappear, eaten away by the sea and by those mollusks that come to be called shipworms. The only thing left will be the cargo, the skeleton of that unlucky voyage. And incredibly enough everything is still there, extraordinarily visible.

But the striking thing is how the scene around the wreck has changed. Right there where the drama took place there is now a long, elegant, exclusive beach near the city of Cesme, with beach umbrellas, a gazebo, kiosks, and even go-go dancers entertaining the customers. But all you have to do is go fifty yards offshore to admire the magnificent capitals sitting on the bottom at a depth of just fifteen to twenty feet. It's one of the most beautiful visions that any scuba diver could have, and it tells this ancient story.

It's not immediately clear why the cargo was never recovered. Perhaps, since it all happened at night, it wasn't possible to relocate the point where the ship went down. Or, given the proximity of the quarry, it was considered less costly to have new capitals made than to pay the famous *urinatores* to find and recover the sunken ones.

Alexis and his friend saved themselves by grabbing onto the little lifeboat on board. And now, still a bit in shock, they're sitting on the beach shivering, as the storm unleashes its wrath out on the water.

Shortly, they'll start walking back to the harbor, looking for help. And what about our sestertius? Is it at the bottom of the sea? No, the merchant still has it; it's still in his purse, hanging from his belt. But it spent a long time in the cold, dark waters of the tempest.

After a long march the two marble dealers and the crew were welcomed and given hospitality at the port. During their stay there Alexis bought some clean clothes with the coins he had with him. And so our sestertius changed hands again. Now it's inside a canvas bag, together with some other sesterces, swinging back and forth on the street to the rhythm of a man's step.

The man is a shopkeeper, a *libertus*, and he's taking the day's receipts to the shop owner, his former master. It's very common to see this type of relationship after a slave has been given his liberty. It's advantageous to both parties, especially to the *libertus*, who gets the help of his former master to enter the world of commerce.

The owner is a rich man who owns a lot of property, including five ships he uses to trade with major ports on the Aegean Sea. Tomorrow, once the bad weather has passed, he'll be embarking for Athens carrying, among other goods, a shipment of precious silk from Alexandria and embroidered fabrics that he's just received from Antioch.

Voyage to Athens

The voyage across the Aegean reveals to us a sea with a surprisingly high volume of traffic. There are always sails on the horizon. The ships carry goods, of course, but also a lot of people. Many of them are traveling for trade and work (functionaries, administrators, soldiers, etc.); others are going to visit relatives. Sometimes goods and people are one and the same, as in the case of slaves being taken to Delos to be sold or coming from other markets.

There are also, as we have already mentioned, tourists. The interesting thing is that, unlike us, they are not in the least bit interested in the great spectacles of nature, such as breathtaking landscapes, snowcapped mountains, or pristine valleys. On the contrary, nature is often considered the source of threats to safety and health (thanks to wolves, malaria, etc.). If anything, the ancient tourists might be interested in those more intimate natural settings where the presence of some divinity can be felt: a spring (after all, who but a divinity can make water gush from the ground?), a sacred wood with its awesome silence, sulfur beds with their hellish fumes, etc. Tourists of the Roman era, in short, prefer places that are circumscribed rather than vast panoramas or overwhelming natural beauty.

The historic sites where they often go usually offer a blend of ancient history and mythology. So, besides admiring the tomb of Virgil in Naples or the tomb of Socrates in Athens, they also visit the tombs of mythological figures such as Achilles and Ajax in Sparta or the place where Penelope decided to make Ulysses her spouse.

In this context, there is no lack of places to visit that feature some curious relics. In Argos, for example, there is a mound under which is buried the head of Medusa. On the island of Rhodes the goblet that Helen of Troy used to drink from is on display, and it has the shape of one of her breasts. In Phaselis, in Asia Minor, we have Achilles' lance. People go to see these relics just the way millions of people today go to see the relics of Christian saints. In the absence of scientific explanations, some of the relics or objects on display have taken on imaginative back stories: for example, the fossil remains of prehistoric elephants are believed to be the bones of giants (of Cyclops, as is the case in Sicily).

Among the ship's passengers there are also people making pilgrimages to shrines, for help with health problems or to get an answer from the oracles. Three shrines in particular are the real engines of pilgrimages: the shrines of Epidaurus, Pergamum, and the island of Kos. Whether on the road or at sea, it is quite common to encounter sick pilgrims on their way to one of these temples. Among the treatments offered at these shrines is dream therapy, as Professor Lionel Casson tells us. After a purifying (and hygienic) bath, the patients enter the temple, they pray, and then they are told to lie down on the ground or on a mat, sometimes in large rooms where they spend the night. Their dreams bring them medical advice, sometimes clear and sometimes obscure, which the priests then interpret. The suggested treatments are always simple: kinds of food to eat or to avoid, baths to take, or exercises to do.

Finally, among the varied humanity transported by the ships, there are also Olympic athletes. We are now in the year 117 CE, and the 124th Olympic games are set to begin in Greece.

Athens

After disembarking at the port of Piraeus, our wealthy entrepreneur is now in Athens. Heliodorus is his name (literally, "gift of the sun"), and he is lying softly on a litter carried by four robust slaves. It's a comfortable way to travel, but it always seems peculiar to our modern mentality. It's a bit like someone picking you up together with the bed you've been lying on and carrying you around the city to do your errands.

As he advances through the crowd (or rather, over the crowd), Heliodorus looks up distractedly at the Acropolis. In its general appearance, the first glimpse will change very little over the course of the centuries, so what Heliodorus sees is very much like what we see today: the Parthenon, then as now, stands out with its forest of gleaming columns.

The litter's little procession passes a point from which the view of the Acropolis is especially evocative. Today it would be the ideal spot for taking a picture. And that's exactly what some Roman tourists are doing. But in the absence of cameras they are using substitutes that worked for millennia: artists. At very low cost, an artist makes a quick sketch on sheets of papyrus, a portrait of the visitor with the Parthenon in the background. Obviously, the artists are not alone; all the tourists are assailed by the *exegetai*, the local guides, who hover like flies.

Stone Twins

After a number of turns around the city, Heliodorus has one last errand to do. And it just may be the one he likes the most. He has to go to the workshop of the sculptor from whom he has commissioned a portrait bust.

In the entryway all kinds of things are on display. There are several statues of divinities, for decoration in the *domus*, marble tubs and pestles, even a sundial in the form of a basin to put in the garden. We go in. Everything is coated with a layer of extrafine powder, and on the ground under our feet we can hear the crunch of slivers of marble.

Around us are many pieces that have been left unfinished, waiting for a buyer before being given the final touch: exactly like what we saw at the quarry. But while in the quarry there were large unfinished objects (capitals, columns, sarcophagi, etc.), here the unfinished works are small. Our eyes skim over gravestones to inscribe, altars without any dedication, a pair of sarcophagi with the figures of the deceased undefined, even statues with the face just barely outlined, waiting for the definitive features. It all makes us think of a sort of "precooked" art, serialized objects waiting for the final touch, different every time.

We follow Heliodorus into the back room. The sculptor is at work, but he jumps up immediately from his stool, takes off his cap, and goes to meet his wealthy patron.

He knows why Heliodorus is here and he points to a bust covered by a cloth. When he uncovers it with a theatrical gesture, Heliodorus raises his eyebrows. The bust that the sculptor has made for him is a very good likeness. This Greek sculptor is good. The bust looks almost like his twin in stone. The only feature that's a little different is the hair. Heliodorus has his hair fixed a little differently. But that's fine, because the bust has the same hair as the official busts of Trajan.

It's interesting to note that both men and women tend to have themselves represented in statues or portraits with the same hairstyle as the empress or emperor. This means that when you see a bust in a museum you can date it simply by looking at the hairstyle (and the beard). The problem is that Trajan just died. Will Heliodorus still be in fashion once the new emperor is crowned?

How to Make Serial Copies

While the two men are bickering over the price for additional copies, we take our leave and go out into the courtyard. Our attention is attracted by the ticking sound of marble being chiseled. We pull aside a curtain and discover the "shop boys" at work.

They're sitting in a line and they're all sculpting the same subject. In fact, they are making identical busts of the same person, an important government official. The statues are identical; it's as if these boys are expert photocopiers in three dimensions. Today, if we go from one museum to another, we can see exact copies of the same subject, down to the last detail. In the case of Emperor Hadrian, for example, we know of no less than thirty marble "twins" of his portrait, scattered in museums all over the world.

How do they do it? Roman sculptors use what we might call geometric techniques. If a statue represents an emperor (Hadrian, for example) with a frontal bust and his face is oriented slightly to the side, a classic pose, the copyist starts shaping the marble by first outlining a cube for the head and a big block for the shoulders. Then he transforms the cube into an oval, and marks some key points of the future face such as the point of the chin, an earlobe, the longest curl of the beard. From one copy to the next these points must always be the same distance from the same point at the top of the forehead, which is the center curl of the hair. This is a crucial step and the distance is established with precision by using a caliper.

Afterward, the sculptor begins outlining the principal features of the face: the forehead, the cheeks, the sides of the nose. . . . Gradually, there emerges from the marble the figure of a sharp-featured, very expressive face. And the work will be easy to copy, precisely because the various facial features are expressed in such a mathematical way, at measurable distances.

The occupation of sculptor and "copyist" was fundamental in ancient Rome. In this era, statues were placed everywhere (which explains why the majority of ancient statues in museums today are Roman). They had several functions. First and foremost, they were celebratory: the serial copies of an emperor will be placed in lots of public places, exactly like photos of the president today are hung on the walls of public offices and army barracks. But the statues actually had a precise objective: to create impressions.

Alone or in a group, for example, in nymphaeums, they were supposed to evoke a theme that then stimulated cultivated conversations on various topics, from war, to the beauty of life, to eros (Laocoön, Venus in the bath, etc.). Or they functioned as sets for religious rituals (statues of Jove) or justified public celebrations (statues of Augustus or other emperors, divinities representing decisions to be made, etc.). In other words, the statues were not only decorative elements for the city, in the same way as ornamental floral arrangements, but rather catalysts for activities that were important moments in daily life.

The demand for statues was enormous, and it wasn't possible to satisfy everyone with original Greek works. For this reason, the workshops started churning out serial copies of Greek masterpieces from the sixth and fifth centuries BCE, and the figure of the sculptor and copyist became fundamental.

Gradually, temples and public spaces began to fill up with copies of Greek masterpieces from the fifth and fourth centuries BCE, perhaps with small Roman variations on the theme, while private villas and houses displayed in their gardens myriads of Greek and Roman heroes, philosophers, poets, and men of power.

At this point, it's clear that being represented by a statue became a status symbol. As a result, famous people or people with a powerful social position, even a modest one, began leaving legacies of busts and statues of themselves and their relatives. Our museums are full of them, and what is amazing about them is the extraordinary realism of their faces and clothing: they are truly three-dimensional portraits in stone. The Romans, unlike the Greeks and the Egyptians, were the first to represent physical defects in their statues: baldness, bags under the eyes, double chins, pudgy faces, etc. This practice has a curious origin. When someone died, a mold of his or her face was made, and from that an original was made to be displayed in the house, like a portrait, in a special place, together with the faces of other ancestors. At the funeral of a Roman from a good family the portraits of his ancestors were carried in the procession behind the deceased to demonstrate to everyone his noble origins. This tradition of the "true" faces gave rise to the realistic style of Roman statues.

One final curiosity to note is that many statues and reliefs were painted: the hair, the eyes, clothing decorations. The ones in our museums today are white simply because the colors have disappeared. But in the Renaissance this was not known, and that's why all the Renaissance statues, sculpted from the whitest possible marbles because of the influence of the "white" Roman statues, are the fruit of a misunderstanding.

The Overly Severe Gaze of Augustus

As we're going back into the sculptor's workshop, we notice a damaged bust of Augustus in the corner, and next to it one of Nero, evidently no longer displayable. We notice a big difference in the impression they transmit: Nero seems alive, almost a person we know. But Augustus has a surprising coldness in his gaze.

The impression is not by chance. Between the time of Augustus and that of Nero about forty years later there was a change in style. The sculptors who were active under Augustus almost all came from Attica and perpetuated the centuries-old classical style of Greek statues. The style was perfect, to be sure, but severe, rigid, lifeless. As the decades went by the style of Roman sculpture changed, perhaps influenced by the work of sculptors from the East; statues acquired warmth and dynamism, with features so alive that when we see them in museums they often make us think: "But I've seen this gentleman somewhere before . . ."

Indeed, the statues in museums present the viewer with a little challenge. If you accept it, your museum visits will become like a game—to guess in what era the statue was sculpted, for example. Think of it in modern terms. Just think of the 1960s, 1970s, and 1980s and of how much the way people appear in public has changed. You can figure out the period of an old photograph simply by looking at how the man has his hair combed or how a woman is dressed. The same holds true for the statues. Artistic styles and ways of dressing changed over the course of the generations, and so you can figure out the era the statue belongs to simply by observing the clothes and the style.

After the realism of Vespasian, Titus, and Domitian, just before and after the tragedy of Pompeii in the year 79, under Trajan and Hadrian the sculptures go back for a short period to a "cold" style: gazes are detached and they never seem to be taking into consideration who they are looking at (frankly, the viewer is made to feel uncomfortable, almost unwanted). Luckily, this style was abandoned almost immediately. Sculptors under subsequent emperors, such as Marcus Aurelius or Septimius Severus, go back to sculpting "live" statues, but with one important innovation: the chiaroscuro effect. It was an ingenious new twist. If you take a good look at sarcophagi or statues from that period you will notice a lot of holes in the hair, beards, mouths, and ears. They look almost like termite holes. Actually they were made by drills and purposely left visible, to create an effect of light and shadow.

Indeed, the statues of this period are no longer all smooth; the sculptors leave rough areas next to polished ones to create a play of light. They even create a textured effect on the skin. The gaze also changes. While the eyes of a statue of Julius Caesar are empty, without pupils (because they were painted), now the pupils are engraved. Imagine the color of the iris to which is added the shadow of a groove: the gaze becomes much more profound, in all senses. (This was a technique initiated under Hadrian, whose eyes were an intriguing deep blue, as suggested by the glass paste inserts of a bronze bust of him conserved in the archaeological museum of Alexandria.) The optical illusion is perfect; the statues become more realistic, yet it's all just a block of stone or bronze. You might say it's the ancient equivalent of CGI and 3-D effects. For centuries this technique enjoyed enormous success.

Another curious thing to note is that the size of the busts changed too, and this allows them to be dated with certainty. In the beginning, the portraits went down to the base of the neck. Then, in the second century CE, sculptors also included the upper part of the torso and arms; later, in the third century CE they decided to include the entire torso. Sometimes they inserted other kinds of marble in a statue: the head of white stone, the clothes with green, red, or speckled marbles. An elegant and prestigious effect.

But at a certain point this surprising vitality of the statues disappeared. This was the last hurrah of ancient statuary. Afterward, the subjects were represented "stiffened" like a dead man, with their eyes wide open and their gaze fixed. Until sculptors arrived at the Byzantine style, that is. To represent the power of the emperors and the superiority of the faith, subjects were portrayed drastically differently from the everyday reality of the common people.

BACK TO THE ETERNAL CITY
~ A Journey Through Time ~

Heliodorus leaves the workshop satisfied with his bust, though he doesn't know that with the new emperor, Hadrian, already in office, tastes will change. Not only will he wear his hair differently, he'll launch the new fashion of the beard—a beard with a precise political and cultural message: not the soldier's beard but the philosopher's. In short, Heliodorus's marble bust is out of style, even before it leaves the workshop. But that's only a detail. What's important is money. And the deals he has made here in Ephesus are excellent. He's managed to sell his whole cargo at a big profit. His business is booming.

Back in the port of Piraeus, he stops in front of the shop of a master goldsmith. A little statuette of Aphrodite in a sensuous pose, on display in the doorway, has caught his eye. It has been the symbol of this little shop for years now, not least because of the ease with which it attracts potential customers. Heliodorus's request is simple: does he have any rings with Aphrodite as the seal? He's thinking one might make a nice present for his daughter's birthday.

The shopkeeper nods, looks around amid the confusion of his work-table and finds a little wooden box. He opens it and takes out two identical rings. The negotiation between Heliodorus and the shopkeeper, two veterans of Aegean commerce accustomed to bargaining over even the most banal things, goes on for a long time. In the end, as a symbolic gesture, Heliodorus adds a sestertius to his offer. The shopkeeper smiles. It's a done deal.

Our sestertius has made it possible for Aphrodite to take flight across the Aegean, but at the same time the goddess allows our sestertius to depart on another long voyage. Indeed, the shopkeeper gives it almost immediately as change to a Roman who has bought his remaining Aphrodite ring. He waited until the negotiation between the two men came to an end, heard the price they agreed on, and paid the same amount, without having to haggle. He's a very bright young man, this Roman. And the ring is his gift for the woman he loves.

His name is Rufus, and now our sestertius has resumed its journey with him, back to Rome. The return trip by ship lasts just a few days, with a brief portage over the Isthmus of Corinth. The narrow canal that today allows ships to pass through the isthmus was not dug until 1892. Before that, ships were dragged overland from one part of the isthmus to the other, and Rufus too had to make the hike. Then he re-embarked on the other side, bound for Brindisi.

From Brindisi our man took the new branch of the Via Appia, only recently completed by Trajan, and rapidly crossed the southern part of the peninsula to arrive in Rome. When the city's skyline of roofs, temples, and statue-topped columns appears before our eyes, we have the sensation of closing a circle. We left here early in the morning; we're returning early in the evening. The streets, alleyways, and atmosphere of the city have remained unchanged. It seems as though just a few hours have passed since we left, but it's been almost a year.

Rufus has left his horse in a stable, outside the gates of Rome. At this hour the streets are empty and everyone has retired to their *insulae*, their windows illuminated by the dim light of oil lamps. These enormous buildings are still pulsing with life. We can hear voices, laughter, arguments that gradually fade to silence, one by one, until all we can hear are the rowdy exchanges coming from the taverns with their world of drunks, gamblers, and prostitutes.

Rufus has arrived at a wide street lined with closed shops. The silence is surreal; the only sound is a neighborhood fountain with the sculpted face of Mercury, a stream of water falling from his mouth into the basin.

From far away, we can hear shouting and the noises of the wagons making their nighttime deliveries in the city, muffled by the buildings. A dog barks in the distance. The latticework of basalt slabs stretching out before us, illuminated by the moon, looks like a tortoise shell.

Up ahead is an intersection, and in the middle of it there is a female figure who is observing us with a hint of a smile. Fair skin, hair gathered up in a bun, a ribbon around her forehead. A devilish lock of curls hangs down to her shoulder. Her arms are open and stretched out in our direction. Her eyes have a faraway look, as though her thoughts have carried her away. . . . She's the Mater Matuta, the "propitious mother," the deity of good beginnings, of fertility, of dawn.

Rufus raises his hand to his mouth, kisses his fingers, and then touches the feet of the statue, staring into her eyes. He thanks her for his safe return.

Then he bangs his fist against the door of a house. A few seconds go by and a voice asks who it is.

"Rufus!" he exclaims.

We hear some decisive turns of the bolt lock and then the door opens, creaking.

A face appears in the darkness, illuminated by a lantern; it's the doorman of the building. He's very happy to see Rufus again. His broad smile opens like a theater curtain to reveal his few remaining teeth, as though they were a sprinkling of spectators watching the show of his life.

With his nose he points upward to Rufus's apartment.

"Everything's in order," he says with a wink.

Rufus climbs the stairs and pushes open the door and is immediately inundated with an intense, ravishing perfume. He smiles. He drops his bag and walks into the semidarkness. In the center of the small living room he sees a woman, standing. Her figure is perfectly outlined against the frame of the open door to the terrace. The moonlight shining through the window sculpts the folds of her tunic in a play of light and shadow.

Suddenly, the dress drops to the floor, revealing the woman's body. Her hips, her breasts are caressed by the moonlight passing through the window grates, painting her body with tattoos of light.

The waiting, the long weeks, the fear of never seeing her again are swept aside by the pure energy of love. In the checkered light of the moon, their bodies press together and become one.

Now they are resting, his head nestled in her arms. We see a tiny reflection on the woman's chest. She lowers her hand to her breast and, as though she were picking a flower, grasps a gold ring with the symbol of Aphrodite.

It's another hot night. Still embracing, the two cross the room, the light sliding over their skin as they walk to the terrace. They remain there for a long time, their arms around each other, looking out at the magnificent panorama of Rome.

Somewhere out there, in a seething hot room, a floor grate is trembling with every blow of a slave's hammer against a die. In those infernal rooms new sesterces are being brought to life, with the face of the new emperor.

Tomorrow morning they will be taken away by couriers—who knows, perhaps even by the same decurion. (No, not perhaps: you can bet that he'll have arranged to be part of the squadron. He has a good reason to return to Scotland.)

And so, new stories will intersect and cross the empire along with these new sesterces, following routes that we can only imagine. Consider that all the inhabitants of the empire regularly handle sesterces. Even the poorest of the poor or the slaves will touch one, at least once in their lives. And these trajectories will repeat themselves for months, years, generations, centuries—even for a long time after the Roman empire will have fallen if indeed it is true that sesterces were used up to the end of the nineteenth century.

A sestertius, therefore, makes the rounds endlessly until . . . it stops. It may be lost, end up under ground or at the bottom of the sea.

And ours? Our sestertius's travels will soon come to an end.

Three days after his return to Rome, Rufus is standing in front of the lifeless body of his maestro, the officer who schooled him in the profession of an *aquarius*, a hydraulic engineer. Despite his young age, Rufus is already highly esteemed in the field for his capacity to discover hidden water sources and keep aqueducts operating efficiently.

He owes it all to this man, who is now lying in a simple wooden sarcophagus, wrapped in a shroud. Before the sarcophagus is closed, he notices that no one has put a coin inside as an offering for Charon, the ferryman who carries souls into the afterlife. His relatives must have simply forgotten, overwhelmed by their sorrow.

Rufus sticks a hand into the little leather pouch attached to his belt and takes out our sestertius. Delicately, he places it on the mouth of the maestro. Then the cover of the wooden sarcophagus is closed.

The ceremony is simple; the burial place is located along one of the consular roads, just outside of Rome. When the ceremony is over and the deceased has been put to rest in the ground, everyone leaves.

Only Rufus stays behind, standing there, staring at the gravestone, a lost look on his face. There is a part of himself under there. He bids a final farewell to his maestro and walks away. After a few steps he joins up with a woman, beautiful, tall, with a refined way about her. She wears an Aphrodite ring on her finger. Now they can let themselves be seen in public. Her ex-husband is no longer a problem; he's gone.

Conclusion

Some 1,896 years have passed: it is now 2013. The tomb of Rufus and Domitia reveals that they were married and had children. Their DNA has come down through the centuries, mixing with that of others. And today, perhaps, part of it is in one of you who are reading this.

All the protagonists of our story are now dust. The horses who accompanied us are also dust; the wooden ships and wagons that took us across the empire have broken up and disintegrated. The city of Rome that we walked through is buried under the new city. The empire itself, history's first great globalization, has vanished.

But a part of this ancient past suddenly returns.

A young woman is kneeling on the ground. She has a brush with which she is delicately dusting the soil, grain by grain. She's an archaeologist. For her it's a passion more than an occupation. Otherwise she wouldn't put up with the miserable pay, the dust, the sore knees and aching back from always being in an uncomfortable position, digging in the dirt.

The object that she is uncovering is a tomb from the turn of the second century CE. The skeleton that is emerging from the ground belongs to a mature man; you can tell from his worn teeth, from the sutures on the cranium by now so well healed that they are almost invisible, from the worn joints of his arms and legs and the chinks in the sides of his vertebrae, evidence of a badly worn back.

The skull that emerges from the ground has an open jaw, as though it were screaming. Actually, it's a sign that the body has decomposed in an empty environment (the sarcophagus), allowing the jawbone to "fall." Over the centuries, soil has entered the tomb and the wood has gradually disintegrated, leaving only some rusted nails.

Brushing next to the head, the young woman notices something. It's a green object. The brush strokes slowly remove centuries of sediment, freeing the object from the clutches of the terrain. It's a coin. After photographing it and transcribing some data, she takes the coin in hand. It is an extraordinary emotion: we feel as though we have made contact with a world that no longer exists, that we have opened a window onto the past.

This coin is our sestertius. It's completely covered by a green patina, caused by oxidation, but in otherwise perfect condition. The young woman turns it in her fingers; she recognizes the face of Trajan. In that moment, even if she doesn't know it, she has set in motion once again the mechanism of exchange that brought this coin to the four corners of the empire. In a certain sense she has brought it back to life. After all the people that we have seen in the Roman era, the story now continues with other people, in the modern one.

She shows the coin to her colleagues on the dig, each of whom holds it for a while before passing it on to another person. Then, in the laboratory, it's handled by an expert who tries to figure out the date it was coined. And finally it is placed in storage. But not for long. Given its excellent state of conservation, the decision is made to display it in a major museum in Rome. And so, a little while later, it is behind glass, and in the light again.

Despite its beauty, however, only a few people, the ones with a true passion, really stop to look at it. Most visitors observe it distractedly or pass by it without noticing. Nobody knows its story and nobody has even the slightest idea of its incredible journey, its odyssey across the empire. That coin, like all the others around it in the glass case, has been handled by dozens of people, and their stories have been, so to speak, crystallized in it, transforming it into a small time capsule.

We have tried to gather those stories and listen to them, learning from each one something about how the world was at the beginning of the second century CE. In turn they have taken us on a journey through the most surprising and modern realm of antiquity: the Roman Empire.

Acknowledgments

I offer my thanks to everyone who has helped me on this long journey through the empire. First and foremost, my gratitude goes to Professor Romolo Augusto Staccioli, for his careful reading of the manuscript, his profound knowledge of the Roman Empire, and his contagious passion for the everyday life of the era.

I would also like to thank Professor Antonio De Simone who, through his great experience of the Roman world, above all in Pompeii, has helped me to better immerse myself in the way the ancient Romans conceived of and lived life.

Many thanks also to Professor Patrizia Calabria, who revealed to me so many secrets of the sestertius and other Roman coins, allowing me to describe our journey through the empire with greater precision.

My heartfelt thanks also go to Professor Giandomenico Spinola, for the explorations that he allowed me to make at archaeological sites. And thanks to Professor Patrizia Basso for the precious information she provided on Roman roads and transportation.

This book deals with a vast horizon, both thematically and geographically. I would like to thank all the researchers and scholars whose comments, observations, and information have assisted me in this adventure.

I will not be able to cite them all and I beg their pardon for that; nevertheless I would like to mention Alessandra Benini, Nicola Cassone, Britta Hallman, Gianpiero Orsingher, Alessandra Squaglia . . . to name only a few.

Obviously, this volume would not have been possible without the work of generations of researchers and archaeologists who through their excavations, publications, and insights, with passion and quiet sacrifices, have brought back to life so many of the empire's sites and so many moments of its everyday life.

For their enthusiasm and their many suggestions, my deep gratitude also goes to Gabriella Ungarelli and Alberto Gelsomini of Mondadori, who believed in and supported this second book on the Roman era. And naturally also to Emilio Quinto for his work on research and revision, and to Studio Gráphen, which reread the manuscript very professionally.

Dulcis in fundo, I wish to thank my wife Monica for her advice and her precious observations on the manuscript as it was gradually taking shape. And, above all, for the patience she routinely demonstrated upon catching me all too frequently with my head in some remote corner of the Roman Empire . . . I'm back home!